Higher Education and Equality of Opportunities

STUDIES IN PUBLIC POLICY

Series Editor: Paul J. Rich, Policy Studies Organization

Lexington Books and the Policy Studies Organization's **Studies in Public Policy** series brings together the very best in new and original scholarship, spanning the range of global policy questions. Its multi-disciplinary texts combine penetrating analysis of policy formulation at the macro level with innovative and practical solutions for policy implementation. The books provide the political and social scientist with the latest academic research and the policy maker with effective tools to tackle the most pressing issues faced by government today. Not least, the books are invaluable resources for teaching public policy. For ideas about curriculum use, visit www.ipsonet.org.

Higher Education and Equality of Opportunities

Cross-National Perspectives

Edited by
Fred Lazin, Matt Evans, and N. Jayaram

LEXINGTON BOOKS
A division of
ROWMAN & LITTLEFIELD PUBLISHERS, INC.
Lanham • Boulder • New York • Toronto • Plymouth, UK

Published by Lexington Books
A division of Rowman & Littlefield Publishers, Inc.
A wholly owned subsidary of The Rowman & Littlefield Publishing Group, Inc.
4501 Forbes Boulevard, Suite 200, Lanham, Maryland 20706
www.lexingtonbooks.com

Estover Road, Plymouth PL6 7PY, United Kingdom

British Library Cataloguing in Publication Information Available

Library of Congress Cataloging-in-Publication Data

Higher education and equality of opportunities : cross-national perspectives / edited by
Fred Lazin, Matt Evans, and N. Jayaram.
   p. cm.
Includes bibliographical references and index.
ISBN 978-0-7391-4669-9 (cloth : alk. paper) — ISBN 978-0-7391-4671-2 (electronic)
1. Education, Higher—Cross-cultural studies. 2. Education and globalization—Cross-
cultural studies. 3. Affirmative action programs—Cross-cultural studies. 4. Minorities—
Education (Higher)—Cross-cultural studies. I. Lazin, Frederick A., 1943- II. Evans,
Matt, 1963- III. Jayaram, N., 1950-
LB2322.2.H513 2010
378.1'61—dc22   2010023509

For Mel Reisfield: An extraordinary teacher and mentor who taught and inspired several generations of youth who later became dedicated teachers at institutions of higher learning.

Contents

1

Introduction

Higher Education and Equality of Opportunities

Fred Lazin, Matt Evans, and N. Jayaram

Public higher education systems in the United States, Europe, and Asia have fostered greater access to a wide range of citizens, providing opportunities that had previously been denied by exclusive elite universities. This was particularly true of American land grant colleges and several public urban colleges which in the late nineteenth and twentieth century provided opportunities for citizens—especially immigrant populations—to obtain necessary academic credentials and training to advance in the economy and labor force. The G.I. Bill following World War II allowed many working-class and lower-class veterans to pursue educational degrees at the more prestigious American universities. The 1970s and 1980s saw a further commitment to equality of opportunity in higher education with affirmative-action programs.

The rising cost of education at the start of the twenty-first century seems to indicate a stark shift in education policies, which raises several important questions: Has the American academic experience changed in recent decades with reliance on the private sector and market forces? Are newer immigrant groups and emerging minorities being given access to higher education? Is equity of class and gender being pursued? Are European, Asian, and African universities following the same trends?

In his 2005 best seller *The World Is Flat*, *New York Times* columnist Thomas Friedman celebrated the fact that globalization was fast leveling the economic playing field. The world of higher education is surely not flat—country-specific cultural norms, economic calculations and political constraints continue to play a major role—but it is flattening. To what end?

From Asia to Europe, Africa to Australia—seemingly everywhere—higher education policy is headed in the same direction. The movement to broaden access to public universities, the dominant strategy during the 1970s and 1980s, has largely shifted to enable the marketplace, rather than the government, to shape the contours of higher education. Government funding is being reduced, affirmative action and other programs designed to ensure broader access are in decline, and personal fulfillment is replacing a public good designed to insure greater equality of opportunities.

The chapters that follow in this book detail how this sea change in higher education has played out in economically developed and developing countries. This book explores the impact of government policies and market forces in different countries to either foster or lessen equality of opportunities in higher education for different racial, ethnic, religious, and gender groupings. A common set of questions guides these accounts: What are the consequences of a market-driven higher education for student access, teaching, and scholarship? What is the impact on the role of the university as an equalizer of opportunities? Is the dominance of marketplace norms and forms inexorable or might governments reclaim some of the authority they have tacitly surrendered?

The chapters in this book present case studies focusing on higher education systems within a particular country or countries. They investigate issues related to access and equity in higher education. Are different groups given equal opportunities? Has equity been neglected with cutbacks in government funding for higher education? Where has affirmative action been effective? Several of the chapters focus on minority groups within the larger societies: How are they treated in terms of access? A few chapters look at funding schemes designed to expand opportunities and access: Have they been successful? Other subjects include the place of foreign students in a national system and access for students with mental health difficulties.

The innovation and attraction of this volume lie in its focus on current cross-national dilemmas in higher education. The research here provides an interesting contrast of the diversity and uniqueness of higher education in the United States, France, Australia, India, Ghana, and several other countries, while at the same time revealing surprising commonalities despite the countries' ethnic and cultural differences. In many countries, across five continents, it is evident that there are worldwide trends in higher education including a cutback in government financing, a decline in access, and a receding of affirmative action.

Thus, the book explores universal phenomena in higher education through the individual experiences of different national systems. The United States experience is most represented in terms of numbers of papers, though it is contrasted with case studies in many other countries: Australia, France, Ghana, India, Israel, New Zealand, South Korea, the Netherlands, and the United Kingdom.

This book is an important addition to the literature on higher education during the age of globalization and the decline of government funding of higher education. The studies are recent and provide important data about the current situation in higher education in countries around the world. Many of the most influential scholars in the field, together with younger researchers, from the United States, Europe, Africa, Asia, and Australia have authored the chapters for this volume. The authors also represent several disciplines in both the social sciences and humanities which contribute to the volume's very interdisciplinary methodology and analysis. This volume should be of interest to students of higher education, higher education policy, development, equity, and globalization. There is also material here which will interest students of public policy of the United States, European Union countries, India, Israel, Far East, Oceania, and Africa.

The eighteen thematic chapters in the book are organized under three sections, dealing respectively with America (5), Asia, the Middle East and Africa (8) and Europe and Oceania (5). The theoretical framework for these chapters is provided by David Kirp's curtain raiser, "The Earth is Flattening: The Globalization of Higher Education and its Implications for Equal Opportunity." Kirp argues that the market rather than government policy has come to shape and determine higher education policy in most countries. From Taiwan to Great Britain, Ghana to Australia, higher education policy is headed in the same direction. The movement to broaden access to public universities, the dominant strategy during the 1970s and 1980s, has largely been supplanted by reliance on the marketplace, not the government, to shape the contours of higher education. As the United States has shifted from an opportunity-driven approach toward a market-driven strategy, other countries have followed suit. The result is a remarkable convergence—a "flattening" of the higher education universe— among developed and developing nations alike. Kirp examines the effect of the shift in educational priorities on institutions, academics, and society and sets the stage for rest of the chapters in this volume.

The five chapters in the first section address issues in higher education in the United States. Carol Schmid's "Challenges and Opportunities of Community Colleges" evaluates the contribution and value of community colleges, which are the least known component of higher education in the United States. Unlike other sectors of American higher education, community colleges provide broad access to education through open admissions and serve a range of college students including those who are most likely to have academic and financial challenges and who are first-generation college students.

They play a critical role, enrolling almost half of the undergraduate students in the United States including almost half of African American and more than half of Hispanic and Native American undergraduate students. Schmid analyzes the community colleges in terms of their demographic profiles, retention and persistence rates by race and ethnicity and immigrant status, and the challenges and opportunities facing community colleges today.

Noga O'Connor's "Minority Access to Higher Education in the United States and the White-Minority Credentials Gap" studies two aspects of changes in minority access to higher education: shifts in degree attainment, and changes in labor market financial returns to education. During the 1970s and 1980s, several policies attempted to promote minority access to higher education in the United States in order to reduce the credentials gap between whites and minorities. O'Connor uses data sets representing three points in time: The National Longitudinal Study of the High School Class of 1972 (the 1970s), The High School and Beyond (the 1980s), and The National Education Longitudinal Study of 1988 (the 1990s). The degree-attainment analysis reveals that the gap remained intact. Surprisingly, however, analysis of financial returns to education (conducted on males alone) reveals that black men with a bachelor's degree during the 1980s and 1990s were at a significant returns advantage over their white counterparts. Thus, though the opportunity structure operates in favor of one group of minorities, access policies have not been successful in eliminating the white-minority credentials gap.

In "Prestige and Quality in American Colleges and Universities" Steven J. Diner looks at the issue of prestige and quality in American universities and colleges. He examines social stratification via a case study of Rutgers University–Newark as an example of a public research university located in an urban area. The growth of popular, consumer-oriented rankings of top institutions, decreasing state and federal support for higher education, and rising tuitions have significantly increased social class stratification in the United States. In writing about these phenomena many scholars and writers have focused on who gets admitted to the elite private colleges. They often neglect public research universities located in urban areas that have had a long tradition of educating research-oriented students from poor or modest backgrounds. Diner urges that more attention be paid to these urban institutions of higher education. He argues that, in today's America and in today's world, diversity is an integral dimension of academic quality. Reversing the growing class and racial stratification of our colleges and universities requires an end to embracing the popular simplistic and elitist rankings of educational quality that so deeply influence American higher education today.

The final two chapters in this section are case studies focusing on Hunter College of the City University of New York (CUNY). One is written by an anthropologist and former dean at Hunter, and the second is by a political scientist. While very different in method and scope, they provide complementary analyses. Both address change in CUNY's admission policies in terms of access and excellence.

In "From Open Admissions to Honors College: Equal Opportunities at the City University of New York" Judith Naomi Friedlander focuses on the debate over CUNY's admission policies and the effectiveness of the Hunter College honors program. In 1970, CUNY's Board of Trustees embraced the ideals of affirmative action, proclaiming that every high school graduate in New York City would henceforth be admitted to CUNY. By the late 1990s the pendulum began swinging back in the opposite direction. Severe pressure from Mayor Giuliani's office and elsewhere eventually persuaded the Trustees in 1999 to put an end to open admissions and to close down remedial programs at the four-year senior colleges including Hunter College. Politically active members of CUNY, long identified with the Civil Rights Movement, argued this would have a negative impact on the diversity and size of the university's student body. These predictions, however, have proved wrong. Since 1999 enrollment has actually grown by 10 percent, and the ethnic and racial distribution of students continues to reflect the diversity of New York City. Friedlander also discusses the success of Hunter's honors program in fostering outstanding academic careers for many of its minority students.

In "The Changing American College Experience: A View from the City University of New York, Hunter College" Charles Tien discusses the way in which changes in access and market approaches have affected minority enrollment at Hunter, especially for African and Asian American students. He utilizes CUNY admissions data to analyze the way in which changes in access and market approaches have affected enrollment for African Americans and Asian Americans. Tien's analysis focuses on data for CUNY's special admission program SEEK (Search for Education, Elevation, and Knowledge) and data on graduation rates. This study also utilizes data from the National Longitudinal Survey of Youth to compare minority students' college experiences with those of white students.

The eight chapters in the second section examine higher education in Asia, the Middle East, and Africa. In "Promoting Access of the Poor through Student Loans in Asia: Prerequisites for Success" Adrian Ziderman examines the effect of student loan schemes aimed at enhancing access of the poor and other disadvantaged groups to higher education in several countries of East Asia. These schemes are often flawed due to a lack of preconditions for success. However, they are often more successful in both reaching the poor and enhancing access if they are appropriately designed and operated. Ziderman argues that student loans can serve an important but limited role in enhancing the access of lower socioeconomic groups. A balanced policy of student support is necessary, incorporating grants for the very poor and subsidized loans for the needy.

Complementing Ziderman is Ka Ho Mok and John Hawkins's "The Quest for World-Class Status: Globalization and Higher Education in East Asia." Mok and Hawkins present an in-depth study of reforms in higher education policies throughout East Asia. To become globally competitive, governments and universities in these countries began searching for new methods to improve university governance. Unsatisfied with the conventional model of state-oriented, highly centralized higher education, coupled with the pressures to improve the efficiency of university governance, many Asian governments have introduced corporatization and privatization measures to run their state/national universities. These moves are designed to make national universities more flexible and responsive to rapid socioeconomic changes. Instead of being closely directed by the Ministry of Education or equivalent government administrative bodies, state universities in Asia are now required to become more proactive and dynamic in looking for their own financial resources. East Asian universities have taken the world university ranking very seriously and therefore they have engaged in the quest for "world-class" university status.

In "The Korean Passage to Tertiary Education for All: Over-Privatization" Ki-Seok Kim and Hwanbo Park examine privatization of tertiary education in Korea. The main driving force behind the rapid expansion of higher education in Korea was not a concerted central planning effort by the government, but rather parents' zeal and willingness to financially support their children's studies. Extreme privatization, with more than 80 percent of students at private universities and colleges, has led to the unprecedented simultaneous transition to universal access to secondary and tertiary education. Korea has one of the highest rates of tertiary education in the world, surpassing the United States. The idea of "tertiary education for all" is closer to reality in Korea than in any other country. This chapter investigates whether this is truly a success story and whether or not there are hidden costs and consequences. The Korean case provides valuable insights for tertiary education policies in other countries.

Two chapters on India follow: one focusing exclusively on India, and the other comparing specific education policies with those of Israel. In "Disparities in Access to Higher Education in India: Persistent Issues and the Changing Context" N. Jayaram focuses on recent changes in the issues of unequal access to higher education in India. The concern with access to higher education is not new, and it has been addressed by policymakers repeatedly since the program of planned development began in India in the early 1950s. However, the context in which the issue was addressed has not remained the same. During the first four decades (1950s through the 1980s), the key strategy was steady expansion of the tertiary sector of education under state patronage. With the adoption of the structural adjustment program and the policy of liberalization (since the early 1990s), the state is gradually withdrawing from the sphere of higher education. The void created by this is being filled by private initiatives and innovations. The shift from state patronage to laissez-faireism in the sphere of higher education has thrown up new issues concerning access and development. This chapter analyzes some of these issues from a sociological perspective, which assumes that education can hardly rise above the socioeconomic context in which it is embedded.

The chapter by Ayelet Harel-Shalev, "Education Policy toward 'Homeland Minorities' in Deeply Divided Societies: India and Israel," compares similar education policies in India and Israel—both divided democracies with a large ethnic/religious minority. She analyzes how each country has determined and implemented language and educational policies with respect to their major minorities. She compares the policies of secular, democratic India, regarding the Urdu language of its Muslim minority, with the policies of Israel, an ethnic democracy, and the use of Arabic for its Arab-Palestinian minority. The findings indicate that both states have consigned the minority language to a marginal position on the public stage. Moreover, while both minority groups enjoy a certain level of autonomy in the educational sphere, their educational status is markedly low in comparison to the majority.

In "Improving Access to Higher Education for Students from Low Socioeconomic Backgrounds in Israel" Miri Amit examines the impact of the Accessibility to Higher Education Program designed to enrich the education of Jewish and Bedouin high school students from southern Israel and to increase their chances of being accepted by a university. The program comprises two main components: one in high schools and the other in a university. The former provides students with extra tutoring within their schools to prepare them for final examinations. The latter gives them exposure to university courses, including scientific laboratories and computer centers. Evaluation of the program shows it to be popular and successful.

The final two chapters of this section focus on higher education in Africa. In the first, "Higher Education in Africa: Challenges of Development and Gender," Pamela Blackmon and Matt Evans examine challenges facing the development of higher education in sub-Saharan Africa, which lags far behind both the developed and the developing worlds in tertiary education. Among the factors behind this region's difficulties in developing higher education are the legacy of colonialism, misguided investment directions from international agencies, funding inefficiencies, and the lack of regulatory oversight. The chapter also looks at sub-Saharan Africa's gender inequalities in higher education in comparison to the rest of the world. The chapter elucidates the need for better management in African institutions of higher education in order to provide this region with the workforce needed to compete in an increasingly globalized world.

In "Development of Corporate and Private Universities in Ghana: Effects on Curriculum, Faculty, Access and Equity" Josiah Cobbah examines Ghana's rapid surge in private universities. The research draws on data from both publicly funded universities and a number of recently established private institutions. Cobbah analyzes the impact of the emphasis on marketing considerations on the curriculum, on access, and on faculty. Also examined is the effect of emerging market trends on the expectations of university students and on their motivation for particular types of university education. This study suggests that an emphasis on marketing is increasingly changing the nature of the university and the commitment of academic staff to the university. Cobbah argues that the trend toward privatization and corporatization may be harmful for Ghanaian higher education.

The final section of the book examines higher education in Europe and Oceania. In "Access to Higher Education in France: Between Equality of Rights and Meritocracy, a Long Walk to Equality of Opportunity?" Gaele Goastellec provides a vivid and broad picture of access in the French higher education system. She explores and explains the organization of access to higher education in France and analyzes the difficulties faced in conceiving and implementing equality of opportunity policies. She focuses on the conflict between meritocracy and equality of rights. She explains that historically the principles regulating access to higher education in France echo a dual higher education system. On the one hand, universities offer open access to all secondary education graduates, in accord with the principle of equality of rights. But, behind this formal equality that led to the tremendous expansion of the university sector, local cooling-outs are organized, and the social distribution of students testifies to a high degree of inequalities. On the other hand, the sector composed of the so-called *Grandes Ecoles* is highly selective and, though based on "pure" academic merit, it largely favors the offspring of the elite.

In "Equal Opportunity in a Public System: Experiences of Ethnic Minority Students in Dutch Higher Education" Rick Wolff and Adel Pasztor examine the increase in enrollment of ethnic minorities in the higher education system of The Netherlands and focus on the issues of social and academic integration. They study national data in order to understand the influence of student characteristics and the learning environment. They then analyze the influence of student characteristics on access, retention and completion: Do ethnic minority students possess specific features that cause higher dropout and lower completion rates, or are general processes leading to either failure (dropout) or success (persistence/completion) reinforced or weakened among this group of students? Subsequently, they evaluate the impact of characteristics of the learning environment, especially the educational structure and culture offered by course programs and institutions: Which features of the educational context either stimulate or hinder study progress of ethnic minority students? Examination of both issues holds social integration and academic integration as key theoretical concepts.

In the final chapter on Europe "Access to Higher Education for Students with Mental Health Difficulties: An Equal Opportunities Issue" Sue Jackson looks at access to higher education problems for students with mental health difficulties in the United Kingdom. A study at the London College of Communication, University of the Arts shows that 50 percent of its students declaring a disability had disclosed a mental health issue by the end of the last academic year. Jackson examines the implications of this situation for those working in institutions of higher education. Her case study identifies the key issues in supporting students with mental health difficulties, offers insights to institutional barriers, and suggests ways to make institutions more disability friendly. Its aim is to ensure the right of students with mental health difficulties to a university education, where they are not disadvantaged by their disability. She argues that the experience of students with mental health difficulties can highlight issues that affect all students from excluded groups.

The final two chapters examine higher education in Oceana. In "Altruism and Avarice: The Place of Foreign Students in Australian Universities" Don Stewart reviews the place of foreign students in the Australian higher education system over the last fifty years. He focuses on the University of Melbourne. The research spans an earlier period, when these students' presence in the universities reflected the "goodwill" of the Australian government and the Australian universities toward less wealthy neighboring countries, to the present time, when they are now the largest source of nongovernment income for those universities. This case study shows how changing attitudes toward equality of opportunities for Australian students have been reflected in attitudes toward foreign students and, perhaps paradoxically, how attitudes to foreign students have been reflected back on the provision (or lack of it) of opportunities for tertiary study for less affluent Australian students.

In the final chapter "A Dual Admission Policy: Enhancing Equal Opportunities in Higher Education in New Zealand Through Merit-based Admission Policy" Boaz Shulruf, John Hattie, and Sarah Tumen discuss various ways of increasing access to New Zealand's higher education system. In search for the optimum model for different groups of students they evaluate alternative models for university entrance. They review the predictive correlations between the New Zealand National Certificate of Educational Achievement (NCEA) systems (the new standards-based assessment for secondary schools) with the grade point averages achieved by first-year students in a New Zealand University. They then evaluate alternative models for university entrance using different attributes of the qualifications for possible entry criteria and ascertain the implications of the best of these models for different groups of students. The best alternative model gives greater weight to excellence and merit in NCEA results and less weight to credit accumulation at minimum pass rates. A combination of this alternative model and the current model provides a merit-based admissions system which would potentially increase the number of under-represented students (Maori and Pacific ethnicities and students from schools in lower socioeconomic communities) who are admitted with no necessary decline in the success rate during the first year of university study.

All but two of the chapters in this book were first presented as papers at the "Hurst Seminar on Higher Education and Equality of Opportunity: Cross-National Perspectives" at Ben-Gurion University of the Negev (BGU) (Israel) in June 2008. More than thirty scholars from six continents and seventeen countries participated in the June 2008 Seminar, which was held in a hotel at the Dead Sea in Israel. Participants also included Israeli faculty members from Bar Ilan University, Ben-Gurion University, Tel Aviv University, and Sapir College.

Cosponsors of the conference included Ben-Gurion University of the Negev (Centre for the Study of European Politics and Society, Center for Research on Higher Education, the Department of Politics and Government, and the Lynne and Lloyd Hurst Family Chair of Government), International Network on the Role of Universities in Developing Areas (INRUDA), Policy Studies Organization (PSO), French Centre for Academic and Cultural Cooperation (CEFIC) in Beer Sheva, The Embassy of France in Israel, and The Committee of Planning and Budget of the Council of Higher Education (in Israel).

Professor Fred Lazin, Lynn and Lloyd Family Chair in Local Government, initiated the conference. Joining him on the steering committee were Professors Nahum Finger (BGU), Sharon Pardo (BGU), Paul Rich, President PSO, Samuel Aroni (UCLA and Co-chair, INRUDA, David Wilmoth (Cochair IN-RUDA), Orlando Albornoz (University of Central Venezuela and INRUDA), and N. Jayaram (Tata Institute of Social Sciences and INRUDA). The steering committee worked together to organize and implement the seminar.

The Hurst Family of the United States, The Centre for the Study of European Politics and Society, the President, Rector, and Dean of Social Sciences of Ben-Gurion University provided financial support. Additional funding was provided by Babette Kabak, Dorothy Kravetz, Mimi Robbins, CEFIC, and Committee of Planning and Budget of the Council of Higher Education (Israel).

2

The Earth is Flattening

The Globalization of Higher Education and Its Implications for Equal Opportunity

David L. Kirp

There is a place for the market, but the market must be kept in its place.

—Okun 1975

From Taiwan to Britain, Ghana to Australia—seemingly everywhere, higher education policy is headed in the same direction. The movement to broaden access to public universities, the dominant strategy during the 1970s and 1980s, has largely been supplanted by reliance on the marketplace, not the government, to shape the contours of higher education.

In his 2005 best seller *The World Is Flat*, *New York Times* columnist Thomas Friedman celebrated the fact that globalization was fast leveling the economic playing field. The world of higher education is surely not flat—country-specific cultural norms, and economic calculations and political constraints continue to play a major role—but it is flattening. To what end?

The chapters that follow detail how this sea change has played out in economically developed and developing countries. A common set of questions animates these accounts: What are the consequences of a market-driven higher education for student access, teaching, and scholarship? What is the impact on the role of the university as an equalizer of opportunity? Is the dominance of marketplace norms and forms inexorable or might governments reclaim some of the authority they have tacitly surrendered?

THE AMERICAN MODEL

During the past half century the United States has taken the lead in reforming higher education—first for the access revolution and latterly for the market revolution. The American experience offers an appropriate starting point for an international investigation.

The American approach is widely celebrated. The *Economist* (2005) describes the "American model" of higher education as setting the international gold standard. Universities elsewhere used to aspire to become their country's Oxford or Cambridge—no longer. When Melbourne University set about to transform itself and claim the status of Australia's premier university, Vice Chancellor Glyn Davis, who designed the new plan, looked to Berkeley and Michigan, America's "elite" public universities, as the template for change. When an Indian multibillionaire dreamed of establishing a world-class private university in his homeland, he wasn't thinking of Oxbridge on the Ganges but of an Indian version of Harvard.

It's hard to argue with America's success. Among the top research universities in the world, according to the widely cited Shanghai Jiao Tong University's rankings of the world's 500 best research universities, eight of the top ten and seventeen of the top twenty are located in the United States. Seven of the eleven universities in the University of California system rank in the top fifty.

The United States was the first nation to develop institutions of mass higher education. At present two-thirds of high school graduates go on to tertiary institutions. And the United States has developed multiple pathways to higher education—second and third chances—rather than using a test that's administered before secondary school to determine a student's educational destiny.

The character of the American university system—better, nonsystem—has contributed to this success. As compared with much of the world, governance is decentralized, with major decisions left to the campuses; together with government the nonprofit sector has a major role (and for-profit schools like Phoenix University have flourished in niche markets); and financial support comes from multiple sources, including government subsidies, tuition, research grants and contracts, and gifts. These structural elements have created opportunities for particular institutions to distinguish themselves.

Access expanded rapidly after World War II, as veterans took advantage of the G.I. Bill to earn college degrees. The research capacity of universities grew apace, as the federal government turned to universities (rather than establishing freestanding institutions or using government's internal capacity, as happened elsewhere), spending billions of dollars on research in the broadly defined domain of national security.

The California Master Plan was the exemplar. It was crafted by Clark Kerr, the first president of the University of California system and the most influential figure in higher education during the decisively important era of the 1950s and 1960s. The Master Plan guaranteed every high school graduate a place in one of California's public institutions. It created a three-tier system—community colleges, which were open to all; state colleges, which admitted students in the top third of their graduating class, and research universities, for which students graduating in the top 12 percent of their class were eligible. The regime was designed to promote student mobility—students who did well in community college were entitled to transfer to a university. Underlying this arrangement was an implicit compact between the state and the public universities. In return for assuring low tuition and substantial infusions of research funds, the state was assured of world-class teaching; a strong institutional commitment to serve the public; and, in the flagship universities, world-class research as well.

Now, however, American higher education is powered more by market forces than government direction. The demise of California's Master Plan reflects major shifts that are visible across the landscape of public higher education in the United States. In California the percentage of the universities' budget that comes from the state has been steadily reduced over the past generation; tuition has tripled; the university has increasingly relied on private funds, which has eroded its commitment to serving the broader community. As California goes, so has gone the nation—and with this shift to privatization the characteristic strengths and weaknesses of the market emerge.

"Winner-take-all" competition for star faculty has greatly strengthened universities such as New York University and the University of Southern California, both of which vaulted into world-class status during the past quarter century (NYU ranks 29th, USC 47th in the Jiao Tong University rankings). At the same time, however, tenure has become a rarity. The number of professors who have no prospect of receiving tenure has ballooned in the past generation. Over 60 percent of new full-time faculty are hired for term, not tenure-ladder, appointments; and many more PhD's can secure only ill-paid, part-time positions. To the university this policy shift may make economic sense, since adjuncts are cheaper, and the university is free to make short-term, rather than lifelong, investments in its faculty. But because the practice makes faculty mobility a necessity and discourages the forging of institutional commitments, it inevitably has profound effects on the character of the academic community.

Americans love rankings—top ten lists proliferate—and higher education is no exception. Ask any college president what she hopes for, and she'll likely list moving up in the rankings among her main objectives. The most influential ranking is published by the *U.S. News & World Report*; it affects everything from student enrollment and faculty recruitment to private giving. Since a school's place in the pecking order depends heavily on student selectivity, the competition for students can be fierce.

To the extent that the rankings rely on criteria that have to do with the quality of education this competition is a healthy thing. But with so much at stake universities have figured out how to "game" the system.

The most important factor in the calculation of rank is selectivity: What percent of those who apply are admitted? What percent of those who are admitted actually enroll? In this consumerist environment students are treated as customers whose preferences are to be satisfied, rather than as acolytes whose preferences are to be formed during their undergraduate years.

Schools across the country have invested billions of dollars in lavish student apartments, sushi bars, high-tech studios for budding sports announcers, and the like. The effect is to divert scarce dollars from libraries, laboratories, and other essential, though less visible, parts of the university; this diversion is particularly worrying at less prestigious institutions, some of which have mortgaged their futures in order to compete in this new market. A shift in students' expressed interest in the past thirty years—away from the liberal arts and toward the "practical arts" such as recreation management and law enforcement—has been abetted by universities' willingness to shift resources.

Competition has changed the character of financial aid. Scholarships and loans used to be awarded entirely on the basis of financial need. But in order to attract students with stronger academic records and so impress the *U.S. News* raters, more institutions are awarding scholarships on the basis of academic performance, regardless of need, through "merit" scholarships. Financial aid is also being used strategically, as a tool to maximize a school's ranking while minimizing the cost to the university. In this new equation the losers are candidates from poor families. Students from poor families have felt the pinch of skyrocketing tuition most acutely, and as the economy worsens, the possibility of their going to college becomes more remote. Confronted with the necessity of earning a living, many cannot afford to invest in their futures.

American higher education has turned into the preserve of the elite. At the 150 most selective universities 75 percent of the students come from the top income quartile, while 10 percent come from the bottom half of the socioeconomic ladder—and only 3 percent come from the bottom quartile. A student whose family income is in the top quartile with aptitude scores in the lowest quartile is as likely to go to college as a student whose family income is in the lowest quartile and whose aptitude tests are in the highest quartile. As Terry Hartle, senior vice president of the American Council of Education, bluntly concludes: "smart poor kids go to college at the same rate as stupid rich kids" (Kirp 2008).

Since the 1970s race-conscious affirmative action has given minority students new opportunities to go to college. But during the past decade, affirmative action has been under siege, from voters and judges alike. The U.S. Supreme Court severely constricted the use of race as a factor in admissions. In several states voters have passed referenda that require public universities to use colorblind admissions standards and this has eviscerated minority enrollment. After California passed an anti–affirmative action referendum, the number of black students dropped from nearly 10 percent to fewer than 3 percent at Berkeley and UCLA, the two most prestigious universities in the state system. The impact on black males is especially devastating. Among the 7,400 freshmen at those schools, only 83 of them are black male students, half of whom have been admitted on athletic scholarships.

Other affirmative action strategies, such as using income as a proxy for race, have been attempted, with only indifferent success. Texas guarantees admission to the University of Texas and Texas A&M, its two most selective public universities, to all students who graduate in the top 10 percent of their high school class. Many Texas high schools have a predominantly minority enrollment and the aim of the policy was to boost the numbers of Hispanic and black students, but there has been less of an impact than was anticipated.

The venerable American belief in higher education as an engine of mobility underlies the 1867 federal legislation that created many state universities and the 1944 G.I. Bill which enabled millions of veterans to earn degrees. But now higher education is increasingly seen not as a public good—a social benefit whose costs should mostly be borne by the taxpayers—but as a private good whose cost should mainly be the responsibility of the individuals who will reap most of the benefits. The impact of this shift, especially for poor and minority students, has been profound.

THE POWER OF MARKET VALUES

As the United States has shifted from an opportunity-driven approach toward a market-driven strategy, other countries have followed suit. The result is a remarkable convergence—a "flattening" of the higher education universe—among developed and developing nations alike. While the particulars differ among nations, the direction of policy change is the same: the market has emerged as a powerful, sometimes dominant, factor in the policy equation.

Until the 1970s the policy differences between the United States and the rest of the world were profound. Even as the United States was moving toward a regime of mass higher education, elsewhere college remained the preserve of the elite—just 5 or 10 percent of secondary school graduates went on to further education. Universities were mostly government-financed, highly centralized, and constrained by uniform rules. Hierarchies of prestige were preserved in the allocation of funds. Tuition was kept low, as were faculty salaries. Though the quality of instruction and research varied greatly, mobility was a rarity. Students were effectively a captive audience and faculty had few opportunities abroad. The main escape route was to be admitted to, or land a job at, an American university (or, for residents of British Commonwealth countries, a British university).

The dynamics underlying the worldwide transformation of higher education are familiar, since they are essentially the dynamics of globalization more generally. The catalyst has been the rise of the knowledge economy— what has been labeled the "soft revolution." Government officials came to appreciate that, if their country was going to succeed in the increasingly global and technologically sophisticated economic market, they needed to expand the number of "knowledge workers." That realization prompted sizeable public investments to expand enrollment. New universities sprouted; within a generation higher education was remade as a mass system (in South Korea and Taiwan access has become nearly universal, with college-going rates above 80 percent).

The Internet contributed to the demise of the old system by making knowledge instantly and ubiquitously accessible. It also inspired the creation of new institutions able to operate across borders. The Massachusetts Institute of Technology (MIT) put its course materials online, giving instructors across the world a benchmark against which to measure their students' skills. Online courses proliferated. Virtual universities emerged, operated either as freestanding entities or as transnational partnerships between universities or as a global web like Universitas 21.

Even as higher education was expanding, its structure was changing apace. The command-and-control model came to seem hidebound when compared with the dynamism of the market.

Here too globalization has been a driving force. As in the United States, competition for students has stiffened. A university's rank in the British government's League Tables or the *U.S. News & World Report* standings establishes its place in the pecking order; and that ranking affects its ability to attract top students, for whom an institution's prestige matters considerably. The Bologna accords have expanded students' options by opening up places to foreign students and developing common degree metrics, requiring universities to look abroad for prospective students. Several nations, most prominently Australia, have taken advantage of the new market opportunities in higher education, aggressively pursuing overseas students and (with less success) opening branch campuses in Asia.

Among elite institutions there is considerable competition for faculty, as star professors are wooed by universities halfway around the world with offers of outsized salaries and lavishly funded labs. Universities have to compete for government research funds, rather than being able, as in the past, to rely on their reputations as a guarantee of quality. Corporate-funded research, which has grown in importance, rarely fits the classic university model—long-term and basic studies whose findings are universally available. Instead, support goes to applied studies intended to yield patentable results that will improve the corporate bottom line. Universities on both sides of the Atlantic competed for a half-billion-dollar biofuels lab underwritten by British Petroleum (a Berkeley–University of Illinois consortium beat out several major British universities to win the contract).

While for most institutions this competition is national or regional, a super-league of world-class universities has emerged. From Chicago to London, Tokyo to Stockholm, these institutions measure their success by their standing in the Shanghai Jiao Tong University 500 top research universities and the (London) *Times Higher Education Supplement*'s World University Global Rankings.

IS EQUITY A SIDE SHOW?

The country analyses that follow cover a wide array of topics. But whether the focus is the role of private institutions or the status of ethnic minorities, the points of similarity are what stand out. In different ways the inquiries pose the same set of questions: What is the role of the market? Does higher education promote equal opportunity or is equity a sideshow in the new higher education bazaar?

Key themes recur in these analyses:

Although higher education is a mass institution—in Korea and Taiwan, more than 80 percent of high school graduates enroll in a university—students from poor families may not enjoy substantial benefits from the expansion. Ethic and economic gaps persist, both in the percentage of students who enroll in universities and in the quality of the institutions that admit them. Among European nations inequality is greatest among the former Soviet bloc countries.

The rhetoric of equality doesn't match the reality of the market. In France, for instance, higher education opportunities are highly stratified, with stratification between the *grandes ecoles* and the universities, as well as among universities.

Widening access to higher education has generated unintended negative consequences. The common intention is to expand opportunities, and improve educational outcomes. But this policy has often been poorly implemented. Many of the new students are less well prepared to meet the academic demands.

When the BA becomes nearly ubiquitous, replacing the secondary school diploma as the signifier of success, as has already happened in such countries as South Korea and Taiwan, degree deflation sets in. Students require a master's degree to distinguish themselves from their peers.

Public funding for higher education has been reduced—drastically in some countries. As compared to a decade ago, most governments provide substantially smaller per-student subsidies to universities, and the percentage of government budgets allocated to higher education has declined.

Demands for institutional "accountability" have increased. In New Zealand, Britain, and the United States, among other countries, the amount of public support is linked to such factors as the percentage of enrolled students who receive degrees, the time to completion, and the number of articles published in refereed journals (U.S. journals are often explicitly preferred.)

Higher education is increasingly delivered by private institutions. As subsidies to public universities have declined, private institutions, either nonprofit or more typically for-profit institutions, have filled the gap. The percentage of university students who attend these schools varies considerably. In Western Europe almost all students still go to public universities, but in Asia and Latin America as many as 90 percent of undergraduates attend nonpublic universities. The implications of privatization for the quality of instruction vary: in some countries, as in Taiwan, they are generally inferior; in others, as in Korea and India, they offer a superior education. These institutions, most of which were founded in the past two decades, do not offer the same range of courses as public universities. Instead they emphasize profitable fields like management, as in Ghana, and law, as in Israel.[1]

THE CEASELESS SEARCH FOR REVENUE

In order to survive in the face of these cutbacks, public universities have looked for alternative sources of revenue. Everywhere except in the United States higher education has historically been regarded as a public responsibility. There is little tradition of private giving, and so universities cannot (at least in the short run) rely on multibillion-dollar capital campaigns

Some countries have avidly gone after the international market. In Australia, one-sixth of the students come from abroad, mainly from South Asia and East Asia; higher education is that country's third biggest export. But the higher education market can be fickle. Foreign students' concerns about the quality of instruction, coupled with the rapid growth of private, and less expensive, alternatives in the home countries, have led to steep enrollment declines in some Australian universities. The influx of international students has also generated resistance among Australian students.

In almost every country tuition has increased, but the long-standing practice of keeping tuition low has proven hard to overcome. In 2005 Britain implemented the most promising strategy to address this shortfall: universities are authorized to nearly triple tuition, to £3,000 (about $5,200), while providing grants and loans to students from poor families as well as loan forgiveness to graduates who earn less than £20,000. Less happily, some Australian universities have lowered admissions standards for students who can pay the full tuition, thus permitting rich and less qualified students to enroll.

There is little tradition of reliance on industry to subsidize research, but that too is changing. The University of Trento (Italy), for example, has developed a partnership with Microsoft, a multimillion-Euro arrangement that has strengthened Trento's international reputation.

In this market-driven environment, efforts to promote equity have been at best a modest success. Even the British high tuition–high loan scheme has proven problematic. While the economic theory underlying the policy is sound, the strategy can work only if the amount of student support is adequate. What's more, students from poor families—who understand short-term costs but have less familiarity with long-term benefits—may need grants rather than loans. "Information poverty" is also a deterrent, as prospective students are put off by the "sticker shock" of high tuition.

As with other equity-promoting initiatives, affirmative-action policies, designed to attract minority students, have had only a limited impact. The Indian government sets formal quotas for castes and tribes that have long suffered discrimination. In New Zealand and Australia, the admissions criteria differ for applicants from indigenous communities. Israeli universities have informally adopted affirmative-action plans to attract Sephardic Jews and Israeli Arabs.

However, cultural and social gaps go unaddressed or, as in the Netherlands, inadequately addressed. Minority students report that they are isolated from their classmates; and, as in France, clashes arise over such cultural totems as head scarves. Not surprisingly, minority students are disproportionately likely to drop out of school. Resentment against what is widely seen as special treatment has stirred backlash among those who haven't benefited from affirmative action, with equity-based claims pitted against merit-based arguments. As the case studies of Hunter College (New York City) show, affirmative-action battles may be a proxy for the deeper issue—the lack of adequate resources.

The institution that has done the best job of expanding access is Open University (OU). Its exemplary track record demonstrates that high-quality mass education can be delivered globally. OU admits all applicants, regardless of their educational background or test scores, and offers instruction that is both intellectually demanding and individually supportive. OU was launched four decades ago in Britain, where it is an institution; one Briton in ten has taken an OU course. The British government ranks its undergraduate education fifth in the nation—that places OU ahead of Oxford. OU has partnered with universities in Africa, Eastern Europe and Asia, and other countries have also adapted the approach. Israel's Open University enrolls one student in six; in India, 1.2 million students, one-tenth of all those in higher education, attend OU. In the equal opportunity domain this is a bright spot—a model deserving of global emulation.

THE CHALLENGE

What, if anything, can be done to shift the balance, away from the increasingly dominant norms and forms of the marketplace and toward greater equality of opportunity? In 1963, Clark Kerr, the visionary who developed the California Master Plan, wrote a justly celebrated account of the new model of higher education titled *The Uses of the University*. That book is optimistic in its account of the academic city, forward-looking in its tone, but in his introduction to the fifth edition, published in 2001, Kerr sounded a pessimistic note. "University leaders have no great visions to lure them on, only the need of survival for themselves and their institutions" (Kerr 2001, 208).

What lies ahead? A glimmer of hope that equity will assume greater importance in policy calculations comes from the United States, the first country to empower the higher education market. Barack Obama has made expanding access one of his highest priorities, and in the aftermath of the 2008 election the federal government may once again treat higher education as an important public good. If there is a substantial infusion of financial aid to poor students, the balance between equal opportunity and the values of the market would once again shift—and perhaps other nations would once again follow.

This much is clear—the equal opportunity battle is lost if higher education is viewed as just another "service," like law and architecture, appropriately subject to "restraint of trade" rules under the General Agreement on Trade and Services. The challenge is to develop a persuasive argument that universities offer something of such great value that they are worth subsidizing even in the teeth of bottom-line pressures—that in certain spheres money should not be the coin of the realm. To do so requires linking what Alexis de Tocqueville, in *Democracy in America*, called "enlightened self-interest" with the interest of the commonweal; linking private good with public purpose; linking a liberal arts education with the development of cultural and economic capital; and linking the acquisition of tools and credentials with the training of responsible and engaged citizens.

If this case cannot be made in a way that's convincing to politicians and taxpayers, then the university will be treated neither as an intellectual commons that generates ideas to the benefit of the society nor an engine of equity but simply as another business—and history teaches that the market is, at best, indifferent to promoting equality of opportunity.

REFERENCES

Friedman, T. *The World Is Flat*. New York: Farrar, Straus and Giroux, 2005.

Kerr, C. *The Uses of the University*. Cambridge: Harvard University Press, 2001.

Kirp, D. *Shakespeare, Einstein, and the Bottom Line: The Marketing of Higher Education*. Cambridge: Harvard University Press, 2005.

———. "College For the Few." *The American Prospect*, December 9, 2008.

Okun, A. *Equality and Efficiency: The Big Tradeoff*. Washington, DC: Brookings Institute, 1975.

de Tocqueville, A. *Democracy in America*. New York: Cambridge University Press, 2009.

Wooldridge, Adrian. "The Brains Business." *Economist*, September 8, 2005.

NOTES

1. Israel's recent experience shows the downside of the market ethos. There, the government reduced the budget for higher education by 20 percent since 2002; 400 faculty jobs have been eliminated, the equivalent of closing one of Israel's seven universities. As enrollment has grown classes have become bigger and the quality of education has declined. New private universities have opened to offer degrees in management, law, and computer science. Tuition is higher than in state schools; and, because these institutions have been able to recruit top faculty by offering higher salaries, the quality of education is often better. Israel's economic success has largely been based on its human capital; now it is losing talent at a worrying rate, with a quarter of Israeli academics migrating to the United States. In protest against government cutbacks, students struck in spring 2007 and professors followed suit the following semester—to no effect.

I

AMERICA

3

Challenges and Opportunities
of Community Colleges

Carol Schmid

The 1,100 American public and private community colleges play an important role in American education. Community colleges enroll almost half of the undergraduate students in the United States. However, they are the least known component of higher education in the United States. This article will offer a critical analysis of the challenges and opportunities of community colleges. It is intricately connected to the theme of higher education and equality of opportunity addressed by David Kirp in chapter 2.

The community college system was established to provide educational opportunities to a diverse population by educating over 10 million students enrolled in credit and noncredit courses (Cohen and Brawer 2002; Phillippe 2000; and Phillippe and Valiga 2000). Unlike other sectors of American higher education, community colleges provide broad access to education through open admissions and serve a range of college students including those who are most likely to have academic and financial challenges and who are first-generation college students. Community colleges have been compared to the "Ellis Island of American higher education" (Center For Innovative Thought 2008). Community colleges enroll almost half of African American undergraduate students and over half of Hispanic and Native American undergraduate students (American Association 2007).

In the century since community colleges were founded they have become the single largest sector of American higher education. Community colleges provide for nearly 80 percent of the first responders in the United States, including firefighters, police officers, and emergency medical technicians. In addition they produce more than half of new nurses and health care technicians (Center For Innovative Thought 2008). However, lurking behind these successes are also significant challenges.

The first section of the paper examines the demographic profile of community college students. The second investigates a comparison of risk factors in community colleges and public four-year colleges. The third concentrates on academic preparation of two-year college students. The fourth part analyzes retention, persistence, and graduation rates by race and ethnicity. This section examines the question: Are minorities being given access to higher education when they begin their student career at community colleges? This work then examines the attitudes of community college faculty and their challenges and sources of satisfaction in teaching. The chapter concludes with an analysis of challenges and opportunities of community colleges in the United States.

WHO ATTENDS COMMUNITY COLLEGES? A DEMOGRAPHIC PROFILE

Community colleges have become an integral part of American postsecondary education. Over the last thirty years two-year institutions have grown faster than any other sector of American higher education. All other sectors of postsecondary enrollment decreased during this time period as a share of postsecondary enrollment (Martinez 2004).

In 2007 community colleges enrolled 46 percent of all undergraduates in the United States. The 1,195 American public and private two-year colleges play a critical role in providing educational opportunities to a large and diverse population. Over six million students are enrolled in credit courses leading to an associate degree or certificate.

A unique and important aspect of these institutions is that they serve a disproportionate percentage of minority students. Nationally almost a third of community college students come from minority backgrounds. Blacks comprise 13 percent of the student population, Hispanics 14 percent, Asians 6 percent and Native Americans 1 percent. Minority students are more likely to start higher education at community colleges than their white counterparts. About half of all Black (47 percent), Hispanic (55 percent), Asian (47 percent), and Native American (57 percent) students in higher education are enrolled in community colleges (American Association 2007).

There is also a great diversity of students with respect to age, gender, family status, and attendance of those new to higher education. Wilson (2004) observes that despite the perception that most community college students are older than traditional college students at four-year colleges and universities, almost half of students in public two-year colleges are eighteen to twenty-four years old. In 2006, over 40 percent of community college students were twenty-one years old or younger. However, two-year institutions also serve nontraditional students, including mid-career displaced workers, single mothers, and individuals looking for a second chance. Nontraditional age students comprise over half (58 percent) of students who attend community colleges (American Association 2007). Women outnumber men at community colleges. This trend has continued for a decade and is projected to continue in the future (Wilson 2004).

Hamm (2004) observes that in contrast with traditional students at four-year colleges and universities, most community college students are torn by multiple roles. The majority work full-time. Almost 30 percent of community college students are married, and over one-third have at least one dependent (Wilson 2004) and 7 percent are single parents. In addition many are new to higher education (39 percent are the first generation to attend college). Almost four in ten community college students have parents who did not attend any postsecondary institution. These students tend to have lower educational expectations. Completion of a certificate is more likely to be a primary educational goal than transferring to senior institutions (Wilson 2004).

Foreign students comprise 8 percent of community college students (American Association 2007). Almost 15 percent of students speak a language other than English in the home. This has led to increasing demand for English as a second language programs in community colleges (Wilson 2004).

The majority of those employed full-time are part-time students. Still over a quarter (27 percent) of community college students attempt balancing full-time studies and full-time work. Among part-time employed students, half are full-time students (American Association 2007). Working students reported that their work schedule limited their class schedule (33 percent), limited the number of classes they could take (39 percent), limited the choices of classes (33 percent), and prevented access to the library (30 percent) (Hamm 2004).

Other demands on the time of these students include commuting to school and their job and caring for dependents. Twenty-three percent commute to class six to twenty hours a week (McClenney 2004). Twenty-nine percent spend more than eleven hours a week and 17 percent spend more than thirty hours a week caring for dependents (Hamm 2004).

RISK FACTORS OF COMMUNITY AND PUBLIC COLLEGE STUDENTS

The definition of an at-risk student according to the National Center for Education Statistics is one who is financially independent, attends part-time, works full-time, delays enrollment after high school, has dependants, is a single parent, or does not have a high school diploma. Using this definition almost 90 percent of community college students had at least one risk factor (McClenney 2004).

Coley (2000) found that the seven risk factors were much more common among community college students than among students who attended four-year public universities. Three-fourths of undergraduates were characterized by at least one of these factors. Students entering community colleges were more likely to have several of these seven factors. Nationally, in the 1995–1996 academic year, 24 percent of students entering community colleges had 4 or more of these factors. In contrast, only about 4 percent of students at public four-year colleges showed this level of risk. Almost one half of beginning community college students had delayed entry (did not enter college in the first year after high school). Almost one half (46 percent) of first-time entrants into the community colleges enroll part-time (taking less than twelve hours) as compared to 11 percent of first-time students attending public four-year institutions. Thirty-five percent of first-time entrants in community colleges work full-time compared to 11 percent in four-year colleges. About 35 percent of community college students were financially independent, and approximately one-fifth had dependents. The Coley (2000) study based on National Center for Education Statistics found that 26 percent of students in two-year institutions had no risk factors in comparison to 70 percent of students in four-year institutions.

Furthermore, Coley (2000) found some significant differences in student involvement in college life, depending on the type of institution the student first attended. Community college students were less likely than other full-time students to participate in study groups, to speak to faculty outside class, and to participate in school clubs.

According to Tinto and Russo (1994), student involvement is difficult to achieve at *most* community colleges. Literature on student retention and attrition suggests that contact with faculty and students outside of class is a crucial factor in a student's decision to remain in college (Chickering and Gamson 1987; Glennen, Farren, and Vowell 1996; and Schmid and Abell 2003).

ACADEMIC PREPARATION: NOT WHAT IT SHOULD BE

Over half of all first-time community college students are underprepared for the academic rigors of college-level courses (Roueche and Roueche 1999). The challenges are even greater for low-income and minority students whose schooling in high school has often been less than adequate. Low-income and minority students overwhelmingly attend secondary schools with fewer resources than wealthier predominantly white suburban schools (Frankenburg and Lee 2002). One of the important consequences of this differential in resources is that in 2000 only one in five high school graduates from families with income less than $25,000 was highly or very highly qualified for college based on their secondary curriculum. In contrast more than half of secondary students from families earning incomes of $75,000 or more were prepared for college (NCES 2000).

Several surveys sponsored by the National Center for Education Statistics have found that community college students are in much greater need of remediation, less likely to graduate, and have lower persistence rates than their counterparts at four-year colleges and universities. The data from this paper is drawn from several sources. Each data set provides a different perspective on community college students.

The 1996/2001 Beginning Postsecondary Students Longitudinal Study (BPS) is a representative sample of all undergraduates, regardless of when they graduated from high school, who enrolled in postsecondary education for the first time in the 1995–1996 academic year and were last interviewed in 2001, about six years later. The 2000/2001 Baccalaureate and Beyond Longitudinal Study (B&B: 2000/2001) provides data on students who received a bachelor's degree in the 1999–2000 academic year, regardless of when they began their postsecondary education. The National Education Longitudinal Study of 1988 (NELS: 88/2000) survey comprises a grade cohort (all the respondents in one grade or about the same age). NELS respondents were first surveyed in 1988 in the eighth grade and were followed through high school and college, and last interviewed in 2000, about eight years after most of the respondents had graduated from high school. Unlike the BPS cohort, which includes first-time students regardless of age, the NELS cohort reflects a more traditional group of college students who enroll in postsecondary education soon after they graduate from high school. A final source of comparison comes from the Achieving the Dream 2002 (AD 2000) cohort of credential-seeking students that attended fifty-eight participating community colleges. This cohort was tracked until 2008. Although not a national sample, it includes 72,392 students. The sample provides a breakdown by race and ethnicity, developmental education status, and persistence rates (Achieving the Dream Initiative 2006a, 2006b, and 2007).

The NELS (88/2000) sample for 1992 high school graduates tracks students who first enrolled in community college within two years of high school graduation. Many of the NELS 1992 high school graduates who entered community college had low ability levels in mathematics and reading. Thirty percent of these students were only able to perform simple arithmetical operations on whole numbers but could not perform simple operations on decimals, fractions, powers, or roots. Forty-four percent of this cohort of community college students had only basic reading proficiency skills. They could not make simple inferences of a text beyond the author's main point. In contrast, based on a variety of measures more than a third (36 percent) entered community college with strong academic preparation that would qualify them to enter four-year institutions (Hoachlander, Sikora, and Horn 2003). This wide disparity in ability levels makes community college courses particularly challenging for instructors.

Overall community college students according to the NELS (88/2000) sample enrolled in the largest number of remedial courses in their first year of postsecondary studies. Sixty percent of community college students took at least one remedial course in their first year in contrast to 29 percent of first-year students at four-year public institutions (Bailey, Thomas, Jenkins, and Leinbach 2005). The 2005 Community College Survey of Student Engagement (CCSSE) confirms this trend. About half of the first-time community college students were unprepared for college. Most of these students were referred to developmental education courses during their first term and 53 percent of the CCSSE respondents had taken or were planning to take at least one developmental education class (Community College Survey 2005).

A breakdown according to race and ethnicity and enrollment in remedial courses in two-year and four-year public institutions found that over three-fourths of black (76 percent) and Hispanic (78 percent) of NELS (88/2000) students at community colleges took at least one remedial course in comparison to 55 percent of white community college students. This trend was also apparent among black and Hispanic NELS students at four-year public institutions who were more likely to take remedial courses than white or Asian students. The small numbers of Native American students attending four-year public institutions were much better qualified than their community college counterparts.

In the AD sample, 35 of the 58 community colleges in the sample participated long enough to provide data on the scope of developmental education by race and ethnicity. Eighty-two percent of students in the 2002 cohort were referred to developmental education. Community colleges with high percentages of minority students were oversampled in the AD cohort. The breakdown of remedial students according to race and ethnicity was: 94 percent Native American, 79 percent Asian/Pacific Islander, 90 percent black, non-Hispanic, 77 percent white, non-Hispanic, and 86 percent Hispanic. Of the 76 percent of AD students who attempted some type of developmental education during their first term of enrollment, 54 percent successfully completed developmental education classes. These rates also varied by race and ethnicity: 58 percent of Hispanic students referred to development education completed at least one developmental education class during their first semester, which was more than the average. Fifty-four percent of both black and Native American students completed at least one developmental education class during their first semester, similar to the cohort average. The percentage of white students completing at least one class was lower than the average, 51 percent (Achieving the Dream Initiative 2006b). The AD sample was not strictly representative of all community college students. However it follows the general trends of previous research. Many community college students struggle with both academic deficits and low income in comparison with students attending four-year institutions.

There is a much larger cohort of poor students among community college students in the NELS study than students attending four-year educational institutions. This may help to explain the anomaly between these two cohorts and remedial education. Students from the lowest SES at community colleges (70 percent) were only slightly more likely to take remedial classes than those in the highest SES quartile (60 percent). In contrast the gap is much larger at four-year institutions. There is a large decline in the proportion of students taking remedial courses from the lowest (52 percent) to the highest income quartile (19 percent) (Bailey, Jenkins, and Leinbach 2005).

An examination of students who are the first in their families to attend college is also linked to remedial education. At community colleges 67 percent of students whose parents had high school completion or less were enrolled in remedial courses in comparison to 58 percent of students whose parents had a BA or higher. At four-year public institutions, 41 percent of NELS (88/2000) students who were first-generation college students took remedial courses compared to 19 percent of students whose parent earned at least a bachelor's degree (Bailey, Jenkins, and Leinbach 2005).

The relatively high poverty rate in the United States is one of the most common barriers to educational attainment and underprepared students. Therefore, "significant numbers of academically unprepared students will continue to enter the doors of higher education; and community colleges will, for the most part, provide the gateway" (Saxon and Boylan n.d.:1). Levin (2001) also observes that the community college is unique among institutions of higher education in accepting these students.

For many students in either large or small communities, the community college is the only public educational institution that will accept them for college-level studies given their high school performance. Furthermore, of the many types of postsecondary institutions facing students who are unprepared for college-level studies, the community college is the only institution whose legal and social mandate is remedial education (Levin 2001:xii).

EMPHASIZING ACCESS OVER SUCCESS:
MEASURING PERFORMANCE

The community college opens its door to all who apply. However, a recent *Community College Week* article has called its persistence and graduation rates "dismal" (Bradley 2007). Berger and Lyon define student retention as "the ability of an institution to retain a student from admission through graduation" (2005:7). Degree completion in this paper refers to actual attainment of a degree or certificate.

Part of the problem of measuring performance is that community college students come to college with very divergent academic goals. The 2006 Community College Survey of Student Engagement documented this diversity of goals. The primary or secondary goal of 48 percent of the sample was to complete a certificate program, 80 percent named their primary or secondary goal as obtaining an associate degree. The major goal or secondary goal of 71 percent of the students was to transfer to a four-year college or university (Community College Survey 2006:5). Because students could name more than one goal, the percentages do not add up to 100 percent. Many community college students change goals over the duration of their college experience (Voorhee and Zhou 2000).

A three-year longitudinal study for all students who entered community college in 2002 by the National Center for Education Statistics found that many students did not accomplish their academic goals. Only 24 percent received an associate degree by 2005 at public community colleges. For blacks the percentage was almost 17 percent. For Hispanics it was 19 percent. The average for Asians was slightly above 25 percent (Knapp, Kelly-Reid, and Miller 2007). Community college leaders have questioned the appropriateness of graduation rates, particularly among students with high demands on their time and a range of personal, academic and financial challenges.

Many students transfer between institutions before completing a degree. As of 2001, according to the BPS study, 40 percent of students who enrolled in postsecondary education for the first time in the 1996/1997 academic year attended more than one institution. Among students in the B&B (2000/2001) sample who started at a four-year institution and obtained a bachelor's degree in the 1999–2000 academic year about 47 percent had attended another institution at some time point with or without transferring (Peter and Cataldi 2005).

Transferring diminishes the chance of completing a bachelors' degree. Holding other risk factors constant, those students who had transferred were less likely to attain a degree or be enrolled in four-year institutions six years after first enrolling in postsecondary education. Beginning postsecondary students who attended a community college at some time during their enrollment were also less likely to persist for six years or to graduate than students who did not attend community colleges during their college career (Peter and Cataldi 2005).

Employing the BPS and NELS (88/2000) samples Dougherty and Kienzl (2006) found that the likelihood of transfer is strongly affected by parents' socioeconomic status. Students whose parents have more advanced education and better paid and more prestigious jobs have a large statistical advantage in transferring to four-year institutions over less economically favored community college students. As we have previously seen in students taking remedial classes a significant advantage is transmitted through differences in high school academic preparation and educational aspirations. Age at college entry also has a very important impact on transfer rates. Older college entrants, especially those over 30 years of age, are much less likely to transfer than community college students who enter postsecondary education right out of high school (Dougherty and Kienzl 2006).

Institutional characteristics also make a difference in community college success rates. Bailey, Calcagno, and Jenkins (2006) found that there was a consistent negative relationship between enrollment size and completion rates. Community colleges with high rates of minority students, part-time students and women also have lower graduation rates. Furthermore they found that greater instructional expenditures are related to a greater likelihood of graduation (Bailey, Calcagno, and Jenkins et al. 2006).

The NELS (88/2000) survey provides a foundation for understanding the disadvantages that community college students and minorities face in completing certificates, associate or bachelor's degrees. Among all NELS postsecondary students who started at a community college, those who took at least one developmental (remedial) course were less likely to complete an associate's or bachelor's degree than students who did not take remedial classes. The only exception was Black students who started at community colleges. They were more likely to earn a certificate, associate, or bachelor's degree if they took remedial classes. Since most Blacks started in remedial classes this finding may be influenced by the small sample size of Black non-remedial community college students. Among community college students who took remedial classes, white students (46 percent) were more successful in earning a credential or transferring to a four-year institution than Black students (32 percent) or Hispanic students (36 percent) (Bailey, Jenkins, and Leinbach 2005).

The cumulative disadvantages of community college students can be seen by examining the class of 1992 eight years later. The representative longitudinal NELS (88/2000) sample paints a picture of perseverance and challenge of community college students. Only 26 percent of students who started at community colleges transferred and 10 percent earned a bachelor's degree within eight years. A more optimistic interpretation shows that the overall success rate (i.e. any credential or transfer) of students who started in certificate programs was 32 percent, while that of associate degree students was 50 percent.

By 2000 of students who began their education at public community colleges, 59 percent of Blacks, 53 percent of Hispanics, and 76 percent of Native Americans had dropped out of postsecondary education. Asians had the best record of completing a bachelor's degree at 30 percent. Whites are a distant second with 17 percent that started in the class of 1992 at the community college completing a degree by 2000 (NELS 88/2000).

Less than half as many black students as white students transferred to four-year institutions. This is one cause of the low bachelor's rate of completion for black community college students (4 percent) in the NELS study (Bailey, Jenkins, and Leinbach 2005). Hispanic postsecondary students who started at community colleges had higher rates of completion than blacks, but not as high as whites and Asians, at nearly all credential levels.

All racial and ethnic groups were more likely to complete a bachelor's degree if they started their education at public four-year colleges or universities. However, even among these students there was a wide range of outcomes in completing a bachelor's degree. Less than 40 percent of Hispanic students and only about half of Native American and black students completed a bachelor's degree in eight years. In contrast 67 percent of white and 73 percent of Asian students at public colleges and universities finished their bachelor's degree (NELS 88/2000).

Few NELS (88/2000) students who started at four-year institutions earned certificates or associate degrees. More students have an opportunity to complete a certificate or associate degree at community colleges. The evidence however points to reduced opportunity to complete a four-year degree if one begins their higher education at a community college. Despite this disadvantage half of the B&B baccalaureate recipients in the United States attended a community college at some time during their college career. Slightly less than half (44 percent) were "casual attendees" who did not start their postsecondary studies at the community college and did not obtain a degree or a certificate from the community college. An equal number (44 percent) of the baccalaureate recipients were "traditional two- to four-year transfer" students who began their undergraduate studies at a community college. The remaining group of "reverse transfer" students (12 percent) started their postsecondary studies at a four-year institution but attended a community college to obtain an associate degree or certificate before obtaining a baccalaureate (McPhee 2006).

The portrait of community college students who complete their education is a very complex one. It is tempered by academic preparation, socioeconomic class background, age, race and ethnicity, and institutional factors. Other factors include hours spent at work and number of institutions where community college students have studied.

FACULTY SPEAK: GREATEST
CHALLENGES AND SOURCES OF SATISFACTION

A survey of faculty at Guilford Technical Community College in Jamestown, North Carolina (GTCC) reinforced many themes we have seen in the literature. GTCC is an urban community college with an enrollment of about 10,600 credit students in fall 2007. Approximately 43 percent of the students are minorities; the largest group is blacks with 36 percent. Slightly less than half (47 percent) of the students were enrolled part-time in 2007. The average age is 27 years.

When the faculty was asked in an open-ended questionnaire about the greatest challenges of teaching at GTCC the highest response was "unprepared and underprepared students for college work." The second most numerous responses were "the problem of work, family conflicts and constraints." A common response was this one from a speech instructor: "My greatest challenge with respect to students is that many of them are unprepared for college work and have other pressing problems that keep them from focusing on schoolwork." Huber (1998) observes that the open-door nature of most community colleges often leads to an instructional challenge in the form of underprepared students. "While faculty at all types of colleges and universities say that their students could be better prepared for college work, under preparation is most marked at community colleges, most of which are open to any who wish to enroll" (1998:19).

Also mentioned by several GTCC faculty were the following challenge: lack of student social skills, lack of good study skills, and varied skill, levels as well as age and generational differences. Too many students also come with disrespectful behaviors.

Although there are great challenges in teaching such a diverse student body there are also sources of satisfaction. By far the largest two responses to this question were "making a positive contribution to students' life" and increasing the joy of learning. Typical of this response was an Emergency Medical Services (EMS) instructor who observed "When you do produce that productive, very well rounded student and I am able to see that he/she did well in my class. That is a great satisfaction." An English professor wrote "The greatest satisfaction comes when, as we often say, "the light bulb goes on." It is very rewarding when students make progress from beginning to the end of class and "find the course actually interesting." Other related responses that received several responses were very appreciative students and witnessing positive changes. The faculty was somewhat divided with respect to the great diversity in the classroom.

CONCLUSION: COMMUNITY
COLLEGES AND THE OPPORTUNITY GAP

Education matters. On average students earning an associate degree have salaries 20 to 30 percent higher than individuals who only completed high school. Students who earned a bachelor's degree resulted in significant re- turns between 56 and 66 percent more than high school graduates (Bailey, Kienzl, and Marcotte 2004). The emphasis in the United States on knowledge acquisition has contributed to a growing wage gap between high school and college graduates.

Community college programs have been able to prepare much of the mid- skilled workforce in the United States, which includes over three-fourths of first responders (firefighters, police officers, and emergency technicians) as well as half of health care technicians and nurses. Two-year colleges are the fastest growing sector in American higher education. There are, however, many academic casualties of the community colleges particularly among the least prepared students.

As we have seen, community colleges have been the institutions of choice for students of color, older adults, those from less affluent backgrounds and stu- dents who work part and full-time. Moore than six million students attend credit classes at almost 1,000 public two-year colleges, located in all fifty U.S. states. While access is increasingly available to a diversified audience via the commu- nity colleges, there remains a large opportunity gap in degree completion.

Minority students trail their white and Asian counterparts on almost every indicator of educational participation and attainment. Blacks, Hispanics, and Native Americans, first-generation college-goers and those from low-income family backgrounds are much more likely to be enrolled in developmental and remedial classes. The number of unprepared students is the greatest chal- lenge of community college faculty.

There is growing evidence of an increasing opportunity gap between stu- dents from different racial, ethnic, and socioeconomic class backgrounds. Black, Hispanic, and Native American students who begin their postsec- ondary education at community colleges are much less likely to complete an associate degree or transfer to a four-year institution than their white counterparts. For all students who start at the community college the path to a bachelor's degree is less probable than among students who start their education at senior public institutions. This trend will have significant impact for the United States. Wellman observes: "Although progress has been made nationwide in closing performance gaps among racial groups in the transition from high school to college, the gaps widen again in baccalaureate completion. . . . Improving the effectiveness of 2/4 transfer will be the key to national progress in closing the gap among racial groups in degree attainment—and it will affect far more students than affirmative action policy" (2002: V).

Projections of a 75 percent increase among the 18 to 24 year olds between 2003 and 2010 of persons of color, primarily Hispanics and blacks, means that education levels may decline in the United States (Kelly 2005). If educational disparities are not addressed, anticipated demographic shifts will have a major impact on educational attainment and earnings in the United States. Some indicators already suggest that the United States is losing its leadership as the most highly educated nation in the world, particularly with respect to the younger population that represents the future workforce.

REFERENCES

American Association of Community Colleges. "Research." 2007. www2.aacc.nche .edu/research/home.htm (accessed March 12, 2008).

Bailey, T., J. C. Calcagno, D. Jenkins, T. Leinbach, and G. S. Kienz. "Is Student-Right-to-Know all you should know? An Analysis of Community College Graduation Rates." *Research in Higher Education* 47, no. 5 (August 2006): 491–508.

Bailey, T., D. Jenkins, and T. Leinbach. "Community College Low-Income and Minority Student Completion Study: Descriptive Statistics from the 1992 High School Cohort." New York: Teachers College, Columbia University, 2005.

Bailey, T., G. Kienzl, and D. Marcotte. "Who Benefits from Postsecondary Occupational Education?" CCRC Brief No. 23. New York: Teachers College, Columbia University, 2004.

Berger, J., and G. Lyon. "Past to Present: A Historical Look at Retention." Pp. 1–27 in *College Student Retention: Formula for Student Success.* Edited by A. Seidman. Westport, CT: Praeger, 2005.

Bradley, P. "Measuring Performance." *Community College Week* (June 18, 2007): 6–8. *Community College Survey of Student Engagement,* Community College Leadership Program, University of Texas at Austin, 2005.

———. "Act on Fact: Using Data to Improve Student Success." *Community College Survey of Student Engagement.* Community College Leadership Program. University of Texas at Austin, 2006.

Center For Innovative Thought. "Winning the Skills Race." Report of the National Commission on Community Colleges, the College Board, 2008. http:// professionals.collegeboard.com/profdownload/winning_the_skills_race.pdf.

38 *Carol Schmid*

Chickering, E., and Z. Gammon "Seven Principles for Good Practice in Undergraduate Education." *AAHE Bulletin* 39, no. 7 (1987): 3–7.

Cohen, A. M., and F. B. Brawer. *The American Community College*, 4th ed. San Francisco: Jossey-Bass, 2002.

Coley, R. J. *The American Community College Turns 100: A Look at Its Students, Programs, and Prospects*. Princeton, NJ: Educational Testing Service, Policy Information Center, 2000.

Dougherty, K., and G. S. Kienzl. "It's Not Enough to Get Through the Open Door: Inequalities by Social Background in Transfer from Community Colleges to Four-Year Colleges." *Teachers College Record* 108, no. 3 (March 2006): 452–87.

Glennen, R., P. Farran, and F. Vowell. "How Advising and Retention of Students Improves Fiscal Stability. *NACADA Journal* 16 (1996): 38–41.

Frankenberg, E., and C. Lee. *Race in American Public Schools: Rapidly Resegregating School Districts*. Cambridge: The Civil Rights Project, Harvard University, 2002.

Hamm, R. "Going to College: Not What It Used to Be." Pp. 29–33 in *Keeping America's Promise*. Edited by K. Boswell and C. D. Wilson. Denver, CO: Education Commission of the States, 2004.

Huber, M. T. "Community College Faculty Attitudes and Trends, 1997." No. R309A60001; NCPI-4-03. Stanford, CA: National Center for Postsecondary Improvement. 1988.

JBL Associates. "Data Notes." *Achieving the Dream Initiative* 1, no. 3 (April 2006a).
———. *Achieving the Dream Initiative* 1, no. 6 (July/August 2006b).
———. *Achieving the Dream Initiative* 2, no. 2 (May/June 2007).

Kelly, P. J. "As America Becomes More Diverse: The Impact of State Higher Education Inequality." Boulder, CO: National Center for Higher Education Management System, 2005.

Knapp, L., J. Kelly-Reid, and R. Whitmore, "Enrollment in Postsecondary Institutions, Fall 2005; Graduation rates, 1999 and 2002 Cohorts; and Financial Statistics, Fiscal Year 2005." National Center for Education Statistics (NCES 2007-154). Washington, DC: U.S Department of Education, 2007.

Long, B. T., and M. Kurlaender. "Do Community Colleges Provide a Viable Pathway to a Baccalaureate Degree?" *Educational Evaluation and Policy Analysis* 31 (2009): 30–53.

McClenny, K. M. "Keeping America's Promise: Challenges for Community Colleges." Pp. 9–18 in *Keeping America's Promise*. Edited by K. Boswell and C. D. Wilson. Denver, CO: Education Commission of the States 2004.

McPhee, S. "En Route to the Baccalaureate: Community College Outcomes." Washington, DC: American Association of Community Colleges, 2006.

Martinez, M. "High and Rising: How Much Higher Will College Enrollments Go?" Pp. 21–23 in *Keeping America's Promise*. Edited by K. Boswell and C. D. Wilson. Denver, CO: Education Commission of the States 2004.

National Center for Education Statistics. *The Condition of Education 2000*. Washington, DC: U.S. Department of Education, 2000.

Perin, D. "The Location of Developmental Education in Community Colleges: A

Discussion of the Merits of Mainstreaming vs. Centralization." *Community College Review* (Summer 2002): 27–44.

Peter, K., and E. Forrest Cataldi. "The Road Less Traveled? Students Who Enroll in Multiple Institutions." *Education Statistics Quarterly* 7, nos. 1, 2 (2005): 1–7.

Phillippe, K. A., ed. *Profile of Community Colleges: Trends and Statistics*. 3rd ed. Washington, DC: Community College Press, 2000.

Phillippe, K. A., and M. J. Valiga. *Faces of the Future: A Portrait of America's Community College Students*. Washington, DC: American Association of Community Colleges, 2000.

Price, D. "Defining the Gaps: Access and Success at America's Community Colleges." Pp. 35–37 in *Keeping America's Promise*. Edited by K. Boswell and C. D. Wilson. Denver: Education Commission of the States, 2004.

Roueche, J. E., and S. D. Roueche. *Making Remedial Education Work*. Washington, DC: Community College Press, 1999.

Saxon, D., P. Boylan, and H. Boylan. "Characteristics of Community College Remedial Students." Prepared for the League for Innovation in the Community College. National Center for Developmental Education (2004).

Schmid, C., and P. Abell. "Demographic Risk Factors, Study Patterns, and Campus Involvement as Related to Student Success among Guilford Technical Community College Students." *Community College Review* 31, no. 3 (2003): 1–16.

Tinto, V., and P. Russo. "Coordinated Studies Programs: Their Effect on Student Involvement at a Community College." *Community College Review* 22, no. 2 (1994): 16–25.

Voorhees, R., and D. Zhou. "Intentions and Goals at the Community College: Associating Student Perceptions and Demographics." *Community College Journal of Research and Practice* 24 (2000): 219–32.

Wellman, J. V. "State Policy and Community College—Baccalaureate Transfer." National Center Report 02-6. The National Center for Public Policy and Higher Education Policy (2002).

Wilson, C. "Coming through the Open Door: A Student Profile." Pp. 25–27 in *Keeping America's Promise*. Edited by K. Boswell and C. D. Wilson. Denver, CO: Education Commission of the States, 2004.

4

Minority Access to Higher Education in the United States and the White-Minority Credentials Gap

Noga O'Connor

As David Kirp has noted (see chapter 2), two-thirds of U.S. high school graduates today enroll in some form of post-secondary institution. Indeed, with 29 percent of the population in the United States today holding a bachelor's degree (U.S. Census Bureau 2007), the importance of postsecondary credentials in the labor market has been increasing steadily. Employers ask for a bachelor's degree for positions that in the past did not require any postsecondary education. By the mid-1990s, an associate degree was as valuable in the labor market as a high school diploma used to be in the 1970s (Tyler et al. 1995; Adelman 1999; and Carey 2004). While it is true that certain sectors of the workforce have experienced deskilling (Lewis 1998), the general trend has been for an increase in the required level of skills for most jobs (Bailey 1989; and Murphy and Welch 1993).

In the United States today, members of minority ethnic groups are significantly overrepresented in blue-collar occupations and underrepresented in managerial and professional occupations compared to whites (Llagas and Snyder 2003). This social disadvantage of minorities goes hand in hand with their lower rates of bachelor's degree attainment.

The reasons for the gap in college enrollment between whites and minorities are varied, and include class (Roscigno 2000), ethnic culture (Ogbu 1994), and the schools themselves (Baker and Velez 1996 and McDonough 1997). The gap has grown between the 1960s and the mid-1980s by about 5 percent, from 13 to 18 percent owing mainly to rising tuition and the decrease in federal financial aid (Orfield 1992 and Baker and Velez 1996). During the

1980s, tuition rose, Pell grants shrank, and loans replaced most grant aid. Minority students were reluctant to take advantage of loan programs, and consequentially their enrollment numbers dropped (Orfield 1992). Minority students were also considerably more financially needy than white students were: between 1973 and 2000, 21 to 28 percent of Hispanics and 22 to 33 percent of blacks, but only 7 to 9 percent of whites, were living below the poverty level (U.S. Census Bureau 2005).

At the same time, several large-scale efforts encouraged minority access to higher education: open admissions, the expansion of community colleges, and affirmative action.

The premise of open admissions is to provide every high school graduate with an opportunity for college admissions—a senior college for top performers and a community college for the rest of the students. Hand in hand with open admissions, the massive expansion of community colleges (Dougherty 1994 and Labaree 1997) promised that through inexpensive, local, and non-selective two-year schools, students could both obtain a two-year associate degree and the possibility to transfer to a four-year college to complete their bachelor's degree. Together with affirmative action—the practice of adding a bonus factor to the admissions scores of minority applicants—these policies were expected to generate meaningful educational gains for minority students and narrow the enrollment gap in postsecondary education between whites and minorities. This study will look at the effect of these policies on minority access to higher education.

SOCIAL POLICIES TO INCREASE MINORITY PARTICIPATION

The implementation of open admissions signified a new role for higher education—instead of the traditional "sorting and selecting" function, colleges now played an egalitarian role, promoting equal opportunity. In its old role, higher education used to be limited to the brightest students, designed to promote scientific progress and social efficiency (Astin 1971 and Labaree 1997). The adoption of open admissions in 1960 by California schools and in 1969 by New York City, and later on elsewhere in the nation, stirred higher education from its old elitist model to its new model, that of an agent of equal opportunity.

In California, the first Master Plan for Higher Education became a law in 1960. The plan instructed the University of California (UC) to admit the top one-eighth of high school graduates, state colleges (CSU) to admit the top one-third of high school graduates, and community colleges to admit everybody else, with 60 percent of UC and CSU undergraduate slots reserved for community college transfers. A successful community college graduate will be guaranteed admissions into a bachelor's program in a California public university, second in admissions priority after continuing students in good standing, and before newly entering students (Richardson 1997 and Richardson, Shulock, and Teranishi 2005).

In New York, a student strike in the spring of 1969, over the underrepresentation of ethnic minorities in one of the city's four-year colleges, resulted in the Board of Higher Education adopting an immediate open admissions policy in the then tuition-free City University of New York (CUNY) system. The policy instructed CUNY four-year schools to admit all high school graduates ranked within the top 50 percent of their class and all graduates with an 80 average in academic courses, while CUNY community colleges were to admit all other high school graduates (Lavin, Alba, and Silberstein 1981 and Fullinwider 1999).

Open admissions were later established in different states across the nation. The policy narrowed inequality in the distribution of ethnic groups in higher education; nonetheless, it resulted in an increase in minority representation at community colleges, while a higher rate of white students attended four-year schools (Lavin and Hyllegard 1996).

COMMUNITY COLLEGES

Community colleges are the primary entry point into higher education for minority students, and have contributed significantly to the increased participation of minorities in higher education (Bragg 2001). During the 1970s and 1980s, community colleges went through the same process that high schools did a half century earlier—as high school attendance became universal, high schools increasingly formed vocational programs alongside their more traditional college preparatory programs. Similarly, as community college attendance became more common, community colleges started offering more vocational programs, channeling an increasing proportion of their students toward vocational and occupational curricula (Hammack 2004). During the 1970s and 1980s, community colleges expanded their vocational programs, and as a result, the percentage of transfers to senior colleges declined between the 1970s and the 1980s (Dougherty 1994; Cohen and Brawer 1989; and Brint and Karabel 1989).

While almost three-quarters of community college entering students state their educational goal as the completion of a bachelor's degree (Kane and Rouse 1999), only 39 percent of bachelor's degree aspirants end up transferring (Choy 2002). This discrepancy could be interpreted as either a positive or a negative trend, depending on where the researcher is located regarding the contention surrounding "substitution effect." The term "substitution effect"

refers to the concept by which community college students would have entered four-year colleges had community colleges not been available; hence,
the low transfer rate is seen as a major challenge. Students from comparable
backgrounds are more likely to obtain a bachelor's degree starting at a four-
year school than starting at a community college (Dougherty 1994); thus,
the availability of the community college reduces their chances of obtaining
a bachelor's degree. As a result, states with more community colleges have
lower bachelor's degree completion rates than states with fewer community
colleges (Dougherty 1994 and Brint 2003).

On the other hand, Rouse (1998) found only weak evidence for a substitution effect, and stronger evidence to support a "democratization effect" of
community colleges: community colleges serve society in opening up higher
education to students who would not have attended college otherwise, hence
even low transfer rates are better than the alternative, which is no postsecondary education at all. As Cohen and Brawer (1989: 48) note, "for most students
in two-year institutions, the choice is not between the community college and
a senior residential institution; it is between the community college and nothing." Minority students tend to delay entry into college and are more likely to
be part-time, and community colleges are designed to serve older, part-time
students. These students are less likely to graduate regardless of which kind
of institution they attend (Metzner and Bean 1987), and community colleges
are always there for nontraditional students, while four-year schools are not
(Cohen and Brawer 1989).

Affirmative Action

Affirmative action toward minorities in higher education has been in place in
the United States since the mid-1960s. The term refers to the practice of promoting minorities in higher education through a favorable treatment during
the admissions process, resulting in a higher rate of admitted minorities.

Affirmative action is usually traced back to a speech given by President
Lyndon Johnson at Howard University in 1965, in which he outlined the ideas
behind affirmative action in the workforce. Within a few years of the speech,
the Department of Labor examined all federal hiring, salary, and promotion
practices for race-based deficiencies, culminating with an enforcement of affirmative action in all federal contracting agencies. In 1971, Harvard University
adopted an affirmative-action program, and in 1978, the Supreme Court ruled in
the famous Bakke case against admissions quotas, but in favor of using race as
a factor in admissions decisions (*The Chronicle of Higher Education* 1995).

Affirmative action was criticized by many, but has persisted. For example,
while community colleges and open admissions were designed to promote equal

opportunity—a framework that promotes blindness to differences—affirmative action is often criticized for accentuating differences. In an equal opportunity (or a meritocratic) society, an organization should not have access to information about a candidate's ethnicity; affirmative action deems this information necessary in order to make a decision (Francis 1993 and Tierney 1997).

Some argue that affirmative action accentuates ethnic differences in admissions criteria—if the criteria for minorities is lowered, there are fewer seats for whites, and consequentially the criteria for whites has to be raised (Astin 1971). Other arguments include reverse discrimination (preference given to less-qualified minorities over more-qualified whites could generate a discriminatory practice against whites); the discrediting of the academic accomplishments of minorities; and weakening standards in academic programs (Tierney 1997 and Harper and Reskin 2005). Professor Kirp (2008) rightfully noted, in the case of affirmative action, two opposing camps are raising equity-based claims versus merit-based arguments. Affirmative-action supporters were able to deflect the criticism by showing results (more minorities admitted into prestigious programs), and by pointing at the additional advantages of affirmative action, such as diverse campuses as better learning environments and compensation for unequal treatment in the past (Tierney 1997 and Harper and Reskin 2005). Nevertheless, since the 1990s, states have slowly been moving away from affirmative action—California in 1996 with Proposition 209, prohibiting public institutions from taking race into consideration in admissions; Washington in 1998 with Initiative 200; and Michigan in 2006 with the Michigan Civil Rights Initiative. In 2008, an amendment to end state-level affirmative-action practices failed in Colorado, but a similar one passed in Nebraska by a significant margin.

CONCEPTUAL FRAMEWORK

While policymakers believe that access engenders equality, many researchers are more skeptical. For example, Raftery and Hout (1993) discussed in their study of Irish male workers the concept of "maximally maintained inequality" (Mare 1980, 1981), showing that the effect of social background remains the same even as the access to education rises, since educational expansion takes place at a certain level only after high-status social groups have reached full saturation of that level and are ready to move on and increase their own educational attainment. Lucas (2001) added the concept of "effectively maintained inequality," showing that even when quantitative inequality (levels of education) seems to halt, inequality is being maintained qualitatively (the kind of education received within a certain level of education). Finally,

Collins (1971, 1979) and Brown (2001) described educational expansion as the result of credential inflation at the top of the occupational hierarchy, as occupational groups are upgrading educational requirements to raise their prestige and autonomy. Consequently, as education expands among lower-status groups, it also expands among high-status groups, and so the gap persists.

Using these approaches as the conceptual framework for this study, the first question I ask is: *Have social policies to increase minority participation in higher education been successful in reducing the gap between whites and minorities in obtaining bachelor's degrees?* My hypothesis is that if "maintenance of inequality" theories are correct, the gap in bachelor's degree attainment will not have narrowed in spite of political efforts to promote minority participation in higher education.

My secondary question in this study is: *Are returns to education equal among ethnic groups?* Financial returns to education will complete the picture of how effective were access policies in improving the life chances and labor market status of minorities. A discriminatory labor market, in which academic degrees held by minorities are not of equal value as those held by whites, will be a counter force to the increased access promoted by the social policies aforementioned.

An equal opportunity structure today, though, may not have been equal thirty years ago, and vice versa. To fully understand the impact of access policies since the 1970s, we need to not only look at returns to education today, but look at returns to education throughout time. Therefore, a third question this study asks is: *In what ways have returns to education changed since the 1970s?*

These three questions are central to our ability to assess the success and potential for success of educational policies in addressing issues of racial inequality. Looking at the shape of the gap is necessary in order to evaluate the success rate in reducing educational inequalities since the 1970s; looking at the shape of labor market returns is necessary in order to evaluate the *potential* for success in reducing educational inequalities.

These questions have not been addressed empirically in a comparative way that utilizes quantitative data from the 1970s, 1980s, and 1990s. This study looks at data collected in the three time periods, using variables that have been standardized across the three data sets.

RESEARCH DESIGN

In order to find whether access policies were successful in reducing the participation gap between whites and minorities, and what the opportunity structure (labor market returns) looked like since the 1970s, this study compares minorities and whites in higher education and in the labor market in the 1970s, 1980s and 1990s. This study utilizes three longitudinal NCES survey programs: The National Longitudinal Study of the High School Class of 1972 (NLS-72), The High School and Beyond (HS&B), and The National Education Longitudinal Study of 1988 (NELS: 88). The first data set follows the high school graduating class of 1972; the second follows the class of 1982; and the third follows the class of 1992. By using the three data sets, I was able to obtain similar data for three points in time, seven years after gradua-tion—1979, 1989, and 1999. By these points in time, the survey respondents are in their mid-twenties, and their earnings are more likely than old workers' earnings to reflect the opportunity structure of their time (Blackburn, McKin-ley, Bloom and Freeman 1990:33, and Loury 1997).

DATA

The NLS-72 is comprised of about 23,000 1972 senior students. Follow-ups occurred after one, two, four, seven, and fourteen years, and postsecondary transcripts were collected after twelve years.

The HS&B survey includes two cohorts: the 1980 senior class, and the 1980 sophomore class. Both cohorts were surveyed every two years through 1986, and the 1980 sophomore class was also surveyed again in 1992 and its postsecondary transcripts were collected. This study used the 1980 sopho-more cohort alone (a cohort of about 27,000 students), to maintain a distance of ten years between the three cohorts included in the study. Throughout the study, the term "HS&B" or "HS&B cohort" will be used in reference to the 1980 sophomore cohort alone, for convenience purposes.

The NELS: 88 is comprised of about 25,000 1988 eighth graders, and over-samples public schools with high enrollment of Asian and/or Hispanic students, to ensure large enough numbers of both groups to enable statistical analysis. A sub-sample of the original sample was selected for follow-ups, occurring after two, four, six, and twelve years. The fourth follow-up includes about 12,000 students.

METHODS

Gap estimates were created by simple descriptive statistics by ethnicity of highest degree obtained by the fourth follow-up for both men and women. Analysis of returns to educational credentials was conducted by a series of ANCOVA general linear models. The dependent variable was earnings from income for the appropriate year for each data set (1979, 1989, 1999), represented in the form of natural log of the earnings in U.S. dollars. Returns to education by ethnicity were identified through an interaction model of ethnicity by education, in which a significant interaction term reflects differential financial returns to education by ethnicity.

VARIABLES

Gender—A variable commonly used in income studies is gender, as returns to education vary between men and women (Tienda and Lii 1980 and Perna 2005), and results of labor market analyses are commonly very different for men and women (Loury 1997 and Morris and Western 1999). For this reason, most researchers choose to conduct their analysis on males only (Tienda and Lii 1987; Card and Lemieux 2001; and Grodsky and Pager 2001). For these reasons this study will include findings for males only.

   Ethnicity—For sample size considerations, American Indians and Asian/PI students were excluded from the analysis. The remaining groups included in the analysis were blacks, Hispanics, and whites (the reference group).

   Parental SES—The term "parental SES" (socioeconomic status) refers to a combination of father's occupation, father's education, and family income. The selected SES variables were created by the NCES and describe SES is terms of z-scores, ranging from -4 to 4, uniformly across the three data sets.

   Ability—An important variable affecting postsecondary success is student ability, as measured in high school. For the NLS-72 and NELS: 88 data sets I used a measure of high school GPA. For HS&B, however, due to an extremely large number of missing cases for the GPA variable, I used the variable BYTEST—the results of an eighth grade aptitude test. BYTEST scores range between 25 to 75 points.

   Highest degree obtained—Highest degree obtained by the fourth follow-up. The variables used were EDATT (NLS-72), HDEG (HS&B), and F4HHDG (NELS: 88). The variables were recoded into three levels: "two-year degree," "four-year degree or more," and "no higher education credentials" as a reference group. Four-year degrees and graduate degrees were combined due to the very small numbers of minorities with graduate degrees. These small numbers were meaningful since this variable was also used for the construction of an interaction term between ethnicity and educational achievement.

Earnings—For the ANCOVA models, natural log of the earnings in constant U.S. dollars was used as the dependent variable.

WEIGHTS

In order to compensate for unequal probabilities of selection and to adjust for the effects of nonresponse in the three data sets, each data set was weighed by the appropriate renormalized weight, designed in each case for the fourth follow-up. In addition, since data for the three survey programs was collected through a multistage sampling pattern involving stratification, the calculation of standard errors through standard methods tends to overestimate the precision of the parameter estimates, which requires the use of design correction. Consequentially, design correction was conducted for each of the data sets using Stata SE/9.2.

FINDINGS

Have social policies to increase minority participation in higher education been successful in reducing the gap between whites and minorities in obtaining bachelor's degrees?

Table 4.1 and Figure 4.1 show the information collected from NLS-72, HS&B, and NELS: 88 on rates of bachelor's degree attainment by the fourth follow-up, seven years after the participants were high school seniors.

While more black and Hispanic students participated successfully in higher education during the 1990s than before, the growth in their rates of obtaining bachelor's degrees was offset by the growth experienced by white students (see table 4.1 and figure 4.1).

Table 4.1   Rates of Obtaining Associate and Bachelor's Degrees

	1979	1989	1999
Bachelor's			
White	23.86%	24.85%	36.88%
Black	13.08%	12.52%	22.41%
Hispanic	9.13%	11.41%	17.66%
Associate			
White	13.96%	7.78%	7.38%
Black	13.40%	5.35%	6.16%
Hispanic	15.31%	6.21%	8.60%

Bachelor's degree

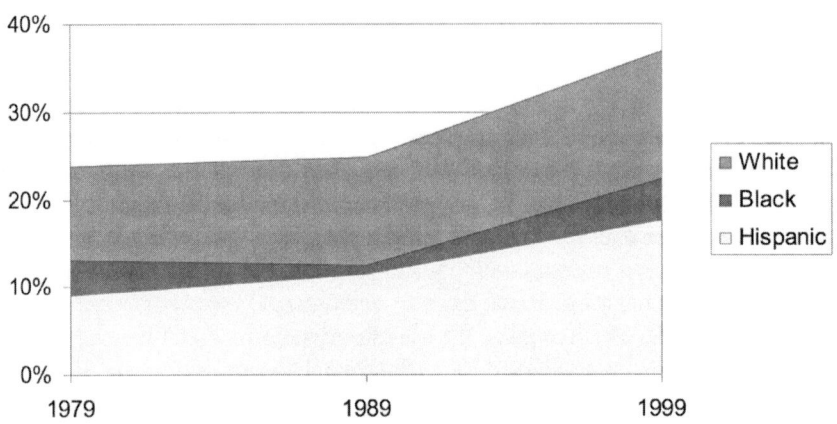

Figure 4.1.   Rates of obtaining a bachelor's degree

Figure 4.1 demonstrates the growing distance between the rates of obtaining a bachelor's degree for whites and Hispanics (the distance grew from 15 percent in 1979 to 19 percent in 1999) and for whites and blacks (the distance grew from 11 percent in 1979 to 15 percent in 1999). Asians and American Indians are not included in the analysis due to small sample sizes.

While the *relative* gains were greater for Hispanics and blacks than for whites (a 94 percent growth for Hispanics and a 71 percent growth for blacks compared to a 55 percent growth for whites), the *absolute* gains of whites were greater than those of any other group. In spite of social policies directed at the advancement of minorities by means of higher education, whites were still overrepresented among degree-holders in the HS&B and NELS: 88 cohorts of twenty-five-year-olds. In 1999, whites were more than twice as likely as Hispanics and 1.65 times as likely as blacks to obtain a bachelor's degree within seven years of their high school graduation.

At the same time, the rates of two-year degree attainment as a final degree dropped sharply for all ethnic groups between the 1970s and the 1990s. In 1979, 13 to 15 percent of whites, blacks, and Hispanics held a two-year degree (and not a bachelor's). In 1989, the rates dropped to 5 to 8 percent, and in 1999, only 6 percent of blacks, 7 percent of whites, and 9 percent of Hispanics held a two-year degree as a final degree. These data go hand in hand with studies on the rise in student expectations (Nettles and Perna 1997; Rosenbaum 1998; and Schneider and Stevenson 1999) and in employers' demands (Tyler et al. 1995; Bailey 1989; Murphy and Welch 1993; Adelman 1999; and Carey 2004).

Are returns to education equal among ethnic groups? In what ways have returns to education changed since the 1970s?

In order to find whether returns to education vary by ethnicity, the same ANCOVA analysis was performed on male respondents in each of the data sets. The independent variable used was the natural log of total earnings.

Table 4.2 shows the importance of controlling for parental SES in the models, as black and Hispanic parental SES in the three data sets differ significantly (p < 0.001) from white parental SES. The table also demonstrates the group differences in bachelor's and graduate degree attainment and in income, as whites surpass blacks and Hispanics in every category, with the exception of associate degrees.

Table 4.3 shows some interesting similarities between the three cohorts, and some interesting differences. GPA is only significant in NELS: 88 and parental SES is not significant at all, though we would have expected both to show consistent significant effects. Both are significant in a unisex data set with a control for gender, and become nonsignificant with the exclusion of women from the data set. Same with the effect of post-secondary credentials, which have a significant and positive effect in the unisex datasets, but no effect—or a negative effect—in the male-only data sets (unisex analyses are available from the researcher upon request).

A constant finding is the one regarding black males, who are at a significant disadvantage in the labor market compared to white and Hispanic males, even after controlling for SES, ability, and education. Hispanic males,

Table 4.2   Means for ANCOVA Variables*

		N	Wage	Logwage	Parental SES	Associate	Bachelor's	Graduate
NLS-72	White	17159	$10,392	9.09	0.07	13.96%	21.46%	2.40%
	Black	3119	$8,573	8.90	-0.60	13.40%	12.12%	0.96%
	Hispanic	986	$9,714	9.04	-0.64	15.31%	8.22%	0.91%
HS&B	White	8624	$18,706	9.75	0.08	7.78%	21.06%	3.79%
	Black	2036	$16,003	9.59	-0.28	5.35%	10.22%	2.31%
	Hispanic	3251	$17,525	9.67	-0.37	6.21%	9.75%	1.66%
NELS: 88	White	8203	$25,889	9.99	0.10	7.38%	32.54%	4.34%
	Black	1120	$20,938	9.80	-0.38	6.16%	20.45%	1.96%
	Hispanic	1687	$22,351	9.86	-0.53	8.60%	15.77%	1.90%

* Means are for the full data sets, and not for the final male samples

52 *Noga O'Connor*

Table 4.3 ANCOVA Models For Log Wage of Males In the 4th Follow-up in 3 Data Sets

	NLS-72		HS&B		NELS: 88	
Constant	9.365	***	9.922	***	10.013	***
Black	-.237	***	-.209	***	-.169	**
Hispanic	-.104		-.066		.161	***
Parental SES	.012		-.015		.010	
GPA^	.022		.001		.051	**
Associate	-.157	***	.002		.044	
BA +	-.186	***	.027		.053	
Black * Associate	.042		.026		-.230	
Black * BA +	.153		.254	*	.197	*
Hispanic * Associate	-.104		-.061		.139	
Hispanic * BA +	.122		.010		.003	
	R^=.015		R^=.010		R^=.020	
	N=5296		N=1537		N=3359	

*** Significant at the 0.001 level
** significant at the 0.01 level
*significant at the 0.05 level
^ GPA is replaced with BYTEST for HS&B (range 25-75 points)
See standard errors in appendix A

though, have a significant advantage in NELS: 88, though the scope of this study is too limited for providing an explanation for this finding.

The main focus of this analysis is on the interaction terms, as they represent the differential returns to education. Nonsignificant interactions would have suggested an equal labor market, while negative and significant interaction effects for either blacks or Hispanics would have suggested a discriminatory labor market. The finding of positive and significant interaction effects for blacks with a bachelor's degree in 1989 as well as in 1999 suggests the opposite—higher financial returns to highly educated black workers in the labor market than the ones whites or Hispanics receive. The fact that the labor market rewards bachelor's degrees held by blacks more than any other bachelor's degree makes the acquisition of the degree more beneficial for blacks than for whites or Hispanics.

To summarize, there is no evidence for lower returns to educational credentials held by minorities in the labor market. Quite the opposite, the only significant finding is the one pointing at higher returns for black bachelor's degree–holders during the 1980s and 1990s. Still, we should keep in mind that only 22.4 percent of NELS: 88 blacks held a bachelor's degree by 1999. The rest of NELS: 88 blacks suffered from lower labor market returns than those of whites and Hispanics at the same degree levels.

DISCUSSION

The data shows that while minority students increased their enrollment in higher education during the 1990s, the increase in their rates of completing the bachelor's degree was offset by the increase demonstrated by white students during the same time period. In 1999, whites were more than twice as likely as Hispanics and 1.65 times as likely as blacks to obtain a bachelor's degree within seven years of their high school graduation, in spite of significant access gains by Hispanics and blacks. How should this data be interpreted regarding the success of social policies to increase minority participation in higher education?

Ostensibly, the higher participation rates of minorities in higher education are evidence for success. In fact, the social agenda behind these policies—reduce social stratification—has not been met. The policies have not been successful in affecting the credentials gap so far, which leads us to conclude that increased access does not necessarily engender educational equity (Raftery and Hout 1993 and Brown 2001).

The heavy reliance of access policies on community colleges may explain the failure in affecting the gap. Though open admissions improved minority access considerably, the majority of the enrollment gains by minority students took place in community colleges (Lavin and Hyllegard 1996). Community college bachelor-aspiring students are significantly less likely to complete a bachelor's degree (Choy 2002) due to low transfer rates and low rates of post-transfer success (Dougherty 1994), which explains why minority access to community colleges did not affect the gap in obtaining bachelor's degrees. In that respect, affirmative action, as a policy designed toward greater equality, makes more sense than open admissions and the expansion of community college. Affirmative action opens up the higher end of post-secondary education to minorities, where they stand a better chance to succeed and complete the bachelor's degree than in community colleges. The move away from affirmative-action policies in higher education in recent years leaves minorities reliant more and more on community colleges as the main entry point into higher education.

This study's findings resonate with the idea of maximally maintained inequality (Mare 1980, 1981)—educational expansion is possible for the disadvantaged only once the dominant social group is ready to take over the next education level, thus guaranteeing itself an advantageous social position. What may seem like equal opportunity is actually "participation for all" and not "equal opportunity" (Lavin et al. 1981); the opportunity to participate is not synonymous with equality of opportunity, since increases in minority participation are being offset by equal increases in white participation. The data presented in this paper supports this claim, as it shows the decline among the three ethnicities in obtaining associate degrees as a final degree (from 13 to 15 percent in the 1970s down to 6 to 9 percent in the 1990s). Once minorities and lower-class individuals gain access to a certain credential, upper/middle class whites conquer the next level of educational credentials to maintain their favorable standing in the labor market. Thus, higher educational credentials remain reliable cultural markers, even—and especially—when education becomes more accessible at the lower levels.

For access policies to be effective in bringing on greater social equality, the labor market cannot be discriminatory toward minorities; otherwise, some may view the focus on access to higher education as unjustified. My investigation into financial returns to education shows higher returns for blacks than for whites with a bachelor's degree. At the same time, blacks are at a significant disadvantage in the labor market, a finding that persisted throughout the data sets. This does not mean, though, that the labor market is discriminatory toward black credentials; instead, it means that other variables may affect black earnings—for example, variables such as lack of labor market connections, or the concentration of blacks in the public sector, where salaries are lower Pollard and O'Hare 1999:32). The data shows no evidence of an opportunity structure that discriminates against minorities. Nonetheless, some researchers (MacLeod 1987; Ogbu and Matute-Bianchi 1986: 84–85; Fordham and Ogbu 1986 and McDonough, McClafferty and Fann 2002) have suggested that minority students *perceive* unequal returns to higher education by ethnicity, and this perception is a powerful force discouraging them from entering higher education. This study joins others (Perna 2003, 2005) in concluding that the source of inequality is not within the labor market, but in the different rates of obtaining credentials.

CONCLUSION

In this paper, I asked whether increased minority access to higher education in the last twenty years has been successful in reducing the white/minority credentials gap, and whether returns for education have changed in the last twenty years.

Has the credentials gap been shrinking? The rate of bachelor's degree attainment by minorities has increased significantly in the last twenty years, surpassing that of whites. Nevertheless, whites remain significantly more likely than minorities to obtain a bachelor's degree within seven years of their high school graduation. Minorities with post-secondary credentials may be gaining valuable human capital, yet the white-minority credentials gap has not shrunk. We have created policies designed to reduce the gaps in education, yet we allowed these policies to direct minorities into community colleges, where only few transfer to four-year schools and complete a bachelor's degree, thus ensuring a "maximally maintained inequality." As long as white students remain one step ahead of minorities in higher education, the educational gap between minorities and whites will remain, in spite of the growth in minority access to higher education.

Labor market returns to the bachelor's degree did not discriminate against minorities for three generations, yet in spite of the major social policies designed to increase minority access to higher education, the gaps in degree attainment did not budge. It is not clear whether in the absence of such policies, the gap today would have been much greater than it is; all the same, the promise of greater educational equality was not fulfilled.

Appendix

Table 4.4   Standards errors for table 3

	NLS-72	HS&B	NELS: 88
Constant	.0447	.0968	.0571
Black	.0508	.0651	.0579
Hispanic	.0571	.0538	.0447
Parental SES	.0167	.0232	.0177
GPA / BYTEST	.0169	.0018	.0189
Associate	.0329	.0696	.0478
Bachelor's +	.0299	.0430	.0310
Black * Associate	.1025	.2335	.1586
Black * Bachelor's +	.0852	.1271	.0987
Hispanic * Associate	.1107	.1386	.1089
Hispanic * Bachelor +	.1302	.1043	.0814

REFERENCES

Adelman, C. *Answers in the Toolbox: Academic Intensity, Attendance Patterns, and Bachelor's Degree Attainment*. Washington, DC: U.S. Department of Education, 1999.

Astin, A. "Open Admissions and Programs for the Disadvantaged." *The Journal of Higher Education*, 42, no. 8 (1971): 629–47.

Bailey, T. R. *Changes in the Nature and Structure of the Workforce: Implications for Skill Requirements and Skill Formation*. New York: National Center on Education and Employment, Teachers College, Columbia University, 1989.

Baker, T., and W. Velez. "Access to and Opportunity in Postsecondary Education in the United States." *Sociology of Education*, Extra Issue (1996): 82–101.

Blackburn, S. M., L. McKinley, D. E. Bloom, and R. B. Freeman. "The Declining Position of Less Skilled American Men." Pp. 31–76 in *A Future of Lousy Jobs?* Edited by G. Burtless. Washington, DC: Urban Institute Press, 1990.

Bragg, D. D. "Community College Access, Mission, and Outcomes: Considering Intriguing Intersections and Challenges." *Peabody Journal of Education*, 76, no. 1 (2001): 93–116.

Brint, S. "Few Remaining Dreams: Community Colleges since 1985." *The Annals of the American Academy of Political and Social Science* 586, no. 1 (2003): 16–37.

Brint, S., and J. Karabel. *The Diverted Dream: Community Colleges and the Promise of Educational Opportunity in America, 1900–1985*. New York: Oxford University Press, 1989.

Brown, D. K. "The Social Sources of Educational Credentialism: Status Cultures, Labor Markets, and Organizations." *Sociology of Education* 74 (Extra Issue) (2001): 19–34.

Card, David, and T. Lemieux. "Can Falling Supply Explain the Rising Return to College for Younger Men? A Cohort-Based Analysis." *The Quarterly Journal of Economics* 116 (2001): 705–46.

Carey, K. *A Matter of Degrees: Improving Graduation Rates in Four-Year Colleges and Universities*. Washington, DC: Education Trust, May 2004.

Choy, S. P. *Access and Persistence: Findings from 10 Years of Longitudinal Research on Students*. Washington, DC: American Council on Education, Center for Policy Analysis, 2002.

Cohen, A., and F. Brawer. *The American Community College*. San Francisco: Jossey Bass, 1989.

Collins, R. "Functional and Conflict Theories of Educational Stratification." *American Sociological Review*, 36 (1971): 1002–19.

Dougherty, K. J. *The Contradictory College: The Conflicting Origins, Impacts, and Futures of the Community College*. Albany: State University of New York Press, 1994.

Fordham, S., and J. Ogbu. "Black Students' School Success: Coping with the Burden of 'Acting White.'" *The Urban Review* 18, no. 3 (1986): 176–206.

Francis, L. P. "In Defense of Affirmative Action." Pp. 9–47 in *Affirmative Action and the University: A Philosophical Inquiry*. Edited by S. M. Cahn. Philadelphia: Temple University Press, 1993.

Fullinwider, R. K. "Open Admissions and Remedial Education at CUNY." *The Institute for Philosophy and Public Policy* 19 (Winter 1999).

Grodsky, E., and D. Pager. "The Structure of Disadvantage: Individual and Occupational Determinants of the Black-White Wage Gap." *American Sociological Review* 66 (2001): 542–67.

Hammack, F. M. *The Comprehensive High School Today*. New York: Teachers College Press, 2004.

Harper, S. and B. Reskin. "Affirmative Action at School and on the Job." *Annual Review of Sociology* 31 (2005): 357–79.

Kane, T. J., and C. E. Rouse. "The Community College: Educating Students at the Margin between College and Work." *Journal of Economic Perspectives* 13 (1999): 63–84.

Key Events Affecting Minority Enrollment, *The Chronicle of Higher Education* (April 28, 1995).

Kirp, D. Keynote Address, Hurst Seminar on "Higher Education and Equality of Opportunity: Cross-National Perspectives," Ben-Gurion University of the Negev, Beer Sheva, Israel (June 3–5, 2008).

Labaree, D. F. *How to Succeed in School without Really Learning: The Credentials Race in American Education*. New Haven, CT: Yale University Press, 1997.

Lavin, D. E., R. D. Alba, and R. A. Silberstein. *Right Versus Privilege: The Open-Admissions Experiment at the City University of New York*. New York: Free Press, 1981.

Lavin, D. E., and D. Hyllegard. *Changing the Odds: Open Admissions and Life Chances*. New Haven, CT: Yale University Press, 1996.

Lewis, T. "Toward the 21st Century: Retrospect, Prospect for American Vocationalism." Information Series No. 373, *Center on Education and Training for Employment*. College of Education, Ohio State University, 1998.

Llagas, C., and T. Snyder. *Status and Trends in the Education of Hispanics*. NCES publication #2003-008, 2003.

Loury, L. D. "The Gender Earning Gap Among College-Educated Workers." *Industrial and Labor Relations Review* 50, no. 4 (1997): 580–93.

Lucas, S. R. "Effectively Maintained Inequality: Education Transitions, Track Mobility, and Social Background Effects." *American Journal of Sociology* 106, no. 6 (2001): 1642–90.

MacLeod, J. *Ain't No Makin' It*. Boulder, CO: Westview Press, 1987.

Mare, R. D. "Social Background and School Continuation Decisions." *Journal of the American Statistical Association* 75 (1980): 295–305.

———. "Change and Stability in Educational Stratification." *American Sociological Review* 46, no. 1 (1981): 72–87.

McDonough, P. M. *Choosing Colleges: How Social Class and Schools Structure Opportunity*. Albany: State University of New York Press, 1997.

———. McClafferty, K. A. and A. Fann. "Rural College Opportunity: Issues and Challenges." Paper presented at the 2002 annual meeting of the American Educational Research Association, New Orleans.

Metzner, B. S., and J. P. Bean. "The Estimation of a Conceptual Model of Nontraditional Undergraduate Student Attrition." *Research in Higher Education* 27, no. 1 (1987): 15–38.

Morris, M., and B. Western. "Inequality in Earnings at the Close of the Twentieth Century." *Annual Review of Sociology* 25 (1999): 623–57.

Murphy, K., and F. Welch. "Occupational Change and the Demand for Skill: 1940–1990." *American Economic Review* 83, no. 2 (1993): 122–26.

National Center for Education Statistics. *Digest of Educational Statistics.* NCES Publications, 2001.

Nettles, M. T., and L. W. Perna. *The African American Education Data Book: Transition from School to College and School to Work, Volume III.* Fairfax, VA: Frederick D. Patterson Research Institute of The College Fund/UNCF, 1997.

Ogbu, J. "Racial Stratification and Education in the United States: Why Inequality Persists." *Teachers College Records* 96, no. 2 (1994): 264–98.

Ogbu, J., and M. Matute-Bianchi. "Understanding Sociocultural Factors in Education: Knowledge, Identity, and Adjustment." Pp. 73–142 in *Beyond Language: Sociocultural Factors in Schooling, Language, and Minority Students.* Los Angeles, CA: Evaluation, Dissemination, and Assessment Center, California State Department of Education, 1986.

Orfield, G. "Money, Equity, and College Access." *Harvard Educational Review*, 62 (1992): 337–72.

Perna, L. W. "The Private Benefits of Higher Education: An Examination of the Earnings Premium." *Research in Higher Education* 44, no. 4 (2003): 451–72.

———. "The Benefits of Higher Education: Sex, Racial/Ethnic, and Socioeconomic Group Differences." *The Review of Higher Education* 29, no. 1 (2005): 23–52.

Pollard, K. M., and W. P. O'Hare. "America's Racial and Ethnic Minorities." *Population Bulletin* 54, no. 3 (1999).

Raftery, A. E., and M. Hout. "Maximally Maintained Inequality: Expansion, Reform and Opportunity in Irish Education, 1921–1975." *Sociology of Education* 66 (1993): 41–62.

Richardson Jr., R. C. "State Structures for the Governance of Higher Education: California Case Study." A Technical Paper Prepared for State Structures for the Governance of Higher Education and The California Higher Education Policy Center, 1997.

———. Richardson Jr., R. C., N. Shulock, and R. Teranishi. "Public Policy and Higher Education Performance in the State of California." Alliance for International Higher Education Policy Studies Report, (New York: New York, 2005).

Rosenbaum, J. E. "College for All: Do Students Understand What College Demands?" *Social Psychology of Education* 2 (1998): 50–85.

Roscigno, V. J. "Family/School Inequality and African-American/Hispanic Achievement." *Social Problems* 47, no. 2 (2000): 266–90.

Rouse, C. E. "Do Two-Year Colleges Increase Overall Educational Attainment? Evidence from the States." *Journal of Policy Analysis and Management* 17, no. 4 (1998): 595–620.

Schneider, B., and Stevenson, D. *The Ambitious Generation: America's Teenagers, Motivated but Directionless.* New Haven, CT: Yale University Press, 1999.

Tienda, M., and D.-T. Lii. "Minority Concentration and Earnings Inequality: Blacks, Hispanics, and Asians Compared." *American Journal of Sociology* 93 (1987): 141–65.

Tierney, W. "The Parameters of Affirmative Action: Equity and Excellence in the Academy." *Review of Educational Research* 67, no. 2 (1997): 165–96.

Tyler, J., R. J. Murnane, and F. Levy. "Are More College Graduates Really Taking 'High School' Jobs?" *Monthly Labor Review* 118, no. 12 (1995): 18–27.

U.S. Census Bureau. *Current Population Survey*. Annual Social and Economic Supplements. Poverty and Health Statistics Branch/HHES Division, Table 4.2: Poverty Status of People by Family Relationship, Race, and Hispanic Origin: 1959 to 2004. Washington, DC: U.S. Department of Commerce, 2005.

———. *Current Population Survey. Annual social and economic supplement. Educational attainment in the United States: 2007*. Washington, DC: U.S. Department of Commerce, 2007.

5

Class Stratification and the Quest for Prestige in American Colleges and Universities[1]

Steven J. Diner

In the second half of the twentieth century, the United States developed one of the most comprehensive systems of higher education in the world, as David Kirp has described in his essay, "The Earth is Flattening." With community colleges, myriad public universities and colleges large and small, independent institutions of every size, and research universities in both the public and private sectors, some form of higher education has been potentially available for at least a generation to all American high school graduates irrespective of their age, how well they did in high school, where they live, or their race, ethnicity, national origin, religion or social class.

Perhaps it is inevitable that such an inclusive system of high education would also be highly stratified. But in the last two decades, as Kirp notes, the growth of popular, consumer-oriented rankings of top institutions, decreasing state and federal support for higher education, and rising tuitions have significantly increased social class stratification. Much has been written about declining state support for public colleges and universities even before the drastic cuts in state funding in the wake of the severe recession beginning in 2008 (Ehrenberg, 2006). Many scholars and writers have described the growing stratification of American higher education, focusing on who gets admitted to the elite private and public colleges in the wake of escalating tuition and declining financial support for state universities (Stevens 2007; Bowen et al. 2005; Soares 2007; Schmidt 2007; Douglass 2007, Thomas and Bell, 2008, Pallais and Turner, 2007). Public research universities located in urban areas have a long tradition of educating students from poor or modest backgrounds with strong, research-oriented faculty, but the literature on stratification of American higher education has devoted very little attention to these institutions.

This essay provides a case study of Rutgers University–Newark, the institution I lead. Rutgers-Newark is somewhat unique in the stratified world of higher education. Rutgers University operates as both a single institution and a state university system. The largest, oldest and best-known campus is in New Brunswick, but Rutgers also has campuses in Newark and Camden. The standards for appointment, tenure, and promotion of faculty are identical on all three campuses. Admissions decisions are made locally, each campus has its own distinctive student culture, and prospective students can apply to each of the campuses.

Faculty and administrators on all three campuses take pride in Rutgers' stature as a major research university and its membership in the highly selective Association of American Universities (AAU). All faculty candidates for tenure and promotion, including new faculty appointments with tenure, are reviewed by a university-wide committee, where the same high research standards are applied to faculty from all three campuses. Rutgers-Newark has PhD programs in all of its professional schools except law (business, criminal justice, nursing, and public affairs and administration), in all of the sciences, and in select areas in the humanities and social sciences. It awards approximately sixty-five PhDs a year.

Rutgers-Newark is one of the "streetcar universities" that emerged in the first part of the twentieth century to provide higher education to working-class commuter students in major cities. The private University of Newark, with schools of law, business, and liberal arts housed in a former brewery and a razor blade factory, was taken over by Rutgers University–New Brunswick in 1946, ten years before the state assumed responsibility for funding Rutgers as the State University of New Jersey. It has a long tradition of educating first-generation college students, students from modest or low-income backgrounds, immigrants, and children of immigrants. Although no longer entirely commuter, Rutgers-Newark remains deeply committed to its historic mission. Rutgers-Newark is thus one of a handful of American universities, mostly public urban research institutions, where students from modest or low-income backgrounds are taught by top research faculty.

Because of its commitment to opportunity, Rutgers-Newark deemphasizes SAT scores in the admissions process. The SAT is a class-biased instrument, and students who can afford expensive SAT-preparation courses and even private SAT tutoring can raise their scores substantially. The correlation between SAT scores and academic success is questionable at best for all students. But it is a particularly poor predictor of success for the kinds of students Rutgers-Newark traditionally has served (Lemann 1999; Sacks 2007, 225–57; and Gilroy 2007, 25–27). At a campus forum a few years ago, one student explained that he was ten years old when he came to New Jersey from the Dominican Republic with his father. He knew no English when he arrived, so he did very poorly on the SAT, but Rutgers-Newark admitted him anyhow through its Educational Opportunity Fund (EOF) program for low-income students. He graduated with a 3.95 GPA, went on to Rutgers-Newark's law school, and clerked for the Chief Justice of the New Jersey Supreme Court before joining a top New York law firm. Another student, who grew up in Jersey City, explained that she always wanted to attend Rutgers Nursing School but in several attempts "could not crack 1000 on the SAT." She too entered through the EOF program and graduated with a 4.0 GPA before taking an excellent job at a nearby hospital.

Many institutions brag about the composite SAT scores of their entering class, citing it as a mark of the quality of their institutions. In addition to its class bias, the SAT cannot measure motivation, interpersonal abilities, artistic creativity, and much more. But more profoundly, the SAT was never intended to be a measure of the academic quality of an institution or its student body. The College Board initiated the SAT in 1926 at a time when many universities tried to limit the number of students who did not come from appropriate old-stock white Protestant social backgrounds, to *predict* the likelihood of academic success. Its proponents argued that it would help identify "diamonds in the rough," intellectually capable students from modest backgrounds who lacked the social polish colleges at the time considered so important, a goal it has never achieved (Wechsler 1977).

Its purpose today, as in the past, is to help evaluate the ability of a single student. The test was never meant to be a composite measure of the quality of colleges. It does not tell us anything about what students actually learn at an institution. But selective institutions across the country now routinely tout their average SAT or ACT scores as a mark of quality, thereby perpetuating the class privilege that these tests foster. The SAT/ACT is, of course, a significant component of the much discussed *U.S. News and World Report* rankings of the quality of colleges and universities. And since students and their parents pay close attention to these rankings, many colleges seek to raise their SAT profiles, further exacerbating the stratification of American higher education (Thacker 2005; Diver 2005: 136–39; Manion 2008: 14–190, Bowman and Bastedo, 2009; and Bowman and Bastedo, 2010).

The same issue arises with *U.S. News* rankings of graduate professional programs. LSAT and GMAT scores figure prominently in admissions decisions of law and MBA programs, for example (Sweitzer and Volkwein, 2009). The Rutgers-Newark law school began the first minority student program in the country in 1968, a year after the Newark riots of 1967. The program remains vibrant today, the law school remains one of the most diverse in the nation, and its faculty, alumni, and students are justly proud of the thousands of graduates of its minority student program who have been highly successful in legal practice. Yet it suffers in *U.S. News and World Report* and other rankings because it assesses LSAT scores flexibly when considering minority and low-income applicants and applicants with disabilities. Whatever value a minimum LSAT score may have in predicting academic success in law school, it surely cannot measure the interpersonal skills, motivation, creativity, and work ethic that are so important in the successful practice of law.

Like many urban and metropolitan universities, Rutgers-Newark admits to its undergraduate programs nearly as many transfer as first-year students. Most of the transfer students come from community colleges, and particularly from Essex County College, located two blocks south of the Rutgers-Newark campus. Essex County College enrolls largely students from Newark and other nearby low-income communities. Rutgers-Newark has long had strong articulation agreements and close working relationships with Essex and other community colleges. Students who transfer to Rutgers-Newark from these community colleges perform very well. Indeed, Rutgers-Newark students who have completed an associate degree at a community college have the same level of academic success as students who begin their college education at Rutgers-Newark. This is one more way in which urban universities work against the prevailing trend toward greater class and racial stratification in American higher education.

Urban universities also have the opportunity to take advantage of the rich array of institutions, populations, and neighborhoods that provide extraordinary learning opportunities for students as well as research opportunities for faculty and students. In recent years, many higher education institutions have developed systematic programs of community engagement and have encouraged "service-learning" or "community-based learning" as a way of strengthening undergraduate liberal education. Since 1985, Campus Compact has promoted "public and community service that develops students' citizenship skills." In 2006, The Carnegie Foundation initiated a voluntary classification of community-engaged institutions. Rutgers-Newark has a long tradition of engagement with its host city. It has built extensive partnerships with corporations and small businesses, arts and cultural institutions, law firms, community organizations, the Newark public schools, social service agencies, health providers, and much more. It has provided modest financial incentives for instructors to take advantage of the city of Newark and its surrounding communities in their teaching. One 2009 graduate commented enthusiastically that "the university is not as secluded as other campuses" noting that students "get a taste of the culture connection that makes the U.S. so unique." Another stated that "the fact that [Rutgers-Newark] is located in such a business-oriented area, having so many buildings and companies located here, can definitely benefit recently graduated students or undergrads looking for an internship." Yet *U.S. News* does not consider these activities in its rankings of quality.

U.S. News and World Report ranks schools in other ways as well. For the last thirteen years, it has ranked institutions by their racial and ethnic diversity. In all thirteen years, Rutgers-Newark has been ranked number one in diversity among national universities (defined as those institutions that award the PhD). This is a source of great pride to Rutgers-Newark faculty, students, and administrators, who brag about it all the time. In fact, it has at least as much to do with the university's location in one of the nation's major clusters of new immigrants as it does with its admissions policies and educational philosophy. Indeed, Rutgers-Newark students are much more diverse than can be revealed by the ratios of African Americans, Hispanics, Asian Americans, Native Americans, and whites calculated by *U.S. News*. English is not the first language for approximately 38 percent of Rutgers-Newark's first-year students. Thirty-three percent of Rutgers-Newark first-year students were born abroad. Ten to 12 percent are Hindu, 10 to 12 percent are Muslim, and 3 percent are Eastern Orthodox. Thirty-seven percent come from families that earn less than $50,000 a year.

Leaders of American colleges and universities have argued for many years before the U.S. Supreme Court and elsewhere that diversity is crucial for academic quality. Yet *U.S. News'* diversity rankings are completely separate from its quality rankings. In other words, *U.S. News* treats diversity as a social descriptor of colleges and universities, but one entirely unrelated to academic quality. Needless to say, this is a sore point for Rutgers-Newark faculty and administrators, which *U.S. News* places in the third tier of PhD-granting universities.

In today's America and in today's ever more global world, diversity is an integral dimension of academic quality. The extraordinary student diversity at Rutgers-Newark is a valuable resource for learning both inside and outside the classroom. Some faculty members have designed courses that specifically draw upon students' cultural and family backgrounds. One theater professor had all of his students produce oral histories of family members and friends who had migrated from abroad, and crafted these testimonies into a theatre production on issues of culture and identity among immigrants entitled "Something to Declare." Another professor has students in a Portuguese studies class interview residents of Newark's Ironbound neighborhood, looking at the often complicated relationships between the older Portuguese residents of the area and newer migrants from Brazil and Central America. Many of the students themselves are from Portuguese, Brazilian, or Central American backgrounds, facilitating their access to neighborhood residents and giving them unique insights into the cultural dynamics. In seminars on public policy issues, students talk freely about their own experiences. In discussions of affirmative action, students discuss their personal encounters, or lack thereof, with discrimination and ethnic stereotyping. When debating bilingual education, students talk about how they themselves learned English. In our global world and our global nation, serious exposure to cultural diversity is an essential element in quality higher education. Indeed, faculty at Rutgers-Newark can participate in a professional development program to enable them to share ideas about how to take advantage of the unprecedented diversity they find in their classes as a pedagogic tool. And the university has begun a systematic assessment of how campus diversity effects learning outcomes.

A growing number of scholars starting their academic careers today deeply understand this development. The unparalleled diversity of Rutgers-Newark's student body is an enormous asset in attracting top faculty. Scholars in all fields get great satisfaction from teaching students with such a wide range of cultural backgrounds. Those in fields like ethnic, urban, and global studies—areas of strategic focus on the campus and of great intellectual ferment generally—say that they find the campus an incomparable place to work.

Students themselves report that campus diversity contributes significantly to their education. A survey of graduating seniors asks if they would recommend Rutgers-Newark to prospective students and if so, why. In the open-ended responses to this question, students repeatedly point to what they have learned from the cultural diversity of their fellow students. A few recent examples:

- "The campus is very multicultural and helped open my eyes to people I otherwise never would have been friends with."
- "Rutgers can make a person believe they are studying abroad because of all of the cultures and diversity encompassed on this campus. I feel as if I have traveled around the world at Rutgers-Newark."
- "I like the fact that I am going to school with different types of people. It allows for many different perspectives and good classroom discussions."
- "If high school students are interested in learning about different cultures, Rutgers-Newark is the school for them. This is the only school where I have learned from other cultures that are extremely different from mine."
- "Rutgers-Newark will not only enrich your knowledge in the major you are focusing in but it will expand your knowledge about different cultures."

- "Rutgers-Newark is incredibly diverse, and therefore, you're able to be exposed to people of other religions, ethnicities, and walks of life, and learn to interact with them, a trait that is needed in the work place."
- "I love the diversity of this campus. As an immigrant, it gives me confidence."
- "I have the opportunity to meet people of all origins and learn about them and their cultures."
- "Rutgers-Newark is a very diverse college, which is quite helpful to all races, particularly immigrants like me and my relatives."

A 2003 graduate, who has been highly successful at Merrill Lynch, spoke in 2007 at a homecoming brunch. He attributed his success largely to what he learned as a student. "The Rutgers-Newark campus, indeed, is a microcosm of the global economy that enables us to interact with students from more than 150 countries and learn about their culture and tradition." he explained. "This has helped me tremendously in my job at Merrill Lynch. I am repeatedly called in to manage projects that are more global," he asserted, "as well as contribute to building my company's multicultural business."

Should not learning experiences like these factor into assessments of educational quality? Should not higher education's hierarchy of quality place special value on the extent to which institutions enroll and graduate students from poor and modest circumstances? If American academic leaders are serious about reversing the growing class and racial stratification of colleges and universities, if they really mean what they say about the educational value of student diversity, then they should stop embracing the popular simplistic and elitist rankings of educational quality that so deeply influence American higher education today. The United States surely will not diminish its growing class and racial stratification if it cannot reverse the stratification of its colleges and universities.

REFERENCES

Bowen, William, Martin A. Kurzweil, and Eugene M. Tobin. *Equity and Excellence in American Higher Education*. Charlottesville: University of Virginia Press, 2005.

Bowman, Nicholas A., and Michael N. Bastedo. "Getting on the Front Page: Organizational Reputation, Status Signals, and the Impact of *U.S. News and World Report* on Student Decisions." *Research in Higher Education* (2009): 415–36.

Bowman, Nicholas A., and Michael N. Bastedo. "The *U.S. News and World Report* College Rankings: Modeling Institutional Effects on Organizational Reputation." *American Journal of Education* (2010): 163–83.

Diver, Colin. "Is There Life After Rankings?" *The Atlantic Monthly*, November 2005, 36–139.

Douglass, John Aubrey. *The Conditions For Admission: Access, Equity, and the Social Contract of Public Universities*. Palo Alto, CA: Stanford University Press, 2007.

Ehrenberg, Ronald G., ed. *What's Happening to Public Higher Education? The Shifting Financial Burden*. Baltimore: Johns Hopkins University Press, 2006.

Gilroy, Marilyn. "Colleges Making SAT Optional as Admissions Requirement." *Hispanic Outlook in Higher Education*. August 13, 2007, 25–27.

Lemann, Nicholas. *The Big Test: The Secret History of the American Meritocracy*. New York: Farrar, Straus and Giroux, 1999.

Manion, Andrew P. "The Rankings: What Board Members Need to Know." *Trusteeship*, March/April 2008, 14–19.

Pallais, Amanda, and Sarah E. Turner. "Access to Elites." Pp. 128–56 in *Economic Inequality and Higher Education: Access, Persistence, and Success*. Edited by Stacy Dickert-Conlin and Ross Rubenstein. New York: Russell Sage Foundation, 2007.

Sacks, Peter. *Tearing Down the Gates: Confronting The Class Divide in American Education*. Berkeley: University of California Press, 2007.

Schmidt, Peter. *Color and Money: How Rich White Kids Are Winning the War Over College Affirmative Action*. New York: Palgrave Macmillan, 2007.

Soares, Joseph A. *The Power of Privilege: Yale and America's Elite Colleges*. Palo Alto, CA: Stanford University Press, 2007.

Stevens, Mitchell L. *Creating a Class: College Admissions and the Education of Elites*. Cambridge: Harvard University Press, 2007.

Sweitzer, Kyle, and J. Fredericks Volkwein. "Prestige Among Graduate and Professional Schools: Comparing the *U.S. News'* Graduate School Reputational Ratings Between Disciplines." *Research in Higher Education* (2009): 812–36.

Thacker, Lloyd, ed. *College Unranked: Ending the College Admissions Frenzy*. Cambridge: Harvard University Press, 2005.

Thomas, Scott L., and Angela Bell. "Social Class and Higher Education: A Reorganization of Opportunities." Pp. 273–87 in *The Way Class Works: Readings on School, Family and the Economy*. Edited by Lois Weis. New York and London: Routledge, 2008.

Wechsler, Harold S. *The Qualified Student: A History of Selective College Admission in America*. New York: Wiley, 1977.

NOTE

1. An earlier version of this essay was published as "Prestige and Quality in American Colleges and Universities," pp. 83–88 in Daniel Little and Satya P. Mohanty, eds., *The Future of Diversity: Academic Leaders Reflect on American Higher Education* (New York: Palgrave Macmillan, 2010).

6

From Open Admissions to the Honors College

Equal Opportunities at the City University of New York

Judith Naomi Friedlander[1]

Affirmative-action policies in the United States have had a profound impact on the nation's colleges and universities since the early 1970s. President John Kennedy was the first to use the term in an executive order in 1961, instructing federal contractors to "take affirmative action to ensure that applicants are employed and employees are treated during their employment, without regard to race, creed, color or national origin" (Kennedy 1961). In 1964 Congress passed the Civil Rights Act, adding sex to the list of protected categories identified in the original executive order (Title VII). Then, in 1972, Congress passed the Equal Opportunity Act, which focused specifically on employment and educational opportunities at colleges and universities. These legislative measures, concerned with fair labor practices and educational access, soon led to the development of special programs to recruit candidates from underrepresented groups and to help them succeed.

Bitter controversies erupted on university campuses across the country over the legality of affirmative-action policies. Although opponents of affirmative action failed to persuade the Supreme Court to rule entirely in their favor, they still managed to limit the effectiveness of Title VII by successfully challenging the use of formal quotas (e.g., *Regents of the University of California v Bakke* 1978). Opponents next took their campaign to the states where they finally won a significant victory in 1996 in California: With the passage of Proposition 209 it is now illegal in that state to consider race, sex, and ethnicity when recruiting employees or students. Other states have since followed suit (Michigan and Washington) and similar propositions appeared on the ballot in 2008 in Arizona, Colorado, Missouri, Nebraska, and Oklahoma (McKenna 2008).

In 1970, two years before the passage of the Equal Opportunity Act, CUNY's Board of Trustees embraced the ideals of affirmative action, while avoiding debates about quotas: Every high school graduate in New York City, they proclaimed, would henceforth be admitted to CUNY. The decision led to heated debates and disagreements persist to the present day. With this sweeping new policy, the Board turned a small, relatively selective institution of higher learning into one that was all-inclusive.

By the late 1990s the pendulum began swinging back in the opposite direction. Severe pressure from Mayor Giuliani's office and elsewhere eventually persuaded the trustees in 1999 to put an end to open admissions and to close down remedial programs at the four-year senior colleges. The new chancellor, Matthew Goldstein, a proud alumnus of City College, promised to restore the historic reputation of his alma mater and that of other colleges in the university system to the distinction they once enjoyed.

Politically active members of CUNY opposed the decision to abandon open admissions. Turning back the clock, they argued, would have a negative impact on the diversity and size of the university's student body. Their predictions, however, have proved wrong.

Since 1999 enrollment has grown by 10 percent and the ethnic and racial distribution of students continues to reflect the diversity of New York City.[2] Difficult challenges, however, remain. For example, although the academic profiles of CUNY students look better today than they did during open admissions, far too many of those accepted still enter without the skills needed to do college-level work. The problem, of course, is national, not local, and CUNY, like other universities around the nation, has been investing more heavily than it did before in the training of primary and secondary school teachers.[3]

As part of his campaign to improve CUNY's reputation, Chancellor Goldstein opened an honors college (Macaulay Honors College) in 2001 and placed groups of specially admitted students at seven of the university's eleven senior colleges. If judged by the success it is having at Hunter, the program is attracting stellar students, reminiscent of those who attended City College in the early decades of the twentieth century, when people referred proudly to the "College on the Hill" as the "Harvard of the Proletariat." But the prestigious new program has also created the semblance of a two-tiered system that critics within CUNY try to expose.

Students at the Honors College are on scholarship and do not have to juggle heavy work schedules to attend classes like other students at CUNY. At Hunter they receive free tuition and board, making it possible to devote themselves full time—or almost full time—to their studies. They also follow a special course of study that provides them with the kind of educational experience associated with the country's most exclusive private colleges.

Although the Honors College receives a great deal of press, the program itself remains comparatively small. At Hunter, for example, which had an undergraduate population in 2007–2008 of nearly 16,000 students, there were 325 participants in the program, and Hunter has the largest number in the system. At Lehman College there were only fifty-two.[4]

THE TERMS OF THE DEBATE

The United States, David Kirp reminds us (2003, 2008), was the first country in the world to offer nearly every high school graduate the opportunity to attend college. Two-thirds of the nation's high school graduates today go to college, he continues, but, he adds, that this is not as impressive as it sounds. Let me mention four of the reasons why: (1) Adolescents are dropping out of high school every year at an increasingly high rate. (2) When we compare the performance of those who remain, to high school students in other parts of the world, young Americans are not competitive with their peers. (3) Expectations in fact are so low in the United States that many high school graduates enter college without the skills they need to do college-level work. (4) Continuing the downward spiral, college professors make modest demands on their students and then pass them along, rewarding them at the end with a bachelor's degree, after six years, or eight, or maybe even ten.

For a number of years, researchers have been tracking the success of open admissions at the City University of New York. Of greatest interest is the work of two sociologists, Paul Attewell and David Lavin (2007), who have recently published to great acclaim the results of a longitudinal study over two generations that demonstrates the positive impact of the experiment, the authors claim, on the lives of thousands of New Yorkers. Lavin published an earlier study as well with David Hyllegard (1996). Basing their arguments on statistical analyses and qualitative research, the first study demonstrates that making college accessible to everyone who graduated from high school has had a positive impact on the lives of the first generation of open admissions students who entered CUNY between 1970 and 1972; the second study carries the story forward, showing that the university's controversial policy has also had a positive impact on the children of these students.

The second study focuses specifically on the experiences of nearly 2,000 women who attended colleges across CUNY. Of those who responded to the questionnaire, 70 percent of them eventually graduated, even if it took them longer than six years to do so. Not only did they finish in significant numbers, many went on for a second degree. According to the authors' findings, having graduated from college and, in some cases, received a master's or PhD were the deciding factors in this cohort's ability to move into the middle class. Thanks to their degrees, they got better jobs, saved more money and acquired other material assets, adopted mainstream childrearing practices, and participated in community activities. Most important, the upward mobility of the graduates led to greater "cognitive and educational success" among their children. Dismissing those who blame programs like CUNY's for lowering academic standards, the authors show in concrete and measurable terms how "open access" has made a real difference in the families of individuals who would never have gone to college, had CUNY not made it possible for them to do so in the early 1970s.

In this chapter, I offer arguments on both sides of the debate in an attempt to move the discussion forward. On the one hand, I take issue with Lavin, Hyllegard, and Attewell for dismissing those who express concern about academic standards. I think the issue is critical. Distancing myself further from those who support open admissions, I also embrace CUNY's efforts in recent years to build high-end programs for gifted students, many of whom come from underrepresented groups and are the first in their families to go to college. I consider these programs very much in keeping with the traditions of the university. But I also believe that open admissions has played a very positive role. At Hunter, as we will see, it gave colleagues the opportunity they needed to extend the college's legacy and build on its historical mission of offering a first-rate education to women, immigrants, and racial/ethnic minorities. The high-end programs created during open admissions made it possible as well for Hunter to respond as effectively as it did to Chancellor Goldstein's call in 2001 to participate in CUNY's Honors program.

Like the new Honors College today, the special programs developed in the 1980s and 1990s have had an impact at Hunter on relatively few students. Based primarily in biology, chemistry, and physics, these programs require students to master sophisticated levels of math and science. Given the challenge, the numbers are still impressive and include students who might never have gone to college, had CUNY not admitted high school graduates with weak academic records. For the vast majority of students, however, open admissions may not be quite the success story that Attewell, Hyllegard, and Lavin have made it out to be.

The data gathered by Hyllegard and Lavin (1996) and Attewell and Lavin (2007) have shown that students who entered CUNY through open admissions in the early 1970s and eventually graduated have enjoyed greater social and economic mobility than those who did not. Their studies are probably the most thorough of any done so far, but they are still very limited, describing, I repeat, the experiences only of students who entered the program in the first three years of its existence. The authors of the CUNY study do not, what is more, systematically look at the work of others that challenges the conclusions they have reached. For example, Nemko (2008) reports on a nationwide study based on a more recent cohort of students than the one used by the CUNY authors and the findings are less optimistic. Articles like Nemko's abound.

Nemko reported on a study that followed students, nationwide, who graduated in the bottom 40 percent of their high-school class—just like those, in other words, who came to CUNY through open admissions. Two-thirds of the students from this group who actually went on to college had still not earned their college degrees eight and half years later. Lavin, Hyllegard, and Attewell also found that the majority of the students in their cohort at CUNY took many years to graduate. The length of time students spent, they argued, should not concern us. No matter how long it took members of the CUNY cohort to graduate, the very fact that they did helped improve their social and economic circumstances. The same does not seem to be the case, however, for their counterparts in the national study. According to Nemko (2008), those who came from the bottom 40 percent of their high-school class and took more than six years to graduate from college "rarely ended up in careers that required a college education."[5]

How do we reconcile such diametrically opposed findings? Are the authors of the CUNY studies arguing that given the scarcity of jobs today, only those with a college degree get anything at all? That is not, I presume, the overriding conclusion they want us to draw.

Lavin, Hyllegard, and Attewell do not offer much insight either on questions asked in national studies about what actually goes on in the classroom. How do CUNY professors, for example, teach college-level material to students lacking the background they need to do college-level work? Attewell, Hyllegard, and Lavin acknowledge the seriousness of the problem—and the difficulty of relying entirely on remedial courses to bring poorly prepared students up to speed—but they do not study it. The authors report only on whether or not the students in the CUNY cohort eventually graduated and how long it took them to do so. In the end, they tell us nothing about what they did in the classroom to earn their degrees, leaving many questions unanswered about the discrepancies between their research findings and the findings of others.

According, once again, to recent studies reported by Marty Nemko (2008), "A majority of the students whom colleges admit are grossly underprepared. Only 23 percent of the 1.3 million high-school graduates in 2007 who took the ACT examination were ready for college-level work in the core subjects of English, math, reading, and science." Given these statistics, how do colleges deal with the problem? Not well, says Nemko, citing the results of research, produced by highly reputable sources. Even for critics of standardized testing these findings give pause:

A 2006 study supported by the Pew Charitable Trusts found that 50 percent of college seniors scored below 'proficient' levels on a test that required them to do such basic tasks as understand the arguments of newspaper editorials or compare credit-card offers. Almost 20 percent of seniors had only basic quantitative skills. The students could not estimate if their car had enough gas to get to the gas station.

Incredibly, according to the Spellings Report, which was released in 2006 by a federal commission that examined the future of American higher education, things are getting even worse:

Over the past decade, literacy among college graduates has actually declined. . . . According to the most recent National Assessment of Adult Literacy, for instance, the percentage of college graduates deemed proficient in prose literacy has actually declined from 40 to 31 percent in the past decade. . . . Employers report repeatedly that many new graduates they hire are not prepared to work, lacking the critical thinking, writing, and problem-solving skills needed in today's workplaces. (Nemko 2008)

The graduates of CUNY in the 1970–1972 cohort may indeed be better off socially and economically than they would have been had they not finished their degrees, but given the current state of higher education, it is difficult for scholars dedicated to the life of the mind to make the case for open access without also addressing the brutal realities of what passes these days for a college education. The history of Hunter, I suggest, may help place this difficult debate in a more optimistic context. From its earliest days the college has stood for equal opportunity and excellence as well. The two, I maintain, can still go together.[6]

HUNTER COLLEGE

The College's Place within CUNY

Situated on the fashionable East Side of midtown Manhattan, Hunter College, which was founded in 1870, is the second oldest college in what became known as the City University of New York. The oldest college is City College, which was founded in 1847. By the 1920s, both City College for young men and Hunter College for young women were educating the children of upwardly mobile immigrants from all over Europe, many of them Jews, and the children of upwardly mobile African Americans. A decade later new colleges opened up in Brooklyn and Queens as well. Together these colleges provided high school graduates in New York City the chance to have a post-secondary education free of charge, an exceptional opportunity in the United States, where almost every other college, be it public or private, charged tuition. In exchange for a free education, these public institutions were highly selective. Taking pride in their academic standing, "Hunter girls" used to say: "If you were smart and rich, you went to Barnard. If you were rich and not so smart, you went to NYU. But if you were smart and not so rich, you went to Hunter."

After World War II, additional campuses opened up. Then in 1961 New York City's public colleges were consolidated into the City University of New York united administratively under a single chancellor and academically through a PhD-granting unit that drew on the faculty from the various campuses. With the creation of the Graduate Center individual colleges were able to recruit to their ranks research-active faculty in greater numbers than they did before, because now they could offer their colleagues the possibility of working with doctoral students. Today the City University serves over 200,000 full-time students. It is the largest urban university of its kind in the country—with eleven four-year senior colleges, six two-year community colleges, and five graduate and professional schools, including the Graduate Center, CUNY Law School, and schools of social work, journalism and public health/nursing.

In 1970, CUNY lifted its demanding college admissions requirements and threw open its doors to any graduate of New York City's high schools who wished to continue his or her studies. In the eyes of those who opposed the change in policy, open admissions contradicted the university's earlier decision to create a Graduate Center and make CUNY more academically competitive. Although weaker students, for the most part, were supposed to attend one of the two-year community colleges before transferring to a four-year institution, students who lacked college-level skills were also accepted at the senior colleges and placed in remedial programs. Complicating matters further, the lines between those who needed remedial work and those who did not were blurring.

During the first year of open admissions, CUNY accepted 35,000 freshmen, which represented a 75 percent increase over 1969. Although new faculty members were hired and facilities expanded, these additions could not meet the needs of the overwhelming number of new students—a third of whom would never have qualified for admission the year before. Shaken to the core, the cherished reputations of City, Hunter, Brooklyn, and Queens plummeted, while the costs associated with the new initiative skyrocketed. Equal opportunity exacted a price, both psychological and financial. Complicating an already very difficult situation, in the mid-1970s New York City and the nation slid into an economic recession, forcing the university to begin charging tuition in 1976.[7]

Twenty-three years later, in 1999, the university ended open admissions and most of the remedial programs at the senior, four-year colleges. Then, in 2001, CUNY opened its highly publicized, tuition-free Honors College. Critics see this latest initiative as the final nail in the coffin—ending CUNY's commitment to equal opportunities—while supporters see it as the rebirth of the university's original mission—making it possible for CUNY to attract once again gifted students from diverse backgrounds, many of whom are the first in their families to go to college.

According to Hunter College's website in the spring of 2008, the families of today's 20,844 students (15,718 of them undergraduates) come from more than 140 countries and speak over 100 languages. More than 50 percent of these students are members of underrepresented groups, making the college eligible to compete for special funding opportunities to support programs in the sciences, primarily, but also in the social sciences and humanities. The fact that Hunter has qualified in recent years to compete for special government grants, available only to institutions with large numbers of minority students, has been critical to the college's success and its ability to weather economic crises and political/cultural upheavals within the university. Today it prides itself in being the most popular college within the CUNY system and it accepts only one out of three applicants.

Although many problems remain, Hunter College today is thriving, enjoying an excellent reputation for preparing minority students to go on to PhD and professional programs at the best universities in the country, particularly, but not exclusively, in the sciences. In 2010 *The Princeton Review* ranked Hunter second in the country as the best buy in undergraduate education, just behind the University of Virginia. For the remainder of this paper, I will look at the circumstances surrounding Hunter College's success and at the challenges the college still faces in a city and nation deeply divided over affirmative action in higher education and over the ways to achieve equal opportunities for students. I begin by summarizing the early history of the institution, for reasons that I hope will become self-evident, before turning to the years when Hunter was transformed by open admissions.

HUNTER COLLEGE'S STORY IN GREATER DETAIL

1870–1945

Hunter College was founded by Thomas Hunter, an Irish schoolteacher from the north of Ireland, who immigrated to New York in 1849. An outspoken defender of Irish nationalism, he was forced to leave home after publishing an article that called for the disestablishment of the Church of England. With the help of an Irish schoolmaster, Thomas Hunter found a teaching position in New York and took up where he left off, embracing progressive causes and calling for change.

In the years following the Civil War, Thomas Hunter established a reputation for himself as an influential advocate for educational reform. By 1868 he had opened the city's first night school for men who were working full time.

Next he sought ways to improve the quality of teacher training programs in New York and provide women with the opportunity to get educated as well. In February 1870, Hunter opened the Female Normal School. Later that same year the school changed its name to the Normal College of the City of New York. In 1914, a year before Thomas Hunter died, the Board of Education decided to change the name once again and call it Hunter College of the City of New York, in honor of its inspirational founder.

Challenging common practice, Thomas Hunter created an academically rigorous program to train schoolteachers. In the early nineteenth century, Hunter noted, at time when normal schools were first being created in Britain and the United States, "a great mistake was made":

> [P]edagogical instruction was based on a narrow education; and raw boys and girls practiced the art of education without the previous training that would enable them to comprehend the underlying principles. . . . The only real normal school was founded in the time of the French Revolution, and though suppressed and reestablished several times, it exists to-day as the best normal school in the world, because its academic course is equal to that of any college in France. With such mental training the professional course is readily understood and assimilated. (Hunter 1931, 177–78)

Taking the Ecole Normale Supérieure in Paris as his model, Thomas Hunter offered his teachers the same kind of academic program that other students received in the best institutions of higher learning. Schoolteachers, he proclaimed, should be well-educated citizens. They would otherwise never be able to prepare young people to meet the challenges of a rapidly changing world. Thomas Hunter was making statements like these when most American children stopped going to school after the eighth grade. By the early twentieth century the Normal College had expanded its mission and become a liberal arts college for high school graduates.

In 1873, eight years after the end of the Civil War, New York State made racial segregation illegal in the public schools. Although nobody paid much attention, Thomas Hunter welcomed the new law and immediately admitted eight African American women to the college. In later years, he took great pride in his institution's commitment to diversity and spoke enthusiastically about the social and ethnic mix of the student body. In his 1886 annual report, for example, he listed the occupations of the fathers of his students—which ranged from bankers to day laborers—and then went on to say: "We have Jews and Gentiles and the children of almost every European nationality; dark-skinned Negroes sitting beside fair-haired Scandinavians. . . . This is the true democratic mingling of the classes which could only exist in a republican country like the United States" (cited in Perkins 1995, 20).

Despite Thomas Hunter's uplifting description of his adopted country, racial segregation, of course, and other forms of discrimination were common practice at the time and remained a problem well into the first half of the twentieth century, preventing African Americans and other racial/ethnic minorities from attending many of the best universities in the country. City College and Hunter College were rare exceptions to the rule and they graduated a remarkable number of gifted young people from excluded groups who went on subsequently to make major contributions to American society. During the 1930s and 1940s, Hunter's alumnae included the African American civil rights activist and lawyer Pauli Murray (class of 1932), and two Nobel laureates in medicine: Gertrude Ellion (class of 1937) and Rosalyn Yallow (class of 1941). To this day, the college remains the only institution of higher learning in the country to count two female Nobelists among its graduates. The list of alumnae from those years included as well the writer Bel Kaufman (1934—the granddaughter of Sholem Aleichem); dancer/choreographer Pearl Primus (1940); actress Ruby Dee (1942); Congresswoman Bella Abzug (1942); and opera singer Regina Resnik (1942), among many more.

1946–1970

In the years following World War II, Americans began going to college in greater numbers than ever. As more families encouraged their daughters to apply to Hunter, the college became increasingly competitive. By the 1950s and early 1960s only applicants with a B+ average or better could hope to be accepted. In 1964 Hunter College opened its doors to men, reducing the number of places for women even further. Then in 1970 the competition ended: Any student with a high school average of 80 percent or higher was eligible. Those with lower averages had to go to community colleges first, with the exception of a handful of students, who entered a special program called SEEK (Search for Education, Elevation and Knowledge).

1969–1999

What was it like during the early years of open admissions at Hunter? Let me try to recreate a sense of the times by quoting extensively from two self-studies prepared by colleagues at Hunter in 1977 and 1986 for the Commission on Higher Education's Middle States Association of Colleges and Secondary Schools. To this day the commission sends evaluators to Hunter and to other institutions of higher learning every ten years to review their academic programs for accreditation purposes. Written to assist outside evaluators in their deliberations, these reports are politically delicate documents.

Successful self-studies provide an honest picture of the challenges an institution faces, while still managing to present the college in a positive light.

The report prepared in 1977 was the first since open admissions and it was written a year after CUNY announced that it would now charge tuition. Given how upbeat self-studies usually sound, the tone of this one was truly alarming. The authors explained that the college had expected the university to implement open admissions slowly, in incremental steps. Having little preparation for the changes taking place, they were trying to adjust as best they could. Like the other colleges in CUNY, Hunter spent the better part of the 1970s, engaged in crisis management, moving from one unanticipated problem to another:

> In the fall of 1970 the policy of Open Admissions was adopted by the City University—five years ahead of the original schedule—offering each new high school graduate entry to some unit of the City University. In the enlarged entering classes that resulted from this decision, although the least well-prepared students were channeled into the community colleges, approximately *one-third* of the students entering Hunter would not have been eligible for admission under former criteria [emphasis added].
>
> With the doors of the City University thrown wide open enrollment expanded rapidly, putting almost intolerable pressure on the College's space and facilities and necessitating the rapid expansion of its faculty and supporting staff [primarily part-time adjuncts].
>
> More recently, with little advance warning, the City of New York was rocked by a devastating financial crisis. The budget of the City University has been sharply reduced in a series of drastic cuts. These cuts have led to a reduction in faculty and administrative staff, the halting of a long-awaited construction program, the abandonment of the University's traditional free tuition policy, the reduction in student enrollment, the sharp curtailment of expenditures for educational equipment, library books, and all Other-than-Personnel-Service items, and movement for greater involvement of the State of New York in the University's management.
>
> Because of these events, as well as the less visible accumulation of minor changes, the college that is now being examined differs from the Hunter reaccredited by the Middle States Association in 1966. (1977)

Ten years later, the 1986 self-study compared the description of Hunter College made in the 1966 report, written before CUNY had introduced its open admissions policy, with descriptions made in the mid-1970s, after the policy had been in place for several years:

> Institutional self-analysis reflects its times, and Hunter College's exercises of this kind over the past three decades offer an important perspective on the changes that have occurred in New York City, as well as in its unique public university, since mid-century.

Thus in 1966, a time of economic growth when Hunter was less than half its present size and admission was restricted to applicants with a high school academic average of close to 90 percent, the self-study prepared for the Middle States Association described the college as seeking "to establish a community of students and scholars engaged in the conservation, transmission and transmutation of human culture" and "to develop in its students intellectual discipline and the effective use of analytical, critical and imaginative reason."

Nine years later, in 1975, surveying a larger and much more diverse student body—the legacy of liberalized admissions policies[8] and an expansionary budget for the City University of New York (CUNY)—the Hunter Senate defined the goal of a Hunter College education a bit differently: "To foster the fullest possible intellectual and personal growth in each student." The emphasis was more individual and personal, focusing on each student according to his or her needs and abilities, and seeming to abandon the tacit assumption in the earlier document that all students enter the college equally well prepared academically. It was also more practical and down-to-earth in its specifics, referring to the college's responsibility "to develop the student's natural, critical and creative powers" and defining as parts of that development "the abilities to conceptualize and analyze, to relate the concrete and the particular to the abstract and general, and to think and write logically and coherently."

Just two years later, on the heels of a wrenching financial crisis, the tone of the [1977] report to the Middle States Association was dour and determined, preoccupied with the problem of survival. The 1977 report summarized two main purposes for Hunter College: "maintaining vigorous academic aims" while "adapting our strong liberal arts tradition to meet the needs of students in today's changing academic climate"—needs that had changed with the admission of larger numbers of academically unprepared undergraduates and the growing emphasis nationwide on vocational and professional work. It concluded by endorsing, as the college's "general aim," the quotation from the 1975 Senate statement: "to foster the fullest possible intellectual and personal growth in each student."

In 1986 the tone of the self-study was considerably more upbeat. Hunter, so it seemed, had turned the corner and things looked a good deal brighter. The document's authors had reason to be optimistic. The economy was stronger and their dynamic new president, Donna Shalala, was moving the college forward in innovative ways. Although many problems remained, the authors focused instead on what was going well—on the achievements of a devoted and enterprising faculty who had succeeded in preserving Hunter College's commitment to excellence. The self-study spoke at great length, for example, about an honors program at the college that had taken on new meaning in the 1970s, since open admissions. Known as the Thomas Hunter Honors

Program, it was mentioned only in passing in the earlier report. By 1986, however, the self-study gives the impression that the program had become a veritable haven, the place where good students could study in the company of peers, in courses taught jointly by two members of the faculty on themes that transcended disciplinary divides and explored new lines of inquiry. The report focused as well on the scholarly activities of the faculty and spoke of the need to create working conditions that made it possible to do serious research. Course loads, it warned, had not been adjusted—the way they had in other colleges and universities across the nation—to help research-active faculty divide their time equitably between their scholarly activities and their teaching obligations to students who were increasingly unprepared for college-level work. Whereas the average teaching load in the 1980s, at comparable colleges in the United States, was four or five courses per year, the official load at the senior colleges in CUNY was seven, and so it remains to the present day!

During these difficult years, the college identified research and teaching opportunities for ambitious faculty and students, particularly in the sciences. In 1985 the Division of Sciences and Mathematics successfully applied to the National Institutes of Health (NIH) for special earmarked funding to support programs in the biomedical sciences for colleges and universities that qualified as minority institutions. Hunter College has since received nearly $40 million from the NIH in RCMI grants (Research Centers in Minority Institutions). Two years after receiving the first grant, the college recruited Erwin Fleissner, a distinguished molecular biologist from Memorial Sloan-Kettering Institute for Cancer Research, to become the new dean and develop the sciences at the college.[9]

The RCMI has helped Hunter recruit gifted new faculty, including members of underrepresented groups, by providing the infrastructural support they needed to build technologically sophisticated laboratories. With these labs up and running, the faculty could then apply individually for government grants to keep their research funded and their record of success has been high. Over the years undergraduate and graduate students have been studying in these labs, side by side with their professors, participating in path breaking work in neuroscience, nanotechnology, and cancer research.

Although the numbers are small in absolute terms, the college is a leader in the country today in launching the careers of minorities in the natural sciences and lab-based social sciences (e.g., biological anthropology and neuropsychology). In addition to the RCMI grants, Hunter receives financial support from eleven other programs that subsidize the training of minority students.[10] Most of the money comes from NIH, but the college has also received substantial funding from private philanthropic organizations, including the

Mellon Foundation for students in the humanities and the Howard Hughes Medical Institute Undergraduate Science Education Program.

Since 1986, the college has lived through a number of crises and changes. In the spring of 1991, Governor Mario Cuomo presented a budget proposal to the State of New York that had serious repercussions for CUNY. The proposal suggested raising tuition, cutting back on state-supported student aid, and reducing the operating costs of the university by 15 percent. Students across CUNY held demonstrations, while members of the faculty and staff met to discuss layoffs and the closing down of small programs. Although the "enemy" was elsewhere, a group of students made Hunter the target of their frustrations. Members of the student government managed to take over the administration building, including the president's office, and hold onto it for nearly three weeks. Classes continued, but the library and central administrative offices were closed down. The main reason given for occupying the building was to protest the proposed tuition hike, but there were local demands too. For example, members of the group wanted the college to fire an adjunct professor, whom they claimed was racist. Students also demanded that the college hire more faculty members of color and allocate more resources to ethnic and gender studies. In response to some of their demands the college implemented a new "diversity and pluralism requirement." Since then, in addition to other requirements, every student at Hunter takes a course on the culture of an American minority, another on gender, yet another on a non-Western society, and finally one on an aspect of European history and traditions (Friedlander 1991).

With open admissions, colleagues in the social sciences and humanities found themselves teaching large, overcrowded classes of students who lacked the basic skills needed to do college-level work. Overwhelmed and demoralized, they were often unable to provide the kind of attention they used to give students when the college was smaller and the student body better prepared. Research-active colleagues receded into their scholarly activities, protecting themselves as best they could from their deteriorating working conditions, which had become far worse than those in other New York institutions. At least CUNY's salaries were comparatively high in the 1970s and 1980s, but soon this advantage disappeared as well.[11]

Colleagues in the sciences and lab-based social sciences had more control over their lives, because their research was funded, making it possible to teach fewer classes by "buying themselves out." Given the academic demands of their disciplines, they also had fewer students and the students they had were better prepared. Aspiring young scientists got a superb education in the labs of their professors.

Given the odds, the stories of students who have succeeded at Hunter are truly inspiring. Erich Jarvis, for example, graduated in the late 1980s in biology and is now a professor of neuroscience at Duke University—specializing in the brains of songbirds. After leaving Hunter he went to Rockefeller University for his doctoral studies. His work is frequently featured in the Science section of *The New York Times*. Most recently he was quoted in an article by Margaret Talbot, in *The New Yorker* (2008). In describing himself, Erich Jarvis has said, "Statistically I should have been a bum." His father was homeless and lived on park benches in New York City. Hunter has also produced more black female physics majors who went on to get their PhDs at MIT than any other college in the country. The numbers, though small, are considered significant by national standards.

Extraordinary students have graduated from Hunter in the social sciences and humanities as well, but they have had to fight harder to stay engaged and gain recognition. All too often they found themselves in overcrowded classes, listening to professors who have "dumbed down" their lectures for students unable to do college-level work.

2000–Present

When Donna Shalala was president of the college in the 1980s, she famously said, "Do you know what I love about Hunter? It's so messy!" And that sentiment continues to attract gifted leaders to the college today. Like Donna Shalala, Jennifer Raab, the current president of Hunter, has turned imposing challenges into great opportunities. Under her leadership the college has built the largest branch of the CUNY Honors program and invested substantially in several areas of academic excellence. The sciences, for one, are stronger than ever. When she arrived in 2001, she committed herself to finding a way to build a new science facility. In the spring of 2010 she is nearing the end of a series of negotiations with the city and a private institution that will make it possible for Hunter to build a new facility within close walking distance of the main campus.[12] Not only are the sciences flourishing, but the arts are flourishing as well, particularly the studio art program, art history, and creative writing. Under her leadership exciting new programs in the social sciences have also begun to take off, including new interdisciplinary courses of study in public policy and human rights, housed in the newly renovated former home of Franklin and Eleanor Roosevelt.[13]

Taking great pride in the achievements of students at Hunter, Jennifer Raab uses the graduation exercises every year to single out several members of the class who have completed their studies with distinction, against unimaginable odds. In 2004, for example, she featured Van Tran, a Vietnamese immigrant who graduated in sociology at the age of twenty-four with a 4.0 average. Discriminated against in Vietnam for being an ethnic Chinese, he spent most of his childhood in a refugee camp in Thailand. Finally he and his family managed to get to the United States in the 1990s. Settling in New York, Van Tran learned English, and worked in a hardware store to help support his family, while he also went to college—first to Hostos Community College, where most of the students speak Spanish, and then to Hunter. The recipient of multiple awards, Van Tran is currently finishing his doctoral studies in sociology and policy at Harvard on a Soros fellowship for new immigrants.

Uplifting stories like Van Tran's abound, but many problems remain. Hunter has still not fully recovered from the damage inflicted on the college during thirty years of a poorly conceived and poorly managed open admissions program. Nine years after CUNY abandoned the policy, the university continues to accept students who are not academically prepared for college-level work. Leaving aside the matter of preparation, there are simply too many students for the size of the full-time faculty, a situation CUNY is trying address, but it has a long way to go. As a result, the college hires armies of adjuncts in some departments. In English, for example, with more than 1,000 majors, part-time instructors have been offering 70 percent of the courses. Without the attention they need, the weak students muddle through, drop out, or transfer. A number of strong students transfer as well. Although the situation is beginning to improve, the college still only graduates in a given year about a third of the students it accepted eight years earlier.

In a valiant effort to turn things around, President Raab has restructured student services to improve the advising of students. She has also received funding from the Mellon Foundation to run a major curricular review of Hunter's general education program and explore ways to improve the quality of college teaching. Although it is still too early to determine whether these initiatives will help in any significant way, colleagues are engaged and energized by the process. Beyond the college itself, CUNY and Hunter have joined the mayor of New York City in a vigorous campaign to recruit and train teachers to work in the public schools. For the time being, however, the faculty at Hunter continues to teach far too many students who lack the background they need to do college-level work.

CONCLUSION

A common response to the challenge of teaching underprepared students is to make fewer demands. Grade inflation is rampant on campuses across the country and weak students flock to generous professors and academically lenient programs. Although the culture is changing, some colleagues at Hunter give students good grades as a matter of principle. As long as they tried, the argument goes, they deserve to get through. It is not fair to punish students for the poor quality of their high school education.

Meanwhile, policy analysts produce dire report after dire report about the state of the nation's schools. The first one came out in 1983. Sponsored by the National Commission on Excellence in Education, "A Nation at Risk" warned Americans in apocalyptic terms that the country was losing its competitive edge internationally. Since then, things have only gotten worse. Marking the twenty-fifth anniversary of the study, Edward Fiske (2008), a former education editor of *The New York Times*, observed that "the report's desperate language may be more justified than ever, for American education is in turmoil":

> The striking thing about the performance of American students on international comparisons is not that, on average, they are in the middle of the pack—which was also true in 1983—but that we have a disproportionate share of low-performing students. We are failing to provide nearly one-third of our young people with even the minimal education required to be functioning citizens and workers in a global economy.
>
> This is particularly distressing news at a time when the baby boomers are aging and a growing proportion of the future work force comes from groups—members of ethnic and racial minorities, students from low-income families, recent immigrants—that have been ill served by our education system. The challenge today is to build access as well as excellence. That's the new definition of "a nation at risk" and ample reason for a new commission to awaken the nation for the need to educate our young people (Fiske 2008).

Many of us, including myself, are long on rhetoric and short on solutions. We need to do more than talk about "access and excellence." We need a plan and we need it urgently. Colleagues in the sciences at Hunter College, I suggest, have led the way, but as they have demonstrated, there are no shortcuts. Labor intensive and costly, Hunter's programs have managed to succeed, despite the odds, by recruiting first-rate scientists to work with highly motivated students, who are frequently the first in their families to go to college.

REFERENCES

Attewell, Paul, and David E. Lavin. *Passing the Torch: Does Higher Education for the Disadvantaged Pay Off Across the Generations?* New York: Russell Sage Foundation, 2007.

Fisk, Edward. "A Nation at a Loss." *The New York Times*, April 25, 2008, A27.

Friedlander, Judith. "Le Muliticulturalisme dans une université américaine. Une étude de cas." *Le Messager Européen* 5 (Fall1991).

Hunter College. Report of the Self-Study Conducted by Hunter College of the City University of New York, to the Commission of Higher Education Middle States Association of Colleges and Secondary Schools, 1977 and 1986.

Hunter, Thomas. *The Autobiography of Dr. Thomas Hunter*. New York: Knickerbocker Press, 1931.

Hyllegard, David, and David E. Lavin. *Changing the Odds: Open Admissions and the Life Chances of the Disadvantaged*. New Haven: Yale University Press, 1996.

Kennedy, John. "Executive Order #10925 of the President of the United States." 1961.

Kirp, David L. *Shakespeare, Einstein, and the Bottom Line: The Marketing of Higher Education*. Cambridge: Harvard University Press, 2003.

Kirp, David L. "The Earth is Flattening: The Globalization of Higher Education and its Implications for Equal Opportunity." Presented at the Hurst Seminar on Higher Education and Equality of Opportunity: Cross-National Perspectives. Beer Sheva: Ben-Gurion University of the Negev, June 3, 2008.

McKenna, Barbara. "Rolling Back Affirmative Action: State Ballot Initiatives Are a Multi-edged Sword," *On Campus* 27, no. 5 (May/June 2008): 10–11.

Murray, Pauli. *Song of a Weary Throat: An American Pilgrimage*. New York: Harper and Row, 1987.

Perkins, Linda. "African-American Women and Hunter College, 1873–1945." *The Echo: Journal of the Hunter College Archives*. In celebration of the 125th Anniversary of Hunter College (1995): 17–25.

Nemko, Marty. "America's Most Overrated Product: The Bachelor's Degree." *The Chronicle for Higher Education* (May 2, 2008): B17.

Spellings, Margaret. "A Test of Leadership: Charting the Future of U.S. Higher Education." Washington DC: Department of Education, 2006.

Report of the Federal Commission on the Future of Higher Education (2006).

Talbot, Margaret. "Birdbrain." *The New Yorker Magazine* (April 12, 2008): 64–75.

NOTES

1. I would like to thank the following people at Hunter College and the Macaulay Honors College of the City University of New York for having helped me gather the data for this paper: Robert Dottin, Anatoliy Kadinsky, Joan Lambe, Theresa Mathis, Vita Rabinowitz, Shirley Raps, Jonathan Schoenwald, Michael Teitel, Peggy Tirschwell, Sylvia Tomasch, Jeanne Waxman.

2. At Hunter College, the number of students has indeed increased, but the percentages of African Americans and Hispanics have dropped. Whether this can be attributed to the change in policy, however, is not clear, given the precipitous drop in the number of African Americans and Latinos attending college nationwide—particularly African American males.

3. CUNY has instituted several new programs to recruit and train teachers, including a special academy to train math and science teachers, offering college freshmen free tuition for four years if, upon graduation, they agree to teach math and

science in the city's schools for several years. In 2005, Hunter College appointed David Steiner as Dean of the School of Education. A bold educational reformer, he began the process of rebuilding the teacher-training programs at the college, with the financial backing of some of the leading financial supporters of educational reform in the country. Soon after she came to Hunter in 2001, President Jennifer Raab opened a special high school, in collaboration with the New York City public schools, for students interested in studying science and math. Finally, since the early years of the twentieth century, Hunter College has been running a school for gifted children, which has a stellar reputation.

4. According to the Macaulay Honors College self-study, prepared in 2008, there were 1,226 students in the program that year system wide, in a university that serves over 200,000 full-time students. After Hunter, the second largest program is at Baruch College with 295 students in 2008. Brooklyn had 162 that year, City 140, Lehman, as noted above, 52, Queens 161 and Staten Island 85. Although Hunter College reported 325 students, the Macaulay self-study claimed that the college had 331. Given this discrepancy, the numbers recorded for the other colleges may also be slightly off. The Macaulay self-study also reported that in the freshmen class entering in 2007, 45 percent of the students were white, 13.4 percent Hispanic, 6.6 percent black, and 34.7 percent Asian/Pacific Islanders. Since 2001, when the first class arrived, the percentages of white and black students have declined and the percentages of Hispanic and Asian students have risen (55.8 percent white, 8.7 percent black, 8.7 percent Hispanic, 26.9 percent Asian/Pacific Islanders). The report also notes that in the graduating class of 2007, 31 percent of the students were the first in their families to go to college and more than 70 percent were either foreign-born or first-generation immigrants.

5. Nemko's article is, admittedly, very provocative. The issues, however, are serious and need addressing. Nemko does not actually identify the study involving students who graduate in the bottom 40 percent of their high-school class, but says that the study is cited by Clifford Adelman, formerly a research analyst at the U.S. Department of Education and currently a research associate at the Institute for Higher Education Policy. Marty Nemko himself is a well-known consultant who offers advice to educators, including—according to his Web site—fifteen college presidents. He is also a media personality who appears regularly on public radio and television, offering advice about educational and other career-related matters. He has published extensively on the subject as well.

6. Although this paper focuses on undergraduates, Hunter College also has MA programs in almost every department in the School of Arts and Sciences and in the School of Education, the School of Social Work, and the Schools of Nursing and Public Health.

7. Undergraduates who were residents of New York State did not start paying tuition until 1978. The annual rate then, for full-time students was $925. In 2008 it was $4,000. The fees for nonresidents went from $1,425 to $8,640. Tuition today in many private colleges is over $20,000 a year. In some of the best, it is well over $30,000.

8. By 1986 only 46.8 percent of entering freshmen had high school averages of 80 percent or higher, 24 percent had averages 75 to 79 percent, 14.8 percent had averages of 70 to 74.9 percent, and 5 percent had averages below 70 percent (Hunter

College Student Profile, 1982–1987, prepared by Hunter College's Office of Institutional Research).

9. Erwin Fleissner served as dean for eleven years, during which time he successfully recruited very talented women and minority faculty. He is credited with having transformed scientific research and teaching at Hunter, turning the college into a national leader in the preparation of young scientists from underrepresented groups.

10. Since the late-1990s, three members of the faculty, two of them African American, have received special honors from the White House, in recognition of the high quality of their research and of their mentoring roles to undergraduate students in the sciences (Presidential Early Career Award for Scientists and Engineers: Jill Bargonetti 1997, Derrick Brazill 2002, and the Presidential Award for Excellence in Mathematics, Science and Engineering Mentoring, Steven Greenbaum, 2005.)

11. CUNY had Al Shanker and the public school teachers' union to thank for their comparatively high salaries in those years

12. Jennifer Raab came to Hunter after serving as the Landmarks Commissioner of the City of New York. Without her knowledge of the complicated political landscape of real estate in New York and her extraordinary political skill, Hunter would never have gotten this far. President Raab also raised money from the central administration of the university and from private donors to renovate the Franklin and Eleanor Roosevelt's House that became part of the College in the 1930s, but had been in terrible disrepair for years. The renovated town house opened in the winter of 2010 and is the home of a new policy institute at Hunter. Finally, in the fall of 2009, Hunter College received the largest gift ever made to CUNY to build a new home for the college's School of Social Work in East Harlem.

13. Some of the distinguished new appointments include the art historian Joachim Pissarro, the great grandson of Camille Pissarro. He came to Hunter from the Museum of Modern Art in 2006 to become the curator of Hunter's art galleries. The Director of Creative Writing is the Australian novelist Peter Carey, the recipient of two Booker Prizes. Peter Carey came to Hunter in 2003.

7

The Changing American College Experience

A View from the City University of New York, Hunter College

Charles Tien[1]

The typical image of a college student is an eighteen- to twenty-two-year-old, going to school full time, with expenses being paid for by parents, and enjoying his or her last phase of youth before starting a career. This is an outdated image, especially since enrollments have increased dramatically over the last thirty years and since minority enrollments have increased as a result of affirmative-action policies. How has the American college experience changed as a result of affirmative action? How is the American college experience different for white students and students of color? What does the minority college student experience look like? Do minorities take longer to graduate? Are minority students more likely to work full or part time to help pay for college? Are minority students more likely to be married with family obligations? This chapter examines how market-driven changes, especially to affirmative-action policies, have altered the student population at the City University of New York and the American college experience.

The City University of New York (CUNY) is the third largest university system in the United States. CUNY began accepting all New York high school graduates in the early 1970s and then tightened admissions standards in the late 1990s. These two changes in admissions policy at CUNY offer an excellent opportunity to see the effects of the "access revolution" and the "market revolution" laid out by David L. Kirp in the introduction of this volume on minority access to higher education. This chapter will analyze admissions data from CUNY to examine minority access to higher education in New York City. It will also analyze data from the National Longitudinal

Survey of Youth (1997) to see how the minority student experience differs from the white student experience in America.

SEARCH FOR EDUCATION, ELEVATION, AND KNOWLEDGE (SEEK)

Lavin, Alba, and Silberstein (1981) explain how CUNY started to expand educational opportunities for minorities in the 1960s. They argue that Albert H. Bowker, who became CUNY Chancellor in 1963, was instrumental in increasing access for minority students at CUNY. He came from Stanford University where he had been dean of the graduate school. "Under Bowker's leadership the movement toward a more inclusive CUNY was begun" (Lavin, Alba, and Silberstein 1981, 5). The city's population was growing and changing to become less white during the 1960s and Bowker started a program in 1964 to admit students outside the regular rigorous admissions process. If CUNY enrollments in the 1960s had remained constant in the face of New York City's growing population, admission requirements would have risen to a 90 percent high school average needed for admission to some of the CUNY campuses. This would have further excluded disadvantaged students. Bowker, however, wanted to expand enrollments and increase opportunities for minorities. New York State responded to Bowker's vision by budgeting for increased enrollments in 1966 and beyond, and establishing a special admission program for minorities. "This program, known by the acronym SEEK (Search for Education, Elevation, and Knowledge), began that fall with a thousand students. It immediately became the major avenue of minority entry to CUNY's senior colleges" (Lavin, Alba, and Silberstein 1981, 5).

OPEN ADMISSIONS

The debates and proposals that marked the change of CUNY's admissions policy in the late 1960s are an excellent reflection of the controversies surrounding affirmative-action programs in general. How far should universities go to open access to higher education for minorities? Does greater access mean reducing academic standards? Are quotas necessary to achieve a student body that looks like society as a whole? Must increasing access be a choice between merit and quotas?

In addition to Bowker's desire for growing enrollments, racial unrest and student activism in the late 1960s also helped push CUNY to revise its admissions policy in 1969. After a turbulent year during which black and

Puerto Rican students at the City College of New York (CCNY) demanded, among other things, that the entering class reflect the black and Puerto Rican population in the city's high schools, the university decided to open its doors wide. The 1968–1969 school year saw CCNY's student auditorium burn, students occupy campus buildings and seal off parts of "the University of Harlem," the closing and reopening of the college, and CCNY's president resign in response to budget cuts that would have reduced new enrollments at the exact time minorities were demanding greater access. After this tumultuous year, the New York City Board of Higher Education voted to implement an open admissions plan that offered a space somewhere in CUNY for all New York City high school graduates. The plan "guaranteed students who graduated from high school with at least an eighty average (in academic, college preparatory courses) or who ranked in the top 50 percent of their high school graduating class a place in a senior college (like Hunter College), if that was their preference; all others could enroll in a community college" (Lavin, Alba, and Silberstein 1981, 18). By using high school rank as a criterion for admission, disadvantaged students were not punished for attending poor performing high schools. In addition, all graduates of community colleges were guaranteed admission into a senior college. The change to open enrollment went into effect in September of 1970. In short, a university with a selective admissions policy had changed to open its doors to any city high school graduate. What were the consequences of this dramatic change in higher education policy?

POST OPEN ADMISSIONS: THE 1980S AND 1990S

What happened at CUNY after open admissions was implemented? This question is answered in two ways by looking at the experience of Hunter College—CUNY's flagship senior college. First, the chapter shows what Hunter College looked like racially and ethnically after this period with data from 1988 to present that was provided by Hunter College's Office of Institutional Research (race and ethnicity data rely on self-identification provided by students). Second, the chapter looks at the performance of these students during the same period by examining Hunter College's six-year graduation rate for SEEK students and non-SEEK students.

Lavin and Hyllegard (1996: table 2.1) report that in 1969, only 4 four percent of students at the CUNY senior colleges (these are the non–community colleges, which at present are Hunter College, City College, Queens College, Baruch College, Brooklyn College, John Jay College, Lehman College, College of Staten Island, Medgar Evers College, NYC College of Technology, and York College) were minority. Minority enrollment at the senior colleges increased to an average of 16 percent for the years 1970 to 1972. The next available data point, which is for Hunter College only, shows that a radical transformation occurred. Each senior college has its own admissions criteria, as do the community colleges, but they were all similarly affected by the open admissions plan. Therefore, changes at the CUNY colleges would reflect the changes at Hunter College described here. By 1988, over 65 percent of the student population at Hunter was minority. The white student population would continue to decline at Hunter College to a low of 35.2 percent in 2003. SEEK and open admissions had sought to increase the enrollments of black and Hispanic students and CUNY achieved this goal immediately. By the late 1980s Hunter College was a majority-minority campus. Undergraduate enrollment at Hunter College in 1988 was 22.9 percent African American and 20.6 percent Hispanic. Asians made up another 11.4 of undergraduates.

Hunter College was transformed by open admissions from a nearly all-white institution to a majority-minority institution. This was the case CUNY wide as well:

> Open admissions brought about one form of equity: the program attracted so many minority students that in the early 1970s they came for the first time to be represented in CUNY freshman classes in the same proportions that they were in the graduating classes in New York City's high schools. Most of these students would not have gone to college had it not been for open admissions. (Lavin and Hyllegard 1996, 196)

CUNY has not been widely or loudly congratulated for transforming itself to give minorities access to the keys of success in America—a higher education. But undoubtedly, CUNY has changed the life paths of thousands of African American, Hispanic, and Asian students by giving them a chance to get a bachelor's degree (Attewell and Lavin, 2007). CUNY succeeded in opening its doors to minorities and did so in a dramatic way over the course of forty years. How did CUNY do in educating and graduating these students once they enrolled?

GRADUATION RATES

Graduation rates provide some evidence of the success of CUNY in educating minority students. Four-year graduation rates at CUNY during the Open Admissions period of the 1980s was abysmally low—around 7 percent, which was well below national averages. The rate of students graduating within five years for CUNY is 34.7 percent, also significantly lower than the national average of 54.3 percent (Schmidt et al. 1999, 57). CUNY students, however, are unlike other college students in many important ways. Over 25 percent work part or full-time to pay for college, 30 percent are or have been married, almost as many are raising children, and half of the freshmen are foreign-born (Schmidt et al. 1999, 25). Thus, a better gauge of graduation success at CUNY might be to look at six-year graduation rates given the higher number of students who are working and supporting families.

The six-year graduation rates of SEEK students at Hunter College during the 1990s are astonishingly low. Cohorts who entered from 1990 to 1994 show steady six-year graduation percentages. That is, on average 13.4 percent of SEEK students entering between 1990 and 1994 graduated within six years. And the average for non-SEEK students for the same period is 28.9 percent. These numbers are not terribly impressive. However, starting with the 1995 cohort (a sixth-year graduation in spring of 2001), SEEK graduation percentages start climbing and do not stop climbing. The 1997 SEEK and non-SEEK cohorts have nearly identical six-year graduation rates of 31 percent. What the numbers suggest is that either changes were made in who was admitted through SEEK starting in 1995 or changes were made to the education experiences of SEEK students starting in fall of 2001. Which was it? Or was it both?

THE CHANGING FACE OF SEEK

Did the student composition of SEEK change over the last ten to fifteen years? While SEEK can be thought of as an affirmative-action program, it actually is a program for all races and ethnicities and is described as a program that was "established to provide comprehensive academic support to assist capable students who otherwise might not be able to attend college due to their educational and financial circumstances. Students are admitted without regard to age, sex, sexual orientation, race, disability, or creed" (Seek Web Page 2010). The CUNY website lists the criteria for eligibility. Among other residency and diploma requirements, students are eligible if they meet New York State income guidelines, and are "inadmissible according to the freshman admissions criteria established for the CUNY senior college" that they want to attend. Thus, while it may be a program primarily for minorities, whites are also eligible to participate in SEEK.

Looking at first-year enrollments through the lens of SEEK provides information on how minorities have gained access to higher education in New York City. Are whites also using a program described to be for minority access to higher education? Are minority enrollments as a whole increasing as the city's minority population has grown? Or is the composition of CUNY's minority enrollment changing to reflect the city's changing minority population? Or are some groups losing access as other groups are gaining access? The following provides a picture of first-year enrollments for SEEK students at Hunter College by race using data provided by Hunter College's Office of Institutional Research.

These data show that white students are a small percentage of the SEEK students who enter Hunter College. This means that the SEEK program is mostly benefiting minorities—the group it was designed to help get into CUNY. Two trends in the data are worth pointing out. First, the percent of white students among SEEK freshmen has increased over time. Before 1996 the average percentage of white SEEK freshmen was 6.04 percent and since 1996 that average has risen to 10.51 percent. This could be the result of increasing Russian and Eastern European immigration to New York City in recent years. Second, white students are a large portion of new transfer students at Hunter College—consistently slightly more than the overall enrollment of white students at Hunter College. For example, in 2007 white students made up 30.3 percent of all Hunter Students while they made up 43 percent of all transfer students. This means that the white students may be benefiting from the open admissions policy that guaranteed a spot in a senior college for all graduates of the CUNY community colleges. Without data on where these new transfer students are coming from, it is not possible to say this definitively.

Black students in 1988 made up 38.9 percent of all SEEK-admitted first-time freshmen students. Data shows that the percent of black students among all SEEK freshmen remained above 30 percent until 1996. The percent of SEEK freshmen who are black has been steadily decreasing since 1996. And in the three years since 2005, the percent of SEEK students who are black has dropped below 10 percent. This is a disturbing trend for a program that was designed to increase black and Hispanic student enrollment in CUNY. Have black students benefited by transferring to Hunter College? The percent of transfer students to Hunter who are black has remained below 20 percent since 1988 and dipped to 10 percent in 2007. Again, not a heartening statistic for a program created to increase black and Hispanic student enrollment at CUNY. The percent of total black first-time freshmen confirms the trend of lower black enrollments at Hunter since 1988. The percent of black students among first-time freshmen (SEEK and non-SEEK, but not including transfers) was 31.5 percent in 1988 and 10.7 in 2007.

What do the data look like for Hispanic students at Hunter College? The percent of SEEK first-time freshmen who are Hispanic has been consistently above or around 40 percent since 1988. However, it was always above 40 percent before 2002 and has only been above 40 percent once since 2002. The average percent from 1988 to 2001 for SEEK first-time freshmen who are Hispanic is 45.21 percent. The average percent since 2002 is 38.08 percent. Thus, Hispanic students have benefited from SEEK, but their share of SEEK enrollments has been steadily decreasing over the last six years. This is evident in looking at data on Hispanic enrollments for first-time freshmen (SEEK, non-SEEK, and total) and new transfer students. As far as the percentage of new transfer students to Hunter College who are Hispanic, there appears to no apparent increasing or decreasing trend since 1988. The percentage of transfer students who are Hispanic has remained around 20 percent, with an average of 19.78 percent over the twenty years.

The data for Asian students at Hunter College reveal an increasing trend of first-time freshmen (SEEK, non-SEEK, and transfers) enrollment since 1988. In 1988, only 10 percent of SEEK first-time freshmen were Asian. By 2007, the percentage of SEEK first-time freshmen who were Asian had reached an astonishing 42.2 percent. The percentage of non-SEEK freshmen who were Asian has also increased, though not as dramatically, from 14 to 19.6 percent. The percent of new transfers who are Asian has also increased: from 12.6 percent in 1988 to 17.9 percent. The increase in Asian students at Hunter College since 2000 has come from Asians benefiting a great deal from SEEK.

The data examined have shown a changing composition of Hunter College's student body. Black student enrollment is down significantly since 2001 and Hispanic enrollment is lower since that time as well, though not by as much. Asian student enrollment has swelled since 2001 and white enrollment has seen a slight uptick. Part of the explanation for these trends is New York City's changing population. The *New York Times* (Roberts 2006) reported that:

> For the first time since at least the 19th century, the black population of both the city and, to a lesser extent, the region, has declined. In the five boroughs, according to the estimates, the number of Blacks declined by about 30,000 since 2000, dipping below 30 percent of the overall population, as the migration of Blacks to the suburbs and areas like the South outpaced immigration from the Caribbean and Africa.
>
> In contrast, the analysis found that while the greater New York region over all lost 162,000 non-Hispanic whites and several hundred Blacks from 2000 to 2004, the region gained 288,000 Hispanic people and 201,000 Asians—more Asians, in fact, than any other metropolitan area.

At Hunter College, changes in minority enrollment began as early as 1996. A changing city population and CUNY's changed admissions policy implemented in the early 2000s seems to have accelerated the minority enrollment changes started in 1996.

CLOSING THE DOORS, AGAIN?

Mayor Rudy Giuliani's Advisory Task Force Report on CUNY in 1999 creates the impression that the consequences of open admissions were disastrous for the university. Its Executive Summary reports that:

> The City University of New York is adrift. An institution of critical importance to New York and the nation, potentially a model of excellence and educational opportunity to policy universities throughout the world, CUNY currently is in a spiral of decline. Its graduation rates are low and students who succeed take a long time to earn their degrees. . . . Academic standards are loose and confused, and CUNY lacks the basic information necessary to make sound judgments about the quality and effectiveness of its programs. CUNY is inundated with New York City public schools graduates who lack basic academic skills, but it has not made a strong effort to get the public schools to raise their standards. (Schmidt et al. 1999, 5)

The report finds that graduation rates at CUNY are well below national averages for four-year public colleges. It reports a four-year graduation rate of between 6 percent and 7 percent and a six-year graduation rate of about 30 percent for the 1980s. This is low in comparison to other New York colleges that report six-year graduation rates between 50 percent and 60 percent.

One of the results of the report was higher admissions standards at CUNY's senior campuses, like Hunter College. The higher admissions standards now require applicants to attain high grade point averages from high school and certain SAT or ACT scores. These higher standards may have resulted not only in the lower black student enrollments at Hunter College, but at other senior colleges, like City College and Baruch College, as well. At Baruch College, black student enrollment dropped from 24 percent to 14 percent, and at City College black student enrollment dropped from 40 percent to 30 percent between 1999 and 2006. It appears that CUNY has shifted its black student population from the senior colleges to its community colleges—total CUNY enrollments for black students (senior colleges and community colleges) have increased since 1999 from 52,937 to 57,791 in 2005 (Aronson 2006).

THE COLLEGE EXPERIENCE THROUGH THE LENS OF RACE

Since individual level data of Hunter College students is not available, this chapter uses data from the National Longitudinal Survey of Youth 1997 (NLSY97) (2003) to examine some of the life situations of minority college students compared to white students. The NLSY97 is a panel study tracking American youth starting in 1997 who were born between 1980 and 1984. Youth were selected randomly nationwide to participate in the study. The original sample included 8,984 respondents. The panel study revisited respondents every year, and this chapter analyzes data from the 2003 round, in which the youngest respondents in the sample are nineteen years of age. Data is only taken from respondents who have attended at least one year of college.

Is the college experience different for minority students? How is it different? Are minority students working outside of school more than white students? Are more minority students married? Supporting children? The answers to these questions may have implications on college success. Students who are faced with work and family obligations in addition to school may find it difficult to graduate in a timely fashion, or at all. To help minority students succeed in college after admitting them may mean changing expectations or changing the definition of success or providing different resources.

First, how does the CUNY student population look in comparison to the nationwide sample? As an institution that enacted aggressive policies to enroll minority students and as an institution serving an urban area with a relatively large minority population, its student body would be expected to be less white than the national average. The NLSY97 data show that nationwide, 17.8 percent of students are Hispanic, 22.4 percent are African American, 2.9 percent are Asian American, and 63.6 percent are white. Comparing the NLSY97 data to Hunter College data shows a striking difference in white and Asian enrollments. Hunter College, reflecting its history of open admissions and urban location, is less white than the national sample, by far. Hunter also has many more Asian students than the national sample. Thus, in terms of diversity, Hunter College's greater diversity meets expectations. The chapter next explores what the college experience is like for minority students compared to white students.

Do minority students work more outside of the classroom? Among white students, only 8 percent did not work at all, whereas 14.2 percent of black students, 20.5 percent of Asian students and 9.1 percent of Hispanic students did not work at all. On the other end of the work scale—those who worked between 49 and 52 weeks per year—25.3 percent of whites worked year-round, as did 17.5 percent of Blacks, 21.4 percent of Asians, and 26.2 percent of Hispanics. Given the rising costs of college, it is not surprising that so many students of all ethnicities had to work for pay, with about 25 percent of students working year-round.

Getting through school can certainly be more difficult if students are raising children as well. Children demand time and resources, commodities that students do not have an abundance of. Among white students, only 6.2 percent had children. The ethnic group with the lowest percentage of children was Asians—only 5 percent of Asian students were raising children. On the higher end, 14.1 percent of Hispanic students and 19.2 percent of black students were raising children. The heavy burden of raising children undoubtedly makes it harder to devote time and attention to one's own education. Universities could help students with children by providing resources like child care on campus.

Typically, college students are single. Of all the college students in the 2003 sample, only 8.2 percent report being married. Being married can certainly have economic advantages, especially if there are no children in the household. Does being married make college easier? This is not clear, and would depend on the circumstances surrounding the marriage. Are both partners in college? Is the spouse gainfully employed? Does he or she help with household chores? Answering these questions is beyond the scope of this paper. However, NLSY97 (2003) data on marital status and race revealed that the overwhelming majority of students are not married. The marriage rate is higher among Hispanic and white students (13 and 9.3 percent respectively) than it is for black and Asian students (5 and 4.4 percent respectively).

DISCUSSION

CUNY's admissions policy has had two major changes over the last forty years. In 1970, CUNY started using an admissions policy whose goal was to have CUNY's students reflect the racial composition of New York City's high schools (Schmidt, 1999, 48). A two-tiered admissions policy was put into place. For the senior colleges, it would admit high school graduates who finished in the top half of their classes or who had averages of 80 percent or above. For the community colleges, it would accept all other high school graduates. This change opened the once closed doors of a selective university system to large numbers of minority students. SEEK was the program designed at CUNY to give access to larger numbers of minorities. By the late 1980s, CUNY had become a majority-minority institution. In terms of giving college opportunities to minority students, CUNY was hugely successful.

What are the implications for the student experience of such a change in enrollment? Data from Hunter College suggest that minority students may take longer to graduate. Part of the explanation for this may be that black and Hispanic students may have additional time demands on their lives as they are more likely to have children. As many as 19.2 percent of black students and 14.1 percent of Hispanic students have children, and this is a significant responsibility for anybody, let alone college students. Policies to admit more minority students need to make allowances for the responsibilities that minority students may have that are different from those of white students, like having children. Some colleges have taken steps to address these differences; for example, Hunter College has childcare available on campus for students with children.

Another concern for colleges is the rising cost of getting an education. Results from a national sample of students suggest that the burdens of working outside of school are no greater for minority students than white students. Whites spend as many weeks of the year working outside school as Hispanic students and more weeks than black or Asian students. This result, however, should raise concerns as well. All universities need to start addressing the high financial costs of obtaining a degree, as well over 60 percent of all students are working at least twenty-seven weeks per year or more.

The results presented here are limited and point to more research that needs to be done. In what other ways are minority students different? What type of economic resources are available to minority students? Do minority students tend to live on or off campus more? How long are their commutes from off-campus housing? Data to answer questions like these would give a fuller description of American student life in the twenty-first century. The results here suggest that affirmative-action policies, like CUNY's SEEK program, can work to bring minority students to college, but that more needs to be done by colleges to help minority students succeed once they are on campus.

REFERENCES

Arenson, Karen. "CUNY Seeing Fewer Blacks at Top Schools." *New York Times*. August 10, 2006.

Attewell, Paul, and David E. Lavin in collaboration with Thurston Domina and Tania Levey. *Passing the Torch: Does Higher Education for the Disadvantaged Pay Off Across Generations?* New York: Russell Sage Foundation, 2007.

Lavin, David, and David Hyllegard. *Changing the Odds: Open Admissions and the Life Chances of the Disadvantaged*. New Haven and London: Yale University Press, 1996.

Lavin, David E., Richard D. Alba, and Richard A. Silberstein. *Right Versus Privilege: The Open-Admissions Experiment at the City University of New York*. New York: Free Press, 1981.

National Longitudinal Survey of Youth. 1997. www.bls.gov/nls. Accessed on March 1, 2008.

Office of Institutional Research. *Hunter College Fact Book 2004–2005*. www.hunter.cuny.edu/ir/. Accessed on April 3, 2008.

———. *Hunter Student Profile 1993–1997*. New York: Hunter College, CUNY, 1998.

———. *Hunter Student Profile 1992–1996*. New York: Hunter College, CUNY, 1997.

———. *Hunter Student Profile 1991–1995*. New York: Hunter College, CUNY, 1996.

———. *Hunter Student Profile 1985–1990*. New York: Hunter College, CUNY, 1991.

Roberts, Sam. "Whites to be a Minority in New York Soon, Data Show." *New York Times*. March 7, 2006.

Schmidt, Benno C. "The City University of New York: An Institution Adrift." *Report of the Mayor's Advisory Task Force on The City University of New York* (New York, 1999).

Seek Web Page. www1.cuny.edu/academics/academic-programs/programs-of-note/seekcd/seek-page.html. Accessed on January 6, 2010.

NOTE

1. I thank Ann Cohen for helpful comments. All errors, of course, remain my own.

II

ASIA, THE MIDDLE EAST, AND AFRICA

8

Can Student Loans Promote Greater Access for the Poor?

Adrian Ziderman

PROMOTING ACCESS OF THE POOR THROUGH STUDENT LOANS: PREREQUISITES FOR SUCCESS

University systems around the world have undergone massive and rapid expansion over the last forty years. As evidenced in the steadily growing proportion of the relevant age-cohort that is enrolled in tertiary education, this expansion has provided the opportunity for numerous youngsters, worldwide, to access and reap the benefits of a university education. Yet, these growing opportunities have not been shared equally by all segments of the population. In most university systems—both in industrialized and developing countries—the ongoing thrust toward expanded university enrollment has left behind such traditionally disadvantaged groups as low-income families, ethnic minorities, and the rural poor. Looking at the participation in higher education of students with low socioeconomic status, a common finding across counties is that the share of this group in total university enrollment has not risen over time.

The central question posed in this chapter is whether the availability of student loans can contribute toward increasing the access to higher education for these disadvantaged groups. A major, but by no means singular, barrier to access of disadvantaged groups is financial; overt costs of university attendance—including tuition fees, other educational expenses, and additional living costs—may place a university education well beyond the reach of many poor families. Yet even where tuition is provided free and the provision of accommodation and food is highly subsidized, the opportunity costs of university attendance (defined as the earnings forgone by the student, and the family, during the years of study) may be formidable.

The expansion in higher education enrollments has been paralleled by a growth in government-sponsored student loans schemes in recent decades, in both industrialized and developing countries. Such loans schemes are now in place in well over fifty countries and their introduction is on the policy agenda in many others. In this chapter, we discuss the role loans schemes can play in easing financial barriers to access. Illustrations and examples are drawn from five detailed case studies that were the focus of a recently completed UNESCO project on loans schemes in South-East Asia (China, Hong Kong region, the Republic of Korea, the Philippines, and Thailand).[1]

ALTERNATIVE LOANS SCHEME OBJECTIVES

Loans schemes vary widely from country to country in terms of the central objectives pursued. In a past paper, no fewer than eleven separate objectives were identified (in five category groupings) that have underscored loans schemes around the world (Ziderman 2002). In the present chapter we emphasize two overall and contrasting purposes of loans schemes which impinge in a major way on university access.

We refer to the first as the cost-sharing model. One central objective of many loans schemes is to facilitate greater cost-recovery (through the raising of tuition fees and other university costs) by countering deleterious effects on enrollment, and especially on the access of disadvantaged groups. The second is what we call the social targeting model, which is explicitly and directly concerned with accessibility for the poor. Where targeted specifically at disadvantaged groups, loans schemes (particularly where subsidized), can lead to greater access of the poor to university education, thus contributing to social equity.

Cost-sharing

We begin with an elaboration of the cost-sharing model. In many parts of the world, problems of access have been aggravated by the ongoing financial crisis facing university systems, the result of parsimony in government budgets. Real resources available to universities have been eroded due to a combination of the dramatic and continuing expansion of student enrollments unmatched by public expenditures on higher education. Universities have attempted to alleviate these financial pressures through the development and extension of nongovernmental sources of funding. Cost-sharing (or greater cost-recovery), where a larger and significant share of the costs of university education is shifted onto the main beneficiaries of university education—students and their families—is the dominant path that is pursued for revenue augmentation. In particular, this has taken the form of the introduction of tuition fees or of raising them to realistic levels. However, greater cost recovery for instruction or for university-provided student housing and meals will have adverse effects on general access. These higher, more realistic tuition fee regimes are likely to result in disincentives to students to continue, or to apply for, university studies. The hardships may be particularly severe for the poor student, who may be hard-pressed already to cover other costs of university attendance. The result is increased dropout, both by current university students and by potential students completing secondary studies and failing to apply for university entry. These effects may be offset, at least in part, by student support schemes, such as the provision of grants and scholarships. But to be effective in facilitating greater access, such measures will need to be introduced on a fairly large scale; this may be overly costly.

Student loan schemes may constitute a more affordable alternative. The disincentive effects of up-front tuition fee increases may be offset also by the availability of loans for students that will cover these augmented costs. Payment is delayed through the receipt of a loan, thus neutralizing the initial disincentive effect of higher fees. Loans enable student-borrowers to avoid up-front payments for higher education (whether for tuition or living expenses) by delaying payment, which will be rendered in manageable installments after graduation. They may also render tuition fee increases politically acceptable. In Singapore, the 1988 university tuition fee rises were accompanied by subsidized loans equivalent to about half the value of the new tuition fees. The much-discussed Australian loans scheme was introduced in tandem with the imposition of university tuition fees in 1989. Similarly, in the early 1980s, large tuition fee increases in Chile were accompanied by the introduction of student loans programs administered by the universities.

Student loans can play a role in mitigating these effects on the poor, and in promoting access, in two rather different contexts.

First, and particularly where loan funds are limited, loan priority may be given to poorer students, i.e., those for whom the access barrier posed by tuition fee increases is particularly high. This is the approach adopted in many countries. But in these cases, where loans allocation is needs-based and directed toward poor students, the central objective of the scheme remains that of cost recovery (and not reaching out to students from low socioeconomic backgrounds). Giving preference to the poor is best seen as a loan-allocation device which is judged to be socially appropriate.

More usually, for loans schemes based on the cost-sharing model, loans are available generally to all students. Preferential treatment for the poor in the allocation process should not be necessary. However, it has been argued that poor students may be unwilling to take up available loan opportunities at established loan conditions. There may be significant debt aversion among the poor and, in particular, a greater reluctance to resort to borrowing to finance higher education.[2] Loan utilization may be low for these disadvantaged groups and difficulties in meeting costs of higher education will deter pursuit of university studies. In this case, it is argued, loans should be made available to disadvantaged students at *more favorable* lending conditions; they would be more highly subsidized than are loans to students generally. Subsidies could take a number of forms, alone or combined: lowered rates of interest, extended grace periods before repayment, longer repayment horizon, and even partial loan "forgiveness" in particular cases.

Social Targeting

A student loans scheme may serve a more active, and deliberate, role in increasing the participation of the poor and of other marginal groups in higher education. In many countries the relatively low enrollment of poor and disadvantaged youth in tertiary education (and also in non-compulsory secondary education) is a cause of social concern. Increasing the access to university education among these segments of the population has become a major element in educational and social policy. While the cause of low access of the poor is multifaceted (and a full discussion is beyond the scope of this chapter), financial constraints evidently play a major explanatory role. There is now a broad consensus on the need to offer clear financial incentives to poor, potential students, not only to overcome the burden of fee payment and living expenses but also to offset both parental resistance to reductions in family income and the fear that the benefits of the educational process may not be sizeable. The provision of financial aid therefore may be regarded as a necessary though not sufficient condition for achieving greater participation of the poor.

But what form should this financial assistance take? The traditional, and most effective, method of enhancing educational access for the poor has been through the provision of means-tested grants to cover tuition fees (where schooling is not free) and (usually) living expenses. However, a widespread grants scheme is likely to be expensive. The use of loans, rather than grants, proactively targeting the poor, offers a method that may both increase access for the poor and reduce, or at least contain, public expenditures on student support over the longer term, as loan repayments build up.

To be effective in increasing educational access for the poor, loans may need to be made available under "softer" lending conditions. While the justification for loan subsidies for all borrowers under the cost-sharing model, and particularly general interest-rate subsidies, is weak (Ziderman 2002), there is wider agreement on the need for subsidized loans for the poor under the social targeting model, in order to encourage them to borrow. Whatever the form that loan subsidies take, the upshot of subsidization is that the student is required to pay back substantially less than the original capital cost of the loan. The part of the loan that is not repaid may be seen as a "hidden grant" to the borrower, the size of which is a reflection of the amount of subsidy built into the loan scheme.

In many loans schemes, the hidden grant element is substantial. In a recent study by Shen and Ziderman (2009), updating Ziderman and Albrecht (1995), interest subsidies were calculated for forty-four loans schemes worldwide. The hidden grant element was less than 20 percent in thirteen of these schemes—a favorable outcome. But in 18 (40 percent) of these schemes the hidden grant was in excess of 60 percent, with graduates repaying less than half of the received loan. A loan offered at market rates and a straight grant may be seen as two ends of a continuum, with subsidized loans (hidden grants) lying somewhere in between. The larger the loan subsidy, the greater is the hidden grant element. Given the need to subsidize student loans for the poor (to offer implicit grants) and, in addition, the higher administrative costs of loans (compared with grants) and the probabilities of repayment default, a significant part of total loans scheme outlays will not be recouped by the loans authorities. Since a grant offers a stronger and more direct incentive for access than does a (partially) repayable loan, the apparent advantage of loans over grants is less clear cut. This highlights a central conundrum in loans policy: at what level of loans subsidy does a grant become a more cost-effective instrument for helping the poor than a subsidized loan? It also suggests that an appropriate financial aid program for the poor is likely to involve a combination of both loans and grants, with a relatively larger overt grant element for the very poor. This is the practice in the Hong Kong scheme, in England and Wales, and in many other loans schemes.

CONDITIONS FOR LOANS SCHEME EFFICACY

The success of a loans scheme in leading to greater participation of the poor in higher education is contingent on many factors. Three, however, are essential ingredients for success:

- *Targeting*: The scheme must be carefully targeted to reach the poor and other disadvantaged groups; otherwise the central objective of the scheme will be lost;
- *Impact:* Student coverage of the scheme must be wide enough to achieve national impact;
- *Adequacy*: The level of individual support must be sufficiently high to cover private educational costs.

These criteria are discussed, in the following three sections. The findings of the five UNESCO case studies set in S.E Asia are used to illustrate the issues of targeting, impact and adequacy. Summary details of these schemes are provided in the Appendix, table 8.3.

TARGETING: DO LOANS REACH THE POOR?

Loans schemes, aimed at needy students to encourage access, tend to be highly subsidized in order to provide strong access incentives. A central challenge in designing and administering these schemes is to ensure that loans are successfully directed to the poor. If targeting is not successful (and loans are also received by the better-off), two undesirable consequences will follow. Not only will achievement of the central objective of the loans scheme be compromised but also the heavy subsidies will not be justified. Yet, in practice, many loans schemes, ostensibly directed toward the poor to increase access, including some of the schemes examined in the UNESCO Asian case studies, are not well targeted to reach the poor student. Targeting thus becomes a critical issue in appraising the efficacy of loans schemes that are directed toward increasing the access of disadvantaged students.

Reaching the Poor[3]

A critical issue, then, is whether the scheme does indeed reach this target group. Targeting the poor requires not only the setting of definitions for loans eligibility (usually in terms of a family income ceiling) but also the ability to check and test the veracity of such information supplied by loan applicants. Where it is difficult to authenticate this information, the scheme may be subject to abuse, with non-poor students gaining access to subsidized loans. This is doubly unfortunate, in terms of the scheme's objectives. It is both wasteful and inequitable to provide students who are not impoverished with these subsidized financial benefits. Without careful targeting, it may well be that the students most in need are the ones that tend to be excluded.

This leads to the important distinction between targeting and screening. A loans scheme that is based on screening (rather than real targeting) focuses on the vetting of applications for their eligibility for inclusion, in terms of the defined entry criteria. It is less concerned with the actual composition of those accepted for a loan—whether they constitute the group *most* in need of a loan or whether self-excluded but eligible individuals have not applied. It is essentially passive in approach, emphasizing legal entitlement rather than satisfying need. In contrast, a well-targeted scheme actively focuses on those most in need; it aims at reaching out to a target population defined in terms of those most deserving of help, including such less readily reached populations as student dropouts in need and the rural poor.

Targeting in UNESCO Case Studies

How well have the Asian case-study loans schemes performed in terms of targeting the poor, as defined in the foregoing discussion? Table 8.1 summarizes the situation for those schemes which were aimed at the poor student. The results are mixed (column 1). The case studies for the Korea (Ministry of Education) and Thailand schemes both indicate a sizeable leakage of loan approvals to non-poor students; this is evidently the case in the China scheme too. The Hong Kong subsidized scheme and the three Philippines schemes are more successful in directing loans solely to poor students.

Defining Eligibility

A loans scheme that targets needy students must define eligibility criteria for receiving a loan. Most student loans schemes aimed at the poor do so in terms of a maximal family income ceiling; this is also the practice in the Asian case study loans schemes aimed at the poor student. The central policy question is: what level of family income should constitute the eligibility ceiling? If this ceiling is set too high, with a consequent enlargement in the number of eligible students, there is a danger that the less disadvantaged among eligible students may be the ones who receive loans rather than those most in need. In this way, the central objective of increasing access of the poor is frustrated. This is likely to arise in those schemes where the number of eligible, and potential, borrowers greatly exceeds the supply of available loans slots. Thus, many schemes define the eligibility ceiling in terms of the official poverty line, to ensure that only those most in need are eligible to take up loans.

In the case studies, the Chinese subsidized scheme and the Philippines schemes confine eligibility to students from families in poverty, as defined

Table 8.1   Loans Schemes Aimed at Increasing Access of the Poor: Asian Case Studies

Case study (loans scheme)	(1) Is there "leakage" of loans to non-poor students?	(2) How is the eligibility income ceiling fixed?	(3) Who provides verification of declared family income?
China (subsidized scheme—GSSLS)	Yes (?)	Local government poverty line	Local authority
Hong Kong region (subsidized scheme—LSFS)	No	Amount of loan offered is in inverse proportion to family income and assets.	Applicant provides documentation such as salary statement, profit & loss account
Korea (Ministry of Education scheme)	Yes	Ministry of Education (eligibility ceiling is above poverty line)	Education institution; banks
Philippines (all three schemes)	No	Official poverty line	Parents' employer
Thailand (current scheme)	Yes	Loans Scheme Office (eligibility ceiling is above poverty line)	Government official (level 4 and above); village head

by the official poverty line (table 8.1, column 2).[4] However, in the Korean (MOE) and Thai schemes, both formally aimed at poor students, the designated eligibility ceiling is an income level *in excess* of the official poverty line; in Thailand, the income ceiling defining eligibility is three times the official poverty line for a family with three children. The policy result is that many students, not drawn from the ranks of the very poor, are eligible to receive a loan.

This issue is compounded by the difficulty in checking the veracity of the information on family income that is provided by loans applicants; this is a central problem where an effective system of income taxation is lacking or where the rural and informal sectors are relatively large. As indicated in table 8.1 (column 3), the case study loans schemes employ alternative methods to check the veracity of declared family income. In some cases, the educational institution certifies that the declared income is correct, on the basis of institutional familiarity with the socioeconomic background of the student-applicant; more usually, a civil servant provides certification.

Table 8.2 Targeting, Coverage and Adequacy: Asian Case Study Loans Schemes Aimed at the Poor

Case study (loans scheme)	1st criterion: Targeting Loans received only by poor students?	2nd criterion: Impact % of poor students receiving a loan	3rd criterion: Adequacy	
			Loans for tuition and/or living expenses?	Loans sufficient to cover designated expenditures?
China (subsidized—GSSLS)	No	Low	Tuition and living	No
Hong Kong (subsidized—LSFS)	Yes	Substantial	Living (tuition covered by grant)	Yes
Korea (Ministry of Education)	No	Low	Tuition	Yes (?)
Philippines (all three schemes)	Yes	Marginal	Tuition	No
Thailand (current)	No	Substantial	Tuition and living	Tuition—yes Living—often not

In Thailand the village head may provide this certification; however, if the loyalty of the village head is stronger toward the student and his family than to the loans scheme, this certification may constitute little more than a rubber stamp.

More generally, the use of family income as the sole criterion for eligibility, whether or not set at the official poverty level, is itself of questionable validity. The family income measure fails to take into account a number of factors such as the number of children or elderly in the family, number of other students in the family, whether the head of household is female, and the amount of private property owned. Over time broader, more sophisticated, measures for defining students in need, probably based on an index related to the foregoing factors, will need to be developed.

Reach of Loans Schemes: Case Study Experience

We turn to the three schemes—all formally aimed at serving the poor—that are implemented inadequately in terms of both targeting and the reach of the scheme.

China[5]

It is estimated that 19 percent of Chinese students may be classified as poor (and 8 percent as very poor). The question is whether those students who are most in need are able to receive a loan. By the end of 2002, some 526,000 students had received a loan; this is nearly 40 percent of all loan applicants and 5.5 percent of total student enrollment. However, even if *only* poor students were in receipt of these loans as intended, this would imply, at best, that less than 29 percent of all poor students received a loan.

Korea

The major purpose of this loans scheme, run by the Ministry of Education, is to aid poorer students; operationally, the aim is that priority be given to children of the unemployed and low-income recipients. In practice, targeting is blunted by malfunctioning of the selection process; any student can apply for a loan and selection (the issuing of letters of recommendation to the participating commercial banks who provide the loans) which is usually made on a first-come, first-served basis. Many non-poor students receive loans (Kim and Lee, 2003). Thus, only some 13 percent of students from the lowest family income group receive a loan (7 percent of all families of students) and 15 percent from the second-lowest tier (19 percent of all families of students). On the other hand, loans were received by some 9 percent of students from the highest income families (constituting 4.3 percent of all student families). While 35 percent of all students receive a scholarship (42 percent for public institutions), the scholarship system focuses on students' academic achievement rather than financial status.

Thailand

The ground rules of the loan scheme require that priority be given to poorer students. This is often not the case in practice. Since loans are distributed by educational institutions, whose loans budgets are not fixed in proportion to the number of poor students enrolled, there are considerable differences, in practice, in the eligibility cut-off point for family incomes across institutions. In the case of upper secondary students, for whom loans are also available, 452,000 loans were allocated in 1999, representing less than a third of eligible students (with family annual income of less than the 150,000 Baht ceiling). We have no data on the reach of the scheme. How many of these loans were allocated to the 313,000 very poor students (in families living below the official poverty line)? Or did most of the loans accrue to the 429,000 better-off, but eligible, students in the 101,000–150,000 Baht family income bracket? Anecdotal evidence suggests that the latter was the case.

The upshot of this section is to emphasize the need to fashion more precise yet operational definitions for eligibility and to develop sharper mechanisms for targeting the poor; these should be combined with steps to generate better data on the reach of loans schemes, as an indispensable tool for appraising and improving the efficacy of loans scheme targeting.

COVERAGE: IS THERE NATIONAL IMPACT?

We now turn to the second criteria for loans scheme efficacy: national impact.

Factors limiting loans scheme coverage

A student loans scheme aimed at increasing access for the poor cannot be regarded as successful in the national context unless it is sufficiently sizeable to achieve an impact nationally. Some country loans schemes remain very small in size and cover only a small percentage of enrolled students. While these schemes no doubt provide a very valuable service to the students who receive a loan, the small coverage size limits their efficacy in achieving the national objectives set for the loans scheme in terms of increased access.

National coverage (measured in terms of the percentage of the target group that receives a loan) may be low for two main reasons:

- The *supply* of loans funds may be constrained, with sufficient funding available to provide loans for only a fraction of the eligible, low-income population.
- The take up of available loan slots by targeted low-income groups may be low, reflecting low *demand* for loans.

Limited Supply of Loans Funds

All loans schemes need to be funded. Funding may come from government, commercial banks, or other financial institutions. Most loans schemes world-wide derive their initial capital funding from the central government (from the current budget or borrowing). A common misconception is that initial loans scheme capital can be regarded as a revolving fund, with the build-up of annual loan repayment receipts over time providing the finance for new loan commitments. But accumulated repayments will fall short of the original sums borrowed because of loans subsidies, repayment default, and government-absorbed administrative costs. Given less than full cost recovery and growing student enrollments, a government commitment of continuing funding will be necessary to ensure loans fund sustainability over the longer term. Government funded loans schemes following the cost-sharing model, which are usually open to all students, are generally adequately budgeted—a political expediency given that all students have the right to a loan. This is the case with well-endowed schemes as in Australia, England, and Wales and the nonsubsidized Hong Kong scheme.[6]

In contrast, government budgeting for loans schemes aimed at social targeting and increasing the access of low-income groups is often circumscribed. There are many reasons for this. Underprovision of budgetary support may stem from poor estimates of need in the planning process, because of a lack of precision in defining the target population, its size, and the extent of loans demand. While the subsidized Hong Kong scheme, aimed at the poor, is well financed and provides adequate loan support for well over a third of student enrollment, the no less extensive Thai scheme has been constrained by poor planning, leading to inadequate government budgeting, thus tempering the growth of the scheme and levels of support. Or the scheme may derive from "showcase legislation": the initial setting up of a scheme of limited scope but with a lack of the political will necessary to follow through with the additional budgetary commitment necessary to establish a larger scheme with national impact. This is the case with the long established "Study Now Pay Later" scheme in the Philippines which has always operated on a very small scale, with little impact on the higher education system as a whole. The meager level of government budgetary support is fossilized in outdated legislation, and the scheme reaches less than 2,000 new students a year.

Nongovernmental sources of loan capital can be employed to fund a loans scheme but usually on a more limited scale than would secure national impact. Commercial banks provide funding for government-sponsored loans schemes in a number of countries (such as in Canada, until 2000). Among the Asian case studies, in the Chinese scheme and the Korean scheme run by the education ministry, initial loans capital is provided by commercial banks. This obviates the need for government initial funding, though not for ongoing subsidy as the government must usually subsidize the interest rate on the loan and shoulder the risks of repayment default. The considerable advantage of employing the commercial banking sector, rather than the government budget, is evident. But there are many difficulties inherent in this approach, particularly in inducing banks to cooperate extensively, and most schemes have resorted to government budgets.

A third option is to use an existing fund or quasi-government financial institution to provide the loan capital. Usually the capacity for these financial institutions to furnish considerable funding is limited. These arrangements have not always worked well. The Korean loans scheme for government employees and their families was financed by borrowings from the government employees' pension fund.[7] Since the scheme is highly subsidized (it provides loans free of interest) and full loans recovery is not possible, it would seem that the overall effect of the scheme was to weaken the financial robustness of the government employees' pension scheme. After temporary suspension in 1999, loans were resumed with the financial resources of government. In the early years of the Study Now Pay Later scheme in the Philippines, an obligation to fund the scheme was imposed on various government financing institutions, including the Social Security System, the Government Service Insurance System, and various public banks. The disinclination of these agencies to disburse funds earmarked for student loans, given the high levels of required subsidy and therefore agency losses, led to the disengagement of these agencies from the scheme and the entry of government as the provider of capital (albeit on a very limited scale) and operator of the scheme.

Low Loans Demand

Even when the number of available loan slots is not limited by funding-supply constraints, low loans take-up by the poor remains a perennial problem in loans schemes aimed at increasing access of low-income groups. However, this problem relates more to the composition of loans demand than to its total size. There may be insufficient demand for loans among the most disadvantaged, the very groups that the loans scheme wishes to reach. This appears to be the case in the Thai scheme. In this case, the need for proactive targeting, including information dissemination, is indicated.

ADEQUACY: DO LOANS FULLY COVER NECESSARY EXPENSES?

The third criterion for efficacy of loans schemes aimed at the poor is adequacy.

Necessary Conditions for Adequacy of Loan Size

A successful loan scheme must provide loans that are sufficiently sizeable to meet the needs of the students at whom the scheme is directed; this includes both tuition costs and living expenses. In many loans schemes, loans are not available for either tuition fees (where these are in force) or for living expenses. Even where both expenditure categories are covered by the loan, the size of the loan may fall short of students' expenditure needs. The implication of small loan size is that higher education remains beyond the means of the very poor, thus largely defeating the purpose of the scheme. In most of the

Asian schemes examined, loan size falls short of student needs for education and living expenses

Three conditions must be present in well-working loans schemes to ensure adequacy of individual loans size. These necessary conditions are: that the total amount of funding available for distribution is sufficiently large; that accurate, up-to-date information on students' expenditure needs is available; and that appropriate loans distribution policies and practices are in place. As the issue of loans funding supply is discussed above, our present discussion will relate to the need for accurate information on students' expenditure needs and the efficacy of policies for loans distribution.

Information on Students' Expenditure Needs

Where loans are provided to cover tuition fees, and particularly where there are standard fees across universities, there is no information gap with regard to loan size needed for tuition. The problem tends to be more serious for loans for living expenses; in many cases, accurate information on students' living expenditure needs is lacking and maximum loans size, which is thus fixed arbitrarily, may fall short of expenditure need. Alternatively, loans may be too generous (and thus wasteful), in putting more money into the hands of students than is necessary. In the Chinese subsidized scheme, loan recipients frequently find that loans are insufficient even to cover tuition fees, given the variation in fees across institutions and study disciplines. The issue is more severe in the budgetary-deficient Philippines scheme; the maximum loan amount, prescribed in outdated legislation, often falls short of the tuition fee. In Thailand, the loan size ceilings set centrally by the Student Loans Committee are, evidently, set arbitrarily and no account is taken of the results of available student education expenditure surveys and costs. Moreover, in the Philippines and Thai schemes there is no linkage to rising educational costs (as there is in Hong Kong), so the real value of loans falls over time. Of all the schemes examined, the Hong Kong case is the most satisfactory in terms of providing an adequate level of student assistance. Loan size (depending on family income) is adjusted periodically, via surveys of student expenses and the compilation of a Student Price Index, to ensure an adequate level of support.

The Hong Kong case

As described by Chung (2003), Hong Kong has adopted an empirical approach to ascertaining the level of individual assistance required. It does so by conducting periodical sample surveys on student expenditures, the first in 1982, and subsequently in 1988 and 1990. A representative sample of students is asked to fill out detailed diaries of actual spending over a fortnight, at different periods of the year. This information is used to construct annual student expenditure patterns. A Student Price Index is developed (similar to a cost-of-living index, but relating only to items used by students, as identified in the surveys) and used to maintain the real value of loans and grants. Subsequent surveys have revealed changing student expenditure patterns over time, thus justifying this approach.

Equitable Distribution Policies

Appropriate loan distribution policies and practices must be in place to ensure that all those who acquire a loan receive the maximal amount to which they are entitled. In this context we may distinguish between centralized and decentralized loan distribution systems. In very many loans schemes—including HECS, England and Wales, and Hong Kong—loans are distributed through a central loans agency, to which individuals apply for loans. The advantage of a system of direct student applications to a centralized agency is that it operates on a level playing field; each applicant receives equitable treatment and the recommended loan size (in relation to need) can be preserved.

At the other extreme, such as in the Thailand case, each university receives a loans budget, which it distributed among eligible student applicants. One advantage of this decentralized system is that it might facilitate proactive targeting, as educational institutions are better placed both to identify students in need and also to encourage potential students to take up loans. Two conditions are necessary for the decentralized system to work successfully in providing adequate size loans to eligible students. First, the loans budget should be distributed to higher education institutions on the basis of objective needs-related criteria, i.e. based on the socioeconomic profile of the student body in each university. Second, actual individual loan size and eligibility criteria (including the cut-off ceiling for parental income) should be standardized across all institutions, to ensure horizontal equity.

Loans inadequacy in Thailand

These conditions are not met in the Thailand scheme. University loans budgets are fixed in relation to enrollment size rather than the number of low-income students; the result is that some universities with large numbers of poor students receive too few funds to provide loans to all students in need, while other universities are able to offer loans to eligible but not highly disadvantaged students. More important, the considerable autonomy granted to education institutions in fixing the size of individual loans results not only in considerable inequities across the system, but also inadequately sized loans.

In particular, some private institutions use the loans system as a mechanism for attracting students, by offering loans for tuition only to a larger number of students, not all of whom are highly disadvantaged. Consequently, many poor students do not receive loans for living expenses at all, or the amounts received fall considerably short of the loan size recommended by the national Student Loans Scheme Committee, with negative effects on access.

TARGETING, COVERAGE, AND ADEQUACY: SUMMARY FINDINGS FOR ASIAN CASE STUDIES

In this section, we bring together our findings on targeting, coverage, and adequacy to draw conclusions on the efficacy of the Asian case study schemes that were aimed at meeting the needs of low-income groups and increasing their access.

These conclusions are from table 8.20. The Chinese scheme does not perform well as a vehicle for assisting the poor (though it should be noted that many changes have been introduced since Shen and Li carried out their study): there is leakage of loans to the non-poor, coverage of the poor is low, and loans are insufficiently sizeable to cover expenses. The Philippines schemes are too marginal in coverage to have any significant impact on the poor, and the Thai scheme, though it does have considerable national impact, is not confined to the poor nor are levels of individual support sufficient in very many cases. The Hong Kong scheme emerges as the most successful in meeting its objective of reaching poor students: there is little leakage of loans to non-poor students, the scheme reaches a substantial percentage of poor students, and loan size is sufficient to cover actual (ascertained) living expenses.

CONCLUSION (AND A CAVEAT)

This chapter has been concerned with the influence of student loans on the accessibility of higher education. The varied experience in Asia with loans schemes aimed directly at enhancing the access of the poor was examined. The conclusion drawn is that these schemes are often to be faulted because they lack a number of necessary prior conditions for success. However, these schemes can be made to operate more successfully in both reaching the poor and enhancing access if they are appropriately designed and operated.

The paper has argued that loans schemes, which aim centrally at making a contribution to the task of increasing the access of the poor and other disadvantaged groups, will fail unless three key conditions are satisfied. These are: that effective eligibility and screening criteria are in place and that proactive targeting measures are employed to reach out to the most deserving sections of the target population defined in terms of those most in need of help; that the scheme is sufficiently sizeable to achieve an impact nationally; and individual loans are sufficiently large to cover the needs of the students at whom the scheme is directed. Unfortunately, these conditions are often neglected.

Finally, there is a need to unify grants and loans policies. We have noted that, due to loan subsidies, student loans usually incorporate a hidden grant which may be sizeable. This emphasizes the complementarities between loans and grants, and the importance of operating unified loans and grants policies. A regime of outright grants for low-income students may be effective in increasing access but is too expensive to be available on a broad basis. Hidden grants (subsidized loans) are more affordable but less efficacious in increasing the access of the poor; poor students may be loath to take up low subsidy loans. A balanced policy of student support, aimed at increasing accessibility to higher education, will need to offer grants and loans in combination, with an emphasis on (mainly) grants for the very poor and subsidized loans for the needy (the degree of subsidy depending on socioeconomic background); student loans for non-equity objectives would carry only low levels of subsidy.

We conclude with a caveat. Student support policies (and loans in particular) cannot act alone; there are other, perhaps more entrenched barriers to access, both at university age and prior to it. Barr (2005) has referred to the *dual* causes of the exclusion of the poor from higher education: financial poverty and information poverty. Loans, grants, and scholarships are aimed at countering financial poverty. But problems of informational poverty are no less acute and should be tackled in tandem. Many youngsters and their families are badly informed about the benefits of university study. For example, a recent study shows that while substantial differences exist in Canadians' perceptions of the costs and returns of university education, the overestimation of costs and underestimation of benefits are particularly striking for low-income Canadians. The author notes that, "The extent to which perceptions differ from reality would appear to be so large that they may form a separate form of barrier to education all of their own" (Usher, 2005).

Poorly informed students (and their families) will be reluctant to borrow. While there is an important role to be played by student support policies (and notably loans) in raising access of the poor, this role needs to be complemented by appropriate action by other institutional players including the universities.[8] Further, it widely recognized that the lack of willingness of large numbers of the poor to enroll in higher education has its roots much earlier on in the education system. This calls for prior action to better inform schoolchildren and their parents and to raise their aspirations.

Adrian Ziderman

Appendix

Table 8.3   Asian Case Studies: General Description

Case Study	Description
China	The major scheme, aimed at the poor, is subsidized by the government. Loans are provided by state commercial banks. Limited coverage but growing.
Hong Kong region	Veteran, centralized dual loans scheme, part of a comprehensive framework, providing grants and subsidized loans for the poor and non-subsidized loans for non-poor students. Broad regional coverage.
Republic of Korea	A number of separate schemes, each run independently and aimed at different target populations. The largest scheme, Ministry of Education and Human Resources Development (MOE), is aimed at the poor.
The Philippines	A very small, long-established national loans scheme, complemented with two new schemes (one in a poor region, the other for high-level institutions). Aimed at the poor but marginal in total size and impact.
Thailand	Highly subsidized, with broad national coverage; aimed at the poor. Includes students enrolled at the upper secondary and tertiary levels. This scheme was replaced recently by the faulted TICAL scheme, which is currently being reformed.

REFERENCES

Andrews L. *Does HECS Deter? Factors Affecting University Participation of Low SES Groups*. Canberra: Department of Employment, Education, Training and Youth Affairs: 1999.

Barr, N. "Financing Higher Education." *Finance and Development* 42, no. 2 (2005).

Chung, Y.-P. *The Student Loan Scheme in Hong Kong*. Bangkok: UNESCO, 2003.

Department for Education and Skills. *Widening Participation in Higher Education*. United Kingdom: 2003.

Kitaev, I., T. Nadurata, V. Resurrection, and F. Burnal. *Student Loan Schemes in the Philippines: Lessons from the Past*. Bangkok: UNESCO, 2003.

Kim, A., and Y. Lee. *Student Loan Schemes in the Republic of Korea: Review and Recommendation*. Bangkok: UNESCO, 2003.

Shen, Hong. "The Most Urgent Problem in Student Loans Scheme in China: Repayment." *Harvard China Review*, Spring 2004.

Shen, Hong, and W. Li. *A Review of the Student Loans Scheme in China*. Bangkok: UNESCO 2003.

Shen, Hua, and A. Ziderman. "Student Loans Repayment and Recovery: International Comparisons." *Higher Education* (2009).

Usher, A., *A Little Knowledge is a Dangerous Thing: How Perceptions of Costs and Benefits Affect Access to Education*. Toronto, ON: Education Policy Institute, 2005.

Vossensteyn, J. J. *Perceptions of student price-responsiveness: A behavioural economics exploration of the relationships between socio-economic status, perceptions of financial incentives and student choice*. PhD dissertation, Center for Higher Education Policy Studies (CHEPS), University of Twente. Brno: VU-TIUM Press, 2005.

Ziderman, A. "Alternative Objectives of National Student Loans Schemes: Implications for Design, Evaluation and Policy." *Welsh Journal of Education*, July 2002.

———. *Student Loans in Thailand; Are They Effective, Equitable Sustainable?* Paris: International Institute for Educational Planning, UNESCO, 2003.

———. *Policy Options for Student Loan Schemes: Lessons from Five Asian Case Studies*. Paris: International Institute for Educational Planning, UNESCO, 2004.

Ziderman, A., and D. Albrecht. *Financing Universities in Developing Countries*. Stanford Series on Education and Public Policy. London: Falmer Press 1995.

NOTES

1. The regional study, a joint endeavor of UNESCO-Bangkok and the International Institute for Educational Planning, consisted of five in-depth studies on the functioning of student loans schemes in Asia. The studies are reported in the following monographs: China (Shen and Li 2003), Hong Kong (Chung, 2003), the Republic of Korea (Kim and Lee 2003), the Philippines (Kiteav et al. 2003), and Thailand (Ziderman, 2003). A synthesis study is provided in Ziderman (2004).

2. Although it is widely held that poor families are debt averse, evidence for Australia and the Netherlands does not support this. Andrews (1999), examining attitudes toward taking up student loans in Australia, failed to find differences in debt aversion between different SES groups. In a more recent study set in the Netherlands, Vossensteyn found no relationship between willingness to take up student loans and SES background (Vossensteyn, 2005).

3. The discussion in this section is based on Ziderman (2004, chapter 9).

4. In the Chinese case, the poverty line is not mentioned in official government eligibility criteria; however, in practice institutions and banks define as priority-eligible borrowers those students whose family income falls below the local poverty line.

5. These figures, taken from Shen (2004), update the data provided in the case study report by Shen and Li (2003).

6. An alternative is securitization of the loans scheme, with loans funding provided by the issue of government-guaranteed bonds. In response to a Thai government announcement that it will not be providing funding for the new TICAL scheme, securitization of the loans scheme is being examined as an alternative funding source. Securitization is unlikely to be appropriate for schemes designed to contain a large hidden grant element, in particular for schemes with strong social targeting objectives.

7. Loans capital in other Korean loans schemes is also provided by existing financial funds: the Ministry of Labour scheme for industrial employees is financed from the Employment Insurance Fund; teachers and their children from the Korean teachers' pension fund; and the Korean Labour Welfare Corporation for industrial accident victims from the Industrial Accident Compensation Insurance Fund.

8. Of interest in this regard is legislation in England and Wales, which came into force in September 2006, together with the system of optional variable tuition fees and tuition loans. Universities wishing to raise fees need to reach agreement with the new Office for Fair Practice on activities to be undertaken by the institution to broaden access to higher education. This includes efforts to reach out to schools with low participation rates in higher education. In parallel, part of the additional income generated by variable tuition fees is to be used by the institutions to establish bursaries (which are additional to the state maintenance grant) for poor students enrolled in more expensive courses (Department for Education and Skills, 2003).

9

The Quest for World-Class Status

Globalization and Higher Education in East Asia[1]

Ka Ho Mok and John Hawkins

GLOBALIZATION: CONTESTED
CONCEPTS AND UNFINISHED DEBATES

In the last decade or so, scholars and writers have repeatedly discussed the nature and impact of globalization at political, economic, social, and cultural levels (see, for example, Held and McGrew 2000; Schirato and Webb 2003). Despite the contested concepts and heated debates on globalization, some scholars have attempted to categorize such discussions into three major schools of thought, namely, hyperglobalists, skeptics, and transformationists (Held and McGrew 2000). Hyperglobalists strongly believe the global economy is dominated by uncontrollable global forces in which nation-states are structurally dependent on global capital that is primarily determined by Transnational National Corporations (TNCs). To believers in this strong globalism, the globalizing economy means a drastic shift in structural power and authority away from the nation-state toward non-state agencies and from national political systems to a global economic system (Held, McGrew, Goldblatt, and Perraton 1999).

Unlike these strong globalists, those who oppose the convergence theory think that globalization is overstated and overgeneralized. According to skeptics, nation-states are more heterogeneous and independent in action than they are given credit for. Since they have never responded to the external changes in the same fashion, there are a wide variety of local and regional responses to globalization. In this regard, they argue that contemporary levels of economic interdependence are not historically unprecedented. In contrast, the global economy is less global in its geographical embrace, especially when compared with the former world empires. Somehow taking a stand between the hyperglobalists and the skeptics, the transformalisits believe globalization is unprecedented but there is no convergence. Instead, they believe the globalizing world has resulted in a kind of global stratification, a new international division of labor. It is against this wider context that some nations succeed at the expense of others and even within nations there are winners and losers. Therefore, the old terms such as the North and the South and the divisions between the first, second, and third world are no longer relevant (Held and McGrew 2000).

The diverse views on globalization outlined above have clearly demonstrated the disagreements among academics and researchers on many aspects of the form or direction, the definitions, and the significance of globalization. Nonetheless, no matter how we assess the impacts of globalization on the contemporary world, no one can deny that the intensification of worldwide social relations which link distant localities in such a way that local happenings are shaped by events occurring many miles away and vice versa, is a reality (Hirst and Thompson 1999). According to Held, "we live in a world of overlapping communities of fate, where the trajectories of countries are deeply enmeshed with one another" (2004: 2). This clearly suggests that we are living in an increasingly interdependent world and therefore we are not immune from the growing influences of the market and the ideas and practices of neoliberalism on many different dimensions of the contemporary world. Yang has succinctly summarized the impacts of globalization:

> Globalization is the result of the compression of time and space that has occurred since advanced technology allowed the instantaneous sharing of information around the world, leading to a cross-border flow of ideas, ideologies, people and goods, images and messages, capital and financial services, knowledge and technologies, creating a borderless world economy. It has a material base in capitalism and an ideological genesis in neoliberalism. (2005: 28)

While some see globalization as an inexorable process of global economic integration (Fukuyama 1992), others see it as a deliberate policy project, which celebrates the market as economic savior (Yang 2005: 28). Central to the ideas and practices of neoliberalism is a shift in the balance between the state and the market, strongly in favor of the latter (Fukuyama 2006: 121). The neoliberal philosophy, with its roots in an intellectual movement promoted by scholars like von Mises and Hayek, advocates the reduction of the role of the state, the opening of national markets, free trade, flexible exchanges, deregulation, the transfer of assets from the public to the private sector, and an international division of labor. This political-economic agenda is often referred to as the Washington consensus although some may argue that it is more an ideology than a consensus (Bayliss and Smith 2001; Stiglitz 2002). In recent years, a major emerging trend from such a political-economic aspect of globalization has been the increased significance of competition. As Watson and Hey have rightly suggested, "national competition has increasingly become a central preoccupation of governance strategies across the world" (2003: 299). Similarly, Jessop (2002), Cerney (1990), and Ball (2007) also argue that modern states are struggling to become "competition states," which aim to "secure economic growth within its borders and/or to secure competitive advantages for capitals based in its borders" (Jessop 2002: 96).

THE QUEST FOR GLOBAL COMPETITIVENESS AND THE WORLD-CLASS UNIVERSITY MOVEMENT

In order to enhance their global competitiveness, governments in different parts of the world have started to conduct comprehensive reviews and implement plans to restructure their higher education systems (Mok and Welch 2003). In response to the growing pressures generated by the globalization forces, modern states have attempted to reinvent themselves by moving beyond the welfare state to become the competition state (Gill 1995; Moran 2002; Jordana and Levi-Faur 2005). Governments across different parts of the globe, facing similar competitive pressures, have undertaken regulatory reforms such as privatization or corporatization of state-owned industries or publicly owned organizations such as the post office and the university, opening up new markets to multiple providers and the introduction of new regulatory regimes under the control of independent regulators (Drahos and Jospeh 1995; Levi-Faur 1998; Scott 2004). To enhance the efficiency of public policies and public management, modern states have deregulated some areas while encouraging competition in others, hence becoming a facilitator or even a generator of markets.

Thus, the role of re-regulation or recentralization in the processes of market restructuring has often been accompanied by the emergence of strong regulatory states and by the entrepreneurial role states play (Chan and Tan 2006; Ng and Chan 2006; and Hawkins 2005). Unlike Cerny's (1997) characterization of the competition state as a basically liberal state, Levi-Faur argues the state (particularly in the intensified global competitive environment, our emphasis) faces a paradox: "the greater the commitment of the competition state to the promotion of competition, the deeper its regulation will be" (Levi-Faur 1998, 676). More important, the actions and mission of the competition state do not necessarily result in the retreat of the state from the market but rather a reassertion of the role of the state under changing social and economic circumstances (Levi-Faur 1998, 676).

In order to promote basic national interests through the creation and enforcement of competition, the developmental states in Asia have taken the opportunity offered by the fundamental economic restructuring processes to transform them into "market accelerationist states" by proactively shaping the market institutions for the benefits of market creation (Mok 2006; M. Lee 2004). Unlike the regulatory state in America that evolved against a liberal market economy context, the regulatory state in Asia has emerged from a context of a combined strong state and a free-market economy, by which the state ideologically commits to an "authoritarian mode of liberalism." As Jayasuriya has rightly pointed out, "this authoritarian liberalism presupposes the existence of a strong (or better described as politically illiberal) state with a capacity to regulate the economy" (2000, 329). In order to promote competition in the markets against the context of authoritarian liberalism, a *market accelerationist state* is forming (Mok 2006). The market accelerationist state has the features of a "dualistic state" as Fraenkel (1941) described: a strong state combined with a liberal market economy. With this kind of state architecture in place, the success of the markets rests heavily upon the presence of strong regulatory institutions. It is against such a wider sociopolitical context that far more pro-competition policy instruments are adopted by modern states to transform the way the public sector is governed. Hence, the higher education sector, like other public policy domains, has gone "private" while ideas and strategies along the lines of neoliberalism and economic rationalism are increasingly influencing the way public policy is managed (Brehony and Deem 2005; Neubauer 2006).

The socioeconomic and sociopolitical environments outlined above have inevitably affected the way higher education is governed. In order to become globally competitive, governments and universities in Asia have started to search for new strategies to improve university governance by the adoption of the corporatization and incorporation strategies of universities. In order to become more globally competitive, Asian universities have taken the world university ranking very seriously and therefore they have engaged in the quest for "world-class" university status.

UNIVERSITY RESPONSES AND STRATEGIES

University Restructuring: Incorporation and Corporatization

To survive in this highly competitive world, universities have to become customer-focused business enterprises (Currie and Newson 1998). As the nation-state acts as a player in the new global marketplace (Currie et al. 2003), universities are encouraged to act in market-like ways and therefore changes begin to emerge in funding, management, and function (Yang 2005, Mok 2006, Hawkins 2005b). Being unsatisfied with the conventional model along the lines of state-oriented and highly centralized approaches in higher education, coupled with the pressures to improve the efficiency of the university governance, a growing number of Asian governments have recently tried to incorporate, or introduced corporatization and privatization measures to run their state/national universities, believing that the transformations of which could make national universities more flexible and responsive to rapid socioeconomic changes (Mok 2006a; Oba 2006; Hawkins 2007). Instead of being closely directed by the Ministry of Education or equivalent government administrative bodies, state universities in Asia are now required to become more proactive and dynamic in looking for their own financial resources.

Similar to their Australian and British counterparts, universities in Asia are now under constant pressures to become more entrepreneurial to look for alternative funding sources from the market, strengthening their partnerships with industry and business (Olsen and Gornitzka 2006; Marginson and Considine 2000). Adhering more toward the market and corporate principles and practices, universities in Hong Kong are now run on a market-oriented and business corporation model. Hong Kong universities have experienced corporatization and privatization processes, whereby higher education institutions have proactively engaged in fostering entrepreneurship to search for additional revenue sources from the market (Mok 2005; Lee and Gopinathan 2005). In order to enhance efficiency of university governance, the University Grant Committee (UGC), the organization which shapes the directions of higher education development in Hong Kong, has recently subscribed to the notion of deep collaboration among universities, believing that synergy could be pulled together if universities in the city-state could better integrate. The UGC even supports university merging or other forms of restructuring to further establish Hong Kong as a regional center for excellence in research and scholarship (Lee 2005; Chan 2007). Turning universities into enterprises and entrepreneurial institutions is becoming increasingly popular in Hong Kong, and university presidents or vice-chancellors have been heavily involved in fund raising activities (Chan and Lo 2007).

Similarly, the Ministry of Education in Taiwan has decided to change the statutory position of state universities into legally independent entities by adopting principles and practices of corporatization. In order to reduce the state burden in higher education financing, all state universities in Taiwan have to generate additional funds from non-state sectors such as the market and private enterprises. In order to generate sufficient funds to finance their institutions, various kinds of market-driven strategies have been adopted. More recently, the Taiwan government has attempted to restructure its state universities by passing a new *University Act* to make state universities independent legal entities. Influenced by the Japanese model, state universities in Taiwan have to establish new governance structures; at the same time they are under immense pressure to search for additional financial support from non-state channels especially when the Taiwan government has significantly reduced core funding (Lo and Weng 2005; Tien 2006).

In facing a new market economy context, the Chinese government has also found the old way of "centralized governance" in education inappropriate (Yang 2002, Hawkins 2000). Acknowledging that over-centralization and stringent rules would kill the initiatives and enthusiasm of local educational institutions, the Chinese Communist Party (CCP) called for resolute steps to streamline administration and devolve powers to units at lower levels so as to allow them more flexibility to run education. In the last decade or so, higher education in the post–Mao era has experienced structural reforms ranging from curriculum design, financing, promotion of the private ("minban") sector in higher education provision, to adopting strategies to develop world-class universities. In order to promote the competitiveness of its higher education in the global marketplace, the Chinese government has introduced various kinds of restructuring exercises to merge universities or to streamline the stubbornly sustained bureaucratic university systems. With strong intention to identify and develop a few Chinese universities into world-class universities, the government has implemented various reform measures such as the "211 project" and the "985 project" to concentrate state resources on a few select top-tier national universities in order to elevate them to leading universities in the world (Min 2004; Mok 2005b; Lo and Chan 2006; Chou 2006).

Like societies in greater China, Japan is not immune from the impact of neoliberalism, managerialism, and economic rationalism, three major ideologies underlying the tidal wave of public sector reforms and reinventing government projects across the world. With the intention of making its state university system more responsive and flexible in coping with intensified pressures generated from the growing impacts of globalization, the Japanese government has incorporated all state universities since 2004. Central to the transformation of the existing national universities into "National University Corporations" are three major reform aspects: increased competitiveness in research and education; enhanced accountability together with introduction of competition; and strategic and functional management of national universities (Hawkins 2007; Oba 2006). Moreover, some universities in Japan are selected as part of the "Flagship University" project, an initiative to promote a selective few to become world-class universities.

Higher education restructuring is popular not only among East Asian states but also among Southeast Asian societies. Having reflected upon the changing university governance models and having evaluated the recent experiences of Singapore Management University (SMU), the Ministry of Education in Singapore has decided to change the governance models of the existing state universities, National University of Singapore and Nanyang Technological University, by making them independent legal entities through the process of "corporatization" (Mok 2005a; 2006b). By incorporatizing these state universities, the Singapore government hopes that universities on the island state will become more entrepreneurial. Similarly, public universities in Malaysia have started a similar project of incorporation and corporatization of national universities since 1998. In the last few years, private universities have grown in number, while public universities are run as corporations in Malaysia. According to Molly Lee (2004), "the structural changes in the corporatized universities show that collegial forms of governance has been sidelined, entrepreneurial activities have increased, and corporate managerial practices have been institutionalized" (Lee 2004, 15).

The Quest for "World-Class" Status and University Ranking

With strong intentions to enhance their global competitiveness, governments and universities in Asia have taken global university ranking exercises very seriously. Recent studies have repeatedly shown that universities in East Asia are increasingly under pressures to compete internationally, and research has obviously become one of the major yardsticks in measuring university performance. University league tables are not only popular in the UK and Canada; various university ranking exercises have also been launched by academic institutions in Taiwan and mainland China (Liu and Cheng 2005; Research Center of Chinese Scientific Evaluation of Wuhan University 2005; Zhejiang University 2006).

Positioning itself as a regional hub of higher education, Hong Kong has placed heavy weight on research performance and this has been reflected in the research performance-led funding formula adopted by the government. Since the 1990s, Hong Kong higher education has gone through several Research Assessment Exercises (RAEs), modeling the UK approach to monitoring research performance. Universities in Hong Kong have gone through major review exercises and have been asked to differentiate themselves in terms of roles and missions, identifying major strengths and developing their centers of excellence. Academics currently working in Hong Kong are confronted with increasing pressures from the government to engage in international research, commanding a high quality of teaching, and contributing to professional and community services. As Hong Kong universities have tried to benchmark with top universities in the world, they are struggling very hard to compete for limited resources, just like universities in central Europe (Kwiek 2004). In a "publish or perish" context, academics in Hong Kong are becoming more instrumental when choosing publication venues and therefore international Social Science (SSCI) and Science Citation (SCI) indexed journals are major targets for getting their works published; while university presidents and vice chancellors in the city state are concerned with their institutions' ranking in the global university league (Mok 2005c; Chan 2007).

In Taiwan, the government has realized that globalization has accelerated competition among higher education institutions globally. With intentions to improve the global competitiveness of Taiwan institutions, the Executive Yuan set out a policy target to develop at least one university in Taiwan as one of the top one hundred universities in the world and at least fifteen key departments or cross-university research centers will become the top in Asia within the next five years (Lu 2004). With these policy objectives, the Ministry of education and the National Science Council have jointly launched the "Programme for Promoting Academic Excellence of Universities," primarily aiming at improving universities' infrastructure and invigorating research (MOE 2000). Well aware of the importance of their international position, higher education institutions in Taiwan have attached far more weight to university ranking exercises. For instance, the Research Institute of Higher Education at Tamkang University has conducted university assessment studies in the last few years. University league tables have been produced and subsequent reports have aroused lively debates in Taiwan (Lo and Weng 2005; Research Institute of Higher Education and University Evaluation 2005; Lo and Chan 2006). Similar to Hong Kong, research assessment has dominated academic life in Taiwan. Despite the fact that the university sector in Taiwan has established the Taiwan Social Science Citation Index (TSSCI) in order to counterbalance the pressures to publish only in SSCI journals, academics confront the reality that special weight is still attached to international publication venues in terms of promotion and research evaluations (Chen and Lo 2007).

In order to enhance the international competitiveness of Chinese universities in the globalizing world, the Chinese government has implemented a few major projects such as the "211 Project" and the "985 Scheme" to enable some higher education institutions to become "world-class universities." For the "211 Project," the government has attempted to develop 100 key universities and key disciplines in the twenty-first century with additional funding allocated to institutions of higher education to improve their teaching and research facilities; while the "985 Scheme" is to transform Beijing University

(Peking University) and Tsinghua University, to be world-class universities by 2015 and 2011 respectively. Realizing the intensified global competition among leading universities and feeling the pressure for better ranking in the global university league, the Chinese government has strategically identified key national bases for humanities and social sciences research and major national laboratories have been established to promote scientific research (Huang 2006). More recently, a research institute of higher education based in Shanghai has recently published a report on *The Academic Ranking of World Universities* which has drawn a great deal of attention and sparked considerable debate among academics in China (Liu and Cheng 2005). In the context of the quest for world-class universities in China, other research institutions in China like the Research Center of Chinese Scientific Evaluation of Wuhan University and College of Education, Zhejiang University, have also conducted research of similar kinds to promote university assessment and performance (Research Centre of Chinese Scientific Evaluation of Wuhan University 2005; Zhejiang University 2006). Most recently, Ngok and Guo have critically reviewed the quest for world-class universities in China, pointing out the gap between the government policy goals and the reality. They also report some malpractices and even corruption among academics resulting from the strong drive for obtaining the world-class status (Ngok and Guo 2007).

In Japan, academics are becoming increasingly aware of the ranking exercises and therefore they have launched a "Flagship Universities" project to identify a few major Japanese universities and develop them as world-class universities. According to Yonezawa (2006), consistent and protracted development of Japan's higher education system has long been driven by strong national initiatives since the late nineteenth century. Heavily invested in its university systems, Japanese universities long dominated the top echelons in *Asia Week*'s annual "Asian University Ranking." Nonetheless, Japanese universities have recently found their positions declining in both the regional and global university league tables. After benchmarking with the world university rankings, the Japanese government has become very concerned about how to reposition Japanese universities in the rapidly changing global environment. Therefore, the government has allocated additional resources to promote internationalization and students and academics are strongly encouraged by the government to engage in international collaborations and exchanges (Furushiro 2006; Yonezawa 2006).

Similarly, universities in Singapore are becoming increasingly aware of their international standing. To strengthen Singapore as a regional hub of higher education, the government strategically identified major top universities internationally and invited them to set up their branch campuses in the city-state. In addition, the government has attempted to attract leading academics to collaborate with local scholars (Mok and Tan 2004). Similar situations can be found in other Southeast Asian societies like Malaysia. The university system there has been going through restructuring along the lines of "neoliberalism" and the present government is very keen to make Malaysia a regional hub of higher education. More overseas academics will be appointed to the system and international collaborations with overseas institutions in terms of research and teaching have received strong support from the state (Interviews by Mok with Professor S. Morshidi and Mr. Abdul Razak, April 2006, Malaysia; Mok 2007a).

IMPACTS OF "WORLD-CLASS UNIVERSITY" MOVEMENT ON ASIAN HIGHER EDUCATION SYSTEMS

Neoliberalism and Academic Freedom

The introduction of more market-oriented and neoliberalist principles and measures to reform university governance was originally intended to empower universities to manage their business with more flexibility and autonomy. But comparative and international experiences of university governance reforms have suggested the adoption of decentralization, marketization, and corporatization strategies have not really liberated universities or empowered academics. Instead, academics and university administrators have only found themselves confronted with intensified pressures to prove their performance through the implementation of quality assurance, international benchmarking, and performance assessment. Hence, it is not surprising that the implementation of decentralization in university governance has resulted in re-regulation and recentralization through various kinds of accountability measures and performance checks. A strong tide of centralized decentralization has significantly affected the way contemporary universities are governed. It is in this context that a growing number of academics have begun to complain about academic freedom being threatened as a result of the decentralization and corporatization of universities.

Our discussion above has indicated how different Asian societies have interpreted the notion of "world-class" university and in what way their higher education systems have responded to the growing impacts of world university ranking. Other recent research has also reported a few major measures being adopted by universities in Asian societies to restructure and transform the university governance through the processes of incorporation and corporatization. Jun Oba's recent work provides a clear policy background for enlightening us about why and how Japanese universities have gone through the process of "incorporation." Unsatisfied with the centralized governance model in university governance, the Japanese government has amended its university law to turn all state universities into legally independent entities, which are supposed to be given more financial and management autonomy in order to make the systems more responsive to rapid changes. Recent fieldwork conducted in Japan has revealed that although state universities have incorporated, front-line academics have not really experienced genuine changes even though university senior management has enjoyed relative flexibility in financial matters (Fieldwork in Japan, January 2006). Oba's article has pointed out the reality and prospects of the incorporation project in Japan, indicating the difficulties involved in changing the highly state-regulated university sector in Japan. Although the Japanese government has a strong intention of transforming university governance in line with corporatization strategies, academics interviewed during various field visits to Japan have repeatedly indicated that the proposed changes have encountered tremendous resistance (Fieldwork in Japan, Mok, January 2006).

Similar to Japan, universities in Hong Kong and Singapore have been experiencing restructuring exercises. In the case of Hong Kong, the post–East Asian financial crisis had significantly affected the finance of the university sector by 2004. Facing severe government budget cuts, the university sector in Hong Kong had to venture into different kinds of income generation activities by launching more self-funded programs and turning their research into commercial products (Lee 2005). In addition, universities in Hong Kong have been under great pressures to perform well internationally by asserting their world-class status through international publications (Mok 2005). More recently, Jan Currie and Carole Peterson have reviewed the "Robert Chung Affair" and the "Amendment of Basic Law," as well as discussing how the university sector in Hong Kong has experienced significant restructuring and governance change. More specifically, they have highlighted the way academic freedom is affected under the pressures of higher education restructuring (Peterson and Currie 2007). Like Hong Kong, Singapore's higher education system has gone through significant transformations, particularly as the government has attempted to introduce internal competition to the university sector in order to enhance the efficiency and competitiveness of the system. Michael Lee and Saravanan Gopinathan examine critically what have been achieved and what are the problems resulting from the university restructuring in Singapore. One of the major challenges that universities in Singapore are facing is the dilemma between accountability and autonomy. Lee and Gopinathan again show how decentralization has gone hand in hand with recentralization, resulting in more control of the state-on-university governance in the context of quality assurance and international benchmarking (Lee and Gopinathan 2007).

Running universities and assessing academics' performance as business-like organizations, especially in neoliberal states, has revealed an observable tendency to emphasize both agency and consumer forms at the expense of professional and democratic forms, particularly when countries are involved in large-scale shifts from traditional Keynesian welfare state regimes to more market-oriented and consumer-driven systems (Peters 2005). One major criticism of such paradigm shifts is "that the agency/consumer couplet instrumentalizes, individualizes, standardizes, marketizes and externalizes accountability relationships at the expense of democratic values such as participation, self-regulation, collegiality, and collective deliberation that are said to enhance and thicken the relationships involved" (Peters 2006: 106). All of this has negatively affected traditional concepts of academic freedom.

Growing Inequalities in Higher Education

With strong intention to position their university systems favorably in different global university ranking exercises, our earlier discussion has already highlighted how universities in Asia have made attempts to concentrate their funding on selective institutions in order to boost them into research-intensive and globally competitive institutions. Not surprisingly, we have heard complaints from academics in Asia about the widening gap between well-established and new universities. It is becoming increasingly prevalent that government funding is linked with the performance and ranking of individual universities, while higher education institutions are under pressures to move beyond the first and the second missions (i.e. teaching and research) to the third mission (serving economic and social developments through the engagement in various kinds of entrepreneurial activities) (Mok 2005).

Preferential treatment and funding based upon selectivity is clearly found in South Korea. Terri Kim has offered a critical analysis of how universities in South Korea are incorporated, identifying the key issues which the universities in South Korea are confronting. But one point which deserves attention here is that unlike other Asian university systems which have experienced reductions in state funding (except Singapore), the South Korea government has increased its financial support to the university sector in order to boost a few universities in South Korea to climb up the world university ranking league tables. For example, Kansei University, aspiring to move up the global university league table, has issued a new personnel policy to recruit faculties from overseas to teach, instead of appointing local Korean scholars. This new staffing policy has raised deep concerns in South Korea (Kim 2006). Similar experiences can be easily found in other Asian societies such as the "211 Project" in Mainland China, "Flagship Project" in Japan, "Brain 21 Project" in South Korea, "Academic Excellence Project" in Taiwan, and "Areas of Excellence" in Hong Kong.

Critically reflecting on the world of globalized higher education, Altbach openly notes that globalization has reinforced existing inequalities and erected new barriers in many ways. Economists Joseph Stiglitz and Dani Rodrik, among others, have argued that globalization has damaged the interests of developing countries in many aspects as the powerful university systems in the developed economies such as those in the United States and the United Kingdom have always dominated the production and distribution of knowledge (Stiglitz 2002; Rodrik 1997, 1999; Altbach 2004). The growing popularity of the quest for the world-class university has further widened the gap between the developed and the developing economies. Although some of the Asian universities have successfully climbed up the ladder in these global university league tables,

> the major international academic centers—namely the leading research-oriented universities in the North, especially those that use one of the key world languages (particularly English)—occupy the top tier. . . . Even within countries at the center of the world academic system in the early twenty-first century— the United States, Britain, Germany, France, and to some extent Australia and Canada—there are many peripheral institutions. (Altbach 2004, 5)

It is clear then that globalization has intensified the problems of disparities between universities in well-established and less developed economies. Therefore, universities in less developed economies would encounter difficulties in performing well in these global university league tables, not to mention those academic institutions at the periphery with insufficient resources to transform into world-renowned universities. Our above discussion regarding how the Asian governments have attempted to enhance their institutions to become world-class and research-led universities clearly suggested the deepening of inequalities and disparities in higher education not only within national systems but regionally and globally as well. Welch, for instance, points out the dilemmas that many higher education institutions in Southeast Asia have confronted in the midst of the quest for world-class-university status. Without sufficient funds, higher education institutions in Indonesia, Malaysia, the Philippines, Thailand, and Vietnam have real difficulties in competing with other well-established universities concentrated in the West and the other wealthier parts of East Asia. Hence, the university systems of these Asian countries are disadvantaged because they fail to assert their academic standing in the global university ranking exercises, patents granted, and papers and citations (Welch 2007). Thus, it is not surprising to see some of the debates over globalization revolve around the problems of social integration and social justice (Held 2004), while the acceleration of globalization has indeed retarded social development and deepened divisions between the North and the South (Welch and Mok 2003). Michael Polanyi even regards the freedom of neoliberalism as a poisoned chalice, liberating us from everything, "even from obligations towards truth and justice" (Polanyi 1975, 14).

International-Benchmarking and a New Cultural Imperialism

International benchmarking and intensifying competition for ranking in the "Global University League" has inevitably influenced the way that Asian universities are governed. Nonetheless, we should not simply understand internationalization in Asia as merely following the American or Anglo-Saxon standards and practices. Although the academic communities in Europe and the United States have been regarded as more "advanced" than their Asian counterparts, higher education institutions in general, and academics in particular, must critically reflect on to what extent and in what way the so-called good practices identified from the West can really integrate well with non-Western education systems.

Our above discussion has clearly shown how Taiwan and Mainland China have attached significant importance to the world university league tables and, therefore, academics working there are under growing pressures to publish in internationally refereed journals and with major university or academic publishers in the United States and the United Kingdom. Although we cannot deny the importance of English as central for communicating knowledge worldwide, we should not simply ignore the importance of publications written in local languages. Nevertheless, we have witnessed the intensification of pressure imposed on professors and academics in Asia to publish in internationally circulated scientific journals, almost by definition in English. In order to assert their authority or to prove their abilities in turning out world-class research and scholarship, Asian scholars are fighting for international venues for publishing their research findings, while increasingly international and regional scientific conferences are exclusively in English, further placing a premium on the language (Altbach 2004, 7). As the pressure for universities to become "world class" increases, it is not surprising that some scholars in China have referred to themselves as "prostitutes," as they find that their work is only recognized if it is published in mostly Western, internationally refereed publications rather than local Chinese journals (Vidovich, Yang and Currie 2007).

As in China, academics in Taiwan have also encountered similar pressures for research assessment and international benchmarking. Field interviews with academics in Taiwan have repeatedly reported that higher education institutions are under tremendous pressure to become more internationalized, while academics continue to experience the publish-or-perish phenomenon. Dorothy Chen and William Lo offer a critical review on research assessment and international benchmarking in Taiwan, arguing that the quality assurance movement taking place in Taiwan has undermined not only the academic freedom of academics but also the values of Asian scholarship.

Putting the observations of these papers together, it is clear that higher education systems in Asia are under great pressures to perform in line with the "standards" prescribed by the Anglo-Saxon traditions. It appears that educational restructuring reforms taking place in Asia have been significantly influenced by new Western managerial-oriented doctrines and neoliberalist ideologies and practices. Responding to the growing impact of globalization, all the East Asian states considered here have reviewed their education systems and launched reforms along the lines of marketization, privatization, and corporatization with the intention of improving their governance and management (Chen and Lo 2007).

Critically scrutinizing the quest for world-class universities, we can easily find that a "Common World Education Culture" or a CWEC approach has emerged, seeing globalization as an emerging movement toward cultural homogeneity, as a cultural end point, a telos leaning toward the neoliberal institutional view celebrating the influence of major supranational organizations such as UNESCO, the World Bank, and the IMF. Central to CWEC approach is the spread of Western values, characterized by hyperliberalism, governance without government, and commodification. For the sake of survival in this highly competitive global marketplace, many states have reinvented themselves by reducing these core activities/businesses, making new arrangements for involving or revitalizing other non-state sectors in public management and social policy delivery (Dale 2000; Mok 2005d). All these transformations have clearly demonstrated how vulnerable the developing countries could become when their economic, social, cultural, and political developments are increasingly determined by supranational organizations.

Despite the fact that many of the Asian societies discussed here have been "decolonized" following World War II, many of them have not really decolonized in practice, since most of them have been influenced strongly by Anglo-Saxon standards or ideologies. The introduction of English as the medium as instruction, the adoption of curricula from Australia, the United Kingdom, and the United States, sending home students to study overseas and establishing international exchanges, coupled with the quest for the world-class universities as predominately defined by the Anglo-Saxon world, have not only created a new "dependency culture" but also reinforced the American dominated hegemony, particularly in relation to league tables, citation indices, and the kind of research which counts as high status. Asian societies seem to have treated "internationalization" as "Westernization" and "modernization" or "Americanization" since the nineteenth century. This represents a potential threat of a new cultural imperialism resulting from the world-class-university movement spreading through Asia (Mok 2007).

CONCLUSION: WALKING ON TWO LEGS

In his analysis of the internationalization and international benchmarking of Asian universities Kazuhiro Ebuchi (1997) suggests that "internationalization" could be interpreted either as an intransitive verb or a transitive verb. The concept of "internationalization as a transitive verb" in English "is a historical concept, which emerged from a nation with 'hegemony' in the international order, while that of 'internationalization as an intransitive verb' is one from a 'smaller nation' which was forced to follow a 'larger nation'" (Ebuchi 1997). Thus not only European but also Asian states should be aware of the potential threat of the rise of a new cultural imperialism or neocolonialism. For example, in the midst of the quest for world-class status, many Asian states may be tempted to change the medium of instruction at their universities entirely to English, while local research and publications written in local languages will face a declining role. Therefore, we need to critically examine the following questions when attempting to internationalize universities: can the standards and practices commonly available in the West be coherently adapted to Asian traditions and cultures? Would the adoption of such Western practices be distorted especially without proper contextual analysis? Most important of all, would there be only one "international standard" as defined solely by or even dominated by the Anglo-Saxon paradigm? Who should be involved in defining the international benchmarks? Without proper contextualization, the adoption of such trendy global strategies or reform measures may prove to be counterproductive.

   In conclusion, we hope with such critical reflections we may become more aware of the danger of new imperialism. Living in a post-colonial context, Asian scholars should be more critical about what they have learned from the West, guarding against the logic of becoming "globalized" meaning "Americanized." Following dominant global practices and ideologies, without developing our own unique systems and honoring the rich traditions, cultures, and scholarships of Asia, may easily lead us to enter a processes of "recolonization." In this regard, learning from other systems is desirable but we should guard against copying without proper adaptation and contextualization. Most important of all, Asia has rich traditions and cultures and we should never look down upon our own scholarly traditions. We strongly believe scholars in Asia should "walk on two legs," internationalizing our academic systems, on the one hand, and cultivating and developing our own paradigms, on the other. Internationalizing with Asian characteristics would be far more challenging and we must commit ourselves to develop alternative academic paradigms for promoting cross-cultural understanding and cross-national policy learning.

REFERENCES

Altbach, P. "Globalization and the University: Myths and Realities in an Unequal World." *Tertiary Education and Management 1* (2004): 1–20.

Ball, S. *Education Plc: Understanding Private Sector Participation in Public Sector Education*. London: Routledge 2007.

Bayliss, J., and Smith, S. *The Globalization of World Politics: An Introduction to International Relations*. Oxford: Oxford University Press 2001.

Brehony, Kelvin, and Rosemary Deem. "Challenging the Post-Fordist/Flexible Organization Thesis: The Case of Reformed Educational Organizations." *British Journal of Sociology of Education* 26(3) (2005): 395–414.

Cerny, Philip. *The Changing Architecture of Politics: Structure, Agency, and the Future of the State*. London: Sage, 1990.

———. "Paradoxes of the Competition State: The Dynamics of Political Globalization." *Government and Opposition* 32 (1997) 251–74.

Chan, David. "Global Agenda, Local Response: Changing Education Governance in Hong Kong's Higher Education." *Globalization, Societies, and Education* 5(1) (2007): 109–24.

Chan, David, and Janson Tan. "Privatization and the Rise of Direct Subsidy Scheme Schools and Independent Schools in Hong Kong and Singapore." Paper presented at the Asia Pacific Educational Research Association 2006 International Conference, Hong Kong (2006): 28–30.

Chen, I. R., and Y. W. Lo. "Critical Reflections of the Approaches to Quality in Taiwan's Higher Education." *The Journal of Comparative Asian Development* 6(1) (2007).

Chou, Prudence. "Taiwan's Higher Education at the Crossroad: Implications for China." Paper presented at the senior seminar, Education for 2020 Project of East-West Center, Hawaii, 6–12 September (2006).

Currie, J., R. DeAngelis, H. De Boer, C. Lacotte, and J. Huisman. *Globalizing Practices and University Responses: European and Anglo-American Differences*. Connecticut: Praeger/Greenwood Press, 2003.

Currie, J., and J. Newson. *Universities and Globalization: Critical Perspectives*. Thousand Oaks, CA: Sage, 1998.

Dale, R. "Globalization and Education: Demonstrating a 'Common World Educational Culture' or Locating a 'Globally Structured Educational Agenda'?" *Education Theory* 50(4) (2000) 427–48.

Drahos, Peter and Richard Jospeh. "The Telecommunications and Investment in the Great Supranational Regulatory Game." *Telecommunications Policy* 188 (1995) 619–35.

Ebuchi, Kazuhiro. *Study of the Internationalization of Universities.* Tokyo: Tamagawa University Press, 1997.

Fraenkel, Ernst. *The Dual State.* Translation from the German by E. A. Shils, in collaboration with Edith Lowenstein and Klaus Knorr. Oxford: Oxford University Press, 1941.

Fukuyama, F. *The End of History.* New York: Penguin, 1992.

———. *The End of History and the Last Man.* New York: Free Press 2006.

Furushiro, Norio, ed. *Final Report of Developing Evaluation Criteria to Assess the Internationalization of Universities.* Kwansei: Osaka University, 2006.

Gill, Stephen. "Globalization, Market Civilization and Disciplinary Neoliberalism." *Millennium* 24(3) (1995): 399–423.

Hawkins, John N. "Centralization, Decentralization and Recentralization: Education Reform in China." *Educational Administration* 38(5) (2000): 442–55.

———. "Walking on Three Legs: Centralization, Decentralization, and Reentralization in the People's Republic of China." In *Decentralization and Education: A Comparative Approach.* Edited by Chris Bjork (2005b).

———. "Some Trends in Public Higher Education: Asia and the U.S." *Chung Cheng Educational Studies*, Special Issue (2005a): 45–62.

———. "Public Good, Commodification and Higher Education Reform: Some Trends in Japan and California, *University Studies*, no. 35 (August 2007): 27–51.

Held, D. *Global Covenant.* Cambridge: Polity Press, 2004.

Held, D., and A. McGrew, eds. *The Global Transformations Reader.* Cambridge: Polity, 2000.

Held, D., A. McGrew, D. Goldblatt, and J. Perration. *Global Transformations.* Cambridge: Polity, 1999.

Hirst, P., and Thompson, G. *Globalization in Question.* Cambridge: Polity Press, 1999.

Huang, Futao. "Difference in the Context of Internationalization by Region: China." Pp. 41–50 in *Final Report of Developing Evaluation Criteria to Assess the Internationalization of Universities.* Edited by Norio Furushiro. Kwansei: Osaka University, 2006.

Jayasuriya, Kanishka. "Authoritarian Liberalism, Governance and the Emergence of the Regulatory State in Post-crisis East Asia." Pp. 315–30 in *Politics and Markets in the Wake of the Asian Crisis.* Edited by Richard Robinson, Mark Beeson, Kanishka Jayasuriya, and Hyuk-rae Kim. London: Routledge, 2000.

Jordana, Jacint, and David Levi-Faur "Preface: The Making of A New Regulatory Order." *The Annuals of the American Academy of Political and Social Science* 598 (March 2005): 1–6.

Jessop, B. *The Future of Capitalist State.* Cambridge: Polity Press, 2002.

Kim, Terri. "The Academic Profession in East Asian Private Higher Education." Paper presented at the International Workshop "Frontier of Private Higher Education Research in East Asia," Hotel Arcadia Ichigaya, Tokyo Japan, 14–15 December 2006.

Kwiek, Marek. "The Emergent Educational Policies under Scrutiny. The Bologna Process from A Central European Perspective." *European Educational Research Journal* 3(4) (2004): 759–76.

Lee, Hiu-hong. "Major Issues of University Education Policy in Hong Kong." *Asia Pacific Education Review* 6(2) (2005) 103–12.

Lee, Hiu-hong, and Saravanan Gopinathan. "Reforming University Education in Hong Kong and Singapore." Pp. 56–98 in *Globalization and Higher Education in East Asia*. Edited by Ka-ho Mok and Richard James. Singapore: Marshall Cavendish Academic, 2005.

Lee, H. H., and S. Gopinathan. "University Restructuring in Singapore: Amazing! Or a Maze?" *The Journal of Comparative Asian Development* 6(1) (2007).

Lee, Molly N. N. *Restructuring Higher Education in Malaysia*. Penang: School of Educational Studies, Universiti Sains Malaysia (2004).

Levi-Faur, David. "The Competition State as a Neo-Mercantalist State: Understanding the Restructuring of National and Global Telecommunications." *Journal of Socio-Economics* 27(6) (1998) 655–86.

Liu, Niancai, and Ying Cheng. "Academic Ranking of World Universities." *Higher Education in Europe* 30(2) (2005) 127–36.

Lo, Yat-wai, and David Chan. "The Impact of Globalization on Higher Education in Taiwan and Mainland China." Paper presented at the International Conference on GDPism and Risk: Challenges for Social Development and Governance in East Asia. Bristol, UK, 12–13 July 2006.

Lo, William Yat-wai, and Fwu-yuan Weng. "Taiwan's Responses to Globalization: Decentralization and Internationalization of Higher Education." Pp. 137–56 in *Globalization and Higher Education in East Asia*. Edited by Ka ho Mok and Richard James. Singapore: Marshall Cavendish Academic 2005.

Lu, Mu-lin. "The Blueprint and Competitiveness of Taiwan's Higher Education." Paper presented at Cross Strait Seminar on Review and Prospect of the Policy of University Excellence held at Taipei, Taiwan, 25–26 March 2004.

Marginson, Simon, and Mark Considine. *The Enterprise University: Power, Governance and Reinvention in Australia*. Cambridge: Cambridge University Press 2000.

Min, Weifang. "Chinese Higher Education: The Legacy of the Past and the Context of the Future." Pp. 53–84 in *Asian Universities: Historical Perspectives and Contemporary Challenges*. Edited by Philip Altbach and Toru Umakoshi. Baltimore and London: Johns Hopkins University Press 2004.

Ministry of Education [MOE], Taiwan. *List of Projects for the First Round of the Program for Promoting Academic Excellence of Universities*. Taipei: Ministry of Education 2000.

Mok, Ka ho. "Fostering Entrepreneurship: Changing Role of Government and Higher Education Governance in Hong Kong." *Research Policy* 34 (2005): 537–54.

———. "Pro-competition Policy Tools and State Capacity: Corporatization of Public Universities in Hong Kong and Singapore." *Policy & Society* 24(3) (2005a): 1–26.

———. "Globalization and Educational Restructuring: University Merging and Changing Governance in China." *Higher Education* 50 (2005b): 57–88.

————. "The Quest for World Class University: Quality Assurance and International Benchmarking." *Quality Assurance in Education* 13(4) (2005c): 277–304.

————. "Globalization and New Governance: Changing Policy Instruments and Regulatory Arrangements in Education." *International Review of Education* 51(4) (2005d): 1–22.

————. "Varieties of Regulatory Regimes in Asia: The Liberalization of the Higher Education Market in Hong Kong, Singapore and Malaysia." Paper presented at the Asia Pacific Educational Research Association 2006 International Conference, 28–30 November 2006, Hong Kong Institute of Education, Hong Kong (2006).

————. *Education Reform and Education Policy in East Asia.* London, Routledge, 2006a.

————. "The Search for New Governance: Corporatization and Privatization Experiences in Singapore and Malaysia." Paper presented at the International Workshop on University Restructuring in Asia, 16 January 2006, Research Institute for Higher Education. Hiroshima University 2006b.

————. "Questing for Internationalization of Universities in Asia: Critical Reflections." *Journal of Studies in International Education* 11(3/4) (2007) 433–54.

Mok, Ka-ho, and Anthony Welch, eds. *Globalization and Educational Restructuring in the Asia Pacific Region.* Basingstoke, Hampshire: Palgrave Macmillan, 2003.

Mok, Ka-ho, and Jason Tan. *Globalization and Marketization in Education: A Comparative Analysis of Hong Kong and Singapore.* Cheltenham: Edward Elgar, 2004.

Moran, Michael. "Review Article: Understanding the Regulatory State." *British Journal of Political Science* 32 (2002) 391–413.

Neubauer, Deane. "On the Public Good." Paper presented at the senior seminar, Education for 2020 Project of East-West Center, (Honolulu, HI: 6–12 September 2006).

Ng, Pak-tee, and David Chan. "A Comparative Study of Singapore's School Excellence Model with Hong Kong's School-based Management." Paper presented at the Asia Pacific Educational Research Association 2006 International Conference, Hong Kong, 28–30 November 2006.

Ngok, K. L., and W. Q. Guo. "The Quest for 'World Class Universities' in China: Critical Reflections." *The Journal of Comparative Asian Development* 6(1) (2007).

Oba, Jun. "Incorporation of National Universities in Japan and Its Impact upon Institutional Governance." Paper presented at the International Workshop on University Restructuring in Asia, Hiroshima, Japan: 16 January 2006.

Olsen, Johan P., and Ase Gornitzka. "Making Sense of Change in University Governance." *IAU Horizons,* 11.4–12.1 (2006): 1–3.

Peterson, C. J., and J. Currie. "Higher Education Restructuring and Academic Freedom in Hong Kong." *The Journal of Comparative Asian Development* 6(1) (2007).

Polanyi, M. *Personal Knowledge Towards a Post-Critical Philosophy.* Chicago: University of Chicago Press, 1975.

Research Center of Chinese Scientific Evaluation of Wuhan University. *How Do We Rank the Scientific Research Competition of the World Universities?* Wuhan: China, Research Center of Chinese Scientific Evaluation of Wuhan University, 2005.

Research Institute of Higher Education and University Evaluation. *University Rankings in Taiwan*. Taipei, Tamkang University, 2005.

Rodrik, D. *Has Globalization Gone too Far?* Washington, DC: Institute for International Economics, 1997.

———. *The New Global Economy and Developing Countries: Making Openness Work*. Washington, DC: John Hopkins for Overseas Development Council, 1999.

Schirato, J., and Webb, T. *Understanding Globalization*. London: Sage, 2003.

Scott, Colin. "Regulation in the Age of Governance: The Rise of the Post-regulatory State." Pp. 145–76 in *The Politics of Regulation: Institutions and Regulatory Reforms for the Age of Governance*. Edited by Jacint Jordana and David Levi-Faur. Cheltenham: Edward Elgar, 2004.

Stiglitz, J. *Globalization and its Discontents*. New York: W. W. Norton, 2002.

Tien, Flora. "Incorporation of National University in Taiwan: Challenges for the Government and the Academics." Paper presented at the International Workshop on University Restructuring in Asia, Hiroshima, Japan, 16 January 2006.

Vidovich, Leslie, Rui Yang, and Currie Jan. "Changing Accountabilities in Higher Education: Education as China 'Opens Up' to Globalization." *Globalization, Societies and Education* (2007).

Watson, David. "UK Higher Education: The Truth about the Student Market." *Higher Education Review* 38(3) (2006): 3–16.

Welch, A., "Governance Issues in South East Asian Higher Education: Finance, Devolution and Transparency in the Global Era." *Asia Pacific Journal of Education* 27(3) (2007): 237–54.

Welch, A., and Mok, Ka-ho. "Conclusion: Deep Development or Deep Division?" Pp. 333–56 in *Globalization and Educational Restructuring in the Asia Pacific Region*. Edited by K. H. Mok and A. Welch. Basingstoke: Palgrave Macmillan, 2003.

Yang, Rui. *The Third Delight: Internationalization of Higher Education in China*. London: Routledge, 2002.

———. "Globalization and Higher Education Restructuring: Issues and Debates." In *Globalization and Higher Education in East Asia*. Edited by K. H. Mok and R. James. Singapore and New York: Marshall Cavendish Academic, 2005.

Yonezawa, Akiyoshi. "Japanese Flagship Universities at A Crossroads." Pp. 85–102 in *Final Report of Developing Evaluation Criteria to Assess the Internationalization of Universities*. Edited by Norio Furushiro. Kwansei, Osaka University, 2006.

Zhejiang University. *A Report on the First Session of the International Academic Advisory Committee for University Evaluation*. Hangzhou: Zhejiang University, 2006.

NOTE

1. Part of the findings reported and analyzed in this chapter are based upon the research project funded by the Chiang Ching-Kuo Foundation in Taiwan. The first author of the chapter wants to thank the Foundation for offering research grant to enable him to conduct fieldwork in Mainland China and Taiwan in 2006 and 2007. Thanks must be extended to the editors of this volume for inviting us to contribute a chapter in this project.

10

A Historical Sociology of "Tertiary Education for All" in Korea

Ki-Seok Kim and Hwanbo Park

This chapter[1] analyzes the unique development of tertiary education for all (*TEFA*) in Korea. Access to tertiary education in Korea has recently reached 81 percent, the highest in the world (Grubb et al. 2006, 7). The transition from elite to universal access to tertiary education was attained in less than three decades, an achievement that took almost half a century in the United States (Trow 1961). As recently as the year 2000, Korean high school graduates were 5 percent more likely to pursue tertiary education, in one form or another, than their counterparts in the United States, a world leader in universal higher education. Korea has also become one of the first countries to have achieved almost universal completion of secondary education, at the highest growth rate of any of the OECD countries (OECD 2009; Grubb et al. 2006, 16).[2] The rapid transition to universal access to tertiary education in Korea occurred almost immediately after, or simultaneously with, the swift transition to universal secondary education. The phenomenon of a simultaneous transition to universal access to secondary and tertiary education is unprecedented (Kim 2007a, 3). Grubb et al. draw attention to the fact that, "the idea of "tertiary education for all" is closer to reality in Korea than in any other country" (Grubb et al. 2006, 16). Is this a success story? In this article, we will address this question by explaining the mechanism and consequences of this simultaneous transition.

The rate of expansion of TEFA in Korea exceeded the government's willingness and ability to provide financial support. The resultant gap was filled by privatization of this new education market, leading to the erosion of the notion of the "public good" in tertiary education. A unique aspect, particular to the case of Korea, lies in the zeal and willingness to financially support their children's studies on the part of parents, and not a concerted central planning effort by the government, as the main driving force behind the rapid expansion of higher education. This has led to a simultaneous shift to increased levels of higher education together with increased privatization.

As will be demonstrated, overprivatization has been the primary mechanism behind the transition since the late 1960s. Due to a heavy reliance on private funding, parents and students must pay a high price, including, "education fever," "examination-hell," and "cut-throat competition." Recent trends reflect a set of deep-rooted cultural norms fostered by this rapid double transition. The reliance on privatization in achieving universal access to higher education places a significant financial burden on families, particularly those of a disadvantaged socioeconomic status. Therefore, the more financial resources that come from the private sector, the more difficult it becomes to attain equitable access. Nevertheless, there is no sign of a narrowing in the gap which exists between regions, socioeconomic status, gender, and family background, all of which have led to inequality of access to universities and colleges.

The global trend toward privatization in higher education has seen such policies have adopted in Western societies, including in former socialist countries, where public higher education systems had been the norm. Critiquing this trend, Altbach (2002, 10) cautions that "while many look to America's impressive private higher education sector, it is more useful to draw on the Asian experience." Countries considering privatization would do well to consider the experiences of Japan, the Philippines, and Korea. More than 80 percent of all students in Korea are currently enrolled at private universities and colleges, compared to only about 20 percent in the United States. Indeed, 83 percent of the national budget for higher education in Korea comes from family funds (Kim 2007a), an unparalleled phenomenon, unseen even in America, where the private sector is far more dominant than the public sector. Furthermore, the distinction between the public and private sectors has been blurred, with even the top Korean national universities relying on tuition fees for more than one-third of their revenue.

The pace of development of Korean higher education is remarkable, especially considering the extremely limited public financial resources and infrastructural support it has been given. Korea has played such an archetypal role before, such as when the Chinese government studied Korea's privatization efforts before launching their own. Thus, the Korean experience is worth examining and may be beneficial to other countries, especially those whose educational cultures and societies are more similar to Korea than America. This article examines policy implications and conditions under which universal access and equity may be pursued by other countries.

FROM PRIVATIZATION TO OVER-PRIVATIZATION

The Historical Origins of Private Higher Education

Both the public and private sectors have traditionally played important roles in higher learning in Asia (Min 2004). As was the case in China, in Korea there existed a dual system of education: public education run by the central and local government and a system of various private education institutes. It was long a common practice among historians of Korean higher education to argue that the first public college, *Taehak* (Great Learning), founded in 372 AD, and its successor, *Sungkyunkwan*, established by the government in 1398, were the Asian counterparts to the Western medieval university as traditional centers of higher education. However, unlike the University of Paris in the twelfth century, *Sungkyunkwan* was not a center of excellence of academic studies, but a governmental institute for lesser degree holders to reside for a certain period of time in order to prepare for their final national examination for the selection of civil officers. It was also the center of Confucian ceremonies and, over time, the ceremonial function prevailed over the educational function. Most of the training of the Korean literati was conducted at a variety of non-formal and less-institutionalized (*NFLI*) institutes, ranging from the family school to the *letter hall*[3] to the private seminary, known as *Sowon*—the most institutionalized of the private schools with governmental authorization.

The origin of private education in Asia can be traced back to the legend of Confucius' teaching practices dating back to around 500 BC. He became a teacher at the age of twenty-nine and his house became a site of pilgrimage and a center of learning for his followers. According to *Confucius Analects*, an early form of his teaching began as follows: "The Master (Confucius) said that from the men bringing his bundles of dried flesh for my teaching, I have never refused instruction to anyone (VII, 7)" (Legge 1892, 61). Dr. Legge, the highest authority on Chinese classics in the English-speaking world, interpreted this phrase as follows: "However small the fee his pupils were able to afford, he never refused instruction. All that he required was an ardent desire for improvement, and some degree of capacity" (Legge 1892, 61). His teaching was not carried out in any formal school or teaching institute established by the government; rather it was a model of private education, whereby a great scholar offered lessons at his house. This form of NFLI private higher education was long practiced in Eastern civilizations (Lee 1984, 220).

While teaching almost anyone who had desire to learn and could pay a nominal fee for tuition, Confucius rigorously selected a small number of disciples among his followers. According to legend, he had at least 3,000 followers. Of these he formally handpicked only seventy-seven, stating, "The disciples who received my instructions, and could comprehend them, were seventy-seven individuals. They were all scholars of extraordinary ability" (Legge 1892, 62). Among those selected, twelve disciples were placed, only one level below Confucius, at the Shrine of Confucius the Saint, where a ritual memorializing him had been observed. Thanks to their continuing scholastic efforts, Confucius' teachings survived various historical upheavals and maintain their place among the greatest classics of higher learning in Asia.

Korean Confucianism is based on Chu His' (1128–1200) Neo-Confucianism, which was revived during the Song Dynasty. The Korean literati found it most appealing, for it sought to establish an ethical base for an enlightened political world with fully developed theoretical studies (Lee 1984, 217). The Korean scholar, T'oegye (Yi Hwang 1501–1570), developed a full explication of *i* (*li* in Chinese) philosophy,[4] which accounts for what things are and how they behave. As a result of his philosophical endeavors, he was revered as a Korean Chu His, a Confucius, or sometimes as both. He presented a philosophical doctrine emphasizing moral self-cultivation as the essence of learning. He was the greatest figure in the history of philosophy in Korea and exerted a huge influence on the shaping of Japanese Confucian doctrine as well.

Under T'oegye, a group of the brilliant Neo-Confucian literati living in the Southern area gathered and devoted their energy to academic pursuits, mainly at the private academies or *Sowon*. They remained in the South for a very long period, in order to avoid being swept up in court politics. The top level of scholarship was passed down through an academic lineage. Among the Southerners, Sungho (Yi Ik 1681–1763) became the model Confucius intellectual. With enough flexibility to embrace Western scholasticism, his teachings made a great contribution to the renaissance of Korean Confucianism in its later days. When he passed away, one of his disciples, and the statesman of the time, Prime Minster Chae, inscribed on his tombstone that "Our scholarship had always grown from an academic lineage. The Korean Confucius, T'oegye, taught his Way to Hangang who taught it in turn to Misu. As a disciple of Misu, Sungho inherited the legitimate academic lineage of T'oegye" (ITKC 2001, 444).

This academic lineage had nothing to do with Sungkyunkwan or the Four Schools established and run by the government. Instead, this lineage was made through private education. The academic linage was transferred to the next generation of scholars. The East and West cultural collision in the early eighteenth century lead to the birth of a variety of new schools of thought, ranging from voluntary conversion to Catholicism, to the birth of a movement rejecting heterodoxy, and to the rise of practical learning.[5]

The main characteristics of private education in the Chosun Dynasty can be summed up as follows: informal, non-institutionalized education; the use of letter halls made study possible anytime for any scholarly teacher and group of students with a minimal level of financial resources but having a desire and capacity for learning; the letter hall was open to virtually all men with a few exceptions; private education functioned as the center of excellence in research and higher learning, coexisting with a network of public education institutes; family, not government, was the main actor in increasing educational opportunities. This archetype of private higher education repeatedly appeared to meet peoples' demands for higher learning under the Japanese occupation, which tried systematically to destroy indigenous private higher education.

The Development of Modern Privatization

The current "modern" education of Korea started from the 1894 Education Reform. Figure 10.1 shows the trend in school expansion at each level during the past decade. The transition from mass to universal access to tertiary education took place only after 1980. As shown in the graph, indigenous forms of private education like letter halls persisted during the colonial period. It is impossible to calculate a reliable participation rate of students attending letter halls, for they took a NFLI form of education which hardly produced any statistics. However, Japanese statistics showed the number of Korean students attending indigenous schools exceeded that of colonized schools until the middle of the 1920s. Sociologists of colonial education have had heated debates in trying to explain why the Korean system collapsed at that particular time.

Contrary to Japanese "official" and propaganda claims, the colonial education was part of an assimilation policy, but designed to liquidate Korean values, culture, and identity. As indicated in Figure 10.1, the colonizers severely limited the Korean people's opportunity for higher education. This policy of repression distorted the development of the secondary education, which functioned as a preparatory program for universities and colleges. Since the late 1920s and early 1930s, primary education seemingly started to expand, not because of the provision of free and compulsory education for all Koreans by the Japanese, but because of its enforcing privatization at the level of primary education. From the beginning, Japanese colonizers shifted the responsibility for financing education to Korean parents. This policy was maintained during the whole period of occupation. In his brilliant historical sociology of the elementary school expansion in the 1930s, Professor Sung-Cheol Oh (2004) showed how Korean parents, resisting Japanese policy for rudimentary vocational education to the Ordinary School (i.e., elementary schools) for producing docile peasants, chose to pay the costs of non-vocation general education and encourage their children to prepare for the entrance examination to the

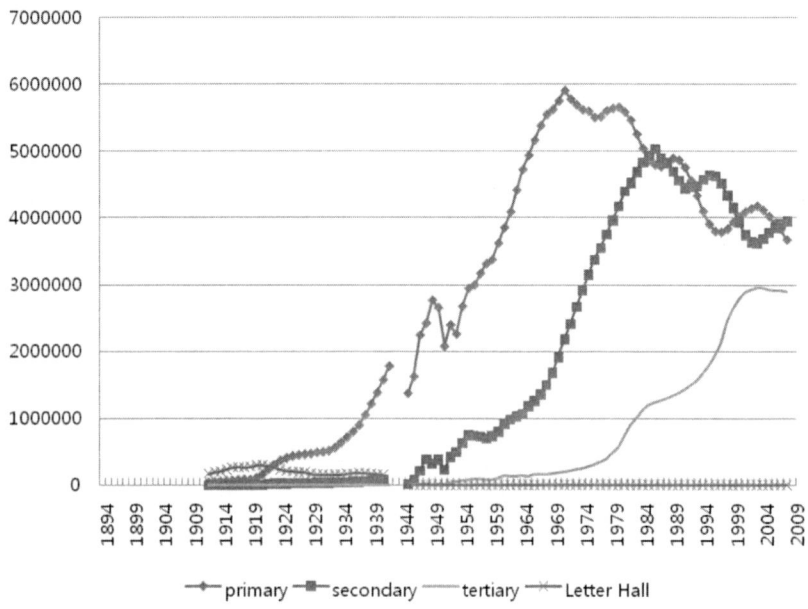

Figure 10.1. Education Expansion by Level of Education 1894-2009, *Source:* Kim, K. S. (1999)

next level of education. Their financial commitment led to school expansion and an early form of "examination-hell" in the 1930s.

Despite a series of education reforms to de-colonize immediately after liberation, the colonial principle of privatization of elementary education was kept and further extended to secondary and higher education. By the early 1950s, the number of students attending private universities and colleges exceeded the number in national public schools. This trend has continued, and has led to an extreme dependence on private education.

Privatization has accelerated school expansions and has led the transition to universal access. The speed of this transition in Korea is unique (and thus difficult to compare to other countries). A comparison between America's "parallel transition" (Trow 1961) and Korea's "simultaneous transition" (Kim 2007a) show some interesting differences. As a result of the simultaneous transition since the 1980s, the educational attainment level of Korea reached the top level among OECD countries. The top level of tertiary educational attainment was facilitated by the recent expansion of two-year private college. As shown in Figure 10.2, the majority of tertiary students attend private universities and vocational colleges.

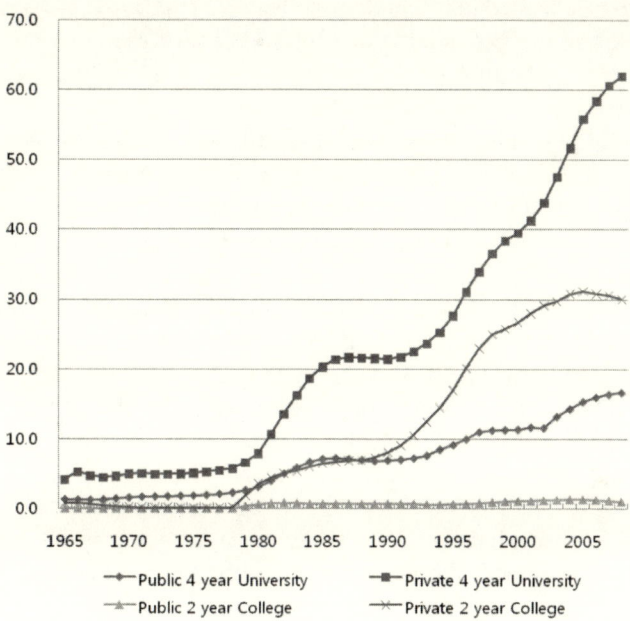

Figure 10.2.   Enrollment Rates by Type of Institution 1965-2008, *Source:* Kim, K. S. (1999)

While all higher educational institutions in Korea rely on private funding, vocational colleges have the highest degree of reliance on the private sector. This pattern differs sharply from the American model where large research universities and elite liberal arts schools show a higher level of reliance upon the private sector than community colleges, which are mostly state-funded public institutions. This dominance of private vocational training creates a greater financial burden on poorer parents, thus eroding the idea of higher education as a "public good."

This phenomenon emerged more than half a century ago. In the early 1950s, UNESCO and UNKRA (United Nations Korean Reconstruction Agency) jointly sent an Education Planning Mission to study the situation of Korean education and make recommendations for rebuilding the education system from the ruins of the Korean War. The Mission's report underscored the fact that a "striking feature of the financing of education in Korea is that secondary and higher education are financed to the extent of at least 75 percent by voluntary contribution from parents" (UNESCO 1952, 103). It also reported that, "Even the unsatisfactory program of education today is maintained, not as a charge upon the whole people through public taxation, but largely through the voluntary support of these families who have at present members to be enrolled in a school or college" (127). Based on these conclusions the Mission recommended that the full cost of primary education and at least 50 percent of the costs of public secondary and higher education be supplied from tax sources (UNESCO 1953, 103).

The Korean government has never implemented UNESCO's recommendation for higher education. It did not start funding even basic education from tax sources until the 1990s. For Korean and foreign education experts the core problem lies in shifting the financial burden away from private funding to public taxation as a basis for the financial support of public education, including tertiary education. Figures 10.3 and 10.4 indicate that dependency on private funding had been increasing over time, resulting in Korea being the most dependent on private funding among OECD countries.

Japan and Korea were the two countries that spent the least amount of public funds on higher education, but Korea's dependence on private funding was considerably greater than that of Japan. Korea is the only country that has let privatization prevail in the field of public education, particularly in tertiary education. The absence of education being defined as a "public good" has contributed to this phenomenon. The increasing proportion of private funding invested in the education market by parents has further diminished the idea of education as a "public good" in the minds of the general population. This vicious circle of privatization was the mechanism which led the simultaneous transition to universal access to secondary and tertiary education to develop as it has.

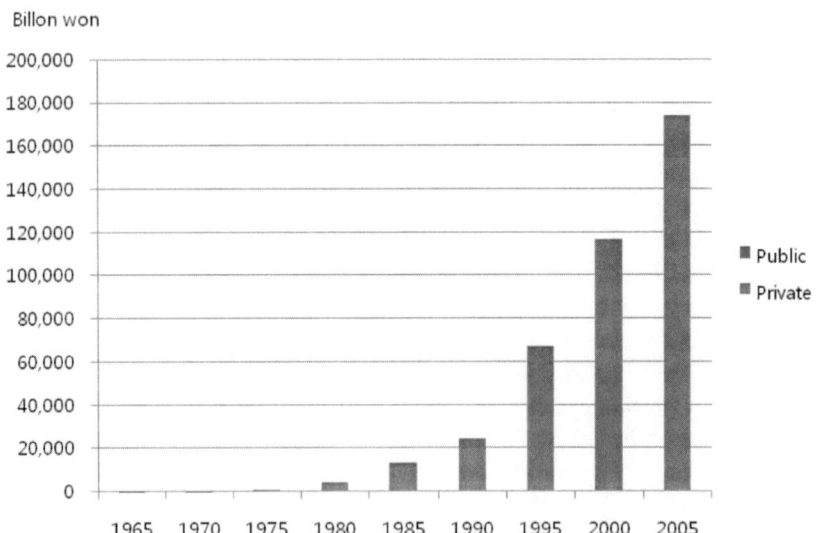

Figure 10.3.   **Expenditure on Higher Education by Funding Source 1965–2005**

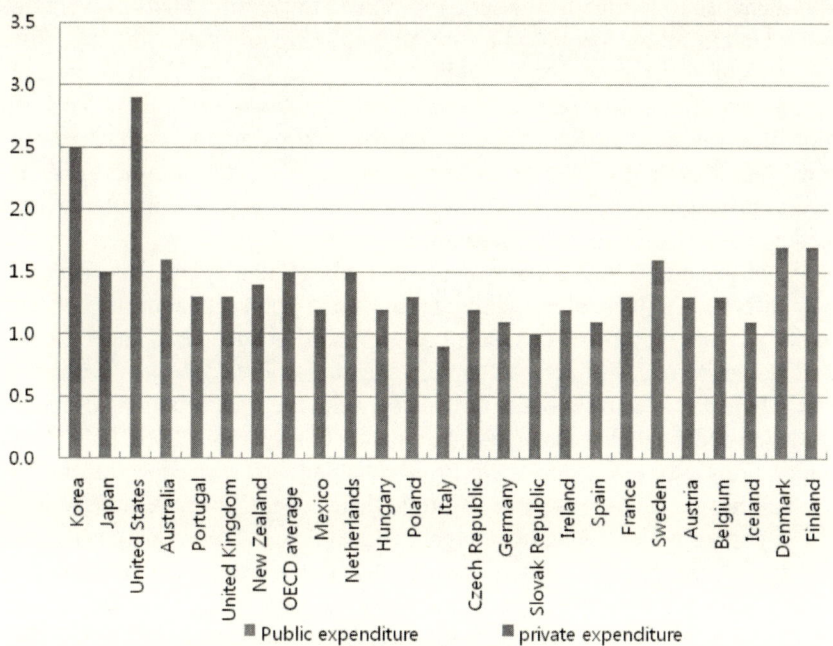

Figure 10.4.   Expenditure on Higher Education as Percentage of GDP, by Funding Source (2006) *Source:* **KEDI & MOE, Education Statistics Yearbook; OECD (2009)**

Consequences of Over-Privatization

The pace of expansion of Korean higher education, which can only be described as explosive, has been particularly rapid since the 1980s (as illustrated in Figure 10.1). One of the consequences of the simultaneous transition was that there was very little time to build up an efficient university system with adequate functional differentiation, between public and private institutions, between metropolitan and provincial universities, between four-year universities and junior colleges, and between research-oriented and teaching-oriented institutions. This also occurred in the secondary educational system, which also failed to develop a reasonable differentiation between college preparatory schools and vocational schools. No efforts were made to make secondary education comprehensive. Instead, vocational high schools separated from academic schools, and were allowed to provide a college track for their students, many of whom went on to receive some type of tertiary education.

Therefore, different universities and colleges in Korea did not develop their own unique missions and functions. All universities aspired to be major flagship universities. It may be understandable that a newly established school would choose to model itself after a top-ranked university. Many universities in the United States have tried to use Harvard University as a model. However, in Korea, all universities (public, private, metropolitan, and provincial) model themselves after Seoul National University. As a result, there has been very little differentiation of functions and purposes among various institutions. One example of the negative consequences of such a process is that several private universities have offered doctoral programs without adequate academic and institutional preparation and support.

The absence of a well-coordinated higher educational system has also critically affected the Korean economy and impacted upon the labor market. The higher educational institutions have not been able to adequately meet the human resources needs of Korea's rapidly growing knowledge-intensive industries. There has been a serious mismatch between the "end products" of higher education and the real needs of the labor market (Grubb et al. 2006). Some large corporations have responded to this by establishing their own educational training facilities where they are able to retrain their college graduate employees.

The past sixty years of Korean higher education can be summed up as low-cost education. In 2006, the Ministry of Education allocated 6.4 percent of its budget to higher education. This amounted to about 0.7 percent of the Korean GDP, about half of the average allocation (1.3 percent) of OECD member countries (OECD 2009). Despite the government's unwillingness to provide adequate resources, the Korean higher education system has expanded rapidly, largely due to intensive privatization.

What has been compromised in the record-breaking growth of higher education in Korea is the value of the "public good" in education. The Korean government has transferred responsibility and commitment for educating the general public to the private sector, more specifically, to the parents and students. This pattern is particularly noticeable in the tertiary education system. As shown in Figure 10.3, only slightly more than 10 percent of the Korean higher educational budget was provided by public funds.

The Korean case is one of the most extreme among OECD countries. The degree of financial responsibility on the part of parents and students far exceeds the case of Japan and the United States, which are known to have the most well-developed private educational systems. This pattern of over-privatization continues unabated in Korea.

LESSONS FROM THE KOREAN MODEL

Korea has transformed from the ruins of the civil war to become the world's eleventh largest economy. In this rapid and impressive transformation, the higher education system has played an essential role. This system can be encapsulated in three salient characteristics: The quantity is impressive, privatization is unprecedented, and the quality is varied. Several lessons may be drawn from the Korean model.

Functional Differentiation Among Universities and Colleges

The most critical issue that emerges from the Korean model is the strong need for rebuilding a coherent system of tertiary education, including lifelong learning, which provides a diversity of higher educational opportunities. To this end, Grubb et al. recommend "a structure that links individual colleges, universities, and other tertiary institutions, rather than simply a group of unrelated institutions" (Grubb et al. 2006, 63). The California State University System is an example of a coherent higher educational system that provides an equal educational opportunity to a student population remarkable for its tremendous diversity in terms of both educational needs and personal backgrounds. As Douglass (2000) points out in his analysis of the Master Plan of the California System, this success is a result of long dialogue and hard-won compromise between the various stakeholders with conflicting views and interests. Like the land grant universities of other states, the California system has successfully established a higher educational institution system with reasonable functional differentiation among colleges and universities that successfully meets diverse and unique educational needs. Thus, the California system has been able to not only meet the expanding demands of higher education but also build several world-class research universities. The California university system has played an essential role in helping California's economy become the world's tenth largest. This is a truly remarkable achievement.

The difficulty in establishing a higher educational system with efficient functional differentiation stems from the fact that the Korean government has relied heavily upon the private sector to meet the expanding demand for higher educational opportunities. It is difficult to establish a coherent and well-balanced educational system when approximately 80 percent of higher educational needs are met by private institutions and private funding. A comprehensive master plan has to be prepared to guide the process of expansion, so that the educational system will not be guided by private sector interests.

A couple of important conclusions may be drawn from the Korean experience. First, the higher educational system has to clearly differentiate between research universities, teaching universities, and vocational colleges. Each individual college and university should develop their own unique system and structure for finance, curriculum, faculty recruitment, and student admission policy according to their missions and functions. The different levels and types of institutions should be coordinated so that, for example, a vocational college graduate would be able to transfer to a four-year university for a doctoral degree. Faculty should also be able to transfer between different types of schools, depending on their ability and interests. However, teaching universities should maintain their commitment to the mission of teaching and instruction by carrying out teaching-related research, education, and vocational training.

Second, there has to be a governance system for universities and colleges of similar types and functions. An autonomous committee of post-secondary education on a central government level should manage the governance system. The committee should be responsible for higher education as well as lifelong education provision for adults and the elderly. Such a committee would be better able to foster and expand the idea of "public good" in education. The central or regional government should be responsible for providing and securing finance, while the individual institutions would manage their funds according to their unique needs and institutional environment. Universities and colleges would be granted freedom in the areas of faculty recruitment, curriculum development, classroom instruction, and student admission policy.

The Renewal of the Idea of the "Public Good" in Higher Education

The greatest challenge for public education in Korea is restoring the *public* aspect of public education. After several decades of the central government's lack of willingness to provide the necessary resources for public education, policymakers, politicians, and even scholars have lost their critical perspective regarding the authentic and real meaning of the "public good" in education. It is the central government's responsibility to fund and provide adequate public education.

The idea of the "public good" in higher education can be promoted and reinforced by the national government providing the necessary resources for all citizens. Interestingly, the only consistent policy in Korean public education during the last sixty years has been the principle of exporting financial responsibility from the government to the so-called beneficiaries, i.e. students and parents. Parents have been forced to share the financial burden with the national government. Consequently, the public's fundamental right to be educated has been reduced to a form of economic behavior, and major educational decisions are made on the basis of profit motives. The element of the public good in education has been replaced by the market principle. An individual's right to education has turned into profit seeking commercial behavior. This has undermined the legitimacy of the public good in Korean higher education.

The trend toward privatization was initially introduced during the Japanese colonial era in order to suppress or limit the public's educational opportunities. Under the American military administration during the second half of the 1950s, privatization was a necessary, temporary strategy used to cope with the rapidly expanding demand for higher education. Unfortunately, what was supposed to be a temporary measure has become permanent. Privatization has its limits in terms of both quantity and quality, especially the quality of teaching and research. Building a world-class university, for example, requires a tremendous amount of funding and resources, which cannot solely be driven by Korean parents' willingness to sacrifice for their children's education.

The Making of an Internationally Competitive Research University

Rapid academic growth, led by privatization, has resulted in a great disparity in the quality of higher education. Korean higher education is a mixture of simple custodial institutions, diploma mills, vocational colleges, comprehensive universities, and a top-level research university. As Kim (2007a) shows, a self-aware and self-empowering program of a particular institution can result in the creation of a leading-edge research university in a peripheral country like Korea. Some of the Korean flagship universities are examples of such a development. The graduate programs of Seoul National University (SNU), Korea Advanced Institute of Science and Technology (KAIST), and Korea University have recently become very competitive by global standards. *The Times* ranked SNU twenty-seventh among the world's top fifty universities for engineering and Information Technology in 2009. The overall ranking of SNU has jumped from ninety-third in 2005 to forty-seventh in the 2009 survey. Kim (2007a) dubbed this impressive ascendance in world rankings "a great leap forward" (Kim 2007a).

A number of factors may help explain this impressive achievement at the top-level universities in Korea. First is the fundamental strength of the secondary educational system. Students enter flagship universities only after top-quality preparation. According to an international comparison published by the OECD, Korean students in the secondary education level ranked among the top three countries in problem-solving skills and mathematical abilities. Thus, it is not surprising that SNU, which admits only the top-tier students, has the potential for becoming a world-class university.

A second factor is the quality of the undergraduate education at SNU. According to the Survey of Earned Doctorates conducted by University of Chicago's NORC, SNU (3,420 recipients), was second only to UC–Berkeley (4,398 recipients), in the number of undergraduates who earned doctoral degrees in the United States between 1997 and 2006 (NORC 2008). SNU's undergraduate programs have been an excellent training ground for graduate programs in American research universities since the 1960s (Jenkins and Riesman 1968).

Finally, the Korean intellectual tradition of a strong and committed relationship between a mentor and his disciples has provided a productive and potent academic force for modern graduate programs. Thus, the ancient native academic traditions have been a vital resource for empowering the international competitiveness of Korean research universities in the modern era of a global information-based economy.

REFERENCES

Altbach, G. "The Private Sector In Asian Higher Education." *International Higher Education* 29 (2002): 10–11.

Douglass, J. A. *The California Idea And American Higher Education: 1850 to the 1960 Master Plan*. Palo Alto, CA: Stanford University Press, 2000.

Grubb, W. N., R. Sweet, M. Gallagher, and O. Tuomi. *Thematic Review of Tertiary Education: A Country Report of Korea*. Paris: Organization for Economic Cooperation and Development, 2006.

Institute for the Translation of Korea Classics (ITKC). "Selected Tombstone Inscriptions." *The Bum-Am' Papers*, vol. 51 (Seoul 2001): 442–63.

Jenks, C. S., and D. Riesman. *Academic Revolution*. Garden City, NY: Doubleday, 1968.

Korean Educational Development Institute (KEDI) and Ministry of Education (MOE). *Education Statistics Yearbook*. Seoul: Korean Education Development Institute (Annual).

Kim, K. S. *An Introduction to Historical Sociology of Education*. Seoul: Educational Science Press, 1999.

———. "A Great Leap Forward To Excellence in Research at Seoul National University 1994–2006." *Asia Pacific Education Review* 8(1) (2007a): 1–11.

———. "The Formation of a Divided Higher Education System in Korea after Liberation 1945–1948: The Rise of Seoul National University and Kim Il-Sung University." *The SNU Journal of Education* 27 (2007b): 1–38.

Kim and Woo. "Is it Pyrrhic Victory?: Over-Privatization and Universal Access in Tertiary Education of Korea." *Asia Pacific Education Review* 10 (1) (2009): 125–37.

Lee, K. B. *A New History of Korea*. Trans. by E. W. Wager and E. J. Shultz. Seoul: Ilchogak, 1984.

Lee. S. H. "Korean Higher Education: History and Future Challenges." Pp. 145–74 in *Asian Universities: Historical Perspectives and Contemporary Challenges*. Edited by P. G. Altbach and T. Umakoshi. Baltimore, MD: Johns Hopkins University Press, 2004.

Legge, J. *The Chinese Classics*. London: Oxford University Press, 1892.

Min, W. "Chinese Higher Education: The Legacy of the Past and the Context of the Future." Pp. 53–84 in *Asian Universities: Historical Perspectives and Contemporary Challenges*. Edited by P. G. Altbach and T. Umakoshi. Baltimore, MD: Johns Hopkins University Press, 2004.

NORC *Survey of Earned Doctorates*. www.nsf.gov/statistics/srvydoctorates/2006/sed06data.cfm. Accessed on August 22, 2008.

OECD. *Education at a Glance: OECD indicators*. Paris: OECD, 2005, 2009.

Oh, S. C. *The Shaping Of Colonial Elementary Education In Korea*. Seoul: Educational Science Press, 2004.

Times Higher Education—QS. *The QS World University Rankings 2009*. www.timeshighereducation.co.uk/hybrid.asp?typeCode=430&pubCode=1&navcode=105. Accessed on October 22, 2009.

Trow, M. "The Second Transformation of American Secondary Education" *International Journal of Comparative Sociology* 2 (1961) 144–65.

UNESCO *Educational Condition In The Republic Of Korea: A Preliminary And Factual Report of the UNESCO/UNKRA Education Planning Mission*. Paris: UNESCO 1952.

———. *Rebuilding Education In The Republic Of Korea: The Final Report of the UNESCO/UNKRA Education Planning Mission to Korea*. Paris: UNESCO, 1953.

NOTES

1. This paper is a revision of first author's paper presented at Hurst Seminar on Higher Education and Equality of Opportunity, Ben-Gurion University, and published on *APER* 10(1) 2009. Funding of this research was in part provided by NRF of Korea (Outstanding Scholars Program) and Academic Leadership Institute for Competency-Based Education (BK21) of SNU.

2. Table A.1.2, p. 37.

3. The "letter hall" is a kind of home-based school or village school. In Korean it is called "Sodang."

4. The other contrasting but inseparable component of Confucian philosophy is *ki* (*Ch'i* in Chinese), which emphasizes the energizing component. See "The Culture of the Neo-Confucian Literati" (Lee 1984, 217–20), for the detailed discussion of Korean Confucian tradition.

5. See Kim and Woo (2009). "Is it Pyrrhic Victory?: Over-Privatization and Universal Access in Tertiary Education of Korea," *Asia Pacific Education Review* 10(1): 125–37.

11

Disparities in Access to Higher Education in India

Persistent Issues and the Changing Context

N. Jayaram

> Education is an essential mechanism for inclusion through the creation of social opportunities. It is, therefore, essential that in addition to ensuring that no student is denied the opportunity to participate in higher education due to financial constraints, access to education for economically and historically socially underprivileged students is enhanced in a substantially more effective manner.
>
> —National Knowledge Commission (2007, 60)

In 2007, three universities in India celebrated the sesquicentenary of their existence. It was in 1857 that the first three universities were established in the country—at Bombay (now Mumbai), Calcutta (now Kolkata), and Madras (now Chennai)—following Thomas Babington Macaulay's *Minute* (of 2 February 1835) and its reaffirmation by Charles Wood's *Despatch* (of 19 July 1854) and the recommendation of a Committee (appointed on 26 January 1855) (Ashby and Anderson 1966, 54–146). For the British rulers, the purpose of higher education in India was clear: it was to evolve a small class of English-educated Indians who may act, in Macaulay's words, as "interpreters between us and millions whom we govern—a class of persons Indian in blood and color, but English in tastes, in opinions, in morals and intellect" (in Sharp 1965, 116). It was never their intention to spread modern education among the masses.[1]

Modeled after the University of London (established in 1836), the three pioneer universities were largely affiliating and examining bodies with very little intellectual life of their own. All the universities that were subsequently established developed in an isomorphic fashion set on the pattern of the original universities. They emphasized English, which not only was taught as a language but also was made the exclusive medium of instruction: while the secondary-school leaving examination was conducted only in English till 1937, English was exclusively used at the university stage right through the colonial period. The content was biased in favor of the languages and the humanities and against science and technology.

The British educational implantation thus succeeded in creating the first generation of indigenous English-educated industrial, commercial, political, and intellectual class in India. This class was drawn mainly from the traditional literati—for example, the Bengali Kayasthas, the Tamil Brahmans, and the Marathi Chitpavans—and the well-to-do in the urban centers. That in due course this English-educated class became the undoing of the British rule in India[2] is a different story. What is important for the theme of this chapter is that the question of inequitable access became an issue right from the inception of modern higher education in the country and has remained alive to this day.

Since independence (in 1947) the Government of India has been addressing the issue of inequitable access to higher education. However, the issue has proved to be intractable, as the context in which it has been addressed has been changing. For brevity as well as for heuristic convenience, two contrasting contexts can be delineated: (1) that of *state patronage*, extending roughly from 1951 (beginning of the program of planned socioeconomic development) to the end of the 1980s, and (2) the era of *laissez-faireism*, following structural adjustment and liberalization, since the 1990s. This chapter examines the vicissitude of access to higher education in these two contexts.

HIGHER EDUCATION UNDER STATE PATRONAGE

The University Education Commission (1948–1949) (popularly known as the Radhakrishnan Commission), appointed immediately after India attained independence, emphasized the importance of higher education in the all-round development of the country. Successive commissions and committees on education and the governmental policy statements (including the National Policy on Education, 1986 and the Program of Action, 1992) following them have highlighted (a) the importance of higher education in establishing an egalitarian society and (b) the need for equalization of educational opportunities. This has naturally meant addressing the inequalities in opportunity for education in terms of caste and class, gender, rural-urban areas, and regions. Assuming the role of patron of higher education, the state embarked on a two-pronged strategy: (i) expanding and broadening the opportunities for higher education through planned development (called Five-Year Plans) and (ii) enhancing the accessibility for sections of the population—scheduled castes, scheduled tribes, backward classes, women, etc.—through protective discrimination policies (reservation of seats in colleges and universities) and ameliorative programs (fee concessions, free hostel facilities, compensatory education, etc.).

Expansion of and Participation in Higher Education

Not surprisingly, under state patronage, higher education has expanded phenomenally: at the time of her independence (in 1947), India had twenty universities and 496 colleges catering to 241,369 students; now it has 437 university-level institutions, 136 research institutes, and 16,009 colleges (see Table 11.1) catering to almost 11.8 million students (see Table 11.2) (MHRD 2007 and 2008)[3]—the third largest academic system in the world (behind China and the United States). In absolute terms, apparently, the opportunity for higher education has expanded.[4] However, the phenomenal increase in the population over the last five-and-a-half decades[5] has negatively impacted on the opportunity structure in higher education.

Estimates of the participation rate vary from a conservative 7 percent (NKC 2007, 43) to a liberal 10 percent. According to the Ministry of Human Resource

Table 11.1   Higher Education Institutions in India (2004-05)

Type of Institution	Number
I—Universities	
1 Central Universities	18
2 State Universities	275
3 Institutions Established under State Legislature Acts	5
4 Institutions Deemed to be Universities	96
5 Institutions of National Importance	13
6 Research Institutes	136
Total	543
II—Colleges	
1 General Education	10,377
2 Engineering, Technology and Architecture	1,302
3 Medical (Allopathy/Ayurveda/Homeopathy/Unani)	817
4 Teachers Training	1,082
5 Others (Law, Management, MCA, IT, Agriculture, etc.)	2,431
Total	16,009

Source: Adapted from MHRD 2007: Table 1, pp. 1-3, 2008: Table 5, pp. 10

Table 11.2   Stage-wise Enrollment in Higher Education

Course	Total Enrollment (000)	% Girls in (2)	SC Enrollment (000)	% Girls in (4)	ST Enrollment (000)	% Girls in (6)
(1)	(2)	(3)	(4)	(5)	(6)	(7)
PhD/DSc/DPhil	55.4	41.2	3.2	27.0	1.3	40.7
MA	469.3	46.6	75.9	34.5	23.1	38.2
MSc	198.7	45.7	20.7	34.8	5.5	39.4
MCom	122.3	34.1	11.0	31.4	3.6	37.0
BA/BA (Hons)	3772.2	43.9	562.9	37.8	196.2	36.5
BSc/BSc (Hons)	1490.8	38.9	168.3	36.2	49.8	33.4
BCom/BCom (Hons)	1465.0	36.6	125.3	32.5	48.4	35.2
BE/BSc Engineering/ BArch.	696.6	23.7	59.3	20.6	21.5	19.6
Medicine, Dentistry, Nursing, Pharmacy, Ayurveda, Unani, etc.	256.7	34.7	29.6	46.4	9.5	41.8
BEd/BT	155.2	43.8	20.0	41.6	9.1	41.7
Others	3095.1	37.9	184.6	44.8	66.2	41.5
Total	11777.3	39.4	1261.0	37.2	434.2	36.3

Source: Adapted from MHRD 2007: Table 3, pp. 9-13, 2008: Table 6, pp. 13

Development (MHRD 2007, 61; 2008, 16), only 9.97 percent of the population in the eighteen-to-twenty-four age-group are currently enrolled in higher education programs. The Government of India itself has set modest targets—of 15 percent by the end of the Tenth Five-Year Plan (2002–2007), and 30 percent by 2020. The National Knowledge Commission (NKC 2007, 43) too recommends a modest target of 15 percent by 2015. If the rate of growth of enrollment during the last two decades is any indicator, even these modest targets appear ambitious (see Parhar 2002). That is, despite the phenomenal increase in enrollment, the vast majority of the youth in the eighteen-to-twenty-four age-group not only remain outside the sphere of higher education but also will remain so for decades to come.

Regional Imbalances

There are regional variations in participation rates in higher education. In as many as eighteen of the thirty-five states and union territories, the gross enrollment ratio in higher education is below the national average of 9.97 percent. The state of Delhi (the national capital) (37.25 percent) has the highest percentage of students enrolled in the eighteen-to-twenty-four years age-group, followed by the union territory of Chandigarh (37.01 percent) and the states of Pondicherry (17.33 percent) and Himachal Pradesh (14.10 percent). The states of Arunachal Pradesh (5.85 percent), Assam (6.94 percent), Bihar (6.02 percent), Jammu and Kashmir (6.54 percent), Nagaland (4.70 percent), Rajasthan (6.04 percent), and Tripura (6.16 percent) have a participation rate of less than 7 percent (MHRD 2007, 61). Thus, not only is the rate of participation in higher education low, but also there is serious regional imbalance in access to higher education.

One aspect of this regional imbalance needs special mention: most institutions of higher education are located in urban areas. Obviously, this favors the urban well-to-do sections of the population, just as it constrains rural people, especially the indigent among them, from accessing higher education. Furthermore, accessing higher education by the rural youth has necessarily meant migration to urban areas. All this has aggravated the social disparities in terms of rural-urban areas.

Streams of Enrollment

Discussing the issue of access, the term "higher education" suggests too much of homogeneity. Level-wise and faculty-wise analyses of the enrollment data for the institutions under the umbrella of the University Grants Commission for 2005–2006 (UGC 2005–06) yield interesting results. The vast majority of students (88.9 percent) were enrolled in undergraduate programs. Students enrolling in postgraduate and research programs accounted for only 9.42 percent and 0.64 percent respectively; the remaining 1.04 percent enrolled in diploma or certificate programs. The affiliated colleges account for most of the enrollment at the undergraduate (90.1 percent) and postgraduate (66.2 percent) levels, the remaining enrolling in university departments or constituent colleges. Faculty-wise, only 16.42 percent of the students were enrolled in professional programs and a whopping 83.58 percent in the "liberal" programs—arts (including humanities and social sciences), 45.12 percent; science, 20.45 percent; and commerce and management, 18.01 percent.

The data on enrollment in higher education in general collated by MHRD (see Table 11.1) confirm these observations. The majority of students (57.13 percent, the single largest category) are in the first-degree "liberal" programs, namely, BA, BSc, and BCom (general or honors). Those enrolled in the "liberal" postgraduate (MA, MSc, and MCom) and research (PhD, DSc, or DPhil) programs constitute 6.71 percent and 0.47 percent respectively. Those enrolled in engineering/technology (5.91 percent), medical (2.18 percent) and education (1.32 percent) programs together constitute less than 10 percent. Faculty-wise, those in arts (36.01 percent), science (14.35 percent), and commerce (13.48 percent) together constitute 63.84 percent of the enrollment.

Thus, the enrollment data from both UGC and MHRD suggest the preponderance of student enrollment in "liberal" programs. With the liberal programs remaining nonvocational in nature, those graduating through this stream contribute to the ever-increasing pool of unemployed or underemployed graduates.[6] For such graduates, while higher education may have some social status significance, it does not seem to necessarily bring economic returns.

The Gender Differential

In 1950–1951, the percentage of women in total enrollment in higher education was only 10, and this percentage has peaked at nearly 40 in 2004. Even at lower (primary through secondary) levels of education, women's enrollment has never crossed 50 percent (see MHRD 2007: x). In 2004, the number of women students enrolled per 100 male students at all levels of higher education was sixty-five, thus revealing the persistence of gender inequality in higher education. Even so, this is almost a fivefold increase in five decades. Thus, gender disparity notwithstanding, women seem to be having greater access to higher education now than ever.

Analyzing the UGC data for 2002–2003, we find that, in terms of level of education, women are marginally better represented in postgraduate (42 percent) and undergraduate (40 percent) programs, than in research (38 percent) and diploma/certificate (33.7 percent) programs. However, as compared to their male counterparts, women students gravitate more toward arts programs (51.1 percent). Twenty percent of them are enrolled in science programs, 16.5 percent in commerce and management programs, and the remaining 12.4 percent in other programs. Similar are the observations from the MHRD data (see Table 11.2). Thus, women seem to be concentrated in programs which, while enhancing their social status, are devoid of employment significance.[7]

However, the access to higher education for women is not the same across the country. There are significant regional variations in women's enrollment in higher education (UGC 2002–03). In the south Indian state of Kerala, which is regarded as a "model state" for social development initiatives, women account for 60 percent of all enrollment in higher education; they are closely followed by their counterparts in the states of Goa (58.5 percent) and Punjab (52.75 percent). In seventeen states, women had higher enrollment than the national percentage of 39.8. The state of Bihar, which has the dubious distinction of having the lowest literacy rate for women, also has the lowest percentage (23.8 percent) of women's enrollment in higher education.

The role of education in empowering women and overcoming their gender-based socioeconomic disabilities has been underscored by several governmental committees and the National Policy on Education (1986). Since education is a concurrent subject (for which both the central and the state governments have responsibility), some states have also been proactive. Thus, there are 1,650 colleges and five universities meant exclusively for women. Many states have opened hostel facilities for girls. In the western state of Gujarat, since 1986, college education is free of cost for all women students. All this notwithstanding, the negative traditional attitude toward women's education persists, especially in rural areas and among the socioeconomically backward castes and classes.

The Caste, Tribe and Religion Differentials

India is a hierarchical society where the modern class system (defined as socioeconomic status and particularly occupational status) is superimposed on the traditional *jati* (caste) system. Socioeconomic inequalities have been cumulative, and the privileges/disadvantages for sections of the population have persisted. To address the inequalities based on primordial basis, the republican constitution of India has identified chronically socioculturally oppressed or indigent communities—scheduled castes, scheduled tribes, and backward classes—for protective discrimination and ameliorative programs. An important component of this discrimination and the related programs to set right the age-old inequalities and disadvantages is higher education.[8]

As per the Constitution of India, based on their population (as in 1961), 15 percent of the seats in all educational institutions, including universities and colleges, receiving financial assistance from the government are reserved for students belonging to the scheduled castes, and 7.5 percent, for students belonging to the scheduled tribes. For candidates from these categories, the maximum age for admission is relaxed by three years and the minimum marks for admission is reduced by 5 percent.

Apart from this, several state governments have reservation of seats for students belonging to backward castes and communities. In some states, almost 50 percent of the seats are so reserved. The current Congress Party–led United Progressive Alliance government has reserved, in addition, 27 percent of seats in all central government run/financed institutions to backward classes.[9] Given the inadequate educational opportunities, especially in the professional realm, this move of the government (as also its proposal to extend the policy of reservation to private educational institutions) has resulted in public protests. The move was upheld by the Supreme Court of India on 10 April 2008 (*Deccan Herald*, Bangalore, 11 April 2008, 1).

Besides the reservation of seats, the scheduled caste and scheduled tribe students enrolling in higher education are extended fee concessions and hostel facilities. To enable them to overcome their academic handicaps and compete with the general category of students, the University Grants Commission

(UGC) has introduced a scheme of remedial coaching. Under the National Overseas Scholarship Scheme, the meritorious students from these categories (seventeen scheduled castes and three scheduled tribes every year) are eligible for financial assistance to pursue higher studies in science, engineering, and technology abroad: since 1954–1955, when the scheme was introduced, in all 751 awards were offered and 545 availed (MSJE 2003–04, 15).

The policy of protective discrimination in higher education has undoubtedly benefited the scheduled castes and scheduled tribes. Steadily, though slowly, the enrollment of students belonging to these categories has been increasing. In 2004, the scheduled castes constituted 10.70 percent of the enrollment in higher education, and the scheduled tribes, 3.78 percent (see Table 11.2). Though these figures are far below the 15 and 7.5 percent reservation for these categories respectively, the scheduled castes appear to have fared better than the scheduled tribes in accessing higher education. This is explained by the fact that the scheduled castes are more urbanized and politically more powerful than the scheduled tribes. Also, the former made a foray into higher education much earlier than the latter (see Chitnis 1981).

The students from the reserved category are concentrated in the arts programs (scheduled castes, 50.66 percent; scheduled tribes, 50.51 percent). More scheduled caste students (14.99 percent) than scheduled tribe students (12.73 percent) access science programs. Those accessing medical and engineering programs are less than 5 percent among these categories. Similarly, only a very small percentage of students from these categories enter the elite institutions of higher learning like the Indian Institutes of Technology and the Indian Institutes of Management. Thus, while there has been noteworthy progress in the enrollment of reserved category candidates in higher education, they still have "a long way to go" before matching the enrollment and participation rates of the general category students (ibid.).

There are significant differences in terms of socio-religious categories. Based on an analysis of the National Sample Survey Organization's (2004–2005) 61st Round data, the Sachar Committee on the status of the Muslim community of India found that "There is hardly any differences between the share in the student and the total population for different socio-religious categories" (Government of India 2006, 72) in the six-to-thirteen years of age cohort. However,

> [T]he gap builds up as one moves to higher age cohorts [see Table 11.3]; the share in the student population for the SC/ST [scheduled caste/scheduled tribe], Muslim and OBC [other backward class] categories become smaller than their shares in the population in the higher age cohorts. The gaps are larger for SCs/ STs and Muslims than for Hindu OBCs. . . . In some cases the deficits are greater for Muslims than for SCs/STs in higher age groups. (ibid.)

It must be noted that other minority socio-religious categories enjoy better educational opportunities. This suggests that the educational backwardness of Muslims (the single largest minority religious community) in India has less to do with its minority status per se than with sociocultural reasons (see Jayaram 1990b).

Open Universities and Distance Education Programs

To increase the opportunity for higher education to the educationally disadvantaged (those without the conventional qualifications for entry into higher education and those who have had no other opportunity to make up for the lost time) and the economically weaker sections of society, the avenue of distance education is now open. As compared to conventional university education, the distance mode of education can have better spread and coverage, its recurring expenditure is low, it is cost-effective, and it is flexible, both for the administration and for the students. Distance education at the tertiary level is offered through open universities specially established for the purpose and directorates/offices in some existing universities.

The Indira Gandhi National Open University (IGNOU) (established in 1985) coordinates the distance education programs at the national level. With 101 different academic programs comprising 900 courses, IGNOU is the largest open university in South Asia. It has a network of forty-eight regional centers, six sub-regional centers, and 1,271 study centers spread over the country. The success of the IGNOU experiment is proved by its steadily increasing enrollment: from less than 4,000 students in 1987 to over 160,000 in 1998 to nearly 1.32 million in 2005.

Table 11.3   **Students Currently Studying as a Proportion of Population by Age-Groups (2004–2005)**

Age-Group	Hindus			Muslims	Other Minorities
	General	OBC	SC/ST		
6-13 years	19.1 (17.3)	36.1 (35.5)	25.7 (27.4)	14.0 (15.1)	5.1 (4.8)
14-15 years	24.3 (19.9)	36.1 (35.2)	21.4 (25.2)	12.2 (14.5)	6.0 (5.3)
16-17 years	28.9 (21.1)	33.7 (35.0)	20.2 (24.7)	10.7 (14.0)	6.3 (5.1)
18-22 years	34.0 (20.8)	30.5 (34.4)	17.7 (25.5)	10.2 (13.9)	7.6 (5.5)
23 years and above	35.6 (23.9)	29.2 (35.1)	18.3 (24.1)	7.4 (10.9)	9.5 (5.9)

Note: Figures in parentheses report the share of each socio-religious group in the total population of that age-group.
OBC = Other Backward Class; SC = Scheduled Caste; ST = Scheduled Tribe.
Source: Adapted from Government of India 2006: Table 4.4, p. 72.

The concepts of open university and distance education are laudable, especially in view of increasing the coverage and equalizing opportunities. However, the way open university programs are run in most universities is far from satisfactory. Whipping up unrealistic aspirations combined with the non-fulfillment of promises leaves many candidates in the lurch. Poor quality of study materials, inadequacy and ineffectiveness of the contact programs, and lack of study-center facilities have virtually ritualized such programs. Obviously, there is a perception that the products of distance education programs are of poor quality.

Social Mobility or Status Retention?

Sociological studies on access to higher education have revealed that the spread of higher education has no doubt benefited the first-generation entrants into the post-secondary phase, and to that extent there has been upward social mobility and embourgeoisement. Given the persistence of socioeconomic inequalities and cultural frameworks for life choices, however, higher education has functioned more as a status stabilizer than as a channel of upward social mobility (see Jayaram 1978; see also Kaul 1993).

It must be emphasized that inequality in educational opportunities does not start at the higher level. The school system in India is hierarchical in terms of both the quality of instruction that the different schools offer and the socioeconomic background of the students whom they enroll. The prestigious schools known for the high quality of schooling they offer are more expensive than government-funded colleges and universities. Obviously, those who can afford spend more on the school education of their wards, and on private tuitions, eventually reap the benefit of the highly subsidized higher education system. Alternatively, private higher education, both in India and abroad, is also open to them. Thus, the operation of the "Mathew principle"—that "to him that hath, shall be given, and he shall have more abundance," as declared in St. Mathew's Gospel (13:12)—in the Indian education system, reinforces inequitable access to higher education

LAISSEZ-FAIREISM AND HIGHER EDUCATION[10]

After a long period of protected expansion with state patronage until the mid-1980s, higher education in India has been passing through a period of stunted growth and uncertain future. A complex turn of events has thrown higher education into a vortex of change. The foremost among such events was the adoption by the Government of India in 1990 of structural adjustment reforms. Influenced by the World Bank–International Monetary Fund combine, structural adjustment has meant the gradual withdrawal of state patronage for higher education and a coterminous privatization of that sphere. However, the government itself is confused and has been dithering about the policy to be adopted on this matter. In this part, I will analyze the implications of the changing context on the issue of access to higher education.

Market Economy and the Changing Demand for Courses

The structural adjustment reforms adopted since the early 1990s have had a significant impact on the demand structure of higher education. It is revealing to analyze the data on the rate of growth of student enrollment in universities and colleges since 1983–1984. For ten years, from 1983–1984 to 1992–1993, there was a steady increase in enrollment: 17.7 percent between 1983–1984 and 1987–1988, and 27.4 percent between 1987–1988 and 1992–1993. However, the next ten years, from 1992–1993 to 2002–2003, have seen a steady decline in enrollment: 23.8 percent between 1992–1993 and 1997–1998, and 21.3 percent between 1997–1998 and 2002–2003 (UGC 2002–03, Appendix III, 255).

At last, the expansion of traditional programs of study seems to have outstripped the demand for them by students. While, generally, the brighter students have always avoided these programs, even the not-so-bright ones appear to be turning their backs on them now, invariably opting for professional programs such as medicine, computer science, information technology, and business management. If they cannot make it to any of these, they would rather try their hand at some courses with narrow but specialized job prospects, such as packaging, plastic technology, fabric designing, and air conditioning and refrigeration. The fact that good students are no longer taking up basic science courses has seriously affected the academic programs of reputed science institutions such as the Indian Institute of Science (Bangalore), which has now come out with incentive schemes to urge meritorious students to take basic sciences at the graduate level.

The lack of link between conventional courses and the job market seems to have become too apparent for students and their parents.[11] At best, the employers—not only in the private sector, but also in the government—use the conventional degrees as sieves for filtering the large number of applicants for the limited number of jobs. The unemployment situation, particularly among conventional degree holders, has worsened over the decades (see endnote 6), with the government no longer able to absorb them in public employment. Aggravating the situation is the economic liberalization program, which demands knowledge and skills generally not possessed by conventional degree holders. It is only natural that those who have been using conventional courses as waiting rooms are either seeking early entry into the job market at lower levels, with the option of obtaining formal university qualifications later, or entering courses that carry better job prospects. Those who still seek conventional graduate courses are generally the leftovers and dregs, or the first-generation students from rural and indigent backgrounds, especially those who are supported by financial assistance from the government.[12]

While the demand for conventional courses has tapered off, the demand for professional and other allied courses has been incessantly increasing, in spite of escalating unemployment even among the professional degree holders. Many educational entrepreneurs are unduly eager to offer such "moneymaking" courses in medicine, dentistry, nursing, engineering and technology, business management, computer science, biotechnology, and education. Many of these private institutions are inadequately equipped to offer any education, let alone professional education.

To enhance their marketability and employment prospects, students taking professional courses try to specialize in a given field or obtain qualifications and skills in some sophisticated courses not generally offered by the universities. A glance at Indian newspapers reveals the number and variety of courses currently offered by various institutions outside the sphere of the university system. These institutions, and the academic entrepreneurs who run them, seem to be extraordinarily sensitive to the variety of knowledge and skills demanded by the changing market economy. They are also extremely flexible, both in what they have to offer and how they go about offering it. While the demand for skills and knowledge is their raison d'être, the maintenance of quality is their badge of success. As in any commodity market, one has to pay more for better-quality education, and this means limited access to such education.

It is important to note that in spite of (or essentially because of) the fact that they are outside the orbit of the university system, such institutions of higher learning have not only survived but even thrived. Some of them have earned a niche for themselves in higher education, and even recognition from academia and employers abroad. As statutorily established academic entities, the Indian universities have sadly lacked competition, and they brook no competition either. With the liberalization of the economy and the state gradually shedding its responsibility for higher education—and with the UGC being no more than a mute witness to the gradual decaying of the university as a public institution—the Indian university system is progressively becoming nominalized and marginalized. Irrespective of one's ideological predilections, it is now conceded that the future of higher education in India will be determined by the market economy and the private sector. This has serious implications for equitable access to higher education, and it is in this context that the demand for reservation of seats in private educational institutions assumes significance.

Decline of State Patronage

While public expenditure on education in India has always been inadequate for meeting the needs of "education for all,"[13] throughout its history the state has highly subsidized higher education (Tilak 2004a). Structural adjustment has meant a drastic cut in public expenditure on higher education: between 1980–1990 and 1994–1995, the share of higher education in development (plan) expenditure decreased from 12.6 percent to 6 percent, whereas the share in maintenance (non-plan) expenditure declined from 14.2 percent to 11 percent (Tilak 1996). Overall, the allocation for higher education, which had peaked at 28 percent in the Fifth Five-Year Plan (1974–1979), has steadily declined in the successive Plans to just 8 percent in the Tenth Five-Year Plan (2002–2007), which is the same as the allocation in the First Five-Year Plan (1951–1956).

The annual growth rate of public expenditure on university and higher education, which was 13.1 percent between 1980–1981 and 1985–1986, had fallen to 7.8 percent between 1980–1981 and 1995–1996 (Shariff and Ghosh 2000, 1400). As a proportion of total government expenditure, the share of higher education declined from 1.57 percent in 1990–1991 to 1.33 percent in 2001–2002. Considering the trends in per student expenditure—from Rs 7,676 in 1990–1991 to Rs 5,873 in 2001–2002 (in 1993–1994 prices)—the decline in public expenditure on higher education would appear even more drastic (Tilak 2004b, 2160–61).[14]

Thus, the state, which had hitherto been the dominant partner in funding higher education, is finding it harder even to maintain the same level of funding for higher education. Financial constraint, however, does not affect all sectors of higher education equally: invariably, non-professional courses are more adversely affected than their professional counterparts. Furthermore, the efforts to privatize higher education by encouraging private agencies to establish institutions of higher learning have enjoyed limited success in general education and non-professional courses. Thus, state universities and their affiliated colleges are the ones in the financial doldrums.

The gradual decline in state patronage of higher education has been accompanied by its inability to address the need for reforms within conventional higher education. The National Policy on Education (1985), its Program of Action (1986), and their review by the Acharya Ramamurti Committee (1991) were all pre–structural adjustment reform initiatives. Neither the phenomenal fall in the demand for conventional courses in the BA and BSc streams nor the remarkable spurt in the demand for courses in such areas as computer science and information technology, biotechnology, and management studies were anticipated. A policy revision taking into consideration the changing context of higher education is still due, and given the dynamics of coalition politics in the country, it will be a long wait!

Private Initiatives in Higher Education

The void created by the waning state patronage for higher education is now being filled by private entrepreneurial initiatives. Two types of private initiatives in Indian higher education can be identified. First, there are private colleges and institutes that are formally affiliated with a university. If such institutions belong to the minority communities, they enjoy certain administrative privileges granted by the Constitution of India. In all academic matters the private colleges and institutes are governed by the university. Many of these private colleges receive financial assistance from the government to the tune of 80 to 85 percent of their expenditure; they collect a small fee from the students to make up the balance. As such, these colleges must observe the grant-in-aid code formulated by the government, including the provision of reservation of seats for students from the scheduled castes and scheduled tribes. At the other end of the spectrum are the unaided private colleges that have to generate their own financial resources. They have considerable leeway concerning administration and the collection of fees from the students; as of now, they are not bound by the rules of reservation.

In contrast are the privately owned and managed colleges, institutes, and academies conducting courses outside the purview of the universities.[15] Typically, they offer courses in such areas as aviation and pilot training, glass technology, plastic technology, packaging, corporate secretaryship, marketing management, financial management, foreign trade, portfolio management, operations research, hotel management and catering technology, tourism administration, software marketing, computer applications, fashion design, and beauty aids. Unlike the diploma courses offered by the polytechnics, some of these courses offered by well-known institutes are accredited with professional bodies in the area, often even outside the country.

Another educational innovation that has come from private initiatives is the concept of the "twinning program." This program involves collaboration between two educational systems, with both systems taking responsibility for teaching and training of students and one of them holding the right to award educational credentials. The program may involve collaboration between an Indian institution and a system abroad (international educational collaboration), or between two systems of education within the country (intra-national educational collaboration).

International educational collaboration is slowly gathering momentum. In India, it was originally devised as a way out of the governmental stranglehold on private institutions of higher learning and the enervating rigidity of the university system. Such international educational collaboration is not, however, confined to professional education. To meet the demand for high-quality first-degree education, especially in areas such as computer science, some private colleges have entered into twinning programs with universities abroad.

Such international educational collaboration involving twinning programs is significantly different from the more direct marketing endeavors of foreign educational establishments. Several universities—not necessarily reputed ones—in Anglophone countries such as Australia, Canada, New Zealand, the United Kingdom, and the United States are enrolling Indian students for their educational programs.[16] Often there is an Internet-based distance education component, but most of them have arrangements with reputed institutes in the country for offering contact programs for students taking these foreign university examinations. Some of these universities even hold educational fairs in Indian cities to familiarize those interested in pursuing their educational programs.

All this necessarily implies opening the sphere of Indian higher education to foreign educational establishments, and the Government of India is now processing a legislation to regulate the establishment and governance of foreign universities in the country. For more than a century, the well-to-do in India have been sending their wards abroad for higher education, with the most talented students obtaining fellowships from the Government of India or foreign foundations. Given the globalization of higher education, such facilities are now being brought into the country. This is akin, no doubt, to the operation of multinational companies in industry and business and as such, it cannot be expected to be free of socioeconomic costs, especially concerning the equitable access to educational facilities. It is well known that such high-quality education involving multinational arrangements, often involving job placements, is expensive, especially as compared to the absurdly low-cost education offered by Indian colleges and universities.

The Uncertain Future

The structural adjustment reforms adopted by the Government of India since 1990 have necessitated a policy of disinvestment of the public sector and open privatization in various spheres of the economy. For higher education, however, the government is hesitant to pursue this policy vigorously. Rather, a different strategy is in operation: there is now a moratorium on the establishment of new educational institutions (especially of the conventional type) under the public sector and an imposition of ceilings on student strength in the existing institutions. The academic profession is being downsized through

a freeze on recruitment, reduction in the number of teachers, and rationaliza-
tion of teachers' work. There is a proposal to introduce the contract system
for hiring teachers in the future. At the same time, self-financing colleges (especially in areas of professional education) are encouraged, and the proposal
to raise fees in the public higher education institutions is on the anvil. These
measures, it is feared, will raise the cost of higher education and make it less
accessible to the masses, on the one hand, and—given the government's inability to regulate the private educational institutions—adversely affect the
quality of education, on the other (Kumar and Sharma 2003).

Closely related to the foregoing trends is the internationalization of higher
education referred to earlier. This is in conformity with the policy of liberalization of education as a service sector under the General Agreement on Trade
in Services (Bhushan 2004). While the requisite legislative provisions are
not yet in place, the education sector "opened up" in April 2004, and foreign
universities and educational institutions (especially from the Anglophone
countries like Australia, Canada, the United Kingdom, and the United States)
have begun to offer competition to the existing educational institutions in the
country. As observed earlier, there is a fear that this might result in draining
resources from India, as well as introduce strong cultural and political influence by foreign countries (Kumar and Sharma 2003: 607).

The lack of a coherent long-term policy perspective is characteristic of
higher education in India today. While the Government of India—irrespective
of the ideological predilections of the party combinations in power—is committed to structural adjustment reforms and liberalization, which necessarily
implies gradual withdrawal of state patronage for higher education and the
privatization and internationalization of this sector, it appears to be dithering
on the issue. Ad hoc policies and the multiplicity of actors—the central and
state governments, the UGC, the All India Council for Technical Education,
the universities and colleges, and the emergent private sector—dealing with
the unfolding exigencies in higher education in their own way portend a period of stunted growth and uncertain future.

CONCLUSION: THE CHALLENGE OF CHANGE

The conventional university system in India, confronting as it is a systemic
crisis, has been incapable of introducing any significant educational innovation
or effectively implementing any educational reform. Given the mounting pressure for increasing accessibility and over-democratization, the trend in the universities is toward reducing everything to the lowest common denominator or
leveling down quality, rather than raising it. The Indian university system is ex-

traordinarily rigid and pronouncedly resistant to change: The impetus to change does not come from within the system. When experiments or innovations are introduced from outside, they are resisted; if enforced, they are ritualized.

The void created by the paralysis and drift of the conventional university system is being filled by private entrepreneurial initiatives. Thus, significant educational innovations and experiments are currently taking place in institutions outside the university orbit and in the private sector. In view of the rapid expansion of (and increasing variety in) knowledge and skills, there is enormous scope for educational innovations and initiatives. The private institutions have been more responsive to the demands of the economy and industry and the changing employment scenario. They have also shown their ability to match relevance with flexibility both in costs and regulation. This does not, however, mean that all private institutions are necessarily good. Many of them are brazenly commercial establishments out to swindle gullible people looking for better-quality education at affordable prices.

Privatization of higher education is apparently a fledgling but welcome trend: higher education requires it to maintain creativity, adaptability, and quality, while the economic trail of liberalization and globalization demands it. Considering the chronic paucity of resources, gradually unburdening itself of the additional responsibility for higher education may be advisable for the government. Instead, it could better utilize the scarce resources for realizing the goal of universalization of elementary education and for improving the quality of school education.

Privatization of higher education, however, is not without social costs. In a polity such as India's, where structured inequalities have been entrenched, privatization is sure to reinforce existing inequalities. This necessitates the social supervision of the private sector and effective measures for offsetting imbalances resulting from the unequal economic capacities of the population. How to advance equality without sacrificing quality? How to control the private sector without curbing its creativity and initiative? Here lies the challenge of change for higher education in contemporary India, 600 million of whose billion-plus population is below the age of twenty-five years.

REFERENCES

Arnold, David. "Globalization of Higher Education: What it means for India." Pp. 48–54 in *Internationalization of Indian Higher Education*. Edited by K. B. Powar. New Delhi: Association of Indian Universities, 2001.

Ashby, E., and M. Anderson. *Universities: British, Indian, and African*. London: Weidenfield and Nicholson, 1966.

Bagga, Chirdeep. "Four-fold Leap in Unemployment: Worse, Education Doesn't Improve Chances of Getting a Job." *The Times of India* (Mumbai), 18 June 2005, 11.

Basu, Aparna. "Indian Higher Education: Colonialism and Beyond." Pp. 167–86 in *From Dependence to Autonomy: The Development of Asian Universities*. Edited by Philip G. Altbach and V. Selvaratnam. Chestnut Hill, MA: Center for International Higher Education, Boston College, 2002.

Basu, Durga Das. *Introduction to the Constitution of India*. 17th ed. New Delhi: Prentice-Hall of India, 1995.

Bhushan, Sudhanshu. "Trade in Education Services under GATS: Implications for Higher Education in India." *Economic and Political Weekly* 39, no. 23 (2004): 2395–402.

Chanana, Karuna. "Accessing Higher Education—The Dilemma of Schooling: Women, Minorities, Scheduled Castes and Scheduled Tribes in Contemporary India." Pp. 115–54 in *Higher Education Reform in India: Experience and Perspectives*. Edited by Philip G. Altbach and Suma Chitnis. New Delhi: Sage Publications, 1993.

Chitnis, Suma. *A Long Way to Go . . .* Report on a survey of scheduled caste high school and college students in fifteen states of India. New Delhi: Allied Publishers, 1981.

Government of India. *Social, Economic and Educational Status of the Muslim Community of India: A Report*. New Delhi: Prime Minister's High Level Committee, Cabinet Secretariat, Government of India, 2006.

Jayaram, N. "Higher Education as Status Stabilizer: Students in Bangalore." Pp. 169–91 in *Process and Institution in Urban India: Sociological Studies*. Edited by Satish Saberwal. New Delhi: Vikas Publishing House, 1978.

———. "Education in India: From Colonial Bondage to Neo-Colonial Dependency." Pp. 45–59 in *Sociology of Education in India*. Jaipur: Rawat Publications, 1990a.

———. "Ethnicity and Education: A Socio-Historical Perspective on the Educational Backwardness of Indian Muslims." *Sociological Bulletin* 39, nos. 1 and 2 (1990b): 115–29.

———. "India." Pp. 747–67 in *International Handbook of Higher Education (Part Two: Regions and Countries)*. Edited by James J. F. Forest and Philip G. Altbach. Dordrecht, the Netherlands: Springer, 2006.

Kaul, Rekha. *Caste, Class and Education: Politics of the Capitation fee Phenomenon in Karnataka*. New Delhi: Sage Publications, 1993.

Kumar, T. R., and V. Sharma. "Downsizing Higher Education: An Emergent Crisis." *Economic and Political Weekly* 38, no. 7 (2003): 603–7.

Mayhew, A. *The Education of India*. London: Faber and Gwyer, 1926.

MHRD (Ministry of Human Resource Development, Government of India). *Selected Educational Statistics—2004–05*. New Delhi: Statistics Division, Department of Higher Education, MHRD, Government of India, 2007.

———. "Higher Education in India." 2008. www.education.nic.in/stats0405.asp. Accessed on 24 April 2008.

MSJE (Ministry of Social Justice and Empowerment, Government of India). *Annual Report*. New Delhi: MSJE, 2003–2004.

Mukerji, Debashish. "The Knowledge Market." *The Week* 23, no. 41 (2005): 36–48.
NKC (National Knowledge Commission). *Report to the Nation—2006*. New Delhi: National Knowledge Commission, Government of India, 2007.
Parhar, Madhu. "Enrolment Projection in Higher Education." *University News* 40, no. 27 (2002): 1–4.
Shariff, A., and P. K. Ghosh. "Indian Education Scene and the Public Gap." *Economic and Political Weekly* 35, no. 16 (2000): 1396–406.
Sharp, H. *Selections from Educational Records—Part I: 1781–1839*. New Delhi: Published for the National Archives of India by the Manager of Publications, Government of India (reprint edition) 1965.
Tilak, J. B. G. "Higher Education under Structural Adjustment." *Journal of Indian School of Political Economy* 8, no. 2 (1996): 266–93.
———. "Privatization of Higher Education in India." *International Higher Education* 29 (2002): 11–13.
——. "Public Subsidies in Education in India." *Economic and Political Weekly* 39, no. 4 (2004a): 343–59.
———. "Absence of Policy and Perspective in Higher Education', *Economic and Political Weekly* 39, no. 21 (2004b): 2159–164.
UGC (University Grants Commission). *Annual Report—2002–2003*. New Delhi: UGC, 2002–2003).
———. *Annual Report—2005–2006*. New Delhi: UGC, 2005–2006.
UNDP (United Nations Development Program). *Human Development Report—2009: Overcoming Barriers—Human Mobility and Development*. Houndmills, Basingstoke, Hampshire and New York: Palgrave Macmillan, 2009.

NOTES

1. The British rulers expected, erroneously though, that "education was to permeate the masses from above." Metaphorically expressed, "drop by drop from the Himalayas of Indian life useful information was to trickle downwards, forming in time a broad and stately stream to irrigate the thirsty plains" (Mayhew 1926, 92). This filtration theory turned out to be a mirage. Meanwhile, the British rule gradually supplanted the pre-colonial indigenous system of education consisting of Buddhist *viharas*, Hindu *pathashalas* and *tols*, and Muslim *madrasahas* by stopping financial aid (Aparna Basu 2002, 168). The net consequence of all this was that only 12.2 percent of the population of British India was literate (in any language) in 1941.

2. The English-educated Indian elite became more and more vocal in its criticism of the Raj. The Sedition Committee which investigated the revolutionary conspiracies in India reported in 1918 that most of the conspirators were educated young men. As it turned out almost all the leaders in the forefront of the nationalist movement belonged to the English-educated elite (in Jayaram 1990a, 49).

3. Besides, there are 1,171 polytechnic institutes with a total enrollment of 388,627 students.

4. It is noteworthy that the rapid expansion of higher education in India has taken place in a socioeconomic context in which a substantial percentage of the population is illiterate (35.2 percent of the +7 year old population, according to the 2001 Census) (cited in MHRD 2008, 24), and despite the low rating of education per se in the order of national priorities (the educational expenditure as percentage of the Gross Domestic Product rose only marginally, from 2.80 in 1980–1981 to 3.93 in 2000–2001). According to the Human Development Report—2009, India's Human Development Rank is 134; Human Development Index Value, 0.612; Education Index, 0.643; Human Poverty Index Value (percent), 28.0; and Annual Population Growth Rate (percent) 2005–2010, 1.4 (UNDP 2009, Statistical Annex, 141–202).

5. According to Census of India—2001, the population of India has increased from 361,088,090 in 1951 to 1,028,610,328 in 2001, that is, by 64.89 percent. The average decadal growth for this period was 23.29 percent and the average annual exponential growth rate was 2.12 percent (MHRD 2007: xxxiii).

6. According to the Census of India 2001, the number of jobless has grown by more than four times since the last census: from 10.8 million in 1991 to 44.5 million in 2001. What is worse, the unemployment rate for graduates (17.2 percent) is significantly higher than the overall unemployment rate (10.1 percent). Nearly 40 percent of graduates are non-workers; the percentage of unemployed among technical graduates (32 percent) is less than that among non-technical graduates (39 percent) (Bagga 2005: 11).

7. According to the Census of India 2001, 74 percent of the non-technical graduates and 49 percent of the technical graduates among women are not working (Bagga 2005: 11).

8. The policy of protective discrimination in education is not a post-independence initiative. In 1855, the Government of Madras had provided for special facilities for students of "depressed classes." In 1918, the Maharaja of the Princely State of Mysore had appointed a committee which recommended special facilities in education for "backward communities." In 1930, the Government of Bombay provided special facilities for depressed classes, aboriginal and hill tribes, and other backward classes (see Chanana 1993: 121). What is new is the extent of its spread and the scope of its coverage.

9. In the landmark *Indra Sawhney versus Union of India (1992)* (popularly known as the Mandal Commission case), the Supreme Court of India has held that reservation of all categories put together should not exceed 50 percent of the total (Durga Das Basu 1995: 93–94). This explains the magic figure of 50 percent in the governmental proposals for reservations.

10. In writing this section, I have relied on my recent status report on higher education in India (see Jayaram 2006).

11. Being aware of the disorientation of the conventional courses, the UGC had recommended the introduction of job-oriented courses at the first degree level. Many universities have introduced a job-orientation component in their undergraduate curriculum mainly to avail the funds provided by the UGC for the purpose.

12. This, perhaps, explains the marginal rise in the enrollment of scheduled castes and scheduled tribes in higher education, even as there is a general decline in the rate of enrollment in that sector.

13. An international comparison revealed that in a list of 86 countries, India (with an expenditure of 3.8 percent of the Gross National Product [GNP] on education) ranked only 32nd in terms of public expenditure on education as a proportion of GNP (quoted in Shariff and Ghosh 2000: 1396).

14. It is significant to note that the Government of India's discussion paper on "Government Subsidies in India" (1997) classified elementary education as a "merit good" and higher education as a "non-merit good" warranting a drastic reduction of government subsidies. The Ministry of Finance has since reclassified higher education into a category called "merit 2 goods" which need not be subsidized at the same level as merit goods (Tilak 2002: 12).

15. The concept of a purely private university (of the American type) is new in India, and the government is yet to put the legal framework for them in order. However, invoking the existing legal provisions (e.g., the UGC Act 1956), several private institutions of higher education have been given the "deemed-to-be university" status. Also, considering that higher education is a concurrent subject under the Constitution, some states have enacted private university acts of their own, but such legislations have been put on hold by the Supreme Court of India.

16. Reliable data on Indian students accessing higher education abroad are hard to come by. Debashish Mukerji (2005: 39) has gathered the following estimates for 2005: United States, 80,000; Australia, 20,000; United Kingdom, 15,000; Canada, 3,000; New Zealand, 3,000; Ireland, 1,000; and rest, below 1,000. According to David Arnold, in 2001, Indians accounted for more than 42,000 students in the United States (2001: 50). "More than 70 percent of Indian students studying in the United States are pursuing post-graduate degrees; only 22 percent are undergraduate students. Business management, engineering, mathematics and computer sciences account for more than 75 percent of all Indian students in the United States" (ibid.: 51). Most Indian students abroad pay full fees, and invariably more than what the students from that country do. The Indian banks now advance loans to Indian students going abroad for higher studies.

12

Educational Policy toward "Homeland Minorities" in Deeply Divided Societies

Ayelet Harel-Shalev

This chapter examines the educational status of what is termed in the academic literature as "homeland minorities." Following the theoretical distinction between immigrant communities and homeland indigenous communities (Esman 1985), this chapter is primarily interested in interactions between the modern nation-state and homeland communities, which articulate and practice ways of life that may essentially contest the state, particularly its public policy and national ideology (Furnivall 1948). Homeland communities, also known as "old minorities," or "indigenous communities" (Kymlicka 2008, 7), are inclined to be non-assimilating minorities, and perceive themselves as having historical rights over their homeland, and therefore they may be inclined to demand some power sharing at the national level.

In this context, it is worthwhile reconsidering David Kirp's argument concerning equal opportunity and access to higher education and democratic norms (Kirp 2009). It is well known that *knowledge is power*. Accordingly, we must ask: Do nation-states want to empower their homeland minorities? On one hand, education might make them better citizens, but on the other, it might also increase the minority members' awareness, as well as demands, for more power as well as group rights.

The demand for substantial autonomy or affirmative action in higher education belongs to a wide spectrum of struggles regarding definitions of the nation-state and the status of homeland communities in deeply divided societies. This struggle stems from continuing dilemmas surrounding finalization of a state's identity, a process that relies on contradictory interests and fights for control, allocation of rights, symbols, and resources among different home-land communities, which also reflect the "competing national imaginations" that these communities produce. Many researchers contend that integration can take place in deeply divided societies only when the state recognizes the concept of "differentiated citizenship" (Barzilai 2003). Therefore, if the state desires to be "a genuine democracy," it should recognize minority group rights, and not merely civic rights (Peleg 2007).

The political "give-and-take" processes that influence the formation of minority group rights in deeply divided societies are not restricted to a certain domain but rather create an equation of balance encompassing all public and political spheres. In India and Israel, we can find, for example, granting religious rights, while preventing some language rights. This political tactic can also be easily discerned in the higher education sphere both in India and Israel: in India, on one hand, one can find Muslim universities, though there is no affirmative action for the Muslim minority, as a disadvantaged social group, in "general universities." In Israel, on the other hand, there is an informal gradual policy of affirmative action for Arab Palestinians in universities in recent years (by the planning and budgeting committee, council for higher education), but the state opposes the request for foundation of an Arab university. Still, in both countries, the relevant minority is underrepresented in higher education at all levels.

This chapter presents a comprehensive, yet focused, comparative analysis of linguistic and educational policies in deeply divided societies that have survived as democracies for a considerable period of time. This research examines positions taken toward the minorities in the linguistic and the education sphere and differentiates between official positions and policy in practice. With respect to the case studies selected, the relevant salient rifts for comparison are the ethnoreligious, dividing Hindus and Muslims in India, and the ethnonational, dividing Jews and Arab Palestinians in Israel.

A primary consideration of the main characteristics of India and Israel proves there is more difference than similarity between the two nations. Of all the enormous differences between India and Israel, the main ones are:

Size—India's landmass is 156 times the size of Israel;
Population—India has over one billion residents while Israel has only seven million;
Language—India has twenty-two official languages while Israel has only Hebrew and Arabic;
Literacy—in India, only 65 percent of the citizens over the age of fifteen can read and write while in Israel 95 percent of the population is literate;

Class—India's economy, while expanding, still ranks it as a developing country with castes as status units, while in Israel there is social segmentation, considerable poverty, and unemployment but Israel is an industrialized country with a developed economic system; and

Structure—India has a federalist system while Israel is a unitary state.

Above all, one of the significant differences within the context of the current research is the attitude of the state toward its citizens, for India is not defined in its official documents as "a Hindu state" but as a secular democracy. In contrast, Israel is defined both legally and practically as a "Jewish and democratic" state, meaning that Israel is a "national ethnic state."[1] These differences have various legal and practical effects on the quality of democracy and citizens' rights and obligations in each country.

In spite of the significant differences between India and Israel, further examination reveals many common features. A few of the most important are: first, both states have upheld the democratic process for more than sixty years. Second, their independence was declared at nearly the same time (India's in August 1947 and Israel's in May 1948), in both cases after the end of British colonial rule. Third, both societies earlier were occupied for a long period of time by Islamic rule, and in modern times both are surrounded by Islamic societies. Fourth, both societies are made up of numerous religious and ethnic communities, including a religious community that includes approximately 80 percent of the population (Hindus in India and Jews in Israel); and both have a large homeland minority (13.4 percent [150 million] Muslims in India, while 19.5 percent of Israelis are Arab Palestinians [about 1.5 million]). Fifth, these countries are not regarded as states with high political stability as they have experienced political assassinations, which democratic literature describes as a hallmark of countries with the highest probability of collapse (Cetron 1980; Diskin, et al. 2005). Sixth, they have been in prolonged confrontations with neighboring states. Seventh, from a cultural point of view, the dominant religions in these states, Hinduism and Judaism, are regarded as ancient civilizations, known for their unique traditions, and they maintain their influence on the governance of these modern countries.

Finally, India, and Israel were founded from the start as democracies, unlike other plural states which were founded as centralized, non-democratic regimes and have gradually developed democratic, free institutions.[2] Moreover, India and Israel deal with similar problems, from splits on religious, linguistic, and national grounds through social classification, incidents of discrimination, economic crisis, and wars, to religious extremism. In spite of the challenges; the democratic ethos in India and Israel has remained a major part of their political systems and self-identities throughout the course of nation building.

Still, in both states, in spite of the formal statement that all citizens are equal before the law without discrimination based on religion, race, gender or caste, equality is not fully realized. This research is designed to analyze these regimes' policy toward minorities in the sphere of language and education.

LANGUAGE AS POWER

In a deeply divided bilingual or multilingual society, the tension that accompanies ethnic or national divisions is reflected in linguistic and educational policies. After all, language is a national symbol and one of the most important social institutions in a state. Language signifies deep cultural associations, employment opportunities, and other important aspects of the state. The state views *language* as a source of power and control. Furthermore, linguistic identity plays a pivotal role in every political and cultural interaction and is of great importance. In a bilingual or multilingual society, certain sectors in society may be regarded as disloyal should they speak the language of the state's enemies or be associated in one way or another with neighboring hostile countries. These facts have a direct effect on the status of relevant minority languages both in India and in Israel—Urdu and Arabic respectively (Harel-Shalev 2006, 2009). Urdu is regarded as the main language of Muslims in India, where it is spoken by half of India's Muslims.[3] Urdu's spread has apparently become limited exclusively to India's Muslims. Hindi and Urdu (generally called Hindustani) should have been the national languages of federal India, along with English.[4] But during the process of partitioning India and Pakistan, and with the choice of Urdu as an official language of an independent Pakistan, a change of perception occurred among Indian leadership. On July 15, 1947 the following proposal was raised in the Indian constituent assembly: "That in clause 21 in the formal language article, the words 'Hindustani' should be deleted . . . and for the words 'Hindustani (Hindi or Urdu),' the word 'Hindi' would be substituted" (Constituent Assembly Debated, Orders of the Day: 18. July 15, 1947).

After long discussions of the constituent assembly, Hindi in Devanagari script was chosen by a large majority as the official—and only—trans-national language (Constituent Assembly Debates IX 34: 1486–491; Schedule 343 [1]). The decision to omit Urdu from the article on the official language in India's draft constitution transmitted the message to the Indian people that Hindi is more national than Urdu. The attitude of the government toward Urdu exemplifies how a significant Islamic symbol was purposely kept out of Indian culture and society. The Indian government assigned Urdu the status of a "scheduled language" but without sufficient protection to enable its development and proliferation.

Although the constitutional term means that Hindi is not a "national language" but the "formal language of the union," Hindi is actually India's national language (*Rashtra Bhasha*). The decision to deny Urdu national status was an insult to Muslims, since they expected independent, secular India was to be uninfluenced by the events of partition and to protect a cherished Islamic symbol—Urdu—as a national symbol of India. India's founders and government were not ready for lingual renunciations in order to integrate the Muslim population into the various social circles. The Indian constitution thus states that Hindi in Devanagari script would be the official language of the union, along with twenty-one other languages (including Urdu), that would be considered as "scheduled languages."[5]

By simple categorization, the Hindu elite legalized Urdu on the individual level while it disempowered the language on the national level, effectively refusing to recognize it as a national language. Among Urdu scholars, it is widely accepted that Muslim Urdu speakers in India have to rely primarily on themselves, and not on the state, to preserve their language (Wright 1966; 2002).[6] Such usage of the rights' discourse has served two purposes. First, it empowered individual rights while disempowering the collective actions of Muslims as a group. Second, it marked a symbolic boundary between Muslim Pakistan and India's Muslim minority. [7]

In Israel, the Jewish government did not cancel the status of Arabic as an official language and did not designate Hebrew as the only official language. Instead of canceling the official status of the minority language, the Israeli government chose a "diplomatic" way, leaving Arabic an official language that has never achieved parity with Hebrew in social reality.

Attempts to pass legislation in the Knesset that would render Hebrew the supreme and sole official language, have to date not succeeded. In 1952, Knesset Member (MK) Raziel-Naor proposed the State Language Bill, designed to make Hebrew the only official language (Knesset Proceedings; 1952, vol. 12, 2520–21, 2528). In the 1980s, MK Ora Namir proposed the Hebrew Language Bill–1981, which would have obligated the government to use the Hebrew language in all governmental and public spheres (Knesset Proceedings; 1981, vol. 92, 719–21, 758–59). Another attempt to render Hebrew the sole official language was made in 1994, MK Shaki once again placed the Hebrew Language Bill on the agenda. The matter was transferred to the Knesset's House Committee and made no further progress (Knesset Proceedings; 12.10.1994). All attempts to legally prescribe Hebrew as the sole official language have come to naught.

Although Israel has preserved Arabic as an official language, Israeli law has not yet formulated a comprehensive normative bilingual regime, resulting in Arabic having a status vastly inferior to that of Hebrew. From a judicial standpoint, the Supreme Court backs the government's policy in the matter of preferring Hebrew to Arabic, while acknowledging the right to language as just an individual right when it comes to Arabic speakers. Hebrew assumes a different place altogether in the Jewish and democratic State of Israel because "Hebrew is the force that unites us as the members of one state. Hebrew is not the legacy of one group or another in Israel. . . . Hebrew is . . . the basis of Israel's definition as a sovereign state . . . a country's shared and uniform language has importance because language is the tool through which the members of society communicate with one another while developing the individual and the collective" (H.C. 4112/99 Adalah v. the Municipality of Tel-Aviv-Jaffa 56[5] P.D.: 393. paragraph 21).

The result is that both minorities (Israeli Arabic speakers and Indian Urdu speakers) were compelled to be bilingual in order to integrate into society, and the minority language remained the minority's only.[8] In practice, the status of Urdu was severely harmed. In spite of India's multilingualism, Urdu is barely taught in secular Indian educational institutions; rather it is learned mostly in religious madrasas and in Islamic universities. In the previous two decades Urdu has been recognized as an "additional official language" in several Indian states. But public education systems still do not support Urdu in a sufficient manner (Farouqui 1994; Bari Abdul 1997, 134–48; Khurshid 2000). Although India grants autonomy of language and education to adherents of the various religions, both these areas are the source of constant dispute between Muslims and central and local governments. In fact, no meaningful steps have ever been made to promote Urdu in India (The Sachar Report 2006, 79).

Israel's policy toward Arabic, the minority's language, in a state that was established as the state of the Jewish people is enigmatic. The decision to keep Arabic as an official language while being involved in a war against Arab countries is important and symbolic. However, in practice the state chose not to actualize the official status of Arabic and kept it at only a secondary status. People in the Arab sector have to attain a high level of Hebrew, sometimes at the price of learning Arabic language credits, if they wish to integrate into the various fields of Israeli society because the central means of integrating into society is the use of Hebrew. From a fundamental legal aspect, the judicial system backs the policy of the state to prefer Hebrew over Arabic. In the Jewish, democratic state of Israel, where "the existence, development, reinforcement and flourishing of the Hebrew language is a core value," (Saban 2003, H.C. RAM Engineers v. Municipality of Nazareth Illit 47(5) P.D. 189, 206). Hebrew is a significant part of national unity and makes up a notable part of the definition of the sovereign state (H.C. 4112/99 Adalah v. the Municipality of Tel-Aviv-Jaffa 56[5] P.D. 393).

GROUP RIGHTS AND EDUCATIONAL
POLICIES IN INDIA AND ISRAEL

India

Except for civil rights, which are provided to all citizens in India, Indian law also provides collective rights to minorities. According to India's laws, minorities' collective group rights give every segment of society that has its own language or culture the right to preserve its culture. Minorities can operate their religious institutions by themselves, with the government's commitment to fund those organizations proportionally. There are separate marriage laws (termed as "personal laws") for the different religious communities, although the constitution says that the state will strive to achieve an equal set of personal laws for all its citizens. Certain scheduled languages are acknowledged in the constitution, parallel to the national language, Hindi, and they are entitled to preservation and development. Minorities may establish and run by themselves educational institutions, with the government's constitutional commitment that they will not be discriminated against in the allocation of funds among the different educational institutions (The Constitution of India, Articles 26; 29; 30; 44; 345–47).

India's collective group rights for its minorities are not provided to the majority group—Hindus. Moreover, Indian law set many limitations on the Hindu community, such as requiring Hindus to open all their religious institutions to all other castes and classes and to avoid restriction on any person (Hindu Code Act of 1956; The Untouchability [offences] Act 1955). No parallel law was legislated for Muslims. Moreover, the state introduced far-reaching changes in Hindu personal law in order to fit the values of equality and democracy, but it left Muslim personal law almost unchanged.

Article 30 of the Indian constitution states that (1) All religious minorities can found and independently manage educational institutions; and that (2) The government will not discriminate between the various minorities' educational institutions when allocating funds. However, the educational achievements of the Muslim minority are much lower than those of the majority group or the achievements of other minorities. Yet the dispute over education in India is centered on another issue: interpretation of the constitution. Although the state grants full educational autonomy to minorities and enables them to establish independent educational institutions funded by the state, the state does not provide for itself the legal possibility to be involved in regulating standards for these educational institutions, nor does it supervise the qualifications of educators, rules of behavior, the level of studied materials, physical conditions in schools, etc.

Thus, essential problems occur when a school's management sets strict rules concerning clothing which limits individual freedom, and the state has no authority to get involved in setting these rules. The government also has no influence on the quality of education, and therefore a severe dispute exists regarding the quality of degrees and diplomas that minority institutions are authorized to give. For example, can a Muslim institute with a faculty of law which lacks high standards give its students a diploma? The issue evokes vigorous public debate and is often raised both in the parliament and in the legal system (Gangwal 1995, 191).

It should be clear that minorities in India, including Muslims, are allowed to establish sectorial universities. Moreover, there are Islamic universities that are entitled to be funded by the state, including Aligarh Muslim University, Jamia Millia Islamia (National Islamic University), and other institutions around India. The parliament explicitly determined by law that these institutions are meant to "promote especially the educational and cultural advancement of Muslims in India."[9] In addition, despite a constitutional prohibition, state-funded institutions do teach religious studies, and at Islamic universities religious studies are required (Brass 1990, 192; The Constitution of India, Article 28). This creates an interesting paradox, because a state with a Hindu majority prohibits the teaching of Hinduism as a mandatory theme in state-funded universities, while Islam is taught as a mandatory subject in several state-funded Muslim universities across India. There have been numerous appeals to the High Court in this matter, and the minority has won most cases (Babu 2002). In this regard, the Muslim minority in India is entitled to widespread collective rights, which causes significant disputes in India. These conflicts expand and spur frequent communal riots, especially in the areas of the controversial universities.[10]

Perceptions of public security among Muslims—partly associated with increasing incidents of communal violence—are intertwined with other spheres of life. For example, the latest Sachar report (2006) indicates that the insecurity Muslims feel in India prevents Muslim parents from sending their daughters to distant schools that require them to use public transport. This is particularly the case when they reach upper primary and middle school, and leads to high drop-out rates among Muslim girls in this age-group (The Sachar Report 2006, 20).

Another important controversy regarding higher education in India relates to the reservation, or affirmative-action, policy that India takes toward lower-caste Hindus. Although India defines itself as a secular democracy, in practice, the Indian polity often shows preference to the Hindu community and displays attitudes opposing equality and universal citizenship. Affirmative action is extended to members of lower-caste Hindus, but Muslims, as a separate, weak and underrepresented community, are ineligible for its benefits. Many researches indicated that Muslims are underrepresented in many elite careers in India, which are ruled by Hindus (Wright 1964, Rajgopal 1987, 58–69; Bose 1999, 113–14). These records represent the situation in the national and state politics as well (Shahabuddin 2004; Brass 1990, 234). Muslims' socioeconomic status and level of education was also considerably lower than that of Hindus or other minorities (Shariff 1995; Wadhwa 1975, 154). Primary data indicates that this was the case in the early years of independence (Reports on Minorities 1983),[11] as well as in recent years (Shariff 1995, 2953; Mahmood 2006). The recent Sachar Report indicates that while Indian Muslims comprise more than 13.4 percent of Indian population, Muslims representation is only 3 percent in India administration service (IAS), 1.8 percent in India foreign services (IFS) and 4 percent in India police service (IPS) (Sachar Report 2006). The share of Muslims in universities is extremely low at all levels. Yet, every current call for affirmative action with regard to the Muslim community has been perceived as a demand for further partition of India (Bhargava 2005). A very limited amount of Muslim communities and classes are listed as OBCs ("Other Backward Classes") that deserve quotas of reservations at the higher education system and in public employment, and even when they do—these affirmative-action rights are hardly implemented (*The Sachar Report* 2006, 189–214).[12]

Israel

There are five important group rights which are given to the Arab-Palestinian minority in Israel (Saban 2002): a formal status for Arabic; a separate Arabic education system, but without independent management; a separate system of matrimony laws for the different religious sectors and the legal right to separate courts, limited by Jewish government control over funding and the appointment of Kadis; Exemption from military service (excluding Druze and Circassian men); and—after the Israeli Supreme Court's judgment a few years ago upholding the right not to be discriminated against in governmental allocation of funds—the first signs of another collective right have developed: the promotion of affirmative action and "appropriate representation" in civil service. At this stage we should not yet regard these civil rights as de facto, as these principles have not yet been fully implemented.

Indeed, the main practical protection of Arabic can be found in the configuration of the Israeli education system. The Arab-Palestinian minority is entitled to a separate education system whose language of instruction is Arabic. But the education system is also controlled, to a great part, by the dominant Jewish-majority government.[13]

In the Arab education system, classes are conducted in Arabic and students also learn Hebrew and English. However, it is precisely this right which the Arab minority in Israel received—to preserve their mother tongue as their leading national symbol—that causes them to be at the periphery of Israeli society, which conducts all its affairs in Hebrew. Because the Arab population's knowledge of Hebrew does not compare with that of their Jewish counterparts, they are left behind in many areas (Kook 2000, 55). In this case, educational autonomy is a double-edged sword. On one hand it can contribute to collective memory, culture, and identity of the minority. On the other hand, it may reduce a minority's participation in majority language-dominated society and politics.

Nonetheless, one cannot ignore the fact that under the Israeli establishment, there has been certain progress in the level of education in the Arab sector and in closing the gaps between the sectors. It was found that, over the years, there has been a significant rise in the level of education among the Arab sector in Israel, including among women and girls (Rouhana and Ghanem 1999, 230–31).

There is no educational autonomy for minorities in Israel, such as that found in India, as borne out by the fact that the Arab school system is controlled by Jewish-dominated institutions. Arab citizens are not regarded as a separate national minority that is able and worthy of being entrusted with the education of its community members, but rather they need to be under constant supervision of the dominant Jewish elites. In fact, because delegating responsibility for the task of education to the heads of the Arab sector is perceived as dangerous to the state, the latter chose to institute supervision over teaching and subject matter in the Arab school system. For that reason, only in 1987 was an Arab first appointed to oversee Arab education in the ministry's pedagogic secretariat, a position previously filled by Jews (Al Haj 2000, 19). Furthermore, the Ministry of Education, which has always been Jewish-dominated, was the sole and exclusive supervisor of curriculum at all the formal educational institutions by virtue of Section 4 of the State Education Law.

Arab registration in Israeli universities began to rise gradually, starting with ten Arab students in 1950, 2,100 in 1977, and more than 11,000 in 1999 (Or Report 2003, Paragraph 113). Despite this meaningful improvement, the gaps between the Jewish and Arab sectors are still considerable (Smooha 2001, 292–94). Despite the fact that Arabs represent 20 percent of the total population, they comprise only 10 percent of the students in higher education institutions. Furthermore, in the year 2000, less than 1 percent of the lecturers in universities were Arabs (Al Haj 2000, 20).

An informal policy of affirmative action for Arab Palestinians has been established at Israeli universities in recent years (by the Planning and Budgeting

Committee of the Council for Higher Education), but the results and implications has not yet been shown. Moreover, the State has opposed requests to establish an Arab university ("The Future Vision of the Palestinian Arabs in Israel," 2006, 27).

CONCLUSIONS

The dominant majority's reluctance to grant rights and privileges to minorities in deeply divided societies has been reviewed extensively in the research literature. Yet, one would expect that the linguistic policy of a state that was defined by its founders as a secular republic would be liberal and more magnanimous toward its religious minorities, as the very definition of the state calls for setting aside religious considerations when determining policy—linguistic policy in particular. One would expect fewer compromises with minorities, such as government recognition of minority languages as official languages, in an ethnic democracy. Interestingly, the Indian secular democracy chose not to grant the Muslim minority language, Urdu, official transnational status, while in Israel, a state defined as Jewish and democratic, Arabic received (de jure) status of a second official language, equal to that of Hebrew.

In fact, the research findings also indicate that India, with its secular definition, and Israel, with its ethnic democracy definition, employ similar public policies means to marginalize certain minority languages while, at the same time, entrenching the status of the language that the regime views as a national asset. In other words, regimes in a deeply divided society, including their various institutions, are inclined to relegate the minority's language to a minor status in the national sphere, whether they are a secular democracy, such as India, or an ethnic democracy, such as Israel. Moreover, this research also shows that the formal decision concerning the minority's language is not as important as how the central and dominant government translates the official policy into actual linguistic policy.

A language's status is inseparable from the status of the education system. When it comes to education and minorities, India and Israel have adopted different policies, from both the formal and practical perspectives. Nevertheless, the outcomes of their educational policies are similar. Minorities in both India and Israel receive a considerably lower level of education compared to the dominant communities. School systems for the minorities are also much less developed than those serving the majority groups. Furthermore, in both cases, the state makes only negligible efforts to bridge the gaps between the sectors.

Because material inequality may have an adverse affect on democracy, it is highly important to bridge the gaps between communities, facilitating genuine equality and social mobility. In the analysis of affirmative-action policy, the minority's socioeconomic status, and its social and political representation, the issue of inequality was examined at length in this study. However, there is no doubt that education also plays a pivotal role in an individual's chances to integrate within society and enhance his status.

Autonomy is a double-edged privilege: it can serve as a means whereby minority communities influence public policy, but, at the same time, it can also deprive the minority community of collective memories or historical claims (Barzilai 2003, 288). This distinction is applicable to the Israeli case. In India, educational autonomy is frequently a tool by which the state shirks responsibility for the minority's inferior achievements compared to those of the majority. The state does not take the necessary steps to bridge scholastic gaps because the schools are run and managed exclusively by the minorities themselves. In India, educational autonomy means that the state views itself as inseparable from the majority community, which defines the state, and to a certain degree, the minorities are regarded as outsiders or foreigners.

Homeland minorities perceive themselves as having rights from time immemorial over their country and homeland, and therefore, they will tend to demand many rights from the state, including group rights (Connor 1987; Jabareen 2002). Moreover, sometimes an indigenous minority will demand a status which is no less than an equal share of the majority community's power. The problem is that global sociopolitical reality shows that a majority community usually refuses these demands. Therefore, a cross-disciplinary pessimism regarding the survival of democracies in plural societies is prevalent in the research literature (Rabushka and Sepsle 1971; Brass 1991). India and Israel have managed to withstand the challenge.

The fundamental ethos in each of these countries, however, has seen several normative transformations since independence. India and Israel have traveled contradictory routes. India, which defines itself as a secular democracy and has granted its minority group citizens numerous rights, collective and civic, and incorporated their symbols in its system of state symbols, has come to lean toward ethnic democracy by adopting Hindu and nationalist elements in its definition of the collective good. "Citizenship defined by civic and universalistic rather than ethnic criteria, which guaranteed a principle of inclusion in India's democracy has been eroded by majoritarian notions" (Hasan 2000, 269). Israel, alternatively, which was established as a Jewish state, and has been classified in the research as an ethnic democracy that did not hesitate to impose military rule over its Arab-Palestinian citizens, has begun to swing toward a more liberal direction and has expanded the rights of Arab citizens during recent decades.[14]

As a part of a wide spectrum of policies toward minorities, linguistic policies and especially educational ones, affect the quality of democracy in segmented societies.[15] As clearly expressed by Michel Foucault and Francis Bacon, knowledge is power. In the cases in this research, knowledge and education are also political power, which can enable gaining more power. Indeed, the linguistic conflict in Sri Lanka, for instance, which was part of a wider struggle for the definition of the state, created the most meaningful threat to national integrity that the state had experienced, and triggered the process that consequently led to the collapse of Sri Lanka's democracy (De-Silva 1998). Struggles on linguistic policies in deeply divided young states—such as Estonia and Latvia—can threaten the stability of a democratizing regime (Andersen 1999; Schmid et al 2004). Such evidence demands future research on linguistic and educational policies in deeply divided non-consociational societies undergoing democratization. In such societies, we can expect to find discrepancies between laws and daily practice due to internal struggles for self-identity, collective rights, and power.

REFERENCES

Al-Haj, Majid. *Education, Empowerment, and Control: the Case of the Arabs in Israel*. Albany: State University of New York Press, 1995.

———. "Identity and Orientation among the Arabs in Israel: A Double Periphery." Pp. 13–34 in *The Jewish-Arab Rift in Israel: A Reader*. Edited by Ruth Gavison and Dafna Hacker. Jerusalem: The Israel Democracy Institute, 2000.

Andersen, E. A. *An Ethnic Perspective on Economic Reform: The Case of Estonia*. Aldershot, UK: Ashgate, 1999.

Apte, Mahadev L. "Language Controversies in the Indian Parliament (Lok Sabha) 1952–1960." Pp. 213–34 in *Language and Politics*. Edited by William O'Barr and Jean F. O'Barr. The Hague: Mouton, 1976.

Babu, Rajendra. Honorable Supreme Court Judge. An Interview with the Author. New Delhi. July 30, 2002.

Bari, Abdul Syed. "Urdu: A Victim of Linguistic Fascism." Pp. 134–48 in *Languages Problems in India*. Edited by Sanghasena Singh. New Delhi: Singh, 1997.

Barzilai, Gad. *Communities and Law: Politics, and Cultures of Legal Identities*. Ann Arbor: University of Michigan Press, 2003.

Baxi, Upendra. *Courage, Craft and Contention: The Indian Supreme Court in the Eighties*. Bombay: Tripathi, 1985.

Bhargava, Rajeev. "On the Persistent Political Under-Representation of Muslims in India." Paper delivered at the conference Multiculturalism and the Antidiscrimination Principle; Ramat-Gan College Law School (December 2005).

Bose, Sumantra. "Hindu Nationalism and the Crisis of the Indian State: A Theoretical Perspective." Pp. 104–64 in *Nationalism, Democracy and Development: State and Politics in India*. Edited by Sugata Bose and Ayesha Jalal. New Delhi: Oxford University Press, 1999.

Brass, Paul. *The Politics of India Since Independence*. Delhi: Cambridge University Press, 1990.

———. *Ethnicity and Nationalism, Theory and Comparison*. Newbury Park, CA: Sage, 1991.

———. *The Production of Hindu-Muslim Violence in Contemporary India*. Seattle: University of Washington Press, 2005.

Cetron, Marvin J. "Forecasting Coups to Come." *Futures* 12 (3) (1980) 262–66.

Connor, Walker. "Ethnonationalism." Pp. 198–220 in *Understanding Political Development*. Edited by Myron Weiner and Samuel Huntington. Boston: Little Brown, 1987.

De-Silva, K. M. "Nationalism and the State of Sri-Lanka." Pp. 62–76 in *Ethnic Conflict in Buddhist Societies*. Edited by De-Silva K. M., Pensri Duke, Ellen S Goldberg, and Nathan Katz. Boulder, CO: Westview Press, 1988.

Dhavan, Rajeev. "Judges and Indian Democracy: The Lesser Evil?" Pp. 314–52 in *Transforming India: Social and Political Dynamics of Democracy*. Edited by F. R. Frankel, et al. New Delhi: Oxford University Press, 2000.

Dhavan, Rajeev, and Fali S. Nariman. "The Supreme Court and Group Life." Pp. 256–87 in *Supreme But Not Infallible*. Edited by B. N Kirpal, A. H. Desai, G. Subramanium, R. Dhavan, and R. Ramachandran. New Delhi: Oxford University Press, 2000.

Diskin, Abraham, Hanna Diskin, and Reuven Hazan. "Why Democracies Collapse: The Reasons for Democratic Failure and Success." *International Political Science Review* 26 (3) (2005) 291–309.

Draft of the Indian Constitution, Article 343. Viewed by the author at the Indian National Archive, Delhi (July 2002).

Dua, Hans R. "Sociolinguistic Inequality and Language Problems of Linguistic Minorities in India." Pp. 355–72 in *Language of Inequality*. Edited by Nessa Wolfson and Joan Manes. Berlin: Mouton, 1985.

Esman, Milton J. "Two Dimensions of Ethnic Politics: Defense of Homelands, Immigrant Rights." *Journal of Ethnic and Racial Studies* 8 (3) (1985): 438–41.

Farouqui, Ather. "Urdu Education in India." *Economic and Political Weekly* 14 (April 2, 1994): 782–85.

———. "Re-defining Islamic Thought." *The Pioneer*, 28 August 2002.

Faruqi, Shamsur Rahman. "Strategy for the Survival of Urdu in India through School Education." *The Annual of Urdu Studies* 21 (2006): 120–38.

Furnivall, John S. *Colonial Policy and Practice*. Cambridge: Cambridge University Press, 1948.

The Future Vision of the Palestinian Arabs in Israel. The National Committee for the Heads of the Arab Local Authorities in Israel, December 2006.

Gangwal, Sunita. *Minorities in India—A Study in Communal Process and Individual Rights*. Delhi: Arihant Publishing House, 1995.

Harel-Shalev, Ayelet. "The Challenge of Survivability of Democracy in Deeply Divided Societies." PhD Dissertation, Tel-Aviv University 2005.

———. "The Status of Minority Languages in Deeply Divided Societies." *Israel Studies Forum* 21(2) (2006): 28–57.

————. "Lingual and Educational Policy toward 'Homeland Minorities' in Deeply Divided Societies." *Politics and Policy* 37(5) (2009): 951–70.

————. *The Challenge of Sustaining Democracy in Deeply Divided Societies: Citizenship, Rights, and Ethnic Conflicts in India and Israel.* Lanham, MD: Lexington Books, 2010.

Hasan, Zoya. "Religion and Politics in a Secular State: Law, Community and Gender." Pp. 269–89 in *Politics and the State in India.* Edited by Hasan Zoya. New Delhi: Sage, 2000.

Israeli Knesset Proceedings—Various debates. Printed by the Government of Israel, Jerusalem.

Jabareen, Hassan. "The Future of Arab Citizenship in Israel: Jewish-Zionist Time in a Place With No Palestinian Memory." Pp. 196–220 in *Challenging Ethnic Citizenship.* Edited by Daniel Levy and Yfaat Weiss. New York: Berghahn Books, 2002.

Jacobsohn, Gary J. *The Wheel of Law.* Princeton: Princeton University Press, 2003.

Jamal, Amal. "Beyond Ethnic Democracy: State Structure, Multicultural Conflict and Differentiated Citizenship in Israel." *New Political Science* 24(3) (2002): 411–31.

————. "Liberal Zionism: Judicial Discourse and the Challenges of Multiculturalism in Israel." *State and Society* 4(1) (December 2004): 789–824.

Khurshid, Salman. "Urdu in India." *Economic and Political Weekly* 8.2 (January 2000).

Kook, Rebecca B. "Towards a Rehabilitation of 'Nation Building' and the Reconstruction of Nations." Pp. 42–64 in *Ethnic Challenges to the Modern Nation State.* Edited by S. Ben Ami, Y. Peled and A. Spektorowski. Basingstoke: Macmillan, 2000.

Kymlicka, Will. "The Internationalization of Minority Rights." *International Journal of Constitutional Law* 6(1) (2008): 1–32.

Mahmood, Syed Zafar. "Sachar Report on Status of Indian Muslims." *The Milli Gazette* 14 (December 2006).

Rabushka, Alvin, and Sepsle Kenneth. "Political Entrepreneurship and Patterns of Democratic Instability in Plural Societies." *Race* 12(4) (1971): 461–76.

Rajgopal, P. R. *Communal Violence in India* (New Delhi: Uppal Publishing House with Center for Policy Research, 1987).

The Report of the Official Commission of Inquiry into the October 2000 Events. Chair Judge Theodore Or (2003).

Reports on Minorities. High Power Panel on Minorities, Vol. I—Religious Minorities. New Delhi, June 1983.

Rouhana, Nadim and As'ad Ghanem. "The Democratization of a Traditional Minority in an Ethnic Democracy: The Palestinians in Israel." Pp. 223–46 in *The Israel/ Palestine Question.* Edited by Ilan Pappe. London, UK: Routledge, 1999.

Russell, Ralph. "Urdu in India Since Independence." *Economic and Political Weekly* 34, nos. 1 and 2 (1999): 44–48.

Saban, Ilan. "The Minority Rights of the Palestinian-Arabs in Israel: What Is, What Isn't and What Is Taboo." *Iyunei Mishpat* 26, no. 1 (2002): 241–319.

————. "A Lone (Bi-Lingual) Cry in the Dark? Following *Adalah et al. v. Tel-Aviv-Jaffa et al.* Case." *Iyunei Mishpat* 27, no. 1 (2003): 109–38

The Sachar Report. High Level Committee (headed by Justice Rajindar Sachar) on Social, Economic and Educational Status of the Muslim Community of India. Notification No. 850/3/c/3/05- Pol. Prime minister office, dated March 9, 2005 (Submitted November 17, 2006).

Schmid, Carol, Brigita Zepa and Arta Shnipe. "Language Policy and Ethnic Tensions in Quebec and Latvia." *International Journal of Comparative Sociology* 45 (2004): 231–52.

Shahabuddin, Syed. "Muslim Representation in the Lok-Sabha, 2004." *The Milli Gazette* 1–15, June. http://www.milligazette.com/Archives/2004/01-15Jun04-Print-Edition/011506200458.htm. Accessed on February 8, 2009.

Shariff, Abusaleh. "Socio-Economic and Democratic Differences between Hindu and Muslims in India." *Economic and Political Weekly* (November 18, 1995): 2947–54.

Smooha, Sammy. "Arab-Jewish Relations in Israel as a Jewish and Democratic State." Pp. 231–363 in *Trends in Israeli Society*, Part I. Edited by Ephraim Yaar and Zeev Shavit. Tel Aviv: Open University, 2001.

Peleg, Ilan. *Democratizing the Hegemonic State: Political Transformation in the Age of Identity.* Cambridge: Cambridge University Press, 2007.

Wadhwa, Kamlesh Kumar. *Minority Safeguards in India.* Delhi: Thomson Press, 1975.

Wright, Theodore P. "Muslim Legislation in India: Profile of Minority Elite." *The Journal of Asian Studies* 23.2 (February 1964): 253–67.

———. "Strategies for the Survival of Formerly Dominant Languages." *The Annual of Urdu Studies* 17 (2002): 168–86.

NOTES

1. For more on the distinction between an ethnic national state and a civil national state see Saban 2002 and Jamal 2002.

2. Nevertheless, India was defined as a democracy from the day of its establishment ("a sovereign democratic republic") and Israel was constitutionally defined as a Jewish and democratic state only in the 1990s.

3. It is worth mentioning that the situation of Urdu quite accurately reflects the situation of the Muslim minority throughout India (Farouqui 2002). Urdu has always been identified more with Islam than with any other religion, although in the pre-independence period, it was not identified solely with Muslims (Russel 1999). In the past, numerous non-Muslims spoke and wrote the language; over time, these numbers have steadily declined.

4. This is to say, Hindustani (a spoken language, near to Hindi and Urdu, which is written in two scripts—Devanagari (Hindi) and Arabic-Persian (Urdu) were mentioned in the Indian constitution draft as the official languages of the Indian Union; and English was recognized as an additional official language for fifteen years. Draft Constitution; Article 343. The Indian parliament prolongs every fifteen years the expiration of the article that says that English is a second official language.

5. English has been recognized as an additional formal language of the union. At the time of independence, Hindi and twelve scheduled minority languages were all acknowledged as trans-national languages. Over the years other languages were recognized, and today there are twenty-two recognized languages in India (including Hindi). For the legislation in this matter see: The Constitution of India, Eighth Schedule, Articles 344; 351; The Constitution (Twenty-First Amendment) Act, 1967; The Constitution (Seventy-First Amendment) Act, 1992. The Constitution (Ninety-Second Amendment) Act, 2003.

6. Simultaneously, some of the blame for Urdu's deterioration as a living language is shouldered by the Muslim leadership. Researchers have complained that in those relatively few cases when the government is willing to allocate funds to promote the language, the Muslim elites have been unwilling to formulate a plan for the appropriate investment of those monies; the existing institutional infrastructure is also of very poor quality. Urdu-speaking researchers and intellectuals like Ralph Russell and Shamsur Rahman Faruqi have contended that "the state cannot do for them what they themselves are incapable of doing for themselves" (Russell 1999, 45–46). However, more recent government efforts to promote Urdu have been decried as "too little, too late."

7. The increasing importance of English and its competition with the vernacular languages are of great importance in both states and require a discussion that is beyond the scope of the current research.

8. The situation in India is more complex than in Israel because of the many spoken languages and many scheduled minority languages. Twenty-one languages in addition to Hindi are recognized scheduled languages, and in some federal states they are official languages (such as Bengali in Bengal, Tamil in Tamil Nadu, etc). A scheduled minority language, which is an official language in a state, has higher status than a minority language that is not an official language in any of the states. Urdu is an official language only in Kashmir, which has a special autonomy status, and this fact demonstrates how far Urdu is an ex-territorial and controversial language in India. Moreover, as Muslim speakers of Urdu are scattered throughout India in various percentages, no other federal state but Kashmir has Urdu as its first official language. To learn more about other Language Controversies in India, read Apte 1976; and Dua 1985.

9. See for example Aligarh Muslim University (Amendment Act), No. 62 of 1981. See also Annexure III Report to the government of India regarding the Aligarh Muslim University (Amendment) Bill, 1978, 1st, Minority Commission Report, 1978, 19–50. See also: Jamia Millia Islamia Act, 1998 no. 58 of 1998.

10. For more details about relations between Hindus and Muslims and the dynamics that led to the eruption of inter-communal riots in India, see Brass 2005.

11. The findings indicate that in various sphere of public employment the Muslim minority is an underrepresented community. For further reading see Harel-Shalev 2005.

12. Muslims are hardly included as Backward Classes, and in limited cases are listed as Other Backward Classes; meaning—the policy of affirmative action is applied mainly to Hindus and not to Muslims. The number of Muslim OBCs, varies from one state to another. The national average of Muslims in public employment, at all levels, does not exceed four percent With respect to these findings, we should be aware that the socioeconomic status of Muslims in India in general is lower than the

status of the Hindus OBCs. Moreover, the latest 2006 Sachar report has argued that even when Muslims are formally included as OBCs, the actualization of their rights has not been realized (The Sachar Report, 2006: 189–214).

13. Due to length limitations of this paper, I will not present a normative evaluation as to the shortcomings and advantages of running a separate education system in Arabic. See more in: Al-Haj 1995; and a concise analysis in: Saban 2002, 269–71; 278–80.

14. This process is also expressed in rulings set down by Israel's Supreme Court given that the courts tend to make decisions that follow the norms established by the country's dominant majorities, Jamal 2004. Like Israel, the character of India's Supreme Court resembles that of other state institutions and tends to adopt similar approaches, Baxi, 1985; Dhavan 2000; Dhavan and Nariman 2000. Many decisions have equated ideas set forth in Hinduism with *Indianization*. Government Institutions, including Supreme Court, have lent a receptive ear to majoritarian notions, See Jacobsohn 2003. The judicial system in Israel, contrary to that of India, has gradually shifted toward universalism and liberalism. For a detailed analysis of these processes, see Harel-Shalev 2005, 312–55.

15. The current research's main goal is to present an analytical comparative study vis-à-vis linguistic and educational policies in deeply divided societies. Therefore, a bilateral discussion is conducted regarding these significant policy fields—language and education. This compound analysis does not summarize the entire gamut of the main factors which are relevant to a minority's civil status. A minority's status—the character of state-minority relations—should be comprehensively analyzed in the course of a multilateral discussion, including other policy spheres as religious rights, socioeconomic status, affirmative action and representation in civil service, and minority treatment by government's institutions as supreme courts, security forces, and so forth. Wide-ranging research regarding all policy spheres is beyond the scope of this particular chapter. For a comprehensive analysis that includes all mentioned policy spheres, read Harel-Shalev 2010.

13

Improving Access to Higher Education for Students from Low Socioeconomic Backgrounds

Miriam Amit

At the dawn of the third millennium, higher education is a basic human right. Equal access to higher education is the democratization of education—the adaptation of democracy to a new world of opportunities. Today's socialism is a republic of learning. . . . We are citizens of two worlds, the geographic one that immediately surrounds us, and the scientific world that lies on the horizon. And just as we learn to traverse our immediate surroundings, so we must learn to explore future vistas as well. . . . The true key to social equality in our time resides primarily in the accessibility of knowledge, in its "rightful allocation" through widely available higher education.

—Shimon Peres, President of the State of Israel

The above statement, made by Shimon Peres, President of Israel and Nobel Prize recipient, reflects the dominant view in Israel today, that education in general and higher education in particular is the key to a promising future for young people and the means for their social mobility—what Kirp (2008) refers to, in characterizing the social role of universities, as an "equalizer of opportunities."

In theory, then, Israeli authorities advocate equal opportunity for higher education to all citizens, regardless of socioeconomic level, religion, or gender. However, in reality this is not the case. A substantial gap persists in enrollment for higher education between different parts of the Israeli society, particularly between the center of Israel and the periphery, and between youths from Ashkenazi and Sephardic origins (The Adva Center for Information on Quality and Social Justice, 2003, Adam Ha'Israeli, 2008).

There are many stumbling blocks on the road to equal opportunity. Major problems include inadequate elementary and secondary school education, unawareness of the importance and potential of higher education, and the difficulty of financing higher education. These issues are naturally more prevalent among lower socioeconomic populations.

The Negev, the southern region of Israel, is home to the lowest socioeconomic populations in Israel, with the highest levels of unemployment, a large percentage of economically challenged new immigrants and many poverty-stricken Bedouin and Jewish communities. A national assessment of educational progress reveals that students of the Negev are, on average, the lowest achieving in Israel. Consequently, Negev students are underrepresented in higher education in general, and in competitive university faculties in particular.

This situation is not unique to Israel. In the United States, 75 percent of the students in 150 top universities come from the top income quartile, and only 3 percent come from the bottom quartile (Kirp 2008). Kirp argues that "A student whose family income is in the top quartile with aptitude scores in the lowest quartile is as likely to go to college as a student whose family income is in the lowest quartile and whose aptitude tests are in the highest quartile. . . . [S]mart poor kids go to college at the same rate as stupid rich kids" (Kirp 2008, 5).

Multiple Paths to Higher Education

Unequal access to higher education is a well known, and researched, problem around the world (Quayle and Essack 2007). A number of different approaches to solving this problem have been proposed. First among these is changing the format of higher education. Since the 1990s, Israel's seven research-oriented universities have been joined by public and private colleges, some of them independent and some extensions of Israeli or foreign universities. These colleges have enlarged the accessibility of higher education somewhat by providing additional platforms for learning, but have simultaneously perpetuated the problem by transferring the same social hierarchies to the higher education facilities themselves, where the universities retain top status, followed by the relatively expensive private colleges, with public colleges bringing up the rear. This hierarchy is expressed in the admission requirements of each academic institution as well. This structure bears resemblance to the educational institutions in the United States, which are divided into community colleges that are open to all, state colleges that admit students in the top third of their graduating class, and research universities, for which students graduating in the top 12 percent of their class are eligible (Kirp 2008, 4). Thus, though the intention of this structure was to make higher education accessible to larger populations, this goal was not realized, and failed particularly in the most prestigious and competitive faculties.

Another approach is to help students in the beginning of their university studies to improve their learning skills. For example, the "Stretch" program "stretches" fundamental semester-long academic writing courses over two semesters, allowing the weakest students a chance to build their basic writing skills to an acceptable level, so that they can continue with adequate confidence and excel in their more advanced courses (Arizona University, 1994).

Another approach is affirmative action in the admission process in order to help students that do not meet the admission requirement get into the university. In the "Broadening Recruitment to Higher Education through the Admission System: Gender and Class Perspectives" in Sweden, for example, the acceptance conditions into university are adjusted for certain minority groups (Berggren 2007). A study researching the effectiveness of these guidelines is currently underway.

In Israel, a program called "Second Chance" enables students who have not finished their high school studies, and did not take final examinations, to complete them after their Army Service or National Service, usually around the age of twenty-one to twenty-three.[1]

While some of these solutions are geared to the populations in the countries in which they are employed, a more comprehensive solution is required to answer the Negev region's problems. According to the Israel's Central Bureau of Statistics, Negev's students have the lowest percentages of achieving a matriculation certificate[2] in general, and more specifically in certain Jewish development towns and Bedouin towns and villages (Central Bureau of Statistics 2008). Even for those who do manage to achieve a matriculation certificate, the quality of the certificate is not necessarily adequate for university acceptance, especially for the more prestigious faculties, notably technological, medical and engineering departments.

Furthermore, there is a high drop-out rate among students of a low socioeconomic population, even among the few who do get accepted into prestigious facilities. These problems often stem from the lack of support and ambition, as academic ambition is not commonly encouraged among families who are stuck in cycles of poverty. Additionally, these students often receive poor basic skills throughout their school education, leading to inability to cope with the high demands of university.

In the past, students from low socioeconomic backgrounds became successful as blue-collar workers in industry. Today, in an era of the global and technologically sophisticated economic market, such students may opt to become "knowledge workers." The project presented below is conducted in

Ben-Gurion University (BGU) in Israel, and is aimed at increasing access to higher education among students from underprivileged areas.

THE "ACCESS TO HIGHER EDUCATION" PROGRAM

Aims

The Access to Higher Education Program (AHEP) aims to overcome the disadvantages mentioned above by intervening at a younger age, thus building skills and academic anticipation that will last throughout high school and higher education. The program is designed to incite excitement about learning in a higher education institute, to familiarize the participants and participants' families with academia, and to decrease anxiety and increase parental support. The program is also designed to improve academic performance and achievements at the school level and in the matriculation final examination, while students are still in high school. This preparation will also save students time and money that they would otherwise waste at a later stage improving inadequate grades to meet university requirements. In short, the program is designed to help lift the students out of a vicious cycle of underperformance and offer underprivileged students an equal chance at higher education.

Scope and Funding

The Access to Higher Education Program was initiated in 2002 by Ben-Gurion University of the Negev (encouraged by school's former President and Rector, Professors Braverman and Finger and their successors, Professors Carmi and Weinblatt) in cooperation with the Ministry of Education, Southern District. Many organizations have expressed support for the importance of this program and have contributed to its successful operation, including: Ben-Gurion University, The Rashi Foundation, Atidim, The Ministry of Education, Bank Leumi, and the Adenauer Fund. Parents pay a small amount of money per year, and the university provides all the facilities including lecture halls, laboratories, computers and logistic support.

Participants

The program started with about 700 students and has grown every year. In 2009, the participant population reached approximately 1,250 students from all over the Negev (see distribution in figure 13.1). All the participants must attend one of thirty-one designated schools, chosen on the basis of a national socioeconomic index (named: Fostering Index). These schools are comprised mainly of students from low socioeconomic backgrounds and all are located in the periphery of Israel, primarily the Negev.

Participants are high school students who begin attending the program in 10th grade and stay until the end of twelfth grade. Students are chosen to participate in the Accessibility to Higher Education Program according to following criteria:

1. Performing in the top twentieth percentile of their class.[3] This ensures that the students have basic academic abilities.
2. Studying mathematics and English at advanced levels, and taking the top two levels of matriculation exams (four or five units) in English and Mathematics, and preferably an advanced science course (for the structure of the Israeli system see Amit and Fried 2002).
3. Teachers recommendations.
4. Demonstration of personal commitment and family support.

STRUCTURE OF THE "ACCESS TO HIGHER EDUCATION" PROGRAM

The project comprises two main components: a school division and a university division called "Towards University." In addition, students also participate in empowerment activities.

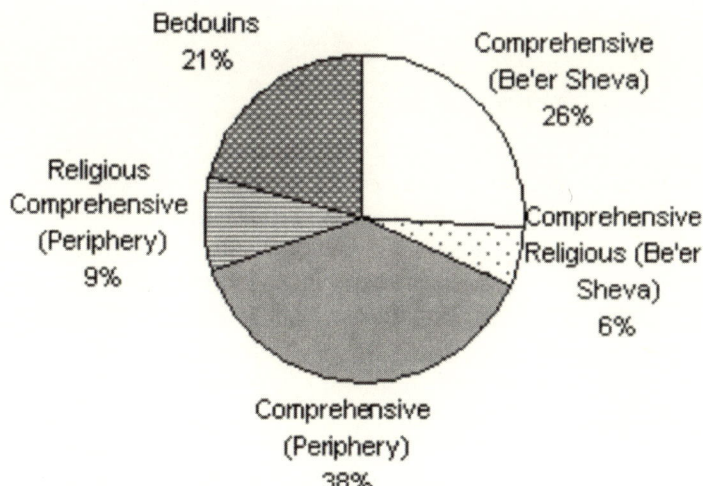

Figure 13.1.   Percentages of School Sectors participating in the Program, 2007, *Source: Myers-JDC-Brookdale Institutes, 2008*

The School Division

The main aim of the school division is to provide reinforcement through tutoring within the school system. Each student receives an extra four to six hours per week (beyond regular school hours) of personal or small group tutoring in the subjects they find most challenging, usually English, mathematics, or science. The extra time allows them to turn to their teachers for help with homework or to fill gaps in understanding—help that many of the students cannot receive at home. The tutoring provides extra training, skills, and knowledge that enable students to elevate their performance, and consequently their grades in the final matriculation examination, and improve their chances of getting into competitive faculties where admission requires extremely high grades.

The school unit also offers the participants an opportunity to complete the national psychometric exam (similar to SATs in the United States), that is required for acceptance into most university faculties. Although many students—regardless of socioeconomic level—opt to take the exam after or during their army service, tutoring and guidance is still offered for students who are interested in taking on the challenge.

Personal Empowerment

Extracurricular activities are organized for program participants, designed to widen their horizons and increase their ambition. The activities include meetings with representatives of different professions, outings, and social activities.

The University Division

The aim of the university component "Toward University" is to expose students to academia and give them a taste of what the university is all about. Bearing in mind that most of them have never been in a university environment (nor have most of their families), the university experience (hopefully a successful one), aims to increase their inclination for forming academic aspirations, foster self-esteem, and expose them to the power and promise of academia.

These goals are implemented in the university division by means of the following features:

- Location: The program is held on the BGU campus, and all of its facilities are open to the participants, including libraries, labs and computers. The students are bused in from throughout the Negev and from other peripheral areas, to the campus, giving them a real university experience; leading one student to proclaim, "here we smell the wisdom of knowledge."

- The courses take place every Friday, when there are few regular courses in the university[4] and therefore less university students around, enabling the high school students to experience the campus without feeling overwhelmed.
- Students learn in relatively small groups, and care is taken to compose these of students from different areas and backgrounds—Jewish and Bedouin, religious and secular, new immigrants and "veteran" Israelis etc. Thus, students form a new social group, with a variety of societal components all focused on a single target: achieving a higher education in competitive fields.
- Activities in university courses take place every Friday morning, from 8:30 to 1:00 (two academic sessions) throughout the academic year. The students participating in AHEP are released from school on this day (in Israel schools operate six days a week), and it is up to the students to make up what they miss in school.
- The academic program is based on courses in a variety of subjects and contents. Special emphasis is placed on the interaction between university content and school curriculum.
- Each student chooses one in-depth course in natural science, mathematics, or technology to take over the entire year, together with two shorter humanities or social science courses, one for each semester. The aim of this combination is for the students to acquire in-depth, comprehensive knowledge of a particular subject in a certain natural science, together with a broader sense of concepts in the humanities.
- The range of courses is extremely wide and rich, with over eighty available courses. Some of the science courses offered are related to subjects learned in school, such as certain advanced mathematics, chemistry or physics courses, while others cover totally new ground, ranging from hematology to the human genome, dinosaur germs and the environment, robotics, visual basics (computer science), critical thinking, logic, etc.
- Humanities courses are similarly rich in variety, including social and developmental psychology, journalism, philosophy of science, practical philosophy, introduction to economics, rhetoric, drama, law, and more.
- Students are entirely responsible for choosing their own courses, which is an experience in itself, as little choice is given in the Israeli high school system. Every year, an "Open Day" is held prior to the start of the academic year, where lecturers present their courses and students can select courses according to their own preferences. This gives students greater responsibility for their learning.

- Each course is given by a senior or junior lecturer or a doctoral student in their area of research and expertise, who can share the processes and progress in the field with the students, so as to give them a taste of practical application of knowledge. Professors are selected for their teaching abilities, as well as their fields of research, so as to be certain that the students will enjoy the lectures, while gaining enrichment from them, and increase their enthusiasm for the academic world.
- Courses are on an extremely high level, the exact teaching methods depending mostly on the students' age. While tenth-grade courses offered may be taught in methods slightly below the rigid academic requirements of a university course, most twelfth graders participate in courses on a par with university levels.
- Accreditation: in an added bonus, the latter courses can be counted as actual academic credits should the students attend the university within seven years. This gives the students a feel of having one foot in the academic world at a young age—which further encourages them to continue to higher education.
- Courses are experienced differently than lessons in school. Besides the excitement of sitting in an actual university lecture hall, the courses are given with visual aids, such as films and PowerPoint presentations, which are not usually used in high school. Additionally, students are given the chance to utilize the university facilities by carrying out experiments in labs, doing research in the library, and using other university facilities in accordance with the courses they take, thus familiarizing them with sophisticated learning methods of higher education to which they have not previously been exposed.
- Accompanying tutors (in addition to the lecturers), mostly engineering students, are assigned to help the students in the more difficult courses by sitting with them in class to make sure they are following, or by offering help after classes. They are also available for contact via telephone and the Internet should the students need help with course homework, as most of their teachers and parents are incapable of helping, due to the specialized nature of the material learned in class.
- The university program is directed academically by a university professor (the author of this paper) expert in science education, with an advisory committee composed of professors from all university faculties.

Reflection and Evaluation

The program was evaluated through an external evaluation process by the Myers Joint-Brookdale Foundation (Bar-Ilan University 2007). A number of revealing findings, presented below, shed light on students' attitude toward the program, and the extreme importance they attribute to the university experience gained through "Toward University."

Student Response

Students' feedback regarding the program, particularly the university component, was overwhelmingly positive.

The first evaluation criterion is the rate of attendance: 92 percent (!) of the students regularly participated in their chosen courses. This rate of attendance is much higher than the average school attendance.

Second, the level of the academic courses: 84 percent were satisfied with the level and said that the course level is "exactly as it should be," 14 percent of the students said that the level of the courses was too challenging and 2 percent reported that the level was not challenging enough.

Third, the quality of teaching: 92 percent felt the courses were well prepared; presentation scored slightly lower, at 87 percent; while two-thirds felt the lecturers were accessible for extra help (see figure 13.2). The latter led to reevaluation of tutors' role and tutoring methods.

The different areas of the courses (natural science and social science) were assessed separately: 76 percent of students reported that they were "very pleased" with their natural science courses, and 83 percent were "very pleased" with their humanities and social sciences courses. This was a pleasantly surprising result, since whereas a large number of participants are scientifically inclined, there was an expectation for there to be greater interest in the natural science and technology courses, and most of the students

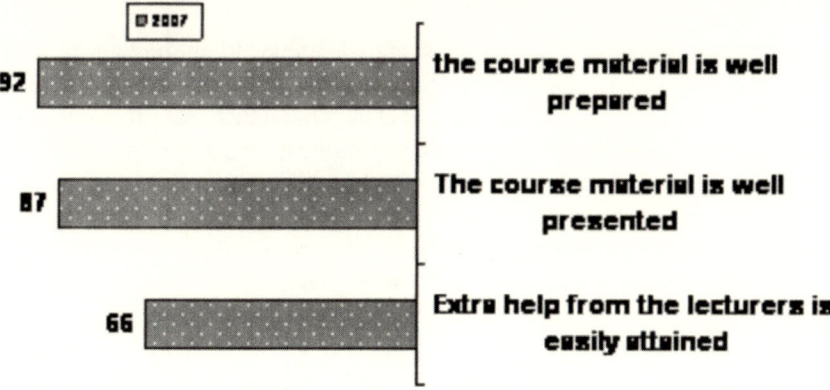

Figure 13.2. Students' response to quality of teaching, *Source:* Myers-JDC-Brookdale Institutes, 2008

had little previous experience with subjects such as psychology, the arts, etc. Furthermore, students from this background tend to perceive the humanities as "a waste of time" due to their more abstract nature, so their enrichment and eager acceptance is very rewarding, showing the broadening of these students' horizons.

Students were asked from which component they gained most, the school division or the university one. The vast majority, 74 percent, reported that they gained most from the university division. 19 percent felt that they had gained the most from the school division and 2 percent chose the empowerment activities (5 percent were undecided).

The school principals involved in the program were asked to assess its influence on the students: 80 percent reported an overall improvement in student performance, including higher grades in school exams; 90 percent said the program increased the students' desire to continue to university.

INDICATIONS OF SUCCESS

Student feedback in the Access to Higher Education Program indicates that they see the university division as much more rewarding than the school-based one. This result is surprising and encouraging, since the school component was directly related to help with schoolwork and actively improved the students' grades, whereas the university unit had almost no immediate benefits. The success of the university division shows that the students were inspired by the academic world. It is reasonable to assume that such attitudes toward academia will motivate them to improve their learning habits, rise to academic challenges and cope with more pressure. These results were also evident from their teachers' responses.

The Access to Higher Education Program is unique in optimizing students' cognitive merits as well as their affective assets. There is currently no other similarly intense program offered in Israel. Although there are other programs for intervention with special guidance toward matriculation and university courses offered for interested high-school students as individuals, there is nothing comparable that combines school assistance with broadening academic horizons and general improvement of learning skills.

A comparison of matriculation grades between schools participating in the program and schools of a similar socioeconomic level showed significantly higher results in the former group. Although other factors may have affected the results, such as teachers' enthusiasm and students' commitment, the possibility of the grades being at least partially affected by participation in the program cannot be overlooked.

Naturally, an important indication of success is how many participating students eventually attend university. This factor is currently difficult to assess as most Israeli students begin university, on average, four years after their high school graduation and the program is in its seventh year, with its first graduates only just out of army service. Follow-up research of program graduates is currently underway. Although there are no concrete results as yet, the feedback from students was extremely positive, and their marked differences in grades and change of attitude toward their schoolwork indicate that they are indeed on the path to higher education.

An important aspect of the AHEP that cannot be overlooked is its affective, social, and emotional impact. As described above, all of Israel's diverse population is represented in this project: immigrants and "natives," religious and secular,[5] Jewish students and Bedouins from the tribes in the Negev area. The program's mixed groups enable the students to learn in a shared social environment, the likes of which they would not otherwise have had an opportunity to experience. The formation of regular, long-term mutual acquaintances, and the experience of striving together toward common goals, fosters in the students an openness and an understanding of those who are different from themselves, something that will doubtless yield rewarding social benefits when these students become part of the adult world.[6]

An additional advantage of the program is the self-confidence and the positive self-image the participants acquire. This self-confidence stems first from the very fact of their acceptance into the program and intensifies as they confront high-level academic challenges and rise to successfully meet them. Such a confidence in one's ability to succeed is important to the entire student population, but is particularly crucial for those parts of it that are more disadvantaged.

CONCLUSION

The students participating in the Access to Higher Education Program come from a low socioeconomic background and most of them, should they be accepted to a higher education institution, will be the first generation in their families to do so. Such students, even if they are accepted into universities, face a high risk of dropping out due to their lack of familiarity with the academic system (Pike and Kuh 2005). After three years of participation in AHEP, however, these students begin their higher education as university veterans, to whom the challenge of university education is no longer a stranger. Naturally, this significantly raises their chances of persevering and completing their academic aspirations.

The Access to Higher Education Program intervenes at an age when shaping educational attitudes and widening intellectual horizons can reap maximum benefit. Rather than offering a crutch to help socioeconomically disadvantaged university-age students battle their way into the university system and then struggle on their own, the program assists younger, impressionable students in improving their cognitive skills and study habits, offering solid foundations for the successful completion of their university education. The taste of university life whets their appetite and increases their ambitions, while gently inaugurating the students and their families into a more academically oriented frame of mind.

The program offers these students a chance to equalize their access to higher education, not by lowering university acceptance standards—a short-term solution that will not ultimately serve their academic ends (Kirk, 2008)—but by providing underprivileged students with the tools and ability to join the ranks of prestigious faculties as honorable academic equals.

REFERENCES

Adam Ha'Israeli. "Grades Are Not Everything: Center, Periphery and Access to Higher Education." Paper presented in Tel-Aviv University, February 2008 [Hebrew].

Adva Center for Information on Quality and Social Justice. 2003. www.adva.org.

Amit, M. and Fried, M. N. "High-Stakes Assessment as a Tool for Promoting Mathematical Literacy and the Democratization of Mathematics Education." *Journal of Mathematical Behavior* 21 (2002): 499–514.

Amit, M., N. M. Fried, and M. Abu-Naja. "The Mathematics Club for Excellent Students as Common Ground for Bedouin and Other Israeli Youth." *The Montana Mathematics Enthusiastic* 4 (2007): 75–90.

Arizona State University. *Stretch Program*. 2008. Arizona State University website. www.asu.edu/clas/english/composition/cbw/stretch.htm. Accessed on April 2008.

Berggren, C. "Broadening Recruitment to Higher Education Through the Admission System: Gender and Class Perspectives." *Studies in Higher Education* 32.1 (2007): 97–116.

Central Bureau of Statistics. *Statistical Abstract*. www.cbs.gov.il.

Kirp, D. "The Earth Is Flattening: The Globalization of Higher Education and Its Implications for Equal Opportunity." Paper Presented at Hurst Seminar on Higher Education and Equality of Opportunity: Cross-National Perspectives, Israel: June 3–5, 2008.

Myers-JDC-Brookdale Institutes. "Report on performance of the Program for Access to Higher Education at Ben-Gurion University for the Years 2006–2007." Jerusalem, Israel (2008).

Pike, G. R. and G. D. Kuh. "First and Second Generation College Students: A

Comparison of Their Engagement and Intellectual Development." *The Journal of Higher Education* 76 (3) (2005): 276–300.

Quayle, M. and Z. Essack. "Students' Perceptions of a University Access (Bridging) Programme For Social Science, Commerce And Humanities." *Perspectives in Education* 25.1 (2007): 71–84.

NOTES

1. In Israel army service is mandatory. Boys and girls are recruited after high school, at the age of eighteen, to serve for two to three years. In special cases army service is postponed for a short period of time and high school students get a "second chance" to improve their grades in the final matriculation examination before their service examination.

2. The Israeli matriculation system requires completing examinations in a number of subjects, including mathematics, English, grammar, history, literature, and a number of other compulsory and optional courses. See also Amit and Fried, 2002.

3. The program "Accessibility to Higher Education" is not designed solely for exceptional students. For mathematically gifted students, an extremely successful program called "Kidumatica," has also been running at the university for the last ten years, with over 420 members of elementary and high school age per year.

4. Regular BGU classes are held Sunday through Thursday.

5. In Israel religious and secular children attend separate schools, as do Arabic-speaking and Hebrew-speaking students.

6. For research on the importance of living together see Amit, Fried, and Abu-Naga, 2007.

14

Higher Education in Africa

Challenges of Development and Gender

Pamela Blackmon and Matt Evans[1]

> To compete in today's knowledge-driven economy and shifting global markets, countries need a flexible skilled labor force, able to create and apply knowledge. This is usually achieved through strong secondary and tertiary education systems.
>
> —World Bank (2009a, 31)

Higher education is widely recognized as a key component for a country's economic and social growth. In an increasingly globally competitive world, nations whose education infrastructures (primary, secondary, and tertiary) lag are at a distinct disadvantage. This creates a cyclical problem. Since poorer countries have fewer economic and social resources, they are in a weaker position for developing institutions of higher education, and their ability to compete in the global economy is weakened further.

Nowhere is this a bigger problem than in sub-Saharan Africa, which suffers from the world's lowest enrollment rates in primary, secondary, and tertiary education (UNESCO 2010, 80). The purpose of this chapter is to examine some of the challenges that sub-Saharan Africa faces in improving higher education. Specifically, we want to determine: why have tertiary education levels in sub-Saharan Africa have lagged so far behind other regions of the world? This is an important question because it is through the tertiary level of education that the greatest contributions to forming a "knowledge economy" are derived (Yusuf et al. 2008).

The first section of this chapter reviews the development of higher education in Africa, from the period of colonial rule to the present. The second section examines how an overemphasis on primary and secondary schooling as having greater contributions to economic development, (as promoted by development economists and the World Bank) may have weakened development of tertiary education in sub-Saharan Africa. The next section elucidates how higher education funding inefficiencies and the lack of regulatory oversight have contributed to the poor quality levels. The last section addresses how persistent gender inequalities at all educational levels are a severe impediment to economic development and poverty alleviation in the region.

BACKGROUND FRAMEWORK FOR HIGHER EDUCATION

Understanding the history of higher education in Africa provides insight into how the current systems operate. The colonial rulers of developing countries including Africa did not initially provide education opportunities for the local populations. Ng'ethe et al. (2008, 14) point out that formal education in the African colonies controlled by Europe was primarily left to missionaries. When institutions of higher education were finally introduced under British and French colonial rule they were not extended to the local population due to the belief that the Africans were inferior (Lulat 2003; Tikaly 2001). This viewpoint changed over time, most notably around the end of World War II when there was greater recognition of the economic value of vocational and industrial training (Ng'ethe et al., 2008).

One problem in French colonial Africa was that the African elites believed their own local institutions of higher education were inferior to French institutions and focused on study abroad rather than improving the domestic institutions (Lulat 2003; Ashby 1966). By the mid-twentieth century, newly educated leaders emerged from these Western institutions to lead independence movements challenging colonial rule and helping to develop national cultures (Tikly 2001 and Kress 1996). Part of this would result in the establishment of national universities "prompted by the nationalism of African states which attempted to assert their independence from their respective colonial powers" (Ng'ethe et al., 2008, 15).

The neglect of higher education in Africa may be seen in UNESCO records, which have no data available for enrollment in higher education in Africa from 1950–1970. Subsequently, in 1980 data indicate one million students enrolled. By 1990, that number had grown to three million enrolled in tertiary education. However, these numbers are still very small when compared to primary and secondary enrollments, which were much stronger for Africa during these same time periods. Primary enrollments stood at 59 million for 1980 and 79 million for 1990 (higher than Latin American enrollments of 76 million for 1990).

Secondary enrollments were at 14 million and 24 million for 1980 and 1990 respectively (UNESCO Statistical Yearbook 1993 and previous years, cited in Gillis, Perkins, Roemer, and Snodgrass 1996, 256). Thus, in a region with more than 700 million people (UNESCO 2010), why have so few moved beyond primary and secondary education to studies in higher education?

OVEREMPHASIS ON PRIMARY AND SECONDARY EDUCATION?

According to Teferra and Altbach (2004, 22), "Africa is the least developed region in terms of higher educational institutions and enrollments. While a few countries on the continent can claim comprehensive academic systems, most have just a few academic institutions and have not yet established the differentiated postsecondary systems required for the information age."

There are many factors that are responsible for a greater focus on primary education levels (even over secondary) in Africa. First, in the economic development literature greater gains were seen from allocating resources for education at the primary rather than at other levels. The argument from an economic point of view was that since developing countries did not yet have an adequate demand for highly educated skilled workers that it was necessary to prioritize forms of education and training, and thus the "proportion of income that should be devoted to education" (Meier 1995, 315). Psacharopoulos (1991 as cited Meier 1995, 322) explains:

> A typical pattern, found since the early days of rate of return estimation in education, is that returns decline by level of schooling. Thus, returns to primary education are higher relative to returns to secondary education, and the latter are higher than returns to university education. This finding, corroborated in study after study, has fundamental policy implications.

These findings resulted in a focus by the international development community, especially the World Bank, that higher levels of economic growth and poverty reduction could be seen by devoting resources to primary (especially) and secondary education over tertiary levels (Bloom et al., 2005, 3). Since the Bank was the most heavily involved in providing advice and loans to the governments in Africa during the 1970s and 1980s they advised increased funding for primary especially and secondary, but not for higher education.

This approach has been criticized by some researchers as being too narrow in scope, in promoting policies that see education less in terms of its social impact and more as an aspect of economic policy (Yang 2003). Critics of the World Bank and International Monetary Fund assail their push for liberalization, privatization, and cuts in government spending in order to make these countries more attractive to foreign investors (Tikly 2001). This has resulted in many countries adopting a business investment approach, as opposed to social welfare, as the primary element in their educational policies (Yang 2003).

Despite this criticism, the focus of the World Bank on primary education was not unreasonable, due to the higher returns and the fact that many developing countries were spending too much of their education budgets on university education of the children of the elite (Stiglitz 2007, 50–51). Researchers have confirmed that in many African nations a small elite has disproportionate access to technology and the best institutions of higher education (Bor and Shute 1991; Teferra and Altbach 2004).

These phenomena have contributed to the lag in the tertiary education sector in Africa. This is unfortunate because despite criticism of inequalities in the provision of education and technology, higher education is still a force for modernization and development in Africa (Teferra and Altbach 2004). In fact, an econometric study by Bloom et al., (2005, 31) suggested that increasing tertiary education for sub-Saharan Africa resulted in faster technological catch-up in addition to improving a country's economic output. Higher order skills necessary for being competitive in a knowledge based economy are acquired at the tertiary level (Yusuf, Saint, and Nabeshima 2008).

Consequently, newer programs developed by the IMF and the World Bank designed to alleviate poverty, which do not reflect an emphasis on funding for tertiary education in sub-Saharan African countries, detract from the competitiveness of the workforce in this region (Bloom et al., 2005). Poverty Reduction Strategy Papers (PRSPs) were developed by the financial institutions during the 1990s largely as a recognition that previous policies supported by the institutions did not promote economic growth or alleviate poverty in the poorest countries (Blackmon 2010). Unlike previous policy frameworks that were developed with little input from the countries themselves, the governments of the countries write their own PRSPs in which they describe specific ways in which they will use the funds provided from debt relief to alleviate poverty in their countries (Blackmon 2008).

Bloom et al. analyzed all of the PRSPs available for African countries for references to higher education. They found that "(a)lthough all countries except Tanzania make some reference to higher education in their PRSPs, only three (Cameroon, Malawi, and Zambia) consider it a way to reduce poverty" (2005, 8–9). Furthermore, they found that six countries were planning to decrease tertiary funding with only Cameroon and Ethiopia planning to increase tertiary education funding levels. The authors speculate that one reason PRSPs do not focus on tertiary level funding is also due to the "brain drain" phenomenon in which large numbers of Africans trained at the university level end up living and working outside Africa. Thus the developing countries lose their intellectual capital, often the brightest of their citizens, and in many cases through an education that was funded by the government (Stiglitz 2007, 51).

FUNDING AND REGULATORY ISSUES IN HIGHER EDUCATION

The formal institutions of higher education in Africa are also beset with a myriad of additional problems. First, World Bank studies have shown inefficiencies, overcrowded classrooms and lack of equipment and computers (Banya and Elu 2001, 29). African universities also suffer from shortages of published materials including books and journals and lack basic resources for teaching, such as laboratory equipment and supplies (Teferra and Altbach 2004).

Other studies have shown African universities plagued with weak management and poor teaching staff. The latter is due to inadequate salaries, poor personnel management, a lack of opportunities to conduct research, and increasing teaching loads resulting from higher student-to-staff ratios (Yusuf et al. 2008). This has been linked to a high student drop-out rate and high percentage who fail to attain passing grades (Bor and Shute 1991, 3).

These problems appear to indicate enrollments far outpacing budgets for tertiary level education. However, an examination of investments and enrollment show a much more complicated situation.

In terms of education enrollment rates, sub-Saharan Africa lags way behind all other regions. From 1999 to 2007, UNESCO reports that gross secondary enrollment rates for sub-Saharan Africa rose substantially. However, at 34 percent, the region lags far behind all others with a secondary enrollment rate that is about half that of all developing countries (see Table 14.1). In higher education, the gross enrollment rate for sub-Saharan Africa lags even farther. Although enrollment in higher education also increased dramatically from 1999 to 2007, the rate for this region stood at only 6 percent—one-third the enrollment rate of developing countries and one-tenth that of developed countries. According to UNESCO, of the ten countries with the lowest gross tertiary enrollment rates all are in sub-Saharan Africa, led by Malawi with a rate of only 0.49 percent (UIS 2010).

In terms of budgeting, sub-Saharan Africa's higher education is affected by its status as the world's poorest region. Twenty-two of the twenty-four countries listed in the United Nation's Human Development Index (HDI) as "Low" were found in sub-Saharan Africa (UNDP 2009). Education in this region is funded at a level similar to other developing regions. A UNESCO study shows that between 1999 and 2007 the amount spent on education in sub-Saharan Africa rose from 3.5 percent of GNP to 4.5 percent. This was the

Table 14.1   Gross Enrollment Ratios in Secondary and Tertiary Education

	Gross Enrollment Ratios in Secondary (percent) School year ending				Gross Enrollment Ratios in Tertiary (percent) School year ending			
	1999		2007		1999		2007	
	Total	GPI (F/M)	Total	GPI (F/M)	Total	GPI (F/M)	Total	GPI (F/M)
World	60	0.92	66	0.95	18	0.96	26	1.08
Developing Countries	52	0.89	61	0.94	11	0.78	18	0.96
Developed Countries	100	1.00	100	1.00	55	1.19	67	1.29
Countries in Transition	91	1.01	90	0.98	39	1.21	58	1.29
Arab States	60	0.89	65	0.92	19	0.74	22	1.05
Central Asia	85	0.99	95	0.98	18	0.93	24	1.10
East Asia and the Pacific	65	0.96	78	1.01	14	0.75	26	1.00
East Asia	64	0.96	77	1.01	13	0.73	25	0.99
Pacific	111	0.99	105	0.96	47	1.24	53	1.31
Latin America & Caribbean	80	1.07	89	1.08	21	1.12	34	1.19
Caribbean	53	1.03	58	1.03	6	1.3	7	1.36
Latin America	81	1.07	90	1.08	22	1.12	35	1.19
N. America and W. Europe	100	0.99	100	1.00	61	1.23	70	1.33
Central and Eastern Europe	87	0.98	88	0.96	38	1.18	62	1.25
South and West Asia	45	0.75	52	0.85	7	0.64	11	0.77
Sub-Saharan Africa	**24**	**0.82**	**34**	**0.79**	**4**	**0.67**	**6**	**0.66**

Source: UNESCO (2010) p. 80

largest increase of any region in the world (see Table 14.2). African spending on education as a percent of GNP went from well below the rate of developing nations to being right in line with the average and close to the worldwide rate of spending. However, while encouraging, these numbers should be regarded with some caution since other regions with faster growing economies may appear to be spending proportionately less, when in fact they have substantially more education resources than Africa.

Similarly, sub-Saharan Africa is the leading region in the world in per capita investment in higher education as a share of GDP, with a rate of 268 percent of GDP per capita. This is well ahead of every other region and above the world average of 90.5 percent (World Bank 2009b). However, as with overall spending, this may be more a sign of low GDP levels rather than significant investment. In addition, when considered with all education spending, and the low rate of enrollment in higher education, the high per capita investment may actually be a sign of inefficient economies of scale.

One problematic issue in budgeting is the unique way in which African universities fund students' education. A significant reason that tertiary education in sub-Saharan Africa costs more than other regions, as a share of the GDP, is that it is publicly funded, with students (or their families) rarely contributing to tuition. According to a World Bank study, the very small percentage of the population able to gain access to higher education receives a large share of the education budget. Among these few, the rich are heavily overrepresented (Bor and Shute 1991). These problems are compounded when university graduates emigrate, taking with them their country's sizable investment in their education and training (Teferra and Altbach 2004).

Another problem lies in the way in which academic funds are distributed. A large share of funding is dedicated to nonacademic purposes, including free student housing, board, and allowances. According to Teferra and Altbach (2004), this may encourage students to take longer to finish their studies. The combina-

Table 14.2   Total Public Expenditure on Education as a Percent of GNP

	1999	2007
World	4.6	4.9
Countries in transition	3.9	3.5
Developed countries	5.0	5.3
Developing countries	4.5	4.5
Arab States	...	4.0
Central and Eastern Europe	4.4	5.1
Central Asia	4.0	3.2
East Asia and the Pacific	4.9	...
East Asia	3.6	3.6
Pacific	6.5	...
Latin America/Caribbean	4.9	4.8
Caribbean	...	5.8
Latin America	4.5	4.1
N. America/W. Europe	5.0	5.5
South and West Asia	2.9	3.8
Sub-Saharan Africa	**3.5**	**4.5**

Source: UNESCO (2010) p. 410

tion of no tuition, free housing, and allowance, together with high drop-out rates and students repeating classes they have failed, has led to lengthy stays at African universities. Banya and Elu report that the average length of time required to complete an undergraduate degree is sixteen years for economics, eighteen years in the humanities, and twenty-seven years in sciences (2001, 13). In addition, a disproportionate share of funding goes to administrative staff. Bureaucratic inefficiencies have led to African universities overstaffed with underqualified and poorly trained administrative staff (Teferra and Altbach 2004). Not only is free housing provided for students, it is also often provided for administrative staff. This has led to high non-faculty costs (Banya and Elu 2001, 11).

A new trend in tertiary education in Africa has been the establishment of a growing number of private institutions. This has been, in part, in response to declines in quality in the public sectors. The period from 1990–2007 saw a doubling in public universities from 100 to almost 200, the number of private tertiary institutions increased markedly from around twenty-four to an estimated 468 (Yusuf et al. 2008, 13). Though still minor in comparison to private education in other regions of the world, the phenomenon of private higher education has been spurred by several factors, including a declining capacity of public institutions to provide for all those seeking higher education, increased student demand, pressure by international agencies for public universities to cut costs, a growing need for a skilled labor force and increased interest by foreign private institutions (Teferra and Altbach 2004, 32).

Most of the new private institutions in Africa focus on skills that can be used in the local job market (not, for example, liberal arts), such as finance, banking, computer science, technology, and secretarial skills (Teferra and Altbach 2004). One of the problems of the growing number of private institutions of higher education is a lack of regulation. Teferra and Altbach contend that, "The status of many private postsecondary institutions in Africa is shady. Many operate without licenses, commensurate resources, or appropriate infrastructure. The quality of service by many is also shoddy, even at a few of the institutions that possess better equipment, newer buildings, and better facilities than the major universities in their country" (2004, 35).

EDUCATION AND GENDER

Evidence that more progress needs to be made in eliminating gender inequality and gender disparities in primary and secondary education can be seen by the inclusion of this goal as one of the Millennium Development Goals (MDGs) that all developing countries are to achieve by 2015 (World Bank 2001/2002, 5). One of the reasons that development economists and the international development institutions such as the World Bank and the United Nations (and by extension UNESCO) focus on increasing the education of girls is the overwhelming evidence that doing so leads to specific increases in economic development and poverty alleviation (Blackmon 2009). Increasing women's education results in fewer births (which would lower the population growth rates in all of these countries) because educated women are more aware of their options for family planning and have a greater role in decision making in the family. For example, while 40 percent of women in sub-Saharan Africa with no education gave birth with no antenatal care, only 6 percent of women with secondary education gave birth with no antenatal care (UNESCO 2010, 2). In addition, female education has one of the strongest negative relationships to fertility, meaning that as the education of females increases their fertility decreases (Meier 1995, 284). This is an important statistical relationship considering that this impoverished region's growth rate is three times the global rate (UNESCO 2010).

Studies have also shown that increasing women's income (through education) results in improvements in the nutrition of children (Apodaca 2010; Behrman and Wolfe 1987; Leslie 1988). This is related to the fact that women make different financial decisions than men regarding how income is spent. Women are more likely to use marginal increases in their income for their families' education, health and nutrition (Coleman 2010, 128). Thus, reducing gender disparity in education not only enables more women to contribute to the workforce, it is also important in reducing poverty and mortality, which are especially problematic in Africa (UNDP 2002).

While the gender gap has been reduced in primary education, women are vastly underrepresented in secondary and higher education in sub-Saharan Africa. With a ratio of seventy-nine women to every one hundred men (0.79) enrolled in secondary education, Africa lags behind every other region of the world. Worldwide, men have a slight edge over women in secondary education enrollment with a ratio of ninety-five women for every one hundred men (0.95). In developing countries the female/male ratio stands at 0.94 while in developed countries the ratio of men and women in secondary education is equal (1.00). Not only does sub-Saharan Africa have the worst gender gap in secondary enrollment, but while most of the developing world saw an improvement in the gender gap during the 1999–2007 period, in sub-Saharan Africa the ratio of female enrollment in secondary education worsened (see Table 14.1).

In higher education in Africa the gender imbalance is even greater. With a female/male ratio of 0.66, sub-Saharan Africa is far behind the global ratio of 1.08. This places Africa far behind the overall rate of developing countries, which have a 0.96 ratio, and even further behind developed nations which have 129 women for every 100 men (1.29) enrolled in higher education. Women outnumber (or are equal to) men in enrollment in higher education in all other regions of the world except for East Asia, and South and West Asia. In the former region the female/male ratio in tertiary education improved from 0.73 to 0.99 (i.e. virtually equal). In South and West Asia the ratio of women remains lower than the world average, but improved substantially from 0.64 to 0.77. By contrast, sub-Saharan Africa was the only region of the world in which the gender ratio for higher education did not improve between 1999 and 2007 (see table 14.1).

Sub-Saharan Africa's lag in reducing gender differences in enrollment in higher education may be tied to gender gaps at lower education levels. According to UNESCO (2010), sub-Saharan Africa and South and West Asia had youth literacy rate for females that were virtually the same in 2007. At 54 percent, sub-Saharan Africa's rate was slightly better than the 53 percent female youth literacy rate for South and West Asia (both were well below the world rate of 80 percent and the developing nation's rate of 74 percent). However, during the period from 1985 to 2007, while the female youth literacy rate in Africa rose nine percentage points, from 45 to 54 percent, in South and West Asia it rose nineteen percentage points, from 34 percent to 53 percent, and in the developing world as a whole by twenty-three percentage points, from 54 to 77 percent (see table 14.3).

Thus, youth literacy rates for females rose at a much slower rate in sub-Saharan Africa than in any other region. This, combined with economic and cultural factors, has likely affected the gender imbalance in secondary education, where the region lagged even further behind the rates of other developing countries and the rest of the world. The gender imbalance in secondary education has subsequently led to an even greater shortfall in higher education in sub-Saharan Africa. Overall, while the average number of years of schooling for females in Africa improved substantially during the period from 1999 to 2007, from 5.9 to 7.9, the region continues to lag behind all other regions of the world (see table 14.4). Thus, the gender imbalance increases as women move through the educational system, and becomes particularly acute at the level of higher education. These trends are unfortunate because investment in the education of females has been shown to yield a higher rate of return (Psacharopoulos 1985, as cited in Meier 1995, 323–24).

CONCLUSION

Sub-Saharan Africa is a vast and diverse region with more than 700 million people in fifty countries, ranging from 87,000 in the Seychelles to 150 million in Nigeria (UNESCO 2010). This region has followed a global trend of declining fertility and growth rates. Population growth has also been affected by wars,

Table 14.3 Youth Literacy Rate (15–24) (percent)

	1985–1994			2000–2007			Projected 2015		
	Total	Male	Female	Total	Male	Female	Total	Male	Female
World	76	82	70	84	89	80	87	90	83
Countries in Transition	98	99	97	99	100	99	100	100	100
Developed Countries	99	99	99	99	99	99	99	99	100
Developing Countries	68	77	59	80	85	74	84	88	79
Arab States	58	70	46	71	80	62	78	86	70
Central & E. Europe	96	98	94	98	99	96	98	99	97
Central Asia	98	99	97	99	99	98	99	99	100
East Asia & Pacific	82	89	75	93	96	91	95	97	94
East Asia	82	89	75	93	96	91	95	97	94
Pacific	94	94	93	93	94	92	93	93	93
Latin America/ Caribbean	87	88	86	91	92	90	93	94	93
Caribbean	66	65	67	75	73	77	78	76	81
Latin America	87	88	86	86	91	92	91	94	94
N. America/W. Europe	99	99	99	99	100	99	100	100	99
South and West Asia	48	60	34	64	75	53	71	79	62
Sub-Saharan Africa	53	63	45	62	71	54	72	77	66

Source: UNESCO (2010) p. 314

food shortages, high child mortality rates, and AIDS. However, sub-Saharan Africa still has by far the world's highest population growth, three times the global rate (UNESCO 2010), and the region's population is expected to double by 2040 to almost 1.4 billion (Tabutin and Schoumaker 2004, 514). Without economic development to match, this will intensify the region's current woes. In fact, during the past several decades, a large share of African nations have been characterized by low (or negative) economic growth. In today's global economy an educated workforce is essential for economic growth.

This chapter has elucidated some of the complex problems facing the development of higher education in sub-Saharan Africa. Some of the problems facing tertiary education in Africa are derived from the local culture

Table 14.4   School Life Expectancy (expected years of education—primary to tertiary)

	School Year Ending					
	1999			2007		
	Total	Male	Female	Total	Male	Female
World	9.7	10.1	9.2	11.0	11.2	10.7
Countries in transition	11.7	11.6	11.8	13.2	12.9	13.4
Developed countries	15.5	15.1	15.8	15.8	15.4	16.3
Developing countries	9.0	9.5	8.4	10.4	10.8	10.1
Arab States	9.8	10.5	9.0	10.8	11.3	10.3
Central and Eastern Europe	12.0	12.1	12.0	13.4	13.3	13.4
Central Asia	10.8	10.9	10.7	12.2	12.2	12.1
East Asia and the Pacific	10.5	10.7	10.3	11.8	11.8	11.8
East Asia	10.4	10.3	10.2	11.8	11.8	11.8
Pacific	14.8	10.2	14.9	14.4	14.3	14.4
Latin America/Caribbean	12.5	12.4	12.6	13.4	13.2	13.6
Caribbean	10.7	10.8	10.7	10.9	10.8	10.9
Latin America	12.5	12.4	12.6	13.5	13.3	13.7
N. America/W. Europe	15.8	15.4	16.2	16.0	15.5	16.5
South and West Asia	7.9	8.8	6.9	9.6	10.0	9.0
Sub-Saharan Africa	**6.6**	**7.2**	**5.9**	**8.6**	**9.3**	**7.9**

Source: UNESCO (2010) p. 339

and political leadership. Authoritarian regimes in much of the region have increased poverty and inhibited intellectual development, diverted resources to corrupt cronies or excessively high military spending, and contributed to violence that has led a large share of the most educated Africans to emigrate, further exacerbating their countries, lack of educated professionals, leaders, and teachers (Harber, 2002, 269).

However, higher education in sub-Saharan countries has also been affected by several outside influences. Colonial rulers for centuries prevented the establishment of institutions of higher education and a culture that could foster intellectual growth. In addition, apparently well-intended pressure from the World Bank led to an overemphasis on primary education at the expense of the development of higher education.

Currently, the development of higher education in Africa faces a number of challenges. First, education funding must become better managed, more systematic, and more effective. Spending priorities must be clearly defined in terms of allocations to faculty, facilities, and supporting expenses. In addition, incentives must be provided to both institutions and students for completion of degrees within a reasonable time frame. Also, higher education planning must figure out the desired role for private education. The rapid spread of private tertiary institutions has been largely unregulated. This is likely to add to inconsistency in the value of education and the degrees obtained, leading to more wasted time and resources.

Another major challenge in sub-Saharan Africa's higher education is the broader changes in the educational system which must be undertaken in order to enhance the important contributions of women to economic development. The low ratio of females to males must be changed so that women can be trained for the skills needed to participate in a knowledge-based economy. In addition to the economic benefits of women's contributions to the economy, increased education levels for women and girls will help reduce the region's high growth rate and further reduce poverty.

Most of the countries of Africa have made substantial progress in increasing the funding and quality of primary and, to some degree, secondary education levels. Now this progress needs to be extended to higher education. With the implementation of effective education policies, sub-Saharan Africa can enjoy the increased education levels—and subsequent economic growth—seen in the rest of the developing world.

REFERENCES

Apodaca, C. *Child Hunger and Human Rights: International Governance*. London: Routledge, 2010.

Banya, K., and J. Elu. "The World Bank and Financing Higher Education in Sub-Saharan Africa." *Higher Education* 42, no. 1 (2001): 1–34.

Behrman, J., and B. Wolfe. "How Does Mothers' Schooling Affect Family Health, Nutrition, Medical Care Usage, and Household Sanitation?" *Journal of Econometrics* 36 (1987): 185–204.

Blackmon, P. "Rethinking Poverty through the Eyes of the International Monetary Fund and the World Bank." *International Studies Review* 10, no. 2 (2008): 179–202.

———. "Factoring Gender into Economic Development: Changing the Policies of the International Monetary Fund and the World Bank." *Women's Studies* 38, no. 2 (2009): 213–37.

———. "International Financial Institutions and Global Justice." In *The International Studies Compendium Project*. Edited by Robert Denemark et al. Oxford: Wiley-Blackwell, 2010.

Bloom, D., D. Canning, and K. Chan. "Higher Education and Economic Development in Africa." http://siteresources.worldbank.org/EDUCATION/Resources/2782001099079877269/547664-1099079956815/HigherEd_Econ_Growth_Africa.pdf.

Bor, W. van den, and J. Shute. "Higher Education in the Third World: Status Symbol or Instrument for Development?" *Higher Education* 22, no. 1 (1991): 1–15.

Coleman, I. "The Better Half: Helping Women Help the World." *Foreign Affairs* (Jan/Feb 2010): 126–30.

Dixon, M. "Globalisation and International Higher Education: Contested Positionings." *Journal of Studies in International Education* 10 (2006) 319–33.

Harber, C. "Education, Democracy and Poverty Reduction in Africa." *Comparative Education* 38, no. 3 (2002): 267–76.

Finkel, S. "Civic Education and the Mobilization of Political Participation in Developing Democracies." *The Journal of Politics* 64, no. 4 (2002): 994–1020.

Kenway, J. "The Information Super-Highway and Post-Modernity: The Social Promise and the Social Price." *Comparative Education* 32, no. 2 (1996): 217–32.

Kress, G. "Internationalisation and Globalisation: Rethinking a Curriculum of Communication." *Comparative Education* 32, no. 2 (1996): 185–96.

Leslie, J. "Women's Work and Child Nutrition in the Third World." *World Development* 16, no. 11 (1988): 1341–362.

Meier, G. M. *Leading Issues in Economic Development*, 6th ed. Oxford: Oxford University Press, 1995.

Ng'ethe, N., G. Subotzky, and G. Afeti. *Differentiation and Articulation in Tertiary Education Systems: A Study of Twelve African Countries.* World Bank Working Paper No. 145 (2008): 1–170.

Okolie, A. "Producing Knowledge for Sustainable Development in Africa: Implications for Higher Education." *Higher Education* 46, no. 2 (2003) 235–60.

Psacharopoulos, G. *The Economic Impact of Education: Lessons for Policymakers.* San Francisco: ICS Press, 1991.

———. "Returns to Education: A Further International Update and Implications." *Journal of Human Resources* 20 (1985): 583–604.

Stiglitz, J. *Making Globalization Work.* New York: W. W. Norton, 2007.

Tabutin, D., and B. Schoumaker. "The Demography of Sub-Saharan Africa from the 1950s to the 2000s. A Survey of Changes and a Statistical Assessment." *Population* 59, no. 3/4 (2004): 457–555.

Teferra, D., and P. Altbach. "African Higher Education: Challenges for the 21st Century." *Higher Education* 47, no. 1 (2004): 21–50.

Tikly, L. "Globalisation and Education in the Postcolonial World: Towards a Conceptual Framework." *Comparative Education* 37, no. 2 (2001): 151–71.

United Nations Development Program (UNDP). *Human Development Report.* New York: UNDP, 1999.

United Nations Development Program (UNDP). (2009) http://hdr.undp.org

UIS. *UNESCO Institute for Statistics (UIS).* (2010) http://stats.uis.unesco.org

UNESCO. *EFA Global Monitoring Report.* London: Oxford University Press, 2010.

World Bank. *World Development Report.* Washington, DC: World Bank, 2000/2001.

———. *Atlas of Global Development*, 2nd ed., (Glasgow: Harper Collins, 2009a).

———. *The State of Tertiary Education around the World: A Global Statistical Summary*, UNESCO Institute for Statistics in EdStats, http://web.worldbank.org/WBSITE/EXTERNAL/TOPICS/EXTEDUCATION/EXTDATASTATISTICS/EXTEDSTATS/0,,contentMDK:21528857~menuPK:4324013~pagePK:64168445~piPK:64168309~theSitePK:3232764,00.html (2009b).

Yang, R. "Globalisation and Higher Education Development: A Critical Analysis." *International Review of Education* 49(3/4) (2003): 269–91.
Yusuf, S., W. Saint, and K. Nabeshima. "Accelerating Catch-Up: Tertiary Education for Growth in Sub-Saharan Africa." Washington, DC: World Bank, 2008.

NOTE

1. The authors' names are listed alphabetically to reflect their equal contributions to this chapter.

15

The Development of Corporate and Private Universities in Ghana

Effects on Curriculum, Faculty, Access, and Equity

Josiah A. M. Cobbah

Traditionally, higher education in Ghana has been limited primarily to the public sector. However changes in the economy and shifts in the demand for higher education have led to an upsurge in the development of private institutions. This chapter examines the shift toward the corporatization and privatization of universities and analyzes the effects of these developments on the future of Ghanaian university students and faculty. Analysis of education policy in Ghana is based on a neo-Gramscian framework.

CORPORATIZATION AND PRIVATIZATION OF THE UNIVERSITY

Over the years universities have become associated with certain traditions. Among these traditions are the proverbial pursuit of knowledge for the sake of knowledge, academic freedom (insulated from state and administrative power), the collegiality of faculty inside and outside the university, the pursuit of careers in academia, a peculiar relationship between university administration and faculty, and peculiar notions of university administrative systems (Bostock 1999; Thornton 2005).[1] More recently, however, a number of scholars have started to sound an alarm about the changing nature of the university and the trend toward corporatization and privatization (Hopper 1998; Lee 1998; Obara 1998; Bostock 1999; Thornton 2005; Cownie and Bradney 2005).

Bostock points out that although some notable universities have successfully operated on what can be considered to be a commercial basis for a long time, universities have not been associated with business and corporate models (Bostock 1999, 2). Altbach posits that this model of state-sponsored higher education is very much a creature of Western Europe. At the time, Altbach observed that, "Africa has few private universities, and public institutions educate virtually all students" (1998, 2). He also pointed out that the majority of African private universities at the time were nonprofit entities that operated under tax exemption status (and enjoyed other privileges) and were expected by the state to serve broad educational and cultural goals (Altbach 1998, 3). In effect, even the private university was not necessarily conceived of as a business. Only in a minority of situations could the commercial motive have been said to be strong, with many such institutions struggling (often unsuccessfully) and on the verge of bankruptcy (Altbach 1998, 3).

What Do We Mean by Corporatization?

According to Bostock, "Corporatization is a process of making a state body into an independent commercial company. . . . Corporatization is often the first stage in a process of privatization where the ownership of a former State body is transferred to private individuals and institutional investors generally through the floating of shares available to the public and subsequent listing on a stock exchange" (Bostock 1999, 2). In the context of education policy Altbach asserts,

> Private higher education has been thrust into the limelight at the end of the twentieth century, largely because of the decline of the state sector. . . . Public institutions are being "privatized" as public funds shrink and universities are forced to find alternative sources of support. Public universities increasingly resemble private institutions in funding patterns. The idea of an academic degree as a "private good" that benefits the individual rather than a "public good" for society is gaining acceptance. The "logic" of today's market economies and an ideology of privatization have contributed to the resurgence of private higher education, and the establishment of private institutions where none existed before. (Altbach 1998, 2)

Thus, corporatization enables the university, which is still a state institution, to behave like a private sector institution. According to Lee, "corporatized universities will be allowed to borrow money, enter into business ventures, set up companies, and acquire and hold investment shares. The government will continue to own most of the universities' assets, and to provide development funds for new programs, and expensive capital projects. But the universities will assume the burden of raising a major portion of their operating costs" (Lee 1998, 7).

This chapter examines how privatization and corporatization will affect higher education in an underdeveloped, dependant country such as Ghana. This research utilizes the ideas of Antonio Gramsci[2] (1891–1937) as a framework for analysis.

GRAMSCI, THE IDEA OF HEGEMONY AND EDUCATION

Gramsci's neo-Marxist ideas today provide a framework, for a number of scholars, for analyzing many social and economic problems. Indeed, Gramscian analysis has been found to be very versatile in providing meaning and insight for a broad variety of applications.[3]

Central to Gramsci's analysis of society was the idea of the hegemony of the ruling classes. In her work on gender and education, Jane Martin interpreted Gramsci's use of the term hegemony to connote "the organizing principle or world view diffused through agencies of ideological control and socializing into every area of social life" (Martin 2006, 38). From this point of view, hegemony is not simply oppressive domination of one group by another. It is rather a sociological reality in which the dominant class uses natural social mechanisms to establish its dominant agenda. Gramsci's key conceptual tool was the notion of cultural hegemony. For Gramsci, it is through cultural hegemony "that the dominant class is able to lay down the terms and parameters of discussion in society; it tries to define and contain all taste, morality, and customs, religions and political principles" (Martin 2006, 38). This is done mainly through education.

A similar perspective is brought by Mayo, who see, Gramsci's thinking on education as "a project that extended far beyond an analysis and discussion of schooling and formal educational issues," thus, "education, in its wider context and conception, played a central role in his (Gramsci's) overall strategy for social transformation since in his view, every relationship of hegemony is an educational one" (Mayo 2007, 2).

For Gramsci, therefore, the entire struggle between classes is really an educational project and education is at the very core of hegemonic relationships (Buttigieg 2002, 69). In Gramsci's architecture of the capitalist state, social institutions (such as universities) are not neutral entities, but "a powerful system of fortresses and earthworks" that protects the state, helping to maintain the prevailing hegemonic relationships (Gramsci 1971, 238). Within the capitalist system, education plays a role to cement the existing hegemony. "It is crucial in securing the consent for the ruling way of life, (and) one that is supportive of and supported by the prevailing mode of production" (Mayo 2007, 3). Thus, for example, Gramsci opposed a proposed separation between

classical and vocational schools in Italy because that was a differentiation that
was eventually going to be achieved on the basis of class (Mayo 2007, 3).

Gramsci's support of both a classical education "and the pursuit of a radical
political education through a traditional curriculum and pedagogy" has been a
source of criticism and debate. Some critics are not able to fathom how Gramsci could champion the liberation of the oppressed and advocate a traditional
education designed by the oppressor to train political progressives who will
bring about the liberation. In his defense, Entwistle concludes that Gramsci
felt that "to emphasize discipline, intellectual order and the authoritative
transmission of the 'thought of the past' is to inoculate the learner against
political authoritarianism, as well as to transmit the skills and knowledge necessary for the pursuit of radical social change" (Entwistle 1979, 86). Indeed
Entwistle's position is that a person's political orientation will not necessarily
be determined by the "ideology of schooling" (Entwistle 1979, 89) and that
"school knowledge is neutral and empowering—thus the need for a disinter-
ested school, and it is up to the individuals to put their knowledge or skills to
the service of status quo or its change" (Entwistle 1979, 89).

The Gramscian approach to education and the state provides a powerful framework for progressive educators and educational policymakers to
analyze educational policy and assess the development of the educational
landscape in a developing country such as Ghana. Gramsci set forth the idea
of education as a transformative process. He argued that one of the functions
carried out by the state, in line with the need to establish cultural hegemony, is
to bring the masses to a particular cultural and moral level. In a sense Gramsci's philosophy of education was akin to John Dewey's (Morrow and Torres
2001, 334). In effect, education should be liberating in terms of the learner's
spontaneous ability to observe, explore, create and reflect. Gramsci felt that
there is a traditional knowledge base that every learner must grasp. His position on the content of education was very pragmatic—striking a fine balance
between "spontaneity and discipline" (Morrow and Torres 2001, 333).

Gramsci believed that education as a transformative process must be made
available to all citizens and so he opposed any system that segregated the
classes. In this work we examine how the processes of privatization and corporatization have affected the traditional university curriculum, the faculty, traditions
of university administration, and access to university education and equity.

EVOLUTION OF THE GHANAIAN UNIVERSITY SYSTEM

At the time of Ghana's independence from Britain in 1957, the country had
one university college (established in 1948). The University College of the

Gold Coast was founded with a relationship to the University of London. In 1961 the school was reestablished as the University of Ghana by an Act of Parliament. A second university emphasizing science and technology, The Kwame Nkrumah University of Science and Technology, was also founded. A third university, The University of Cape Coast, was established in 1962 to focus on education and the production of graduate teachers.

In 1993, the University College of Education, Winneba, and the University of Development Studies were founded. The university in Winneba consolidated several advanced teacher training institutions and was designed to organize campuses across the country to help strengthen teacher education in Ghana (Daniel 1996, 1). The University for Development Studies was established in the Northern Region with a mission to combine academic work with practical training and community service (Daniel 1996, 1).

Since the establishment of University of Winneba and the University for Development Studies a number of public institutions of higher education have achieved university status. The old School of Mines in Tarkwa in the Western Region and the Ghana Institute of Management and Public Administration (GIMPA) in Accra became universities in 2004.[4] Several other public institutions now provide university-level education and grant degrees (see table 15.1). These include the Ghana Institute of Journalism (GIJ), the Institute of Professional Studies (IPS), and the National Film Training Institute (NAFTI).[5]

FINANCIAL CONSTRAINTS, ACCESS, AND EQUITY

The principle of equal access to university education implies "making it possible for everyone that desires a university education to receive it. For this to be possible it means that enough classrooms, laboratories and instructional facilities should be provided for everyone" (Oyabade et al. 2007, 41). In the early years of independence the public universities were generously funded (Sawyerr 1994; Manuh et al. 2007). Over time, the demand for university education in Ghana has remained very high, and although the government has made more investments to establish new universities, supply has not been keeping up with demand (Manuh et al. 2007, 3). In addition, there are serious "structural inequalities based on age, region, social class, gender, ethnicity and rural/urban origin that determine access to university education" (Manuh et al. 2007), with those from areas in the country with better access to basic and secondary education having an advantage over their counterparts from less developed regions (Addae-Mensah 2000).

The situation was worsened by the government's education restructuring program, which increased the number of candidates seeking admission to

Table 15.1   Publicly Funded Institutions of Higher Education in Ghana

Name	Gender	Certificate/ Diploma	First Degree	Post- Graduate	Total
Kwame Nkrumah	M	97	14,656	1,168	15,921
University of Science	F	16	6,359	264	6,639
and Technology					
(KNUST)	Total	113	21,015	1,432	22,560
	M	126	11,017	380	11,523
University of Cape	F	169	21,572	108	5,449
Coast (UCC)	Total	295	16,189	488	16,972
	M	163	8,188	200	8,551
University of Education	F	47	4,387	102	4,536
(UEW)	Total	210	12,575	302	13,087
University of	M	111	4,536	27	4,674
Development Studies	F	74	1,880	1	1,955
(UDS)	Total	185	6,416	28	6,629
University for Mines	M	37	752	94	883
and Technology	F	-	77	1	78
(UMAT)	Total	37	829	95	961
	M	875	14,524	1,147	16,546
University of Ghana,	F	717	10,409	564	11,690
Legon (UG)	Total	1,592	24,933	1,711	28,236
	M	1,409	53,673	3,016	58,098
Total	F	1,023	28,284	1,040	30,347
	Total	2,432	81,957	4,056	88,445

Source: National Council for Tertiary Education, 2008

the universities. Within a few years, the number of students graduating from secondary schools tripled. As a result, publicly funded university enrollments increased, from 9,997 in 1990 to 47,589 in 2002–2003, and 63,576 in 2003/4, an average growth of about 12 percent per annum (Manuh et al. 2007, 44).

Access to university education in Ghana is quite limited. In 2000, out of the more than 600 secondary schools in Ghana, 50 schools produced more than 70 percent of students admitted to publicly funded universities (Addae-Mensah 2000). A survey carried out by Manuh and others involving 1,500 students suggested that approximately 50 percent of university students came from twenty-nine secondary schools (Manuh et al. 2007, 82). The survey also showed that nearly 70 percent of the students in the five universities reside in three southern regions—Greater Accra, Ashanti, and Eastern Regions (Manuh et al. 2007, 82).

Supply difficulties also affect access for adult students, those who for one reason or another were not able to enroll at a university directly after their secondary school education, or those who missed out on traditional secondary education. University educational structures in Ghana have traditionally focused on secondary school graduates, with very little attention paid to the educational needs of working adults who try to combine a working life and educational studies. Such a situation results in limited opportunities for adult late starters (Assie-Lumumba 2001).

The financial challenges facing these institutions have led to overcrowded lecture halls and lack of space (Manuh et al. 2007, 83). In addition, students are forced to pay exorbitant rents to landlords in accommodations near university campuses. Although decent private hostels are being developed, they are not adequate and the rents are usually beyond the reach of the average student.

Funding for public universities is a major problem for the government. Between 1991 and 2000 the average annual dollar value of government support per university student declined by 75 percent, from $2,360 to $566 (Addae-Mensah 2001). The government adopted a cost-sharing formula to fund university education, under which the government would pay 70 percent of the cost with the other 30 percent coming from the universities' own internal revenue generation, private donations, and student tuition payments (Manuh et al. 2007, 98). This formula has been a source of much conflict between student bodies and the government.

ARRIVAL OF PRIVATE INSTITUTIONS

These problems set the stage for the corporatization of universities and the advent of commercialized private universities. Ghana's higher education framework changed considerably in the early parts of the 1990s. Many private sector and religious bodies who had previously only involved themselves in pre-tertiary education have founded institutions (Appendix 15.1). This led authorities to establish the National Accreditation Board (NAB) in 1993 (Ofori-Attah 2006, 1).

A number of questions about the new educational framework have emerged, including: Will the new institutions help address issues of access, or will they just create more room for privileged groups within Ghanaian society? Will these institutions become comprehensive universities, where academics provide comprehensive university education and carry out research, both basic and applied, to a broad spectrum of students? Table 15.2 lists private institutions and a sampling of the fees they charge (as compared to publicly funded universities). Clearly these institutions are not in any way making it easier for the underprivileged to gain access to a university education. A regular student at a publicly funded institution pays about $313 for the year. Comparatively therefore these private institutions are very expensive and out of the reach of many Ghanaians.

A GRAMSCIAN ANALYSIS OF GHANAIAN HIGHER EDUCATION

Commercialization, the University Curriculum, and Teaching

Gramsci's assertions on education are useful for analyzing Ghanaian higher education. One of the main characteristics of Gramsci's analysis of education was his abiding faith in the power of education to liberate the human mind and cause the oppressed to confront their oppression and create a new reality for themselves. Gramsci himself came from very humble beginnings, and his university education taught him that there should not be one type of education for the elite and another for the masses (Burawoy 2003, 201). Gramsci believed that the oppressed should have a say in their hegemonic relationship with the dominant class. They are capable of doing so only if they have the capacity to confront and negotiate through the machinations of the hegemonic structures. This is only possible if the masses acquire a comprehensive education. They cannot do so if they are only trained vocationally to provide the limited services that the dominant classes require of them. In this sense Gramsci's philosophy of radical education has been likened to that of John Dewey (Morrow and Torres 2001, 334).

By today's standard, Gramsci's assertions on education do not seem "radical" and have even been characterized by some as conservative. Morrow and

Table 15.2 Sampling of Fees of Private Institutions

Schools	Fees
Ashesi University College	Ghana Nationals $2772
	Other Nationals $2772
Methodist University College	$ 962
Regent University	$1,070
Knutsford University College	$938
Valley View University	$1,024
Wisconson International University	$700
Islamic University	$726
University of Ghana (Public)	Fee Paying $1352
	Regular Student $ 313

Data collected February, 2008

Torres (2001) cite E. D. Hirsch's[6] contrast between the radical educational program of Paolo Friere and the "conservative" ideas of Gramsci:

> Like other educational progressives, Freire rejected traditional teaching methods and subject matters. . . . He called for a change of both methods and content—new content that would celebrate the culture of the oppressed, and new methods that would encourage intellectual independence and resistance. . . . Gramsci took the opposite view. He held that political progressivism demanded educational conservatism. The oppressed should be taught to master the tools of power and authority—the ability to read, write, and communicate—and to gain enough traditional knowledge to understand the worlds of and culture around them. Children, particularly the children of the poor, should not be encouraged to flourish "naturally," which would keep them ignorant and make them slaves of emotion. They should learn the value of hard work, gain the knowledge that leads to understanding, and master the traditional culture in order to command its rhetoric, as Gramsci himself had learned to do (Hirsch 1999, 3).

At a recent assembly at Regents University College, Ghana's head of state while celebrating the contributions of these new institutions lamented the lack of focus on the sciences and asked the new institutions to pay more attention to the sciences in their curriculum.[7] Many of these new institutions are very sensitive to the university education market and are cashing in on the perceived demand for business and information technology graduates (Appendixes 15.1 and 15.2 show private institutions' emphasis on business and information technology).

The demand for business courses may be related to the growth of the service sector in the Ghanaian economy. The Annual Report of the Institute of Statistical, Social and Economic Research of the University of Ghana reported that 2006 saw very impressive growth rates within the service sector of the Ghanaian economy. For example, the Finance, Insurance, Real Estate and Business Services sector saw an average growth rate of 5.7 percent from 2002 to 2006. Within this period the number of banks in Ghana increased and competition within the banking sector has been very keen. Altogether, the service sector's contributions to the Gross Domestic Product increased from 24.3 percent in 2005 to 30.1 percent in 2006 (ISSER 2007). As the service sector expands, new higher education institutions have responded with business courses, and university courses in business and finance are aggressively sought by students. The effect has been that even students without an aptitude for business have been enrolling in business courses.

Consequently, business programs have been flourishing, to the detriment of the arts, sciences, and social sciences. Currently, many students are reluctant to take required humanities and social science courses. The attitude has become one of giving the student (customer) what he or she wants—and is willing to pay for. This trend is dangerous because in an era of competition there is a tendency for the institutions to be concerned more with attracting more students than with the content of the education the students are receiving.

Gramsci was convinced, not unlike the advocates of liberal education and cultural literacy in the United States, that every citizen is entitled to a comprehensive education, especially those who need a revolutionary education in order to liberate themselves. In effect, students and progressive educators have to resist the vocationalization that is taking place with privatization and corporatization. Those who have been involved in academic counseling know firsthand how difficult it is to counsel a student with little aptitude for business subjects but who is determined to earn a business degree because in his view business expertise is what the market wants. Indeed one may wonder how many artists, historians, and physicists have been lost to the business craze.[8]

Commercialization, the Faculty and University Administration

Many Ghanaian institutions of higher education do not have nearly a full complement of professional intellectuals, whose duty it has always been to maintain the integrity of the university curriculum. It may well be that they are simply giving their customers what they are asking for with little or no sense of a fiduciary responsibility toward the student. The new private or corporatized university operates strictly within a tight budget, and the budget does not always allow for the time-honored but sometimes expensive traditions we have come to associate with the university. In many of these institutions there is no tenure for academics. The university would rather hire a number of less expensive temporary or part-time faculty. These employees are less likely to demand higher salaries or seek an active role in the university's administration. A similar phenomena, the increased use of adjunct faculty in the United States, has been criticized because, "permanent class of gypsy scholars threatens to be created. . . . This practice is particularly shameful when it is also employed to compensate for exorbitant salaries paid to a few 'superstars.' That market pressures should have so distorted the research university is a measure, of course, of its moral collapse" (Wilshire 1990, 251).

The commercialized university has no use for traditional faculty tenure. In terms of the university's human resource base, the cumulative effect is "increasing casualization, juniorization and 'churning' of academic staff" (Bostock 1999, 11). What for the university are market-oriented, cost-controlling, and cost-cutting measures, are, for the progressive university academic, steps that emaciate the ability of the university and its faculty to provide the total organic education that Gramsci indicated was necessary for the mental liberation of students. Similar concerns expressed by Mabizela regarding Kenyan universities are very applicable to Ghana (Mabizela 2004).

The new commercialized universities have little or no interest in research, and if there is a research agenda, the emphasis is on research with commercial value. Faculty members are now under pressure not simply to increase their intellectual and research output but also to conduct their affairs such that students will not be turned away. Hence, for example, faculty increasingly complain of the use of student evaluations for faculty appraisals. This has resulted in a trend whereby those who teach the subjects that are in higher demand have more clout and command more resources.

The trend toward corporatization is also affecting the manner in which university administrators run universities. According to Bostock, "the university administrator was traditionally a detached figure whose role was to uphold standards of probity in such matters as appointment, examination and handling of money. In the corporate university, administrators are expected to behave as would the executives in any other large commercial enterprise" (Bostock 1999, 13). The university campus was traditionally a terrain of equals, with the administrators essentially performing as the firsts among equals. The pressure to attract more resources, to attract more students and retain them in the face of competition, is now driving university administrators to be more authoritarian. As a result, the tradition of reliance on a committee system of shared governance is becoming a thing of the past.

The university president is gradually becoming more like a chief executive officer of a for-profit company. For example, the process of change and commercialization that the Ghana Institute of Management and Public Administration (GIMPA) has experienced has raised eyebrows in Ghana and elsewhere.[9] However the mechanisms of change that were set in motion on the campus could not have been easily implemented on a regular university campus. A consultants' report on the change process remarked:

> There is the argument that if the leader is put in an Organization/Institute/Establishment where the leader/Director-General cannot get a leeway or get his way through he could not have performed as he had done. Especially in an environment—a university for example, where rules, regulations, procedures and structures are well established/laid down, where one cannot easily circumvent the existing rules, procedures, structures, only little could have been achieved (ED&M Consulting 2007, 27).

According to Bostock "the former administrative style of gentlemanly (admittedly sexist) collegiality among tenured and mostly respected citizens . . . seems to have given way to a more robust even cut-throat style known as managerialism" (Bostock 1999, 14). He further remarked that this new style of administration, "with its emphasis on flexibility and avoidance of commit-tees, carries with it an increased risk of corruption and malpractice that the earlier paradigms strove so hard to eliminate" (Bostock 1999, 14).

What corporatism seems to be achieving is the creation of institutions within which professional academics, who used to be the custodians of the university, are now reduced to field hands who are dispensable and may be replaced according to the whim of high-handed bottom-line observers. The effect is really a waste of intellectual resources, teaching, and research expe-rience on a lot of campuses. There is evidence that these trends tend to dis-courage potential faculty from university employment. Academia is therefore continually hemorrhaging in terms of good quality faculty, to the detriment of the university and its students.[10]

There are further concerns that this trend is not only affecting what students are taught, it is also increasing control of universities by external interests. Economic difficulties have made universities desperate to find ways to stay in business, making it more difficult for university administrators to stand up against the interests of major funders, including the government.

The university has traditionally been a place where all shades of ideo-logical and philosophical persuasions are represented, enabling lively debates among faculty and students. The question is how viable this model is in the face of the realities of these new institutions of the developing world. In ef-fect, we may just end up with university faculty who produce a reserve army of business graduates who go out into the world to compete for increasingly nonexistent jobs, and who themselves are being forced on a daily basis to question their own philosophical and disciplinary commitments and to realign their commitments in order to survive within the commercialized university.

For students, corporatization is increasingly altering their relationship with the government, particularly as regards students' concerns over inadequate funding of the publicly funded universities.[11] Even after various stakeholders, including student groups, reached what was named the Akosombo Accord in 1997, there has been tension between student groups and the government over fees and cost-sharing. Students of the publicly funded universities routinely voice disappointment at the government and university authorities each time new user fees are announced. The fact is that it is still very much a privilege to receive a university education from the publicly funded universities, and the government and university authorities are increasingly high-handed in the manner in which they handle student agitation and unrest on campuses.[12] The situation is also affected by politicians' perceptions about the political inclinations and affiliations of student leadership.[13]

Ghanaian academics in the past constituted a bastion of political analysis and critique.[14] The current state of affairs casts doubt on the ability of the university in Ghana to act as a social critic, and the extent to which executives of corporatized Ghanaian universities will allow faculty to play this role. In addition, there has been a push for African universities to form alliances with industry (Atta-Mills 2004; Yamson 2004; Abeasi 2004 etc.). Partnerships with industry elsewhere have led to situations where could "individual academics essentially become entrepreneurial partners of industry" (Brownlee 1996, 6). This further compromise academics' role as societal watchdogs.

The traditions of the university have always been such that campuses usually have a fair share of academics of all ranks who confront pressures from within and without in order to avoid a situation where dominant interests can pay the university piper and call the tune. The traditional campus has been home to faculty of all stripes, with everyone (elite and the masses) having a voice on campus.

In Ghana, religious bodies have begun to wield a greater influence over universities. There is growing evidence that religious institutions that have established universities are interested in advancing the cause of their respective religious denominations, and there are signs that there might be a need for the accreditation body to outline a policy on what the academic authorities of religious institutions can require of students and staff on campus with respect to religious affiliations. Recently students of a religious university in the suburbs of Accra complained about the imposition of a dress code for students and the prohibition of certain types of music on campus. There are also reports of religious intolerance on the part of a number of institutions that are affiliated with religious groups, with instances where faculty members are required to attend religious services on campus.[15]

In a Gramscian sense, the faculty of a university is very crucial to any possible emphasis on academic discipline, intellectual order, and a transmission of the thought from the past. The university has always been a place where faculty have shepherded students and provided "school knowledge which is neutral and empowering" (Entwistle 1979, 89). The trends toward corporatization and privatization are damaging the traditional university environment within which students can receive liberating education.

CONCLUSION

It appears that Africa has entered the era in which an academic degree is increasingly considered a "private good" that primarily benefits the individual rather than a public good that benefits society (Altbach 1998). As African, and particularly Ghanaian, politicians assert that government alone cannot bear the burden of the cost of university education and rationalize the dawn of privatized university education and the increased corporatization of the publicly funded universities, it is important for students and for educators to subject these utterances to scrutiny.

Ghanaian universities have been struggling with issues of funding and human resources that have historically created difficulties with access and equity. With the advent of the corporatized university and the private university we are now confronted with a process of vocationalization and erosion of the traditions and conditions that enabled the university to carry out its mandate. The trend toward privatization/corporatization is breeding university students who attend university simply to acquire a vocation. This raises a host of questions for future research. For example, in these times of corporatization, privatization, and commercialization, are the private universities churning out graduates who are qualitatively different from the graduates of the traditional publicly funded universities? Given the funding difficulties faced by the institutions, are they able to provide the rigor and mental and attitudinal liberation that one expects of a university?

This chapter has examined the processes of corporatization and privatization from a progressive perspective, influenced by the thinking and writings of Antonio Gramsci and a number of neo-Gramscian scholars. There is no doubt that the higher education landscape in Ghana is in flux. It is important that students, members of the academy, and policymakers be made aware of these changes. These changes must be scrutinized because they pose specific challenges for classic university education and to long-standing educational traditions. Further scrutiny of this phenomenon will help inform and influence policy for the benefit of a truly accessible and equitable higher education system.

Appendix

Table 15.3   A Sample of Courses Offered by Private Institutions

Schools	Program
Ashesi University	Business Administration
	Management Information Systems
	Computer Studies
Methodist University College	Faculty of Business Administration
	Accounting, Marketing, Banking and Finance, Human Resource Management
	Faculty of Social Studies
	B.Sc. Economics
	B.Sc. Psychology
	B.Sc. Information Technology
	B.Sc. Mathematics/Statistics
	Faculty of Arts and General Studies
	BA English
	BA Religious Studies
	BA French
Wisconson International University College	Dept. Of Information Technology
	BA in Computer Science And Mgt.
	Department Of Business Studies
	B.Sc. Management and Computer Studies
	BA Business
Valley View University	Bachelor of Business Administration
	Accounting
	Marketing
	Human Resource Management
	Business Management
	Banking and Finance
	B.Sc. Computer Science
	B.Sc. Nursing
	B.Sc. Information Technology
Knutsford University College	B.Sc. in Business Administration
	Accounting and Finance
	Banking and Finance
	Marketing Management
	Human Resource Management
	B.Sc. Computer Science
Islamic University	BA in Religious Studies
	BA in Business Administration

Data collected February, 2008

Table 15.4   Student Enrollment for Private Universities by Gender and Faculty, 2006 / 2007

Faculty / Department	Gender	Certificate/ Diploma	First Degree	Post-Graduate	Total
Computer Science	M	-	350	-	350
	F	-	67	-	67
	Total	-	417	-	417
Engineering	M	-	755	-	755
	F	-	42	-	42
	Total	-	797	-	797
Information Communication Technology	M	38	786	-	824
	F	13	201	-	214
	Total	51	987	-	1,038
Agriculture	M	11	-	-	11
	F	3	-	-	3
	Total	14	-	-	14
Mathematics	M	-	7	-	7
	F	-	2	-	2
	Total	-	9	-	9
Business Administration	M	569	6,251	166	6,986
	F	497	5,214	95	5,806
	Total	1,066	11,465	261	12,792
Theology / Religious Studies	M	135	523	5	663
	F	10	79	1	90
	Total	145	602	6	753
Arts / Social Studies	M	15	1,516	4	1,535
	F	2	860	5	867
	Total	17	2,376	9	2,402
Education	M	-	24	2	26
	F	-	29	1	30
	Total	-	53	3	56
Total	M	768	10,212	177	11,157
	F	525	6,494	102	7,121
	Total	1,293	16,706	279	18,278

Source: National Council for Tertiary Education, 2008

REFERENCES

Abeasi, Kwasi. "Higher Education and Industry Partnerships." Pp. 53–64 in *African Universities, the Private Sector, and Civil Society*. Edited by George Benneh, Mariama Awumbila, and Paul Effah. Accra, Ghana: Universities Press, 2004.

Addae-Mensah, Ivan. "Education in Ghana: A Tool for Social Mobility or Social Stratification?" J. B. Danquah Memorial Lecture, Ghana Academy of Arts and Sciences, Accra (2000).

———. "Matriculation Address." *Proceedings of the Matriculation of the University of Ghana*. University of Ghana Special Reporter no. 699, 40.4 (2001).

Altbach, Philip G. "Private Higher Education: Themes and Variations in Comparative Perspective." *International Higher Education* 10 (Winter 1998): 2–4.

Assie-Lumumba, N. T. "Demand, Access and Equity Issues in African Higher Education." Background Paper for the Joint Colloquium on the University in Africa in the 1990s and Beyond, Association of African Universities, Accra (1995).

Atta-Mills, J. E. A. "Opening Address, Conference on African Universities: The Private Sector and Civil Society: Forging Partnerships for Development." Pp. 13–19 in *African Universities, The Private Sector, and Civil Society*. Edited by George Benneh, Mariama Awumbila, and Paul Effah. Accra, Ghana Universities Press, 2004.

Bostock, William W. "The Global Corporatisation of Universities: Causes and Consequences." *AntePodium Journal of World Affairs* 3 (1999) 1–27.

Brownlee, Peter. "Competitive Advantage and the University." *Campus Review* (February 1996): 15–21.

Burawoy, Michael. "For a Sociological Marxism: The Complementary Convergence of Antonio Gramsci and Karl Polanyi." *Politics and Society* 31.2 (2003): 193–261.

Buttigieg, J. A. "On Gramsci." *Daedalus* (Summer 2002): 67–70.

Commission on Higher Education in the Colonies. *Report*. Chairman: Hon. Mr. Justice Asquith (1945).

Commission on Higher Education in West Africa. *Report*. Chairman: Rt. Hon. Walter Eliot (1945).

Cownie, Fiona, and Anthony Bradney. "Gothic Horror? A Response to Margaret Thornton." *Social and Legal Studies* 14.2 (2005): 277–85.

Daniel, G. F. "The Universities in Ghana." *The Commonwealth Universities Handbook 1997–98*, vol. 1 (1996): 649–56, www.users.globalnet.co.uk/~univghana/ghanahed.htm.

Enterprise Development and Management Consulting Ltd. (ED&M Consulting). *Assessment of the Overall Impact of Reform on the Operations of Ghana Institute of Management and Public Administration, Draft Report*, Accra (2007).

Entwistle, H. *Antonio Gramsci—Conservative Schooling for Radical Politics*. London: Routledge and Kegan Paul, 1979.

Fischman, Gustavo E., and Peter McLaren. "Rethinking Critical Pedagogy and the Gramscian and Freirean Legacies: From Organic to Committed Intellectuals or Critical Pedagogy, Commitment, and Praxis." *Cultural Studies—Critical Methodologies* 5.4 (2005) 425–47.

Gramsci, Antonio. *Selections from the Prison Notebooks*. Edited by Q. Hoare and G. Nowell Smith. New York: International Publishers, 1971.

Hirsch, E. D. Jr. "Reality's Revenge: Research and Ideology." *Arts Education Policy Review* 99 (1999): 3–16.

Hopper, Richard. "Emerging Private Universities in Bangladesh." *International Higher Education* 10 (Winter 1998): 5–6

Institute of Statistical, Social and Economic Research (ISSER). *The State of the Ghanaian Economy in 2006*. Legon: University of Ghana, 2007.

Lee, Molly N. N. "Corporatization and Privatization of Malaysian Higher Education." *International Higher Education* 10 (Winter 1998) 8–9.

Manuh, Takyiwaa, Sulley Gariba, and Joseph Budu. *Change and Transformation in Ghana's Publicly Funded Universities: A Study of Experiences, Lessons and Opportunities*. Oxford: James Curry Ltd., Accra: Woeli Publishing Services, 2007.

Martin, Jane. "Gender and Education: Change and Continuity" Pp. 22–42 in *Education, Equality and Human Rights: Issues of Gender, Race, Sexuality, Disability and Social Class*. Edited by Mike Cole. London: Routledge Taylor & Francis Group, 2006.

Mayo Peter. "Antonio Gramsci and His Relevance for the Education of Adults." *Educational Philosophy and Theory*. Journal Compilation (2007): 1–17.

Morrow, Raymond A., and Carlos A. Torres. "Gramsci and Popular Education in Latin America: From Revolution to Democratic Transition." *International Journal of Educational Development* 21 (2001): 331–43.

Obara, Yoshiiaki. "A Presidential Perspective from Japan." *International Higher Education* 10 (1998): 11–12.

Ofori-Attah, Kwabena D. "Expansion of Higher Education in Ghana: Moving Beyond Tradition." *Comparative and International Education Society Newsletter* 142 (September 2006).

Oyebade S. A., S. A. Oladipo, and J. A. Adetoro. "Access to and Equity in University Education: A Status Report in Nigeria and Sub-Saharan Africa." Pp. 42–53 in *Access, Equity and Quality in Higher Education*. Edited by J. B. Babalola, G. O. Akpa, A. O. Ayeni, and O. Adedeji. Abuja: Nigeria Association for Educational Administration and Planning, 2007.

Sawyerr, A. "Ghana: Relations Between Government and Universities." In *Government and Higher Education Relationships Across Three Countries: The Winds of Change*. Edited by G. Neave and F. V. Vught. Oxford: Pergamon Press, 1944.

———. "Challenges Facing African Universities—Selected Issues." *Newsletter of the Social Science Academy of Nigeria* 5.1 (2002): 25–30.

Thornton, Margaret. "Gothic Horror in the Academy." *Social and Legal Studies* 14.2 (2005): 267–76.

Wilshire, Bruce. *The Moral Collapse of the University: Professionalism, Purity and Alienation*. Albany: State University of New York Press, 1990.

Yamson, Ishmael. "Forging Relations Between African Universities, Business and Industry for Development." Pp. 13–19 in *African Universities, The Private Sector, and Civil Society*. Edited by George Benneh, Mariama Awumbila, and Paul Effah. Accra, Ghana: Universities Press, 2004.

NOTES

1. This article was inspired by, and draws heavily on the ideas ably expressed in publications by these two authors.

2. An Italian sociological Marxist scholar who left the world a legacy of Marxist writings that were published as *The Prison Notebooks* (Gramsci 1971).

3. An example is the application of Gramscian analysis to popular education in Latin America by Raymond A. Morrow and Carlos Alberto Torres.

4. The School of Mines had operated as a campus of the Kwame Nkrumah University of Science and Technology. GIMPA was established in 1960 by the United Nations to serve as a training institution for senior public sector managers.

5. GIJ and NAFTI were formerly diploma-granting institutions. Perhaps the two institutions can be said to have trained the bulk of the nation's journalists and other media personnel. IPS was initially a professional accountancy school that started as a private institution.

6. An advocate of cultural literacy in the United States.

7. Reported in the *Daily Graphic*, May, 2008.

8. A colleague in the United States once remarked on how many of our business graduates from a predominantly minority university campus we found working on retail shop floors for very low wages after struggling through a business degree.

9. A full research study of GIMPA is ongoing.

10. A young colleague recently returned to Australia. His concerns had as much to do with wages as with what he saw as a culture of high teaching loads, little time for research, and the lack of involvement of faculty in the Institute's administration.

11. In spite of agreements reached between student organizations and the government, student groups complain any time the universities announce new student user fees.

12. An example is a recent case of unrest at a student residence, Casely-Hayford Hall at the University of Cape Coast.

13. There is currently a lawsuit involving a student leader who believes he has been denied admission to law school because of his student activism.

14. Ready examples of activist critics are Professor Ebo Hutchful in the early 1970s and Dr. Paul Ansah, whose writings in the erstwhile *Legon Observer* are still much talked about.

15. There is some speculation as to whether the NAB would involve itself in issues of religious and academic freedom.

III

EUROPE AND OCEANIA

16

Access to Higher Education in France

Between Equality of Rights and Meritocracy, a Long Walk to Equality of Opportunities?

Gaële Goastellec

Historically, the French higher education system is characterized by its duality: on one hand, elitist *Grandes Écoles* register the elite of the nation, following their own rules and organizations, among others, for access, which is mainly ruled by academic merit. On the other hand, universities are embedded in a national and legal framework that claims equality as its basic value: equality between institutions, equality between diplomas, equality between curricula, and, of course, equality of access to universities for all high school graduates, regardless of their academic achievement, constitutes the ideal on which the higher education system was built.

French university students are thus characterized, above all, by the fact of not being part of the elite; the elite have been set apart in the *Grandes Écoles*. This duality of the French higher education is one of its main characteristics. The multiplication of higher education institutions (IUT, BTS, "small" *Grandes Écoles*, and engineering schools inside universities) diversifies the system. But it does not change its duality (Berthelot 1990). The entrance to some degree programs comes with institutional competition: selective degrees tend to transform themselves into elitist ones. The generic right to study—implemented by the university sector—transforms the first degree into a relegation path. To put it differently, equality and merit are values warranted by the higher education sector, but those who are entitled to equality are not entitled to merit.

The initiative of the Parisian Institute of Political Science, in 2001, to open its admission to students from high schools identified as underprivileged through a specific admission process represents an important innovation in France. This institution, emblematic of the social reproduction (students coming from the upper class represent more than 80 percent of the enrollment) diversifies its recruitment to manage diversity and a new form of excellence. This practice, fashioned after affirmative action in vogue in the United States, has met with resistance. Depending on the student's former high school background to compensate social inequalities implies abandoning the principle of merit as the exclusive criterion for admission. Candidates not being regarded as equal per se, the previous formal equality of a unique entrance examination is modified by variables such as schooling and territorial and social origins. Following this innovation, an increasing number of elitist schools are developing specific schools to widen their recruitment.

Indeed, the distinction between merit and democratization is not the only frontier characterizing the French higher education sector. Patent sociodemographic characteristics, such as type of high school degree, gender, and economic, cultural, and social capital, impose limits on equality of opportunities. While these variables are known to regulate higher education access since the researches of Pierre Bourdieu and Jean-Claude Passeron (1964), they do not cover all the inequalities.

Another level of inequalities appeared during the last few decades, as new tools of analysis were developed: "institutional effects" and other "site effects" have evaded notice for long in the traditional understanding of the university, centralized and thus supposed to be homogenous. But a homogenous higher education system would imply, for example, an equal probability for a student, others things being equal, to obtain his or her degree in any university. As a matter of fact, researches on access to universities reveal this not to be the case. In fact, the probability for a student to obtain a degree from one institution can sometimes be twice as high in another institution (Felouzis 2000 and 2001). Students' social background, thus, is not the only characteristic weighing on their academic careers.

EQUALITY OF RIGHTS, INEQUALITIES OF RESULTS

The opposition between the *Grandes Écoles* and the French university is the product of what has long been perceived as the absence of universities. Legally, universities disappeared between 1797 and 1896; they were suppressed by the French Revolution until the Third Republic gave them a moral personality again. Universities are still in the process of giving access to the majority. This process has been implemented by several laws and, more recently (1989), by the contractualization of the relations between the state and the universities (Musselin 2001). The specificity of the Napoleonic University is its uniqueness: setting up in all places of the national territory the same fields of studies. The center of the university organization is Paris; each faculty in the provinces depends upon a referring Parisian faculty. The power of the faculties is thus stronger than that of the university. The organization can be summarized as follows: a single university (the Imperial University), a single territory, a single model of student. The organization of access to universities echoes this principle: the roots of the formal governmental policy related to the question of access and equity are laid down in the *Code de L'Education* (Article L612) of 1989:

> The first higher education degree is opened to all the high school graduates. . . . [A]ll the candidates are allowed to register in the institution of their choice. . . . All dispositions related to the repartition between institutions and curriculums exclude all form of selection.

The originality of the French universities, revealed by this law, consists in the official lack of selective access. This aspect of the French higher education is not the result of a policy, but the translation of a situation into norms. The propaedeutic year was used by the universities to select the best students until the reform Fouquet (1966) implemented a two-year diploma instead. A first attempt to organize the student's access was initiated by the President General De Gaulle in April 1968. But the riots of May 1968 put an end to this attempt, and the principle of a nonselective university sector is, thus, the result of a historical context more than an outcome of a political decision.

Searching for uniformity, centralized and dedicated to massification, the French university is deprived of the elite production by the *Grandes Écoles*. The creation of the *École des Ponts et Chaussées* and the *École des Mines* in the eighteenth century, and the dual movement initiated by the French Revolution—the suppression of universities by decree (15 September 1793) and the creation of the *École Polytechnique* and *École Normale Supérieure*—set the base for a two-stream higher education system. The French state, suspicious of its universities, has localized research in other institutions: the *Collège de France* (1650), the *École Pratique des Hautes Etudes* (1868), the *École Libre des Sciences Politiques* (1872), etc. The national intellectual identity is built outside the universities. The higher education landscape in France is thus structured with the universities training teachers, lawyers, and doctors, on one hand, and the *Grandes Écoles*, being places of innovation and of production of elites, registering the best secondary education students, on the other.

The higher education system thus remains unfinished, and this contradiction favors a massive increase in access to higher education: between 1960 and 1970, the number of students increased by 174 percent, then by 38 percent between 1970 and 1980, and by 44 percent between 1980 and 1990. This growth continued during the first half of the 1990s (25 percent), probably favored by the Orientation Law of 1989, aimed at enrolling 80 percent of the relevant age-group in the baccalaureate programs. Between 1997 and 2001, their number slightly decreased (0.7 percent), mainly due to a demographic decrease and stagnation in schooling rates. This trend was counterbalanced in 2000–2005 by a slow increase (1.1 percent per year) mainly due to foreign students, whose entry was facilitated by the Bologna process. With the diminution of their number in 2006 and the slight diminution of the proportion of high school graduates continuing to higher education, the overall number of students started decreasing again. The overall process of massification, while important, must be weighted: in France, only 54.5 percent of the relevant age-group graduates from high school and 45.1 percent access higher education. The first level of inequality thus differentiates those who get into higher education from those who stay out of higher education. A second level of inequalities concerns access to the selective institutions. How does massification influence access to the selective and nonselective sectors?

ACCESS TO THE SELECTIVE SECTOR:
THE POWER OF ACADEMIC AND CULTURAL CAPITAL

Grandes Écoles: Hiding Social Reproduction

There has not been much research on admission to elitist institutions in France (see Bourdieu 1989; Charles 1987; Julliard 1997; Lazuech 1999). The national databases on access to universities mix real selective institutions with less prestigious ones, making it impossible to study institutional admission patterns. It is as if the French society was not concerned with the elite nature of student recruitment. One of the few relatively recent research available (Euriat and Thélot 1995) traces, over a period of thirty years, the evolution of social recruitment of the four most prestigious French schools: the *École Polytechnic*, the *École Nationale d'Administration*, the *École Normale Supérieure*, and the *École des Hautes Etudes Commerciales*. Each of these schools represents the most elitist training in the following four spheres: industrial, administrative, intellectual, and economic studies. This research reveals a singular inertia of social inequalities in these schools: at the beginning of the 1990s as well as at the beginning of the 1960s, students coming from the working class[1] were twenty-three times less probable to access these schools compared to those coming from the upper class. The gap between the *Grandes Écoles* and universities was not only maintained but also increased, testifying to the refusal of the *Grandes Écoles* to be involved in the massification process. Furthermore, the decrease of inequalities in universities makes the *Grandes Écoles* even more elitist than they were.

We can compensate for the lack of information on the recruitment into *Écoles* by analyzing the students' profiles in the preparatory classes of these schools and compare it with those of the universities. This comparison, however, remains an approximation, as not all the preparatory classes' students access these elitist institutions.

Preparatory Classes' Recruitment: An Inherited Distinction

In 2006–2007, the preparatory classes (CPGE) registered 73,456 students, representing 7 percent of the first of second years' higher education students (Daverne and Dutercq 2008). Men (58 percent) are better represented than women (42 percent), but what differentiates the profile of preparatory class students from their university counterparts are their social origin and their parents' educational level. Table 16.1 shows that children of parents who are in senior management are more represented in the CPGE (50.8 percent) compared with the university (31.4 percent). Their overrepresentation in the CPGE makes for an underrepresentation of children of all the other social categories, and mainly children of workers.

This quantitative domination of the highest social class is correlated with an overrepresentation of the children whose fathers have the highest degrees:

Table 16.1 Social background of university students and CPGE students

Fathers' occupation (in percent)	University	CPGE	Difference
Peasants	1.9	2	-0.1
Craftsmen, merchants, company directors	6.7	7.8	+1.1
Senior management, liberal professions	31.4	50.8	+19.4
Intermediary professions	15	13.9	-1.1
Employees	13.4	9.7	-3.7
Workers	10.5	5	-5.5
Pensioners, unemployed	11.7	7.2	-4.5
Unknown	9.4	3.6	-6.8
Total	100	100	

Source: Ministère de l'Education Nationale et de la Recherche, 2007: "Socio-professional background of the French students," Table 6.14.

55 percent of the CPGE students have fathers who have at least a two-year university degree, compared with 27.9 percent of those who are registered in the university first cycle (including in medical and law degrees). At the same time, 56.3 percent of the university students' fathers did not finish their secondary studies, compared with 31.1 percent of those studying in CPGE. The academic capital of the student's family thus plays a determinant role in her/ his orientation, so much so that it seems to go beyond the student's own academic achievement: when comparing students' orientation in relation with the grade they obtained for their high school diploma, it appears that 56.8 percent of the sons (24.2 percent of the daughters) of company directors, liberal professionals or senior management personnel register in CPGE, compared with 29.4 percent of workers' sons (14.6 percent of workers' daughters). These inequalities of access to CPGE are probably behind what similar measurements in the *Grandes Écoles* would show. But they reveal their role in the selection of elite based on inherited social and academic capital.

This opposition between the selective sector and the university sector is not the only one structuring the French higher education system. Universities also reveal a differentiated orientation of students linked to their social background.

UNIVERSITIES AND INEQUALITIES OF ACCESS

Access to higher education remains linked to social background. If the gap has been reduced, it remains important: children of senior management personnel graduate from high school nearly twice more numerously compared with children of workers and are 2.2 times more likely to access higher education (Ministère de l'Education Nationale 2001). Inequalities within the universities thus represent a second level of inequality.

Inequalities in Orientation

The study of the students' social background in the different subjects reveals inequalities: 82.9 percent of the children of senior management personnel and liberal professionals register for university compared with 67.7 percent of the children of workers. The latter students (20.5 percent) choose the STS section more than the former (4.5 percent). There has been a change in the profile of students registering in the IUT. Historically, the IUT registered students from the lower classes, but since the 1980s, middle- and upper-class children have tended to be more represented (Erlich 1998). Academic careers and school preferences thus vary according to social origin: the lower-class students are more represented in the short and professionalized curricula, while the upper-class students tend to go for selective curricula, or, at least, long studies.

Similar trends can be observed in enrollment into various subjects. Students from the upper class are more often registered in subjects where the *numerus clausus* is used (Law and Medical studies). Children of senior management personnel and liberal professionals account for 36 percent of law students, 43.4 percent of health sciences students, and 30 percent of the higher education students. By contrast, workers' children account for 8.7 percent of law students, 5.3 percent of health sciences students, and 11.2 percent of all students (Ministère de l'Education Nationale et de la Recherche 2007). These inequalities are more significant in the light of the fact that workers represent 25 percent of the French population while the upper class account for only 11 percent.

How can we analyze these social inequalities? The organization of the *Grandes Écoles* admission, based on formal equality in a selective entrance examination, leads to a transformation "of the privileges into merit, as it allows social action to play, but through more secrets paths" (Bourdieu and Passeron 1964: 104). The university sector, though more open regarding social background, still uses the same principle. Cultural capital and family knowledge of university organization and its prerequisites produce the same opacity. In these two worlds, equality of chances characterized by the entrance examination, by the differentiation between short and long studies and subjects, produces social inequalities in the orientation and, later on, in rates of success. In the university sector, inequalities in access and orientation are reinforced by academic career inequalities: the probability to obtain the first university degree in two years varies between 40.7 percent for the students coming from the lower class to more than 50 percent for those coming from the upper class (Ministère de l'Education Nationale 2002).

The aggregation of these inequalities produce a differentiation in the probability of students to pursue their studies: students from working-class backgrounds represent 12.3 percent of the *Licence* (the first three-year cycle), but only 7.3 percent of those accessing the master's degree and 4.4 percent of those registered for doctoral work. Meanwhile, students from the upper class increase their proportion from 28.7 percent to 38.3 percent (Ministère de l'Education Nationale et de la Recherche 2007). The unequal probability of accessing higher degrees according to social background shows the progressive selection operating in the university:

University contributes this way to the reproduction of a class domination, it plays a role of selection of the individuals and transmission of the ruling class culture . . . , conforming itself to the cultural order of the ruling class, the university allows the reproduction of social structures and classes hierarchy by hiding the social origin of academic performance inequalities, and by naturalizing them through a gift ideology (Lapeyronnie, Marie 1992:122).

Thus, social background represents the cornerstone of university achievement. It affects the type of high school degree obtained and the choice of studies. Besides this long-known dimension of educational inequality, new social issues reveal other kinds of inequalities.

Geographical Inequalities: "Institutional Effect" and Academic Principle

The study of the "institutional effect" goes against the secular tradition of the French higher education system that is supposed to be equal in all places of the territory since the Imperial University and that still allows universities to refuse access for students coming from another academy (the only legal cause of refusal). To reveal disparities in access to degrees could thus transform these refusals into unfairness. The research carried by the Ministère de l'Education Nationale (2002b) analyses the probability of obtaining the first university degree in seven subjects taught in eighty-one universities. The national probability to obtain the two-year diploma in two years reaches 45.5 percent, in five years 79.7 percent. A comparison of the success rates among universities shows that the real rate varies, as the "weighted rates" neutralize the effect of age, type of secondary degrees, and university subject.

Depending on the university, the real rate of graduation in five years varies from 41.8 percent to 99.1 percent. These universities do not register the same public, which fact explains, at least in part, the inequalities in success in the first degree. Older students graduate less often than their youngest counterparts, and those who obtain a scientific secondary education degree have a better graduation rate compared with those who graduated in economics, literature, and, even more, technology. Nevertheless, all these indicators being identical, the graduation rate dispersion between universities remains strong. The "added value" that determined the probability of graduating among students reveals an "institutional effect": it varies from −28 points to +23.6 points.

Another researcher (Felouzis 2000) arrived at the same conclusions regarding the different subjects: the probability for a given student to leave the system without a degree in the three universities studied varies from 19 percent to 39 percent in law, from 5 percent to 11 percent in geography, and from 49 percent to 56 percent in material sciences. This research testifies to local inequalities, which go against the principle of university uniformity and the constraint of students' regional registration it is supposed to legitimate.

These success rates measure the probability to obtain a degree that is only national by name. These studies do not consider the quality of the training, the level of examinations, nor their adequacy to the academic and professional future of the students. Nevertheless, they underline the nonpertinence of the principle of belonging to an academy (that is, the place where the students obtain their high school diploma strongly influences their university registration), which produces inequalities when geographic disparities appear.

Geographic inequalities revealed by various studies question the principle of equality and homogeneity vis-à-vis the French higher education system. While "schools" are always more numerous, universities become more heterogeneous. The transformation of university policies, historically based on the acknowledgment of faculties and subjects, but now reoriented toward a taking into account of institutions, and the researches questioning the "institutional effect" seem to demand a redefinition of the role of universities and critical thinking about the different ways toward equality.

RECONCILING MERIT AND EQUITY, NEGOTIATING EQUALITY OF OPPORTUNITIES

Confronted with the dissociation of equality of rights and merit, the French higher education institutions are slowly attempting to modify their practices.

Institutional Reactions

Introducing discreet meritocratic practices in universities

We have previously shown how universities, required to register all secondary school graduates regardless of their characteristics, later offer them unequal probabilities to graduate. This can be linked to different certification practices and to different admission practices. Indeed, while selection is formally prohibited, fieldwork in two faculties of a provincial university has revealed cooling-out processes aimed at specifying the type of students registered (Goastellec 2002). This cooling out has been previously described by Burton Clark (1960) as a succession of stages "aimed at reinforcing students" lucidity regarding their own ability by putting to test not only their academic aptitudes but also their motivations, and, finally, their self-esteem. Confronted by specific student demands for access, each department produces its own rules of registration, defined to encourage some students and discourage others. These processes are the consequence of more or less framed departments' projects.

For example, in the biology department studied, the cooling-out process is highly formalized. At a first level, the website stipulates that entrance is reserved for students having a scientific secondary degree (while this type of requirement is nationally forbidden) and that the number of seats is limited. At a second level, students requesting registration are obliged to present a registration file including information on their previous academic achievement (report card of the previous years) and a letter of motivation. A third level requires the potential students to make an appointment with the professor responsible for registration. Only during this appointment will he/she receive the registration file. The purpose is to make sure the student understands the university requirements. During the meeting, the professor explains the organization and difficulties of the curricula, looks at the student's previous results and advises her/him to register or not, and to prepare for the year by working on specific subjects during the summer. In fact, everything is put in place to test the student's motivations and make sure he/she will fit in the department's project. As for the "registration authorization," it is provided by the pedagogical committee, after taking into account individual files. "How do we select them? But it is the natural selection that is operating, if I dare to say. There are those I see once and those that, finally, once they have heard the discourse, leave on running!" (Interview with professor in charge of admissions, September 2001).

This cooling-out process has two advantages for the department. It favors the less motivated students' self-elimination and confronts the most "resistant" to their field of study requirements, so that they are able to prepare for their ensuing studies. Since the universities are not authorized to operate a direct selection process, this process does not involve *real* selection; it makes the candidates *believe* that they are considered for selection after due process of ascertaining motivation and aptitude.

Of course, the lack of transparency regarding these cooling-out processes makes it difficult to measure their effects on the building-up of a student profile. But comparing the student profile in the department with the national student profile in this subject allows us to grasp some specificity that may be linked to the cooling-out process. For example, if the year after the creation of this biology department (in 1999), women were more numerous among the students (62 percent), the proportion of men has quickly increased to reach 53 percent, while at the national level women remain better represented with 58 percent. The opposite trend in this department is the consequence of a deliberate elitist image, men being on an average more attracted by elitist degrees than women.

In the same vein, students coming from another academy have always obtained a scientific secondary degree, while 10 percent of those coming from the university academy have obtained a technical one. The biology department thus uses the legal framework to select, on the margin, students with the best academic results.

This department has developed an "admission project." Conformity with the legal framework—the acceptance of graduates of all high schools from the academy—is balanced by a cooling-out process that favors self-elimination of the less motivated students. This practice tends to attract strategically advantaged candidates. Beside, the cooling-out process can also be analyzed as a warming-up process: while it discourages candidates who have low self-esteem, it also attracts those who are self-confident. If self-confidence is linked to academic success, with an identical academic level, boys and children of the ruling class often show stronger self-esteem. Finally, the specificities of these students—men with coherent and homogeneous academic careers, coming from middle and upper classes—are the product of this "admission project."

Introducing equity within meritocracy

During the last seventeen years, attempts have been made by elitist institutions to widen their recruitment. The first innovation in this regard has been implemented by the Parisian Institute of Political Science. This institution advertised itself as the flagship institution regarding these procedures by adopting a specific admission process for students coming from areas identified as having disadvantaged high schools (ZEP [Priority Education Zone]). In 2001, it adopted conventions with high schools from the ZEP, probably to increase the republican legitimacy of its admission process.

De facto, this institution's reputation (the traditional path to access the National School of Administration, leading to the most prestigious careers), the coherence between the education provided and the marketplace, and the internationalization of its curricula explain this institution is a real added value. The qualitative study of the social origin of the students of this institution (Cheurfa and Tiberj 2001) reveals that, in 1998, children of the working class were twelve times less numerous than within university. Furthermore, the children of workers were six times less represented, while the children of the senior management personnel (53.5 percent as against 35.5 percent) and those of company directors and liberal professionals (28 percent versus 9 percent) were overrepresented. Beside, these inequalities of access appear to be increasing, as children from the upper class become more represented.

The sole registration for the entrance examination already presents itself as a form of self-selection largely indexed on social and cultural capital, and statistics also reveal that the examination modalities require a specific type of cultural and economic capital. Private training also improves the probability to succeed, as well as linguistic immersions, recommended to face the linguistic test. Surely, the redactions required in the examination mobilize a cultural capital that reinforces the weight of social origin. Children of senior management personnel and those in the intellectual professions and teaching are the only ones to see their proportion increase after the examination: they represent respectively 53.5 percent and 10.5 percent of the students taking the examination, and 56 percent and 15.5 percent of those who are admitted.

In this context, a second path of admission has been implemented to reduce the social reproduction characterizing this institution. Before its implementation, this path of admission was at the core of strong debates at the national level. The National Assembly first approved the project and then rescinded it under pressure from a student union. The Constitutional Council called by some senators questioned the legality of the dispositions. When finally it was adopted, the Institution started to delegate to teachers of the identified high schools the choice and preparation of candidates, if possible three years before high school graduation. The central role of the teachers consists in the diffusion of strategic knowledge. It seeks to compensate a lack of knowledge that is not strictly linked to school but to schooling strategies. The recruitment criteria used in this recruitment are part of a holistic approach: cultural, social, and economic capital are taken into account to analyze student academic achievement. Academic value is measured by former academic results and secondary education grades, and students are orally tested on the basis of a file prepared during the year. The jury then considers "qualities related to the mastering of oral expression, intellectual curiosity, and motivation of the candidate" (*Le Monde*, 28 March 2001).

These criteria, evaluating individual qualities, favor the admission of candidates who are not from the same mold. During the years following this innovation, an increasing number of students have been selected through this second path of admission, and there has been a seven-fold increase in the number of high school partnerships—forty-eight ZEP high schools are involved in this project.

Correcting inequalities through this preferential recruitment questions the principle of social justice: what is collectively fair is not necessarily individually fair. To implement the second path of admission has reduced the number of places dedicated to the students taking the first path of admission. Marginally, this also leaves out students who would have been taken in the normal course. This explains the polemics about these practices. Students also worry that this opening could generate a depreciation of the academic prestige they used to benefit from. For the last two centuries, French schools have been characterized by Malthusianism and their focus on specific academic criteria was reproducing social elite. The opening of the recruitment, though only marginally, represents at least symbolic rupture of elitism.

This practice has been accompanied by the reorganization of tuition fees and funding. Tuition fees have increased from €1,000 per year to €5,000, which is closer to actual costs. The rationale behind this increase may be that, in the French context, students in the highly elitist sector of the "preparatory classes" leading to the *Grandes Écoles* are supported by public taxes to a greater extent than their university counterparts. Considering that most students enrolled in those institutions come from high-income families, the unfairness of the system become obvious. While tuition fees were raised, the administration of the Parisian Institute of Political Science opted for indexing them on family income. This policy has resulted in the same 20 percent of students benefiting from fee exemptions, while another 12 percent are charged less than before (€500 instead of €1,000). This policy had the consequence of maintaining 20 percent of the students benefiting from fee exemptions, while another 12 percent are charged less than before (€500 instead of €1,000), and the richest 29 percent, coming from the top 2.5 percent wealthiest families at the national level are charged tuition fees five time higher. The added income provided by this increase is then used by the institution to match the 50 percent fellowships provided by the national government to low-income students. Fairer admission practices lie in a wide interpretation of students' needs and of their ability to afford higher education.

An increasing number of elitist institutions are implementing innovative ways to provide access to socially "disadvantaged" students. About thirty *Grandes Écoles* and high school "preparatory classes" are today part of this trend, each one developing their own practices (Allouch 2008). For example, one of the most prestigious French high schools, the *Lycée Henri IV*, has started tutoring (by its students) the ZEP high school students to help them access its "preparatory classes."

These innovations, no doubt, only have a marginal effect. The number of students so helped is small, as these higher education institutions also struggle to preserve their elitism. Moreover, these innovations have other purposes than social justice: they are about increasing the efficiency of these institutions by taking in academically gifted students. The students benefiting from these actions share the same academic excellence as the traditional elite (Daverne and Dutercq 2008).

While the French higher education system is characterized by free education, it does not warrant equity: although French students and their families oppose tuition fees and selectivity in access, EUROSTUDENT research (2005) reveals that the French higher education system is plagued by one of the highest levels of inequality by social group in Europe (along with Austria, Germany, and Portugal). In this context, the Ministère de l'Education Nationale has introduced new fellowships for academically gifted students, introducing an equity principle, where equality was traditionally the only rule.

National Incentives toward Admission Regulations

The national framework still makes it difficult to change admission rules, and students' lobbies are vociferous when it comes to protecting what they perceive as a right: accessing universities and subjects regardless of their academic background. As a result, the articulation of merit and equity only operates in the margin. Students' funding is one of these discrete tools.

If changes in admission process contribute to the widening the student enrollment in higher education, they cannot be dissociated from funding issues. In France, open access to universities for high school graduates is sustained by free studies and fellowships based on parental income, family size, and distance between the place of study and the family residence. This translates the principle of equity of rights, setting merit to the side. But, in 1998, merit fellowships were implemented to help academically talented students coming from the working class and willing to prepare for entrance examinations to the *Grandes Écoles*. In all, 186 fellowships amounting to €6,000 per year were granted in the first year, and 400 fellowships in the second year. This attempt to compensate for economic inequalities reminds one of the old merit fellowships provided to the best students of the republican schools to access secondary education. It illustrates a basic understanding of school justice: it only combines acknowledgment of academic merit and correction of some highly visible economic inequalities. In this process, social and cultural causes weighting on higher education orientation are hidden.

Another attempt deals with the centralization of students' registration. During the last few years, besides the implementation of the Bologna accord and the changes it envisaged in the degree structure and quality assurance process, the government began redefining the rules of the higher education system, providing universities with more autonomy, introducing new possibilities for academic recruitment, and introducing more possibilities for institutional differentiation. The national frame of formal uniformity is being slowly abandoned. This institutional differentiation also calls for a differentiation of the student body. At the same time, the question of student admission is becoming more formalized at a central level, through a process named "active orientation." Since 2007, the Ministère de l'Education Nationale has created a national website to centralize and rationalize students' preregistration. Echoing the practices of the biology department previously described, the preregistration requires that each student presents the results he/she obtained during the last two years of high school, submits a professional project, and explains which subject he/she wants to register for. Universities then give a consultative opinion, conforming to the student's choice or orienting her/him toward others studies. The purpose is, on the one hand, to facilitate the preregistration for the students by making it more transparent, and, on the other hand, to advise students as regards their orientation, if not to use a cooling-out process to control the students' distribution within the system.

At a national level, thus, reorganizing higher education involves introducing an element of merit where equality of rights would be the leading rule. At the institutional level, elitist institutions are today more open to implement equality of opportunities practices, whereas historically it was only merit that governed their admission process. This attempt to balance and reconcile merit and equality marks a redefinition of the original republican ideology and an attempt to join other higher education systems emphasizing greater equity.

CONCLUSION

The massification of the higher education system is often perceived as a form of democratization, as it allows a larger number of students to access higher education. Meanwhile, two dimensions reveal that, at a qualitative level, this democratization is to be nuanced: the strongest increase has taken place in universities (with student numbers increasing by 5.8 times between 1960 and 2000) while the preparatory classes increased their numbers by 3.6 times (Ministère de l'éducation nationale et de la recherche 2000). Selective higher education institutions, educating the elite, have been preserved, while the overcrowded universities had to adapt to a new public policy.

Even more, research demonstrates that massification tends to reproduce inequalities instead of promoting social justice: the opening of higher education to a larger number of students merely displaces inequalities in the world of education (Duru-Bellat 2005). The choice of different academic paths according to social background creates a "segregated democratization" (ibid.), and intensifies the diploma race between students and social groups, as degrees become positional goods.

Concern, thus, shifts from expanding access—increasing the number of students entering higher education—to widening access—focusing on providing equal access to higher education for previously underrepresented groups. This is what institutions belonging to the selective sector—which have historically benefited from more autonomy than universities—have the opportunity to implement, while the university sector is the place of a slow and discreet reorganization. If "adapt through differentiation or perish" is the new motto of the universities, "improve efficiency through increasing social justice" is the new motto of the elitist institutions.

In this context, changes in the French organization of admission reveal that the principle of equality of right is slowly challenged by the principle of equity, or equality of opportunities. Although the process is very slow, both the diffusion of international practices reinterpreting affirmative action and the researchers' questioning of the French social reproduction through school push toward rethinking fairness in higher education. Some changes are being observed, but equity is still a long and complex way to go.

REFERENCES

Allouch, Van Zanten. "Formateurs ou 'Grands Frères'? Les tuteurs des programmes d'ouverture sociale des Grandes Ecoles et des classes préparatoires." *Education et Société* 21 (2008): 49–65.

Berthelot, Jean-Michel. "Les effets pervers de l'expansion des enseignements supérieurs, le cas de la France." *Sociétés Contemporaines* 4 (1990): 109–22.

Bourdieu, Pierre. *La noblesse d'Etat, grandes écoles et esprit de Corps*. Paris: Minuit, 1989.

Bourdieu, Pierre, and Jean-Claude Passeron. *Les héritiers, les étudiants et la culture*. Paris: Minuit, 1964.

Charles, Christophe. *Les Elites de la République, 1880–1900*. Paris: Fayard, 1987.

Cheurfa, Madani, and Vincent Tiberj. "Le concours d'entrée à Sciences Po: inégalités d'accès et inégalités sociales." Website of l'Institut d'Etudes Politiques de Paris, 2001.

Clancy P., and G. Goastellec. "Questioning Access and Equity in Higher Education: Policy and Performance in a Comparative Perspective." *Higher Education Quarterly* 61, no. 2 (2007): 136–54.

Clark, Burton R. "The Cooling Out Function in Higher Education." *American Journal of Sociology* 65 (1960): 569–76.

Daverne, Caroline, and Yves Dutercq. "L'implication des responsables d'établissement dans la formation scolaire des élites." *Education et Société* 21 (2008): 33–47.

Duru-Bellat. "Democratization of Education and Reduction in Inequalities of Opportunities: An Obvious Link?" Communication, ECER Dublin (2005).

———. *L'inflation scolaire. Les désillusions de la méritocratie*. Paris: Seuil, 2006.

Erlich, Valérie. *Les nouveaux étudiants, un groupe social en mutation*. Paris: A. Colin, 1998.

Euriat, M., and C. Thélot. "Le recrutement social de l'élite scolaire en France. Evolution des inégalités de 1950 à 1990." *Revue Française de Sociologie* 36, no. 3 (1995): 403–38.

EUROSTUDENT. "Social and Economic Conditions of Student Life in Europe, 2005: Synopsis of Indicators." Jannover: HIS Hoschschul-Informations-Systems, 2005.

Felouzis, Georges. "Les inégalités à l'université. Des inégalités sociales aux inégalités locales dans trois disciplines universitaires." *Sociétés contemporaines* 38 (2000).

———. "La condition étudiante, sociologie des étudiants et de l'université." Paris: PUF, 2001.

———. "L'enseignement supérieur en France: l'émergence de l'établissement comme objet de recherche." Bordeaux: Colloque du RESUP, 2002.

Filâtre, D., and M. Grossetti. "La carte scientifique française." Pp. 21–44 in *La territorialisation de l'enseignement supérieur et de la recherche: France, Espagne, Portugal*. Edited by M. Grossetti and P. Losego. Paris: L'Harmattan, 2003.

FQP. "Formation Salaries: Enquête sur la formation et la qualification professionnelle." Paris: INSEE, 2003.

Goastellec, G. *Egalité et Mérite à l'Université: une comparaison Etats-Unis, Indonésie, France*. Thèse de Doctorat, Bordeaux, 20020.

Goux, D., and E. Maurin. "Démocratisation de l'école et persistance des inégalités." *Economie et Statistique* 307 (1997): 27–39.

Julliard. *La faute aux elites*. Paris: Gallimard, 1997.

Lazuech, Gilles. *L'exception française, Le modèle des grandes écoles à l'épreuve de la mondialisation*. Rennes: PUR, 1999.

Merle, P. *La Démocratisation de l'enseignement*. Paris: Repères, La Découverte, 2002.

Ministère de l'Education Nationale. *La socialisation des étudiants débutants, Expériences universitaires, familiales et sociales*. Paris, 2000.

———. *l'Etat de l'Ecole*. Paris, 2001.

———. "La réussite au DEUG par université et par discipline, session 1999." *Les dossiers* 127. Paris, 2002a.

———. "Note d'information 01.31." *Profils et devenir des élèves inscrits dans une classe préparatoire aux grandes écoles*. Paris, 2002b.

Ministère de l'éducation nationale et de la Recherche. "Evolution des effectifs d'élèves et d'étudiants." *Repères et Références Statistiques*. Paris, 2000.

———. *Repères Références Statistiques sur les enseignements, la formation et la recherche*. Paris, 2007.

Musselin, Christine. *La longue marche des universités françaises*. Paris: PUF, 2001.

NOTE

1. The authors have built aggregated categories. For example, in "working class" they included workers, employees, peasants, merchants, and craftsmen.

17

Equal Opportunity in a Public System

Experiences of Ethnic Minority Students in Dutch Higher Education

Rick Wolff and Adel Pasztor

David L. Kirp (see chapter 2) argues that a public higher education system offers more equal opportunity for underrepresented groups than a market-driven higher education system. A system that is (highly) subsidized by government makes entrance and participation of individual students less dependent on their socioeconomic background. This offers students from poorer families, such as large groups of ethnic minority students, the opportunity to reach the top of the educational ladder. Moreover, in a public system, higher education institutions are more alike, competing for future students only on the basis of content and quality of courses. In a market-driven system, institutions try to attract students either by offering all sorts of fancy commodities or by being very selective, enrolling only students who are extremely talented and/or can afford high tuition fees. As a consequence, a variety of institutions arise, from prestigious, rich universities to academically low-standard institutions, whether popular or less affluent.

Dutch higher education is mainly public and the quality of higher education institutions is considered relatively equal (for example, there is no Dutch equivalent of the Ivy League institutions in the United States). In general, higher education institutions have to admit all students with a Dutch secondary education diploma that qualifies them for higher education. Furthermore, all students receive financial assistance from the government and can apply for additional grants. These features make Dutch higher education relatively open and accessible on both the national and the institutional level and have, together with demographic developments (in Amsterdam and Rotterdam ethnic minority persons have become the majority in the age-group fifteen to twenty years old), contributed to the increase of the number of ethnic minority students entering Dutch higher education during the last decade.

In 1997, some 7,100 first-year full-time students of ethnic minority background (students of Moroccan, Turkish, Surinamese, Antillean/Aruban, or other non-Western origin [roughly all countries in Latin America, Africa, and Asia with the exception of Japan and Indonesia], defined as ethnic minorities [*allochtoon,* in Dutch] by the Statistics Netherlands' definition as a person at least one of whose parents was born in one of these countries) enrolled in either an institution of higher professional education or a university institution. In 2006, this number has more than doubled to almost 15,000 students. In 1997, 7 to 8 percent of the first-year full-time students had an ethnic minority background. This percentage increased to some 13 percent in 2006 (Statistics Netherlands 2007). The increase in the number and share of ethnic minority students raises the question if a public system that offers equal opportunity in terms of access also offers equal opportunity in terms of retention and completion. Figures are not very promising: national data show that dropout rates of ethnic minority students are higher while graduation rates are (much) lower compared to those of Dutch majority students (students with both parents born in the Netherlands) (Statistics Netherlands 2008; Wolff 2007).

These outcomes seem to nuance Kirp's argument that a public system provides equal opportunity for different groups in a diverse student body. In this chapter we will elaborate on this nuance by investigating these general outcomes more thoroughly. The second section presents the basics of the Dutch education system as background to the position of ethnic minority students in it. We will focus also on the composition of the body of first-year ethnic minority students on several characteristics and compare these with that of first-year Dutch majority students. The third section will look at the national dropout and completion figures and try to relate them to the entry profiles of both ethnic minority and Dutch majority students. Section four focuses on higher education experiences of ethnic minority students. How do these experiences relate to the (poorer) academic performance of these students? The fifth section will further explore the outcomes of the previous section in light of capital theory. The closing section will relate our findings to Kirp's views on public higher education systems and present some points for discussion.

THE ROAD TO DUTCH HIGHER EDUCATION

The Netherlands have a binary higher education system consisting of (research) universities and institutions of higher professional (or vocational) education (HBO) (Figure 17.1). Access to universities requires higher secondary education qualifications than to HBO-institutions. Only students with a pre-university diploma (VWO) are granted access to universities. The pre-university track takes six years without repeating. Entrance into higher professional education is more open. Qualified students from both the general (Havo and VWO) and vocational (MBO) track have access to HBO-institutions. The vocational track takes longest to get into HBO: seven to eight years without repeating. Havo is the shortest road into HBO: five years without repeating.

Tracking starts after eight years of primary education, at the end of which pupils are twelve years old. Basically, pupils are tracked by two criteria: scores on national tests (Entry and/or Cito-test) and an advice by school. On basis of the national test scores and the school advice, pupils are directed to either the vocational track (VMBO) or the general track (Havo/VWO), which is considered as a very important decision in one's educational career. First, because it determines the learning environment for the coming years—whether a student's education will be more practically or academically orientated. Second, because it determines the number of years before one is qualified for higher education. In principle, it is possible to switch from the vocational to the general secondary education track (Havo), which is a promotion in the educational career, but because of national education reforms track-switching has become more difficult and most vocational students remain in their track. Pupils who continue in the general track after primary school can go directly to senior general secondary education (Havo) or to pre-university school (VWO). However, there is also the opportunity for a bridging year at the end of which it is decided whether a pupil will go to either Havo or VWO. HE-qualified students have access to every public higher education institution, regardless of their average exam grade. This means that with the right qualifications almost all higher education institutions are accessible.

There is no broad first year where students can follow subjects from a range of disciplines and choose their course program after the first or first two semesters. At the end of secondary education, students select a specialized course program. Right from the start undergraduate students, who, for example, have selected economic studies, follow economics or economics-related subjects, undergraduate law students follow law or law-related subjects, and so on. Implicitly, there has to be some connection between the chosen secondary education examination subjects and the higher education training. For example, students who did not do a secondary education physics examination cannot enter the physics course program. Some course programs like medicine studies or dentistry have a *numeris fixus*.

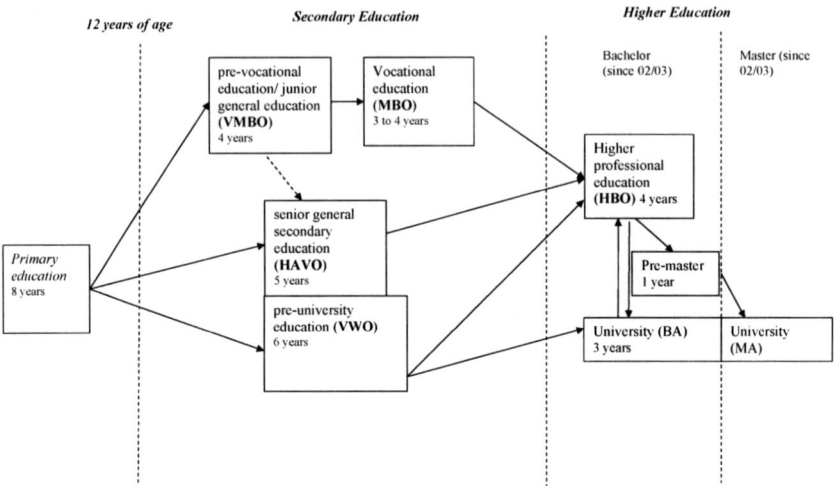

Figure 17.1.   The Road to Dutch Higher Education

Students in higher professional education can switch to university before graduation on the condition that they have gained all first-year credits of their HBO course program. In this case they are qualified to start in the first year of a university program. University students can switch to higher professional education without this condition: students who are eligible to go university also have qualified for higher professional education (students with a VWO–pre-university diploma).

The current higher education system is a bachelor/master system introduced in the academic year 2002/2003. HBO students can graduate within four years for a bachelor's degree, without repeating. University students can reach their bachelor's degree within three years of study, without repeating. Generally, HBO-institutions are not authorized to grant the master's degree, while university institutions are. The master's phase takes one extra year after the bachelor's phase, without repeating. University students can reach their master's degree within four years of study. Generally, HBO-bachelor's can access university master's via a pre-master's year. So, in regular circumstances, an HBO-student can reach the master's degree within six years of study (four years bachelor's, plus one year pre-master, plus one year master's).

Having said this, our graduation data do not apply to the bachelor/master system since the analyzed graduation-cohorts fall under the old system, when both HBO and university course programs were divided in a "propedeuse phase" of one year, followed by a "head phase" of three years (for some university studies four years), without repeating. In this system, students from most course programs could graduate within four years of study.

The entry profile of many ethnic minority first-year full-time students in the Dutch higher education shows that they had a different school career than most of the Dutch majority first-year full-time students. First, more ethnic minority students enter higher education with an MBO-diploma (between 30 and 35 percent of the ethnic minority HBO-intake) than Dutch majority students (some 25 percent of the ethnic Dutch HBO-intake). This implies that the vocational track is a more important road to higher education for ethnic minority than for Dutch majority students.

As a consequence, ethnic minority students commence more often a course program at an institution of higher professional (or vocational) education. Around 70 percent of the ethnic Dutch first-year students are HBO-students; for Turkish and Moroccan students, this figure varies between 75 and 80 percent, for Surinamese and Antillean/Aruban students, between 70 and 75 percent (Statistics Netherlands 2008).

A second consequence is that ethnic minority students enter higher education at an older age than Dutch majority students. Between 30 and 40 percent of the ethnic minority students starts at the age of eighteen or younger in higher professional education, while the same holds true for 50 to 60 percent of the ethnic Dutch first-year full-time students. Also the university-level ethnic minority students start at an older age. While 75 to 80 percent of the ethnic minority students enter university at the age of nineteen or younger, for Dutch majority students this percentage is more than 90 percent. These differences show that, on average, the road to higher education takes longer for ethnic minority students.

Apart from the school career, there is another striking difference between the two groups. Ethnic minority students are more concentrated in a few course programs. For example, 50 percent of the ethnic minority HBO-first-year full-time students start at an economics course program against one third of the Dutch majority HBO-first-year full-time students. At the university level, the corresponding percentage is 20 to 25 percent of the ethnic minority intake in economics course program, and about 18 percent in law studies. Among Dutch majority first-year students, these figures are respectively 17 and 11 percent (Wolff 2007). This shows that ethnic minority students and Dutch majority students differ in the process that leads to a choice of field.

Within ethnic minority groups, one striking development has taken place in the last ten years. The share of second-generation ethnic minority students (students from ethnic minority origin who were born in the Netherlands) has increased enormously. In 1997, around half of the ethnic minority students were born in the Netherlands. Currently, over 75 percent of the Surinamese,

Moroccan, and Turkish first-year HBO-students is second generation. At the university level, this number even exceeds 80 percent for the same ethnic groups. In all ethnic groups (including the Dutch majority group), women have a slight majority among the first-year students (Wolff 2007).

ACADEMIC SUCCESS: DROPOUT AND GRADUATION RATES

As noted in the introduction, academic success in terms of retention (or formulated negatively: dropout) and graduation rates is less among ethnic minority students. At the HBO-level, dropout rates after two years of study of Dutch majority students vary between 15 and 18 percent, depending on the cohort, while this figure lies structurally 4 to 5 percentage points higher among ethnic minority students (here, dropout means genuine dropout, that is: dropping out of the Dutch higher education system. This differs from switching: dropping out from one course program and continuing at another course program). Broken down by the different variables, the most striking differences in general are by entry age and preparatory schooling. Older starters and students with an MBO-diploma have the highest chances to drop out. These at-risk groups are relative large among ethnic minority students. To illustrate this point, we present figure 17.2, where dropout rates are related to ethnic origin and preparatory schooling for full-time HBO-students. There seems to be a relation between preparatory schooling and droping out: students with pre-university training (VWO) have lowest dropout rates, especially Dutch majority students (in the figure referred to as ethnic Dutch students), followed by students with a senior general training (Havo). It is clear that dropout rates are highest among MBO-students, especially MBO-students from ethnic minority descent (even though dropout rates have decreased over time).

At the university level dropout differences are smaller compared to higher professional education: between 7 and 9 percent of the Dutch majority students drop out within two years of study, which is 1 to 3 percentage points lower than that of the ethnic minority group, depending on cohort. The lower dropout rates in general for university students indicate that these students have an easier transition from secondary to higher education.

Dropout rate differences between ethnic minority and Dutch majority students may seem modest with only a gap of a few percent. However, ethnic majority students drop out structurally more often than Dutch majority students. Moreover, differences in academic success are more striking when graduation rates are monitored. Figures 17.3 and 17.4 show these differences after six years at HBO-level and seven years at university level by ethnic origin and preparatory schooling. Graduation rates of ethnic minority students are between 15 to 20

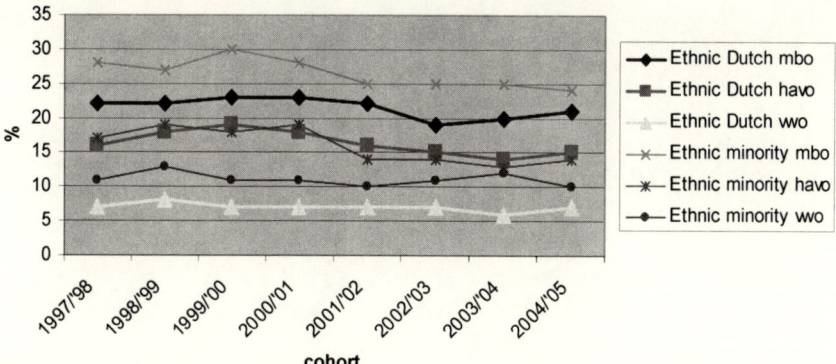

Figure 17.2. Dropout Percentage—by cohort, ethnic origin, and preparatory schooling (within two years of study of full-time HBO-students) *Source:* **Statistics Netherlands, processed by IMES**

percent *lower* compared to the graduation rates of Dutch majority students with the *same preparatory schooling*. This is odd considering the formal equality in pre-HE-training (in figure 17.4 students with HBO-preparatory schooling are HBO-graduates who continued at a university institution). The graduation-rate gap is smaller among university students with pre-university schooling (VWO), but still remains more than 10 percentage points.

Apart from these differences on the same level of preparatory schooling, another striking trend appears. Graduation rates of HBO-students with Havo and MBO training are fairly equal, while the differences in dropout rates were substantial between these groups. Apparently, in the first two years of study, a group of students with MBO training persist that later on perform just as well as, or even better, than students with Havo training. Selectivity at the start of course programs seem to work out well, fulfilling its purpose in Dutch higher education. However, what is striking is that this selection mechanism seems to work *within* an ethnic group but not *between* ethnic groups. Even ethnic minority HBO-students with pre-university training, who were the most promising students based on the low dropout figures, perform less well compared to Dutch majority HBO-students with Havo and MBO-training, who are relatively poor performers within the group of Dutch majority students. The same holds true for university students. Graduation rates of students with HBO- or VWO-preparatory schooling are almost identical within the group of Dutch majority students, but ethnic minority students with VWO-schooling are performing less than ethnic Dutch HBO-graduates.

Next to preparatory schooling, gender also relates strongly to graduation. Graduation rates are highest among Dutch majority female students, and

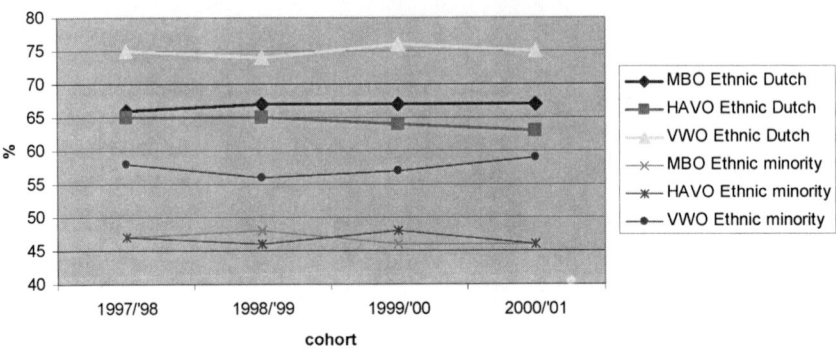

Figure 17.3. Graduation rates—by cohort, ethnic origin, and preparatory schooling (after six years of study, HBO-students) *Source:* CBS-StatLine, processed by IMES

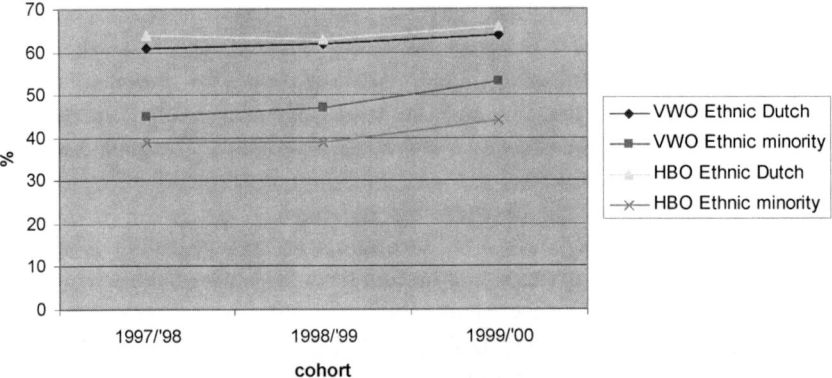

Figure 17.4. Graduation rates—by cohort, ethnic origin, and preparatory schooling (after seven years of study, University-students) *Source:* CBS-StatLine, processed by IMES

lowest among ethnic minority male students. Both at the HBO and at the university level some 70 percent of the Dutch majority women graduate within six and seven years respectively, while among ethnic minority men the graduation rate is only 40 percent. Graduation rates of ethnic minority women and Dutch majority men are comparable and situated between the two extremes. Again, a selection mechanism is revealed that works within groups, but does not bring equal graduation rates to students of different ethnic groups.

In sum, national data show that preparatory schooling, gender, and entry age are related to academic success. Schooling and entry age are possible causes for higher dropout rates and lower graduation rates of ethnic minority students because of the relatively large amount of at-risk students within this student group. However, when the level of preparatory schooling is taken into account, the differences in academic success between ethnic minority and Dutch majority students remain. The gender distribution is comparable between the different ethnic groups. The share of women among first-year Dutch majority students resembles the share within the ethnic minority student group, so the group composition by gender does not account for the differences in academic success between ethnic groups. Similar to preparatory schooling, the relationship between gender and academic success indicates that performance-related processes differ between ethnic minority and Dutch majority students.

National data give (descriptive) information about the academic success of ethnic minority students compared to that of Dutch majority students. But it is clear that these data only shed limited light on what is going on. The next section will give more detailed information on the higher education experiences of ethnic minority students in Dutch higher education.

THE HIGHER EDUCATION
EXPERIENCE OF ETHNIC MINORITY STUDENTS

National data on dropout and completion were a reason to study more thoroughly the higher education experience of ethnic minority students. Why is it that ethnic minority students are dropping out more often, are less successful in completing their studies, and take longer to graduate? Here, we present results of three research projects, partly based on work by Vincent Tinto (1993), who introduced the concepts of social and academic integration. While social integration refers to the process of making social contacts with teachers and peers, academic integration refers to the process of learning. To most students, the feeling they are part of a community is an important factor in deciding to stay and complete the program. In turn, good academic integration means that students identify positively with the field concerned, that teachers and peers invite students, as it were, to participate in the profession. We present the results of these research projects because they offer an opportunity to look behind the world of dropout and completion data and, therefore, contribute to a better understanding of processes that lead to dropout, retention, and completion.

Research by R. Wolff and M. Crul (2003), in which higher education experiences of students and dropout-students of ethnic minority background were compared, shows that attrition is caused by an accumulation of factors. In some cases students get entangled in a negative spiral, which ultimately leads to their attrition. Students can also find themselves lifted in a positive spiral and as a consequence are confident they will graduate. Of course, there is a whole range of situations in between these extremes. There are both general (applicable to all students) and specific (for ethnic minority students) mechanisms at work. General mechanisms are related to factors such as the (wrong) *choice of course program* and (insufficient) mastery of *study skills* (planning), but also to the *socioeconomic background* of students. Relatively more ethnic minority students are from a low-income environment. Most are first-generation entrants, the first of their families to enter higher education. This means that they do not exactly know what to expect from higher education. Another general factor is *networking skills*, an important factor that distinguishes those who persist from the dropouts. Students with adequate networking skills use these in the pre–higher education phase to choose a fitting course program and apply them during their studies to create and maintain a network that is supportive in gathering information and in overcoming problems (planning, decreasing level of motivation). Probably, ethnic minority students lack these skills more often because they are not acquainted with the higher education institutional culture.

Three specific factors were found for ethnic minority students. First, the *migration history*: Some first-generation migrant students who came to the Netherlands after secondary education found it hard to get used to a new society. The second factor is related to *language skills*. A shortcoming of language skills can hinder reading Dutch study books, writing papers and theses, and communicating with peers, teachers, and student support staff. The third factor lies within the area of *interethnic interactions*. Most of the informants (students and leavers) refer to ethnic issues when talking about contacts with faculty and, especially, peers. Experiences range from innocent observations and situations (e.g., being different, a tighter bond of understanding with other ethnic minority students) to cases of overt discrimination and exclusion. However, almost all persisters and dropout students in this research were very reluctant in framing these experiences as forms of racism or discrimination, mostly because in their eyes unpleasant peers, teachers, or counselors treat ethnic Dutch students equally badly.

S. Severiens, R. P. Wolff, and S. Rezai (2006), studying the learning environment of first-year students at both higher professional education and university course programs, find differences between ethnic minority students and Dutch majority students on three domains. First, students differ by background characteristics. On average, parents of ethnic minority students have lower education qualifications than parents of Dutch majority students. Ethnic minority students, especially at the HBO-level, have to study more often in a less facilitating home environment (for example, no study room and/or a computer at home). Ethnic minority students also have more difficulties in reaching higher education. More frequently than Dutch majority students, these students have school careers that caused a delayed higher education entrance. Second, study progress (measured by number of credits after one year of study) of Dutch majority students is related to other characteristics than among ethnic minority students. Study progress of Dutch majority students is positively related to intrinsic motivation, gender, and (at the university level) average secondary education exam score and negatively related to informal social integration (social contacts between students outside class, or, in other words, student life). But for ethnic minority students, study progress is negatively related to time spent on a job and positively related to formal academic integration (contact with teachers during class) and the quality and quantity of student support and advice. Third, ethnic minority students report different higher education experiences than Dutch majority students. They feel less at home at their course programs, are less satisfied with the quality of cooperation with peers, and (at the HBO-level) have a stronger preference for group work assisted by and in the presence of a teacher and for practice-oriented tasks. Finally, ethnic minority students are more of the opinion that teachers pay insufficient attention to the personal background of students. The authors conclude that academic success of ethnic minority students seems to be more dependent on the learning environment, while Dutch majority students can rely to a greater extent on their "own" capital in order to be successful.

Research targeting students at higher professional education in general and teacher education students in particular (Severiens et al. 2007) also confirms that the wrong choice of course program is the main cause of dropout for both ethnic minority and ethnic Dutch students. At the same time, ethnic minority students report less support in the course program choosing process. To a lesser extent they visited information days, did course program choosing tests and consulted family and friends about possible course programs. Furthermore, ethnic minority students felt less at home at their course programs (again!) and more than two third of the ethnic minority respondents experienced unequal treatment to some extent at their course program. These outcomes were even more extreme in the case of teacher education programs for primary education. Finally, teacher education students from ethnic minority background seem to have more problems in finding an internship at primary schools and report more often problems with their internship primary school mentor or the team of teachers at their internship school.

The findings of the three studies show that many factors influence academic success, but also, and more important, that the higher education experiences of ethnic minority students seem to be very different than those of Dutch majority students. Moreover, ethnic minority students seem to meet more difficulties in the transition process into higher education and beyond. Partly, these difficulties are due to general mechanisms and processes, though possibly reinforced among ethnic minority students, but some difficulties seem to be related to mechanisms and processes specific for ethnic minority students.

CAPITAL THEORY AND ACADEMIC SUCCESS

How the observations of the three studies can be conceptualized in order to understand differences in academic success between ethnic minority and Dutch majority students in a more systemic way? By addressing the perspective of individual students, we concentrate on the question how (well) students are prepared for higher education and whether their personal "equipment" suffices to have a satisfying and successful higher education experience. Differences in dropout rates, graduation rates, and other measures for student success suggest that there is "diversity in equipment." One can argue that ethnic minority students seem to be less well prepared and equipped to persist and perform successfully in Dutch higher education. This brings us to the concept of "capital" as a key theoretical approach. We assume that every individual student has his or her own backpack of knowledge, skills, and capacities to navigate through the higher education system. This backpack can be "unpacked" into different packages, representing the different forms of capital.

In an overview of theories on the structural minority underperformance in American higher education, D. S. Massey et al. (2002) mention the "Theory of Capital Deficiency." This theory postulates that ethnic minority student groups are less successful because they have less access to and disposal of the necessary forms of capital (financial, cultural, and social) to be successful in higher education. How do these different forms of capital relate to minority underperformance? Massey et al. define financial capital as economic resources of students, in particular parental economic resources (parents' income). If anything, money buys time and other resources: when you do not need to spend time on earning money, you can focus on your education. When money is available, you can buy study-supporting facilities (computers, books, means of transportation, extracurricular training, etc.). Since relatively many ethnic minority students come from lower socioeconomic background, they do not have access to the advantages offered by financial capital.

The concept of cultural capital is extensively elaborated on in the work of Pierre Bourdieu (1996, 1997; see also Bourdieu and Passeron 1979), who uses the concept of cultural capital to explain stratification in both society and the education system. Cultural capital refers to (knowledge of) styles, tastes, norms, and values of the highly educated, the elite, and the people who are part of High Culture. The initial internalization of cultural capital depends on the parents' abilities to socialize their children into this high status (or higher education) culture. However, cultural capital can also be influenced by other realms of socialization, for example, by peers or teachers in secondary education or from community-based organizations like churches or sporting clubs (Rhamie and Hallam 2002). Once in higher education, a student will experience that higher education is a system or field where specific codes, values, and norms rule. These codes, values, and norms—mostly unwritten and even unconsciously present—refer to what is "done" and "not done," to what is "hot" and what is "not." Students from groups that are traditionally recruited by HE-institutions will feel like "fishes in the water" because of their cultural capital. They have more knowledge of the dominating codes, norms, and values at their course program than students from nontraditional groups, who will feel more frequently like "fishes out of the water" (Bourdieu and Wacquant 1992). In Bourdieu's view, the role of cultural capital for student success cannot be underestimated: "Academic success is directly depended upon cultural capital and on the inclination to invest in the academic market" (1973, 96).

The effect of cultural capital on academic persistence and success has been proven empirically. Cultural capital can be linked to "the fit between a student's values and belief system and his or her academic environment" (Nora 2004, 182). A finding by A. Nora (ibid.) is that students who feel at home and feel personally accepted at their institution or department are more prone to persist than students who lack this feeling of fitting in. Although this mechanism seems to be a general attribute of students, in practice the majority of faculty, staff, and students at most higher education institutions in Western countries are white. Consequently, the ethnic composition of these institutions is such that many ethnic minority students experience a lack of cultural capital to sufficiently fit into the academic environment. Several studies show that Hispanic/Latino, African American and Asian Pacific American students have a less strong sense of belonging to the college community than white/Caucasian students (Hurtado and Carter 1997; Johnson et al. 2007). E. T. Terenzini and P. T. Pascarella (2005, 394) argue that black students at historically black colleges and universities are "more likely to complete their bachelor's degree than similarly qualified Black students at predominantly White institutions." This is probably caused by a more positive and supportive environment or, in other words, an environment in which these students feel more accepted and supported.

Results for the Dutch situation indicate that processes and mechanisms related to cultural capital are also at work in Dutch higher education. Indications for this are the repeated result that ethnic minority students feel less at home at their institution and course program (see also de Graaf et al. 2006) and feel excluded because of perceived acts of unequal treatment, and their status as first-generation student (the majority of these students are the first of their families studying in higher education).

The last form of capital we address is social capital. Social capital refers to social contacts and networks (which have influence on academic success). For example, a student who has access to valuable information on ways to be successful in higher education through her or his social networks of peers, friends, and family has increasing chances of academic success. This example shows a few aspects of the concept of social capital as emphasized by James S. Coleman (1988) and Robert D. Putnam (2000). First, social capital has both a social and an economic component. In the social sense it deals with interactions between individuals or between individuals and groups. Basically, social capital emerges from the exchange of information between people. Economically, social contacts or networks are meaningful as social capital if these contacts or networks are of any *value* for specific goals. In this sense, social capital is a means "to get things done," whether in the short or long term, whether direct or indirect. Second, a person can be part of different social structures or communities. A student can be seen as part of a family, and may belong to different communities such as the community of the neighborhood of residence and/or the student or academic community.

These social structures can be related to study success in different ways. In the first place, the attitudes or *norms* toward education and study success can vary between social structures. Seemingly, it goes without saying that no one can oppose the psychological, social, and economic benefits of educational attainment. Good educational results enhance one's self-esteem, open door to social networks, and improve chances on the labor market. However, J. U. Ogbu (2003) showed in an ethnographic study on black students from a middle-class high school that academic success can also be framed negatively. Among these students, academic success was seen as "acting white," as conforming to norms and values of the white part of the American population; in other words, as acting as the "other." In the second place, a social network provides channels to circulate and get to helpful *information* to facilitate study success. For example, peers can inform each other about which chapters are important to read, where good abstracts are available, how to deal with certain assignments, how to make tests, and how to plan the studying of material. Conversely, a social network can lack this informational advantage, for example, the family network in the case of first-generation students (students who are the first in their families that are in higher education). Third, social capital of social structures can be what Putnam sees as one of the most important distinctions between the different forms of social capital, *bonding* or *bridging*. The bonding-function aims to enhance togetherness, to promote a sense of belonging to community among separate members. Bonding can have an empowering effect, but at the same time sends the message of exclusion toward nonmembers. Bridging is aimed to connect different social structures and, simultaneously, their respective functions of social capital. In other words, bridging makes it possible to combine the best (but also the worst) of both worlds. Coleman refers to bridging as the closure function of social capital. Two social structures can be connected by one or several persons who are members of both structures. The importance of closure is its accumulating strength in the effectiveness of norms. A norm can be more effective if it is supportive in both social structures.

What do we learn from the concept of social capital applied to the case of ethnic minority students in Dutch higher education? Earlier, we saw the importance of networking skills for persistence in higher education (Wolff and Crul 2003). This indicates that the ability to create and maintain a network and thus to invest in social capital, also plays a role in study success of ethnic minority students. However, data suggest that relatively many ethnic minority students lack the social capital needed to be successful. It seems plausible to say that the networks these students are part of do not have enough value of improving one's academic skills. For example, this group of students may come from families and communities where there may be a positive norm toward education, but where at the same time, useful, helpful, and concrete knowledge and information about higher education in general and about course programs in particular is lacking. Their family and community may be strong in bonding, while bridging capacity with highly educated groups may be of more use to these students. Based on the distinction of Granovetter between strong and weak ties, Putnam, summarizes the bonding function of social capital as "getting by," while the bridging function of social capital is "getting ahead." The case of ethnic minority students suggests that there is no closure between the different networks they are part of, which means that, once in higher education, they are on their own. Or they may be in social structures of students with similar background who, in a sense, are on their own, too. This "on their ownness" probably lies behind the outcome of Severiens et al. (2006) that ethnic minority students prefer to study in a learning environment where formal academic integration is facilitated, where there is close personal and frequent contact with teachers and faculty, both in the classroom context and in working group situations. For these students, the perceived lack of social capital among peers can be compensated for by more and clearer instructions by and the presence of teachers and faculty. In this light, it is interesting that, in Putnam's view, informal networks seem to be more beneficial than formal networks. It can be argued that successful students are those students with much cultural and social capital, who have the advantage of being part of highly valued informal networks and of having access to the different forms of capital through informal channels (family, community, friends, and peers).

Focusing on the perspective of student characteristics in relation to study success, we conclude that capital theory opens up a promising direction for further research in order to get a more systematic grip on research findings concerning ethnic minority students in the Dutch higher education system. Furthermore, capital theory gives the foundations to construct a conceptual framework that can be helpful in our understanding of the educational position and experiences of these students.

CONCLUSION

In our introduction, we summarized Kirp's views on the benefits of a public higher education system, especially in terms of equal opportunity. To some extent we agree with Kirp's argument. A public system tends to have more equal (access to) institutions and in such a system students can choose between these institutions on matter of taste ("Does this institution and course program fits me?") rather than on, for example, financial conditions ("Can I afford to study at all and can I afford to study at this specific institution?"). However, national data and research findings on the Dutch situation show that equal opportunity in access does not guarantee equal opportunity in terms of retention and completion. Ethnic minorities drop out more often and have lower completion rates than Dutch majority students. The experiences of both ethnic minority and Dutch majority students indicate that ethnic minority students more often lack the appropriate cultural and social capital to be successful in higher education. Strikingly, the level of preparatory schooling does not compensate for this: an ethnic minority student who has the same secondary education diploma as a Dutch majority student, and—in a formal sense—has a comparable chance of succeeding as his/her Dutch majority peer, still has a higher chance of dropping out and a lower chance to graduate (within the same time span). One can argue that especially in higher education, success must primarily depend on the talents and skills of students. However, apart from students' own responsibilities to perform well, higher education institutions (management, teachers, and student support staff within these institutions) also have a responsibility to create a learning environment where students from different ethnic backgrounds have an equal sense of belonging and feel equally at home at their course program. In our view, this will contribute to better study progress and more study success of all students, regardless of their background. This point must perhaps be emphasized even more in the case of public higher education systems. Equal access also bears the promise and expectation of equal opportunity. If a system creates these promises and expectations, than this system and its institutions should be responsible to do their utmost to meet them the best they possibly can.

Finally, we highlight three subjects of discussion in order to clarify some limitations of our contribution. Firstly, as Massey et al. (2002) argue, one problem of capital theory is the close relationship between the different forms of capital, which makes it very difficult to isolate the impact of these separate capital forms. Students from lower economic backgrounds usually do not have parents who can socially reproduce cultural capital. These students come from social structures (communities) with hardly any social capital relevant to academic success. Moreover, there is a large space where low socioeconomic status overlaps with ethnic or racial background. In other words, the ongoing debate whether class or ethnic/race differences are responsible for inequalities in the field of education is not at all solved by capital theory. However, from a pragmatic point of view, the different forms of capital offer the opportunity to reorganize our research findings in such a way that, to a greater extent, systemic observations of the higher education position of ethnic minority students in the Netherlands are possible.

We considered the group of ethnic minority students as a homogeneous group. Of course, this is an oversimplification of reality. In fact, the group of ethnic minority students comprises many separate ethnic (or racial) groups. Some of them perform better than others. For example, the group of students from "other non-Western origin" is the most successful student group of all ethnic minority groups (but still is underperforming compared to Dutch majority students), while Antillean/Aruban students have the lowest scores on the indicators of academic success (Statistics Netherlands 2008). We did not emphasize the ethnic heterogeneity within the total group of ethnic minority students, because the purpose was to convey research outcomes from the Dutch case (differences in success, experiences, and acquired capital) in as straightforward and simple a manner as possible. Having said this, a more detailed analysis of separate groups probably brings up more knowledge on processes that lead to academic success or failure. These processes may be specific for certain ethnic groups. This knowledge can be used to refine, redirect, or even change the (theoretical) approach proposed in this chapter.

By focusing on student characteristics in this chapter, we did not bring into the analysis one equally important field of research. The impact of characteristics of institutions and course programs, especially their educational structure and culture offered, has been left out. We know these characteristics can have much influence on study success (Tinto 1993; Yorke and Longden 2004). Moreover, characteristics of institutions and course programs (the

288   *Rick Wolff and Adel Pasztor*

influence of teachers, faculty, and student support staff on sense of belonging and academic success) are one of the main features in our own research (see Wolff and Severiens 2005; Severiens et al. 2006; Severiens et al. 2007). In order to keep our analysis as clear as possible, we chose to focus on the student perspective in this paper, not least to emphasize the ethnic minority student voice.

REFERENCES

Bourdieu, P. "Cultural Reproduction and Social Reproduction." In R. Brown (ed.), *Knowledge, Education and Cultural Change: Papers in the Sociology of Education* (London: Tavistock, 1973): 71–112.
———. *The State Nobility. Elite Schools in the Field of Power* (Oxford: Polity Press, 1996).
———. "The Forms of Capital." In A. H. Halsey, H. Lauder, Ph. Brown, and A. Stuart Wells (eds.), *Education: Culture, Economy, and Society* (Oxford: Oxford University Press, 1997): 46–58.
Bourdieu, P., and J. Passeron. *The Inheritors: French Students and Their Relation to Culture* (Chicago: University of Chicago Press, 1979).
Bourdieu P., and L. Wacquant. *An Invitation to Reflexive Sociology* (Chicago: Chicago University Press, 1992).
Coleman, J. S. "Social Capital in the Creation of Human Capital." *American Journal of Sociology* 94 (Supplementary) (1988): s95–120
de Graaf, D., U. de Jong, and I. van der Veen. "Staken of switchen binnen het hbo: kunnen instellingen hun studenten behouden?" *Tijdschrift voor Hoger Onderwijs* 24, no. 4 (2006): 218-28.
Hurtado, S., and D. F. Carter. "Effects of College Transition and Perceptions of the Campus Racial Climate on Latino Students' Sense of Belonging." *Sociology of Education* 70 (1997): 324–45.
Johnson, Alvarez, Soldner Longerbeam, and Leonard en Rowan-Kenyon Inkelas. "Examining Sense of Belonging among First-Year Undergraduates from Different Racial/Ethnic Groups." *Journal of College Student Development* 48, no. 5 (2007): 525–42.
Massey, D. S., C. Z. Charles, G. F. Lundy and M. J. Fischer. *The Source of the River* (Princeton: Princeton University Press, 2002).
Nora, A. "The Role of Habitus and Cultural Capital in Choosing a College: Transitioning From High School to Higher Education, and Persisting in College among Minority and Non-Minority Students." *Journal of Hispanic Higher Education* 3, no. 2 (2004): 180–208.
Ogbu, J. U. *Black American Students in an Affluent Suburb* (New Jersey: Lawrence Erlbaum Associates, 2003).
Putnam, R. D. *Bowling Alone: The Collapse and Revival of American Community* (New York: Simon & Schuster, 2000).

Rhamie, J., and S. Hallam. "An Investigation into African-Caribbean Academic Success in the UK." *Race, Ethnicity and Education* 5, no.2 (2002): 151–70.

Severiens, S., R. P. Wolff, and S. Rezai. *Diversiteit in leergemeenschappen: Een onderzoek naar stimulerende factoren in de leeromgeving voor allochtone studente in het hoger onderwijs* (Utrecht: ECHO, [2006]).

Severiens, S., R. P. Wolff, M. Meeuwisse, S. Rezai, and W. de Vos. *Waarom stoppen zoveel allochtone studenten met de Pabo?* (Den Haag: SBO, (2007).

Statistics Netherlands. www.cbs.nl/en-GB/menu/organisatie/default.htm (2008).

Terenzini, E. T., and P. T. Pascarella. *How College Affects Students: A Third Decade of Research* (San Francisco: Jossey-Bass, 2005).

Tinto, V. *Leaving College: Rethinking the Causes and Cures of Student Attrition* (2nd edition) (Chicago and London: The University of Chicago Press, 1993).

Wolff, R. *Met vallen en opstaan: Een analyse van instroom, uitval en rendementen van niet-westers allochtone studenten in het Nederlandse hoger onderwijs 1997–2005* (Utrecht: ECHO, 2007).

Wolff, R., and M. Crul. *Blijvers en uitvallers in het hoger onderwijs* (Utrecht: ECHO, 2003).

Wolff, R., and S. Severiens. *Structure and Culture of Learning Environments and their Influence on Study Progress of Foreign Background Students: A Qualitative Research at Three University Course Programs in the Netherlands*. Paper presented at the Earli conference in Cyprus, August 2005.

Yorke, M., and B. Longden, (eds.). *Retention and Student Success in Higher Education* (Maidenhead/Berkshire: Open University Press, 2004).

18

Access to Higher Education for Students with Mental Health Difficulties

An Equal Opportunities Issue

Sue Jackson

> The EU Disability Strategy emphasizes equal access to quality education and lifelong learning. These two areas enable disabled people to participate fully in society and improve their quality of life.
>
> —European Communities (2007)

For many years equal opportunity has been about gender or women's issues, race and/or ethnicity, language or social class. It is only in the last few years that disability has become an issue that has required government action to ensure that it is included in the area of diversity. In the United Kingdom, legislative changes affecting the rights of students with disabilities in higher education, i.e., the Disability Discrimination Act, 1995, have opened the door for a key Labour government policy called "Widening Participation" at the tertiary level. It is part of their agenda for social inclusion and universities have been strongly encouraged to open their doors to students who have been traditionally excluded, including students with disabilities. John Selby (2007:1), the Director of Widening Participation, promised,

> HEFCE (The Higher Education Funding Council for England) is committed to ensuring that all those with the potential to benefit from higher education have the opportunity to do so, whatever their background and whenever they need it. As part of this commitment, we have been funding initiatives aimed at improving access and progression of disabled students . . .

This is, therefore, a key time to consider improvements to provision and thinking around institutional culture.

Traditionally, higher education in the United Kingdom was only for the elite and very small numbers. Thirty years ago only 8 percent of the population went to university. The massive expansion in the last twenty years and the government's drive toward 50 percent take-up of places has led to a number of difficulties and pressures on institutions. There has been a rapid rise in staff-student ratios, and teaching groups are now very large (Trowler 1998), which puts students, in general, under pressure (Yorke and Longden 2004), and teaching staff do not have the time to be available to students outside the timetabled curriculum. Some students seem to be less prepared for the demands of university education and the expectations of higher education, particularly those who come from families where they are the first to attend an institution of higher education, or those who enter as mature students, having worked for some years prior to attending the course.

This has led to some rethinking of university teaching and learning methods and the realization that good practice for a particular group of students can often be cited as best practice for everyone. Teaching staff are more willing to adapt their curriculum, to offer a variety of ways of assessing and evaluating the courses, modifying their ways of teaching, putting lecture notes on the Intranet, allowing students to tape-record lectures, offering extra time for assignments, and making special arrangements for exams. Sheila Riddell, Teresa Tinklin, and Alastair Wilson (2005) have recorded that this has all helped students with disabilities.

The students who seem to have the most disadvantages are those who have the "hidden" disability of mental illness. Students with mental health difficulties have been a growing concern for us in recent years in our study support team. The United Kingdom Higher Education Statistics Agency indicates that, in 2003–2004, 0.2 percent of the total numbers of students declaring a disability (on their application forms) disclosed a mental health problem. At the London College of Communication (LCC), which is one of the campuses of the University of the Arts London, the largest specialist art and design educational institution in Europe, our statistics showed that 29.5 percent of our students declaring a disability had disclosed a mental health issue by the end of the same academic year. By the end of the academic year 2005–2006 this number had increased to 50 percent of our students who had disclosed having disabilities, subsequently disclosing the nature of that disability to be a mental health issue.

We know that students generally do not disclose their disability before they apply for a course, because they are worried that this would prevent them from being accepted into a degree program. However, we have found that the initial onset of a mental health breakdown may happen during their time at university. Statistics show that one in three students is likely to suffer some kind of mental health difficulty (MIND). Sixty-three percent of universities report an increase in psychological distress among students (Association of University and College Counseling, 1996/1997). In a survey, possible clinical anxiety was recorded in 46 percent of male students and 64 percent of female students, with possible clinical depression in 12 percent and 15 percent respectively. This compares unfavorably with lower levels reported in 1987, where between 1 and 25 percent showed signs of emotional disturbance (The Mental Health Foundation 2001). Suicide accounts for almost 23 percent of all deaths of people aged fifteen to twenty-four years; suicide is the second most common cause of death in young people after accidents. It has been estimated that 7 to 14 percent of adolescents will self-harm at some time in their life, and as many as 20 to 45 percent of older adolescents say they have had suicidal thoughts (MIND).

In this chapter, I will examine the implications of this situation from the perspective of someone with experience of giving academic support to a number of students with mental health issues. I will offer insights from this experience and use these examples to identify key issues around equal opportunities and suggest ways to make institutions more disability friendly. My main aim is to ensure the right of students with mental health difficulties to a university education, where they are not disadvantaged by their disability.

Universities need to change structurally if they wish to become more inclusive. Many universities expect the students to fit in with them, but this often presents barriers to participation and access. So, in the spirit of the government directive, we are continuously looking for ways of making adjustments so that disabled students are not prevented from taking full part in the university life.

We can do this if we operate within a social model of disability, concentrating on the need to remove these barriers, whether they are environmental or social. It is important to be flexible and to recognize the need to build a relationship between the individual student and the university as well as considering the requirements of society as paramount (Riddell, Tinklin, and Wilson 2005). This is in contrast to the medical model, which suggests that, if we "fix" the student, then we can disregard the disability. For example, if you allow a student to record lectures, as s/he is unable to concentrate due to the medication s/he is taking, then the situation would be "fixed." But the situation is somewhat different from the student experience.

The social model will ensure that the university structure can adapt to the diverse needs of its student population. In the United Kingdom, teaching staff, course designers, and curriculum development teams are all responsible for ensuring that the students have access to the curriculum. The arrangements for the assessment (i.e., grading and feedback) of students, however, are dealt with by the university at strategic level, so an examination of structural factors will also give insight into the type and nature of the barriers that are faced by the students. Disabilities are not medical conditions that can be cured, and it is important that this is recognized and considered. We need to learn to adapt to suit the individual.

This recognition of the social model puts pressure on the institution and presents challenges. Within this context, mental health issues present even more of a challenge. The behavior of some students is difficult to manage at times: for example, a student who interrupts inappropriately or one who continuously makes demands that teaching staff or support staff cannot meet. This will raise the anxiety of both teaching and non-teaching staff. At LCC we are trying to make a difference to the learning experience of all students. Students with mental health issues still need to receive extra support to help them cope with the environments that they find themselves in. By making changes and adjustments, the right balance may be achieved. If universities and institutions of higher education look at the difficulties presented by the learning environment as well as the support of individual students, a positive outcome for all students could result. We are trying to achieve structural and cultural change within the university, such as methods of teaching and assessment (grading), rather than focusing on helping students to cope with existing practices.

In 2002, the Disability Discrimination Act came into force in the United Kingdom. This Act defines a disabled person as someone who has a "physical or mental impairment which has a substantial and long-term adverse effect upon his ability to carry out normal day-to-day activities" (Disability Discrimination Act, 1995). This includes students with mental health difficulties. To qualify, the disorder has to be a form of mental distress which is "clinically well-recognized" (ibid.), even if it is controlled by medication. These disorders include depression, bipolar disorder, schizophrenia, phobias, obsessive compulsive disorder, and eating disorders. Students with hidden impairments such as mental health difficulties do not want to be classed as "disabled," but will have to accept this, in order to gain reasonable adjustments. They need to have a letter from a medical practitioner to begin the process of claiming for Disabled Student Allowance (hereafter referred to as DSA) which recommends to the university the kind of adjustments that should be made. However, this only covers students from the United Kingdom. European Union students and international students are not eligible to apply for DSA. Nor are those United Kingdom students who do not want to be seen by a medical practitioner or who do not want to take traditional medication.

The Higher Education Funding Council for England awards funding to higher education institutions on the basis of the number of United Kingdom students applying for DSA in their first year of a degree course (Higher Education Statistics Agency [HESA]). However, as students are not obliged to disclose that they have a disability, these statistics are not necessarily representative of the total student population. Also LCC attracts a large number of overseas students, some of whom have mental health difficulties, which often manifest during the course of their educational program. These students are not able to apply for funding, nor does the institution have a stream of funding available for their support. At LCC, we do support these students by offering extended deadlines for assignments, extended library loans, and one-to-one academic and emotional support. Along with other disabled students, their needs are assessed, albeit by me, and recommendations made to the course teams. We are not able to recoup the money, but we feel that we would not be offering them an equal opportunity if we did not adopt this strategy.

The Disabled Student Allowance is the government's way of attempting "to level the playing field" for students with disabilities. Any "home" student (i.e., resident in the United Kingdom) that can prove that s/he has an ongoing medical condition will be offered a Needs Assessment, which will attempt to examine the best way to match assistive technology to the difficulty. The Disabled Student Allowance is not based on an individual's income background.

Katy, a student with obsessive compulsive disorder, often finds herself checking that she has locked everything up twenty or thirty times and then unable to get out of the house. Her DSA gave her a computer and the ability to access the Internet and, therefore, the university intranet. She is able to at least be in contact with her tutors and continue to work from home, especially if lecture notes are posted on the intranet. The Disabled Student Allowance also covers extra mentoring or study support to help Katy to make up the lost hours.

J. Borland and S. James (1999) felt that DSA is an effective way to design support for individual students, but it seems to have a limited impact on practice and provision. In 2004, Greg Hampton and Richard Gosden likened universities to the competitive environment found on the sports field. However, disabled students are expected to compete in the same "games" as their nondisabled peers and are given a range of accommodations to compensate.

According to the Disability Discrimination Act, a student with a disability cannot be treated less favorably for a reason relating to her/his disability and the university has to make "reasonable adjustments" that can be either individual—for example, by allowing an assessment in a different format (this is sometimes called accommodated assessment)—or it can be an adjustment that is offered to all students—for example, offering a variety of assessment formats to all students. For students with mental health difficulties, this could be interpreted as recognizing that some situations put such students under intolerable pressure. In the case of the above student with obsessive compulsive disorder, she might be allowed to e-mail her assignments, if she is unable to actually bring them in herself.

Other stressful situations might include being with large groups of people, group work, presentations, having to absorb information under pressure and having rigid deadlines. Even group trips to exhibitions can be terrifying for those suffering from phobias or obsessive compulsive disorders. Universities are now required to be proactive in identifying barriers and work to remove them. Offering all students a variety of ways of achieving the same learning outcomes would take away another pressure from the disabled student who does not wish to be seen as being different and singled out.

In 2006, the legislation in the United Kingdom was strengthened by a new statutory responsibility to promote disability equality. The disability equality duties require universities to consider disability equality in everything they do. They now have to report on what educational opportunities are available to students with disabilities and also how well these students achieve. An action plan must be included to implement measurable improvements and disabled students need to be involved in considering what actions must take priority. This ties in with the similar focus on ethnic minorities and students from lower social classes.

An increasing number of people are declaring mental health difficulties in the United Kingdom. There are various possible explanations for this. It would seem that there is now less stigma attached to such difficulties and more government legislative and funding support, so people are more willing to declare. Some areas of modern life, such as increased drug use, might indicate an actual increase. In the spirit of widening participation, there is more encouragement to support students for whom being successful at a university is really problematic. "The university recommends early disclosure and provides reassurance that this will not affect the application process . . . [However,] this attitude ignores the valid reasons for non-disclosure, such as fear of unfavorable treatment or the wish not to be treated differently to their peers" (Shevlin et al, 2004:18)

Many students will not disclose a disability unless they have to. Some students will arrive at university with excellent Advanced Level (school leaving) qualifications, in spite of their mental health issues. Many students do not even realize that mental health difficulties are a disability category under the Disability Discrimination Act. *Effi* talked about her "condition," but never mentioned the diagnosis by name. *Masako* talked about her "emotional epilepsy" and declared that several members of her family had the same problem. It took two years before she finally submitted her medical evidence, which clearly stated a very severe personality disorder. For *Steve*, telling us his diagnosis of schizophrenia was a concern, because he thought it would change the working relationship he had with his tutor. Others disclose and then swear us to secrecy, which, no doubt, is their absolute right; under the Disability Discrimination Act, everyone has the right to ask for their condition to remain confidential.

Students with mental health issues will often make a very late application for a course. Some find the completion of forms quite daunting, others are unable to make a phone call without support or end up making too many calls to many people because of their anxiety. One member of staff felt he was being "harassed" by a student who was totally overwhelmed by the anxiety of knowing whether or not he would be accepted on the course. Some students create such a fuss that some staff may bypass the usual complex process of admissions and allow students to start courses which they may not be ready to begin. This then causes difficulties later on when the student is unable to manage and then highlights more anxieties. By recognizing these difficulties and recommending that admission-tutors put these students in touch with me, and possibly acting as an intermediary, I am often able to relieve the stress on all sides.

Students often begin their courses full of confidence until suddenly something happens to challenge them:

> In the first lesson we were asked to get ourselves into groups of three. . . . I couldn't do this. For me to speak to someone was just too much. In the end I was put with the other "losers" who were also too shy or too scared, which did not help our communication at all (a student with disability).

There is a very simple strategy to remedy this situation. Teaching staff need to take on board that many students often struggle to make friends. Why not organize the students into different groups for the first six weeks, so that they gradually get to know each other and find out who they can work with and who they cannot? This is something that would help all students, not just those with anxieties.

Another student with a disability said,

> Our first assignment was to go around the campus picking up anything that had been thrown away. We had to collect twenty pieces and bring them back to the studio in order to look at the packaging and typographical design. . . . This really upset me. My mother has schizophrenia and she picks up rubbish daily and piles it in our house, under my bed etc. I do not need to come to university to do such things . . .

I was confident that the university lecturers had never considered that this task might cause anyone anxiety. But, when I pointed it out to them, they were able to think of any number of ways of gaining the same information that they required for their assignment. I stressed that giving the students choices allowed everyone to find their own best method of working.

Teaching staff working with students continue to be concerned about how to respond to students with mental health difficulties who express such high levels of anxiety in a variety of explosive ways, given the extra time and work needed to assist these students. Providing suitable boundaries for the student with mental health difficulties is also important. Very often their life is in chaos, and ensuring that they are contained and know where to come to if they have a problem ensures that fewer staff are involved and levels of anxiety are lowered. It is important to realize how vital confidentiality is in this area.

Additionally, there is often still a stigma attached to mental health difficulties. This means that such students should never have their problems discussed or referred to in any public way. All discussion should be limited to appropriate professional conversations and, for a more general discussion, the student should be anonymized.

There is, however, another side to confidentiality. It is important not to let students tell you very serious things, such as suicidal tendencies, and then swear you to secrecy. In such circumstances the best thing to do is say to the student that you cannot agree to keep such information secret, but you will pass it on with care to people who can help. It is important then immediately to tell your line-manager and whoever you have identified with this responsibility within the wider university.

It is also important to remember that some of the indicators of behavior described can also be found in students who do not necessarily have a mental health problem. It is always a matter of judgment to decide whether or not a particular form of behavior is a matter of concern in any individual student. This judgment should not be made by one individual. Some tutors might think that they should be responsible for their students, but it is important to stress that this might not be their area of expertise and they must call for assistance. By offering my support in a regular feedback session to staff, I hoped to be able to train them to listen to their students with more empathy.

Some teaching and non-teaching staff were very concerned about the mental health problems/issues and what may happen. It was important to resolve the difficulty by reminding staff of the Disability Discrimination Act, that they could not treat students less favorably for a reason related to their disability and to work to a reasonable conclusion. *Carl* is a student who would not come into the classroom. He has a history of phobias, which manifested themselves sometimes in his being unable to come into a room where there is more than one other person. He felt desperate and wrote a letter to the lecturer describing his anxieties. After speaking to the lecturer who contacted me and explaining that the student used the class as a distraction against his suicidal thoughts, the lecturer felt that the situation was out of control and the student should not attend the course.

Under the Disability Discrimination Act, we have to find ways to enable disabled people to gain access to education. I was able to organize a weekly tutorial with the course director for the student, so that he would be able to know what was happening during that week's activities and could decide what he would be able to manage on-site and what he would do at home. This reasonable adjustment enabled the student to complete the course and continue to further courses.

In the United Kingdom, students are assessed (graded) by coursework, extended essays, and presentations as well as examinations. One reasonable adjustment for all disabled students is recognizing that they are likely to have periods when they are in too much pain or unable to manage their difficulties. At our university, students are then given an extra two weeks to produce their assignments. Some teaching staff worry about the fairness to all students and the standards if some students are given extra support or extended deadlines. They are also concerned that disabled students are not developing attributes of independent learning. However, students with mental health difficulties are often battling with blockage and lack of creativity possibly caused by strong medication or even intrusive thoughts and voices. These students need the extra time and support to show that they can do work that is up to standard and of value.

Sally, a student diagnosed with severe depression, would often complain that she could not start to write. She said,

> I am frightened of being judged because if I receive a low grade I will fail my course, drop out, my family will reinforce my own fear that I am a "loser" and that I will not be able to make a living. I will end up hungry, homeless, and living in the gutter.

Sally's tutors were full of praise for her work and often said her work was the best in the class. It was very difficult for her to hear this praise and believe it. Without support she would definitely have not completed her course successfully.

Research at Plymouth University in the United Kingdom (SWANDS 2002) has shown that, by offering all students a choice of type of assessment that has been agreed before the start of the course, fewer adjustments, if any, need to be made for disabled students. These types of changes require cultural as well as structural change, since such changes in teaching and learning can only work with the cooperation of teaching staff and administrators. M. Shevlin, M.

Kenny, and E. McNeela (2004, 21) point out that there are issues of both attitude and awareness: "support was generally conceived as the provision of assistive personnel and technology. However, [students] had by far the most difficulties in overcoming lecturer suspicion, indifference or lack of awareness."

With her writing, *Geraldine* often felt overloaded and did not know where to begin, in which order to plan her work, or how to structure her assignments. She had had a particularly difficult school experience while she was battling with her eating disorder and found people in authority difficult to manage. She would do anything she could to avoid getting started on her work and often the stress would make things much worse. She felt so bad that she was unable to attend class. She concentrated on minutiae, like clothes, to distract herself from bigger problems but the minutiae then also become stressful and important.

My strategy was to offer *Geraldine* one-to-one weekly tutorials to help structure and plan assignments, to ensure all deadlines were met and procedures correctly followed, and to give emotional support. Contact was maintained as often as required (sometimes daily) to try and contain the anxieties and create boundaries. I also contacted other staff who taught *Geraldine*, so she knew we always had her in mind, whenever there was a problem.

Of course, procrastination is a universal problem for all students, but for those with mental health issues it can become a bigger difficulty if it is not kept under control. These students need support from a member of staff, who has an understanding of all the issues involved and the likely effect of the blurring of boundaries on such a student. S. Jackson and M. Blythman (forthcoming) found that by basing this member of staff in a study support team, which supports the academic needs of all students, less stigma was attached and other academic staff were inclined to be supportive:

> In the University of the Arts London this means that academic support for students with mental health difficulties is located within an academic unit rather than within a student services unit. This has a number of advantages. It means that we are recognized and respected (mainly!) by other faculty as fellow teachers. We often have more teaching experience and pedagogic knowledge than many of our colleagues elsewhere in the university who have been appointed for their disciplinary expertise rather than their knowledge of teaching and learning. These factors mainly make much easier any negotiations around changes in the way a course is delivered although there can occasionally be difficulties with faculty whose approach to teaching is radically different from ours.

An issue requiring both structural and cultural change is the need to make both teaching and learning methods and modes of assessment/evaluation more inclusive. Tinklin, Riddell, and Wilson (2004) point out that this requires challenging fundamental, conventional notions of what counts as effective teaching and learning. This makes changing assessment (grading) one of the hardest aspects to achieve. Structural changes might include less dependence on attendance at large formal classes, a wider variety of possible ways of learning, and the use of varied assessment/evaluation methods. If these are open to all students, then this normalizes a number of things that are really helpful to students with mental health difficulties. Assumptions of normality are central to an inclusive approach (Shevlin, Kenny, and McNeela 2004; Tinklin and Hall 1999). At the same time there may be a need to take on board an individual request; for example, a student may need to take an examination in a room alone.

Universities need to do considerable work with all employees, both teaching and support staff, to give them a greater understanding of mental illness and how to cope with students with mental health difficulties. We have found that people working at the university, at all levels, at times misinterpret behavior and are also made to feel uneasy, leading to fear. "Sometimes staff were apparently well-meaning but ill-informed, or were operating on assumptions about a student's needs without checking with the student concerned . . . many staff had a positive attitude but insufficient experience or knowledge" (Tinklin and Hall 1999, 191).

Sometimes the behavior of a student brings up anxieties for the tutors themselves and maybe we do not do enough to support staff with their own worries. In the United Kingdom, current thinking among professionals is that we need to recognize the normative nature of what is perceived as "normal behavior." But such perceptions are contingent on social, cultural, and historical factors and vary considerably across different national, social, and cultural groups.

Universities also need to become more flexible around opportunities for students to take time out and return later to the same course. Recent research, in the area of social class participation but equally applicable to students with mental health difficulties, suggests that the United Kingdom is not good at this (Quinn et al. 2005). Currently, universities and colleges in the United Kingdom are rewarded financially and in terms of reputation for getting students through in the minimum period, which is three years for a bachelor's degree in England.

Administrators and funders need to recognize that some students cost more to educate than others because of their additional support needs. It is not possible to work on a model of "the universal student." There needs to be a part of the university which identifies all available external funding to support this work, but it is important not to be entirely reliant on "special" money. Rather the needs of some students should be seen as a question of social justice. However, there is also a danger in large amounts of additional support of failing to develop students' independent learning. Greg Hampton and

Richard Gosden (2004) argue that students who do receive additional support in various ways should still be encouraged to "minimize their reliance" on assistance for this reason. However, for some students, in-class support is vital if they are to achieve their potential and teaching staff are to be supported.

CONCLUSION

To sum up, my argument is that universities have to have mechanisms to support individual students such as those with mental health difficulties, as shown in the case studies above. However, universities also need to be willing and able to make structural changes at Teaching and Learning Committees and the Academic Board, as these are the teams who are responsible for creating access to the curriculum. They will need to consider preadmission interviews, learning and teaching environments, funding, flexibility with attendance, and, above all, awareness training for all staff. Arrangements for the assessment (grading) of disabled students need to be considered at the course-validation stage and written into the examination policy and design of assessment methodology of each course. I would argue that such changes will benefit all excluded or marginalized groups and contribute to social justice.

REFERENCES

Borland, J., and S. James. "The Learning Experience of Students with Disabilities in Higher Education: A Case Study of a United Kingdom University." *Disability and Society* 14, no. 10 (1999): 85–101.

European Communities. *Including People with Disabilities: Europe's Equal Opportunities Strategy*. Italy (2007).

Hampton, Greg, and Richard Gosden. "Fair Play for Students with Disability." *Journal of Higher Education Policy and Management* 26 (2004): 225–38.

Jackson, S., and M. Blythman. "Just coming in the door was hard': supporting students with mental health difficulties." In R. D. Babcock, S. Daniels, and J. Inman (eds.), *Writing Centers and Disability* (Southern Illinois University Press, forthcoming).

Mental Health Foundation. "Promoting Student Mental Health." *Student Mental Health Update* 2, no. 1 (2001).

Quinn, Jocey, Liz Thomas, Kim Slack, Lorraine Casey, Wayne Thexton, and John Noble. *From Life Crisis to Lifelong Learning: Rethinking Working-Class "Drop Out" from Higher Education*. (York, UK: Joseph Rowntree Foundation, 2005).

Riddell, Sheila, Teresa Tinklin, and Alastair Wilson. *Disabled Students in Higher Education* (Oxford: Routledge, 2005).

Selby J. "Widening Participation" (Circular letter number 31/2007). Higher Education Funding Council for England (2007).

Shevlin, M., M. Kenny, and E. McNeela. "Participation in Higher Education for Students with Disabilities: An Irish Perspective." *Disability and Society* 19, no. 1 (2004): 15–30.

SWANDS (South West Academic Network for Disability Support). *Compliance in Higher Education: An Audit and Guidance Tool for Accessible Practice within the Framework of Teaching and Learning* (Plymouth, UK: University of Plymouth, 2002).

Tinklin, Teresa, and John Hall. (1999) "Getting round Obstacles: Disabled Students' Experiences in Higher Education in Scotland." *Studies in Higher Education* 24: 183–94.

Tinklin, Teresa, Sheila Riddell and Alastair Wilson. "Policy and Provision for Disabled Students in Higher Education in Scotland and England: The Current State of Play." *Studies in Higher Education* 29 (2004): 637–57.

Trowler, Paul R. *Academics Responding to Change* (Buckingham: SRHE and Open University Press, 1998).

Yorke, Mantz, and Bernard Longden. *Retention and Student Success in Higher Education* (Maidenhead, UK: SRHE/Open University Press, 2004).

Websites

AUCC (Association for University and College Counseling). http://www.aucc .uk.com/annual_survey.html. (2004).

Disability Discrimination Act. *Office of Public Sector Information.* http://www.opsi .gov.uk/acts/acts1995/1995050.htm. (1995).

Equality Challenge Unit. *Disability Home Page.* http://www.ecu.ac.uk/guidance/ disability/. (2006).

HESA (Higher Education Statistics Agency). http://www.hesa.ac.uk/index .php?option=com_datatables&Itemid=121&task=show_category&catdex=3. (2006).

MIND (National Association for Mental Health). http://www.mind.org.uk/ Information/Factsheets/Suicide/#Suicide_in_young_people. (2006).

National Disability Team. *Briefing: Supporting Students with Mental Health Difficulties.* http://www.natdisteam.ac.uk/documents/ Supportingstudentswithmentalhealthdifficulties. (2004).

Open University. *Making Your Teaching Inclusive.* http://www.open.ac.uk/ inclusiveteaching. (2006).

19

Altruism and Avarice

The Place of Foreign Students in Australian Universities

Don Stewart

Australia is the third largest English speaking destination for international students after the United States and Great Britain. In 2006–2007, a total of 228,592 offshore student visas were granted. This was an increase of 19.89 percent over the 2005-06 figures and, in fact, yearly increases of this sort have occurred each year since 1994. These international students have been a major source of income for Australia, generating Australian \$3.7 billion in 2000 and thus becoming Australia's third largest export earner. The proportion of international students in Australian universities currently stands at 17.3 percent (Australian Government: Department of Immigration and Citizenship 2008). This is the highest proportion of any OECD (Organization for Economic Cooperation and Development) country (cf. the United States, the largest recipient of international students, at 3.4 percent). It would be fair to say that no other country has pursued the recruitment of international students with such passion as Australia, with virtually every Australian university having an active and well-resourced recruitment organization to recruit international students and the Australian organization IDP providing a worldwide network of agents and recruiting offices.

To understand the Australian situation, it is important to understand that all but two of the forty Australian universities are public institutions. They were set up by individual state legislations, but rely on the federal government for most of their funding. This poses a number of questions: How and why has this situation developed? Are the international students well-treated and getting a good education in Australia? And what has this influx of international students meant for Australian students, the quality of their education, and their access to university studies? In answering these questions, I will draw on my experience over the last twenty-five years as an educator, a counselor, a recruiter, and administrator of international students and their programs, and a negotiator of agreements relating to such students.

The Colombo Plan

The first intentional and official involvement with international students came with the signing of the "Colombo Plan" agreement at a meeting of British Commonwealth Foreign Ministers in Colombo in January 1950. The original concept was the provision of development assistance by the richer members of the British Commonwealth to less-developed Commonwealth members. Quite quickly the scheme was extended to other Asian countries, and scholarships to Australian universities became an important feature of the program. By 1969, over 8,000 students had come to Australia under this scheme (Humphreys 2004). While this is a very small number compared with current numbers, it was significant to the Australian universities at that time and, in fact, to the Australian society at large, during the 1950s and 1960s.

Malaysian Students

Another significant source of international students for Australia during this period, in this case privately funded students, was the ethnically Chinese citizens of Malaysia. Because of positive discrimination policies by the Malaysian Government in favor of *Bumiputra* (literally, sons of the soil), i.e., Malays, it was very difficult for those who were not ethnically Malay to gain entry into Malaysian government universities, so Chinese families sent their offspring, for the main part, to either Great Britain or Australia. Even after restrictions were eased in Malaysia in the 1990s, a tradition had been built up in Malaysian Chinese families and the second generations of these families continued to go to Australia. To illustrate this point, while I was Head of the International House at The University of Melbourne, a young man I interviewed for residency explained that both his parents had been residents in the House. In fact, he said, he was conceived at the International House. Needless to say he was accepted!

Commonwealth Scholarships

During the 1950s, the Australian Government (led by the Liberal Party, i.e., a conservative party in Australian terms) introduced a generous scholarship scheme for Australian students which paid university fees and a means-tested living allowance. Because the number of Australians entering university education at this time was quite small, a large proportion of those seeking tertiary studies received scholarships; this scholarship scheme became an opportunity for upward mobility for many children of poorer families at that time. The Prime Minister, Sir Robert Menzies, was a strong supporter of universities (he was Chancellor of The University of Melbourne during most of that time) and universities were comparatively well funded. Unfortunately, the number of scholarships was not increased in the following years, even when the Australian population grew and also as the proportion of young people of university age seeking university education increased. Because of this, university fees had once again become a significant barrier for many poorer students by the time that a Labor government was elected in 1972. This government promptly abolished all university fees.

HECS (Higher Education Contribution Scheme) Fees for Australian Students

University enrollments in Australia grew by a factor of over twenty in the years from 1949 to 2000 (i.e., from 31,753 to 695,485) and, in particular in the years from the abolition of student fees in 1972 to 1988 enrollments increased from 182,337 to 420,850 (Australian Government, Department of Education, Employment and Workplace Relations 2008). The cost of supporting universities was becoming a noticeable burden on government and, recognizing that university education is both a public and a private good, the then Labor Government believed that students should bear part of the burden and so, in 1988, introduced the Higher Education Contribution Scheme (HECS). The plan was that fees would not be charged upfront but that when students graduated and were earning a reasonable amount, a levy would be charged through the tax system. Initially, when the scheme was introduced, repayments were fairly modest at Australian $1,800 per year of study and repayments cut in at a taxable income of $22,000. However, repayment amounts were increased yearly and, in 1997, after the election of a conservative government, differential rates of HECS charges were introduced, recognizing the different costs of mounting different courses and, to some extent, the relative financial benefits of having degrees in different disciplines. In 1997, the threshold taxable income for repayment was also reduced to Australian $20,000. By 2006, the annual HECS fees had increased to Australian $4,900 for the cheapest courses and up to $8,000 for the most expensive courses, although a modest attempt at manpower planning was introduced with HECS fees for teaching and nursing set at $3,900 (Australian Vice-Chancellors' Committee 2008).

Full Fees for International Students

The introduction of the HECS system for Australian students in 1988 left the foreign students in an anomalous position. They clearly could not be part of the HECS system since they would, in all likelihood, not be subject to the Australian tax system upon graduation. The decision was made that these students would, in future, pay full-cost-recovery fees. This meant that all direct and indirect costs would be included in the fees. The fees would also include a capital component which covered the depreciation costs of the capital, buildings, equipment, and libraries which had already been paid for by the Australian taxpayer. This meant that the authorities could say that foreign students would not and could not displace Australian students, since once a situation was reached where any class was above capacity, new plant and buildings could be acquired and more staff hired. At this time, there were 18,000 foreign students in Australian tertiary institutions, out of a total of 440,000, i.e., 5 percent. Despite predictions that the fees would discourage international students, international student numbers grew by 18 percent in 1990 and continued on an upward trajectory from there on (Australian Bureau of Statistics 2007).

Reasons for the Growth of International Student Numbers in Australia

There are several reasons why international student numbers continued to increase in Australia even after the introduction of full-cost-recovery fees.

- Australia provides an education in English, which is sought after by a majority of students looking for an international education.
- The universities have developed from a British system and standards are high. In fact, standards vary very little among the forty universities.
- Over the last fifteen years, fees for international students have compared very favorably with major competitors, the United States, Great Britain and Canada. Changes in exchange rates, however, have reduced this advantage.
- Australia's proximity to Asia, the major source of international students at present, is also important. Airfares and travel times are much less and, therefore, a cost advantage. It also means that students can return home more frequently and parents can visit. Time zones are close, another aid in communication between the student and home. For example, Perth is in the same time zone as the major cities of Asia and the other areas of Australia are no more than two hours different.
- Australia is seen as a safe environment as against the perceived dangers of living in the United States.

While the above reasons might all be legitimate, they need to be brought to the notice of potential students and Australian universities have pursued this task with great vigor.

Why have they done this? The OECD figures show that, during the period 1995 to 2003, the share of GDP going to tertiary education decreased by 7 percent as against an OECD average increase of 48 percent (National Tertiary Education Union 2007). This decrease in funding for Australian universities was coupled with an increase in bureaucratic control over them, thereby limiting the opportunities universities have had to develop new funding sources. The monies returned by students to the universities through the HECS system grew only slowly, since students had to graduate and then earn a sufficient salary to be required to pay funds back through the tax system. On the other hand, full fees from international students went directly to universities in the year they studied. The older, more prestigious universities, the so-called "sandstone universities" often won significant funds for contract research; whether this was a financial benefit or a further drain on resources was a subject of constant debate within universities. Also, gifts and bequests to one's alma mater have never been a feature of life in Australia, a country with a strong socialist heritage. Because of the above reasons, and the aggressive recruitment of international students by Australian universities, it was only a short period of time before the full fees of international students became the major nongovernment source of funding at all Australian universities. As an example, the Australian $200 million received from international student fees by the University of Melbourne in 1997 was 16 percent of its total income, with around 25 percent coming from recurrent government grants (the University of Melbourne 2008). Other Australian universities would show an even greater proportion of their income coming from international students.

The focus of Australian universities' international recruitment was first on Asia. Traditional sources of international students such as Malaysia and Singapore were the target of vigorous marketing. Some universities developed "twinning" arrangements with local institutions in order to provide a captive flow of international students and one university set up a branch campus each in Malaysia and South Africa, while another set up a campus in Vietnam. The heavy competition between Australian universities then moved to other Southeast Asian countries: Indonesia, Thailand, and Vietnam. Australian universities then looked further afield—the Middle East and Central and South America. Study abroad students from the United States also became an important contribution for some universities. More recently, numbers from the more traditional Southeast Asian countries have declined, but have been more than made up for by an increase in students from India and China. In 2006–2007, students from India made up 17.3 percent of all overseas students in Australia, 15 percent came from China, 8 percent from Korea, and 5.5 percent from the United States. The traditional major source of international students, Malaysia, had now dropped to fifth with 4 percent, while no other country made up more than 3 percent of the numbers. It should be added that many students also go to Australia for intensive English courses, while others enter "bridging" programs to bring their academic standard up to a level acceptable to the universities (Australian Bureau of Statistics 2007).

The Education Received by International Students

The decision to send one's children abroad to study is one which entails considerable expense and often great family hardship, and so the financial return from this son or daughter acquiring an overseas degree is often a significant factor in the choice of the field of study. Overwhelmingly, the choice made in Australia by international students has been in the area of management or business studies (48.5 percent in 2000). A further 25 percent studied science or engineering in 2000 and many of these students were in the information technology field (Australian Bureau of Statistics 2007). Because of international agreements, such as the Washington Accord in engineering, Australian degrees have international recognition in these areas; so, the graduates can be said to have gained "value for money."

Another guarantee of value for money for these students has been the Australian Government's National Code of Practice, set up to ensure ethical treatment of international students, which all universities must agree to if they are to market their courses overseas (Australian Government, Australian Education International 2007). There have been some cases where international students have been taken advantage of, but they have not been numerous. A more common complaint has been that these international students have been treated in a more favorable way compared to Australian students because of their position as "paying customers."

Full Fees for Australian Students

More recently, the existence of places in Australian universities for full-fee-paying students from overseas, with apparently somewhat easier entry conditions than for Australian HECS students, not surprisingly, has led to a call for Australians to be admitted to the universities under the same conditions as their overseas classmates. It was a call which many of the cash-strapped universities were only too happy to support, and, in 2002, the government allowed universities to admit a limited number of Australian undergraduate students on a full-fee-paying basis (universities had been allowed to charge full fees for postgraduate courses from 1992). The conditions were eased further in 2005 (Australian Government, Department of Education, Employ-ment and Workplace Relations 2005) when more than 3 percent of Australian students were paying full fees, paying an average of Australian $20,000 per annum each. More and more students have taken up the full-fee option since that time, particularly in the more prestigious universities and in the most lucrative professions such as medicine and law.

In November 2007, a new Labor government was elected which has a policy position of opposing full-fees for Australian students. This new gov-ernment has reiterated its position since coming into power, saying that it will start to phase out full-fees for Australian students in 2009. This has created a predictable outcry from the universities asking that they be compensated for the consequent loss of income (*The Age*, 2008).

Case Studies

To illustrate the changes which have occurred over the last 50 years in at-titudes to international students in Australia, two organizations of which the author has personal experience are briefly described: International House (the University of Melbourne) and the International Development Technologies Centre.

International House: The University of Melbourne

The story of the start of International House at the University of Melbourne is helpful in illuminating societal attitudes in the 1950s and the impact the arrival of Colombo Plan students had on those attitudes. This was at a time when the notorious "White Australia" policy was still in force and Austra-lian city dwellers never saw anyone who was not of European origin. It is not surprising, therefore, that the new arrivals found severe discrimination in seeking accommodation. In one case, when a group of Colombo Plan students complained about their inadequate housing to the housing officer at the university, this officer not only managed to get these students better ac-commodation, but also recognized their isolation and loneliness. He started to invite them out on social occasions with his university student friends and on one notable occasion they were refused admission to a hotel because "We don't serve colored people."

From this experience was born the idea of an International House, like that in New York, where Australian and international students could live together and gain, as well as satisfactory accommodation, mutual understanding. This idea became a cause célèbre among the liberal intelligentsia of Melbourne who set about fund-raising until they were able to buy land and seek support from the governments of Australia, Malaysia, Singapore, and Brunei. The International House opened to students in 1958, with fifty-five students. In 2008, it celebrated its golden jubilee, with 270 students. Unfortunately, this is now a pitifully small proportion of the international students at The University of Melbourne.

Although owned by the University of Melbourne, the International House is fully self-supporting on the basis of the fees paid by the residents. By tradition, these are 50 percent Australian and 50 percent international, and in a reversal of the situation when the International House started, the international students are the more affluent, while the Australian students, coming, as they mostly do, from rural areas in the grip of drought and economic downturn, are struggling.

The International Development Technologies Centre (IDTC)

From 1980 until 2007, the above center, under various names, operated in the Engineering Faculty of the University of Melbourne. It grew from a desire of faculty members to contribute to the development of the poorer countries of the world. After a study (commenced in 1978) of ways in which they could contribute, they decided that a master's program for engineers, which was specifically directed to the needs of developing countries, would fill a gap. This, it was felt, would contribute to the development of technology and technological manpower, and hence development, in the students' home countries much more effectively than any research or technological innovation.

The Australian Government aid organization (AusAID) decided that this program fitted its aims and so provided a grant to the University of Melbourne to sponsor up to twelve students under the program. Students came not only from South and Southeast Asia, but also from Africa and the West Indies. This sponsorship continued until the introduction of full fees for international students in 1988. At that time AusAID said that it would no longer provide a direct grant to the university, but would pay full fees for students they put into the program. This led to the growth of the program from twelve to twenty students in the next year. Continued growth followed, additional degree programs were offered, and the numbers grew to over 200 in 2007.

The composition of the student cohort in IDTC has changed during that time. While scholarship holders have continued to be part of the cohort, they have become a small minority, with most students, or their families, paying full fees. The mix has also changed in other ways: more Australian students and students from North America and Europe have joined the program because of their desire to train to work on development issues. Over the last five years,

Chinese students have become the biggest national group. This program has also become a significant income earner for the Faculty of Engineering.

Commencing in 2008, The University of Melbourne has radically restructured its teaching programs into what it refers to as The Melbourne Model. This is based on the Bologna Declaration (a joint declaration of the European Ministers of Education in June 1999) which aims to promote a system of tertiary education worldwide that allows for comparable university degrees internationally. In actual fact, the model is not very different from the familiar U.S. system, where a liberal undergraduate degree is followed by graduate study in the student's chosen professional area. With all engineering subjects now postgraduate, the IDTC offerings have lost their distinctiveness and the Centre has ceased to exist. The program was built on close personal contact and concern for students by staff and the loss of this distinctive character may well mean that the value of the suite of subjects will diminish, even if they continue to exist.

CONCLUSION

This chapter has traced the evolution of attitudes toward international students from one of altruistic concern for the people from poor counties to the commercialization of these international students into a major source of income for universities and, indeed, one of Australia's major income earners. In doing this, Australia has capitalized on its position as a country "with a European history and an Asian geography." The Colombo Plan students who came to Australia in the 1950s were curiosities. Apart from a few U.S. soldiers of color during World War II and indigenous Australians, who were kept well in the background, Australians had never seen anyone not of a European ethnicity; a far cry from today. Australia is now the second most ethnically diverse country after Israel. Australia has embraced its Asian location with vigor and the hundreds of thousands of Asian students who have come to Australia, and the many who have stayed, have played no small part in this. Australia has been greatly enriched, and not just in financial terms.

Throughout this chapter several influences on access to higher education for Australian students have become apparent. The 1950s, when the first international students started to come to Australia, was also a time when university education became accessible to many Australians who previously would not have thought it possible. These doors started closing until 1972, when the abolition of university fees again opened the doors.

The growth of the number of international students during the 1980s and 1990s had two paradoxically different effects of equity of opportunity for

Australian students. On one hand, the international students provided income for cash-strapped universities and enabled them to continue to provide reasonable university education for all students, international and local. On the other hand, the full fees for international students have provided a compelling model for a similar arrangement for Australian students which opened the door wider for the offspring of the affluent, particularly into study for the more lucrative professions, a move definitely opposed to equity.

Altruism and avarice when looking at international students? The altruism has definitely been there and continues to this day. Avarice is probably too strong a word. The commercialization of international student education has provided a lifeline to university administrations faced with an unsympathetic government which restricted their opportunities to find other sources of income. Who can blame them if they took it?

REFERENCES

The Age. "Unis Slam Abolition of Full-Fees." http://www.theage.com.au/education-news/unis-slam-abolition-of-full-fees/2008/02/27 (accessed April 24, 2008).

Australian Bureau of Statistics. "Perspectives on Migrants, Overseas Students–2007." Canberra, 2007.

Australian Government: Australian Education International. *National Code of Practice 2007* (2007). http://aei.dest.gov.au/AEI/ESOS/default.htm (accessed April 24, 2008).

Australian Government: Department of Education, Employment and Workplace Relations. "'Our Universities: Backing Australia's Future'—Policy Paper." Canberra, Australia, 2005.

———. *Students 2007 (First Half Year)—elected Higher Education Statistics* (2008). http://www.dest.gov.au/sectors/higher_education/publications_resources/profiles/students_2007.htm (accessed April 28, 2008).

Australian Government: Department of Immigration and Citizenship. "Fact Sheet 50—Overseas Students in Australia." (Commonwealth of Australia, 2008). http://www.immi.gov.au/media/fact-sheets/50students.htm (accessed April 29, 2008).

Australian Vice-Chancellor's Committee. "History of HECS-to-2008." 2008.

Humphreys, L. R. *Of Many Colours: A History of International House, The University of Melbourne* (Melbourne: International House, The University of Melbourne, 2004).

National Tertiary Education Union. "The Funding of Australian Universities, 1996–2005: An Examination of The facts and Figures." South Melbourne: National Tertiary Education Union, 2007.

20

A Dual Admission Policy

Enhancing Equal Opportunities in Higher Education through Merit-Based Admission Policy

Boaz Shulruf, John Hattie, and Sarah Tumen

Equity in higher education has been a major concern of educational policy makers in New Zealand and worldwide (Anae et. al. 2002b; Dobric 2005; Halsey 1993; Ministry of Education 2002, 2005a, 2005b; Scott, 2004, 2005; Smyth et al. 2006). The major concerns have been the inability of educational systems to close the gap between well-established populations, mostly Europeans or European descendents in Europe, North America, Australia, and New Zealand, with middle and higher income who have traditionally achieved higher educational attainment than other groups, largely immigrants, indigenous people and people from low-income families who are traditionally underrepresented in higher education (Anae et. al., 2002a; Brown and Burkhardt 1999; Epple et. al. 2005; Gray et. al. 2000; Guri-Rozenblit 1989; Jones et. al. 2002; Lipset et. al. 2003; Ministry of Education 2004, 2005b; Morgaman et al. 2002; Scott 2005).

David Kirp's overview of the development of higher education policies (see chapter 2 in this volume) sheds light on the tension between the economic and the social drivers, which determine those within the society who acquire higher education and who destine to remain out of this still exclusive club. Historically, higher education institutions and policy makers have addressed inequality in higher education largely through modifying admission policies as they believed that the barrier to equality lies with the gatekeeper, i.e., the admission criteria. Hence, a range of admission policies have been implemented aiming to increase the number of students from traditionally underrepresented populations in higher education (Rigol 2003; Skilbeck and Connell 2000).

Among these the most popular admission policies are the open-admission policy (Friedlander 2008; Schmid 2008), and ethnicity-based affirmative-action policies (Bucks 2005; Donnelly 1998; Loury and Garman 1993; Tienda, Alon, and Niu 2008). Nonetheless, these admission policies attracted criticism from two different fronts. One front was legal, as demonstrated in a California case where the High Court abolished any affirmative action in admissions to higher education institutions arguing that it is unconstitutional (Mohr et. al. 2004). The other type of critique argued that enabling students to enroll in higher education institutions based on sociodemographic criteria rather than on their secondary school achievements would increase the number of students who fail and thus damage the quality of education (Deaton and Schutz 2001).

In New Zealand most universities have applied special admission policies for traditionally underrepresented populations, particularly enabling students of Maori and Pacific ethnicities to enroll in degree programs even if they have not met all the admission criteria. Nonetheless, a comprehensive synthesis of the evidence of the New Zealand tertiary education outcomes indicates that, though the educational attainment of all New Zealanders has increased over the past fifteen years (1991–2005), the gaps across ethnic groups remains the same (Smart 2006). Hence, the dual admission model concept as introduced in this chapter may provide an improved method for enhancing equity in higher education.

THE NEW SECONDARY SCHOOL ASSESSMENT SYSTEM IN NEW ZEALAND: NATIONAL CERTIFICATE OF EDUCATIONAL ATTAINMENT

Until 2003, New Zealand students who graduated from high schools were assessed by a norm-based assessment (Black 2001; Dobric 2005). This required obtaining a grade of "C" or higher plus a Higher School Certificate, of an "A" or "B" Bursary (University of Auckland 2001, p. 13). (There are other paths into universities, such as mature-age entry, which are not investigated in this chapter.) From 2002 to 2004 the assessment system was progressively changed from this norm-based assessment to a standard-based assessment model, named the National Certificate of Educational Achievement (NCEA). This change was the result of a lengthy discussion which was influenced by arguments that the norm-based assessment system had disadvantaged students from certain ethnicities, particularly Maori and Pacific and students from lower income families (Dobric 2005; Strathdee 2003).

The NCEA is a standards-based system that measures students' performance against standards of achievement or competence. The NCEA achievement standards assessments include two major components: some undertaken during the year and some completed nearer the end of the year. The ratings for the NCEA are "excellence," "merit," "achieved," and "not achieved." This system closely mimics first-year university study, in which the level of competency is measured via assignments during a course and often an examination at the end of the course. The NCEA also includes another form of credits, unit standards, which only rate the level of performance as pass/fail (NZQA 2004).

The NCEA standards offered in secondary schools are usually at levels 1, 2, and 3, depending on their level of difficulty. Typically, but not necessarily, level 1 is assessed at year 11, level 2 at year 12, and level 3 at year 13. Every standard achieved is worth a set number of credits based on the expected number of hours that students need to study to achieve the credit (NZQA, 2005b). To be awarded a NCEA level 1, a student must achieve eighty credits, including eight in numeracy standards and eight in literacy. To be awarded a NCEA level 2, a student must achieve sixty credits, plus twenty credits at any level, even if gained for any other national qualification. To be awarded a NCEA level 3, a student must achieve sixty credits at level 3 or above, plus twenty credits at level 2 or above, even if gained for any other national qualification (NZQA 2005b; Strathdee 2003).

The NCEA included a Grade Point Average (GPA) based on the grade achieved for achievement standards, allowing admission decisions based on this GPA to be made for limited entry tertiary qualifications where there is competition among applicants for limited numbers of places. In calculating the GPA, zero was assigned for not achieved, two for achieved, three for merit, and four for excellence. The difference between achieved, merit, and excellence is 1, but the grades 0, 2, 3 and 4 do not represent a continuous scale. In this system, merit is proportionally worth 1.5 more than achieve (3/2) and excellence is worth 1.3 more than merit (4/3). The NCEA framework also includes unit standards, which can score only not achieved or achieved. Thus, the contribution of the unit standards for the NCEA GPA cannot exceed 2 points per Standard.

The universities of New Zealand and the NZQA agreed on a set of criteria for University Entrance (UE) that differs for open entry and limited entry programs (NZQA 2006). For open entry programs, a minimum of forty-two credits at level 3 or higher must be attained, including a minimum of fourteen credits at level 3 or higher in each of two subjects from an approved subject list, together with a further fourteen credits at level 3 or higher taken from no more than two additional domains on the National Qualifications Framework. In addition, a minimum of eight credits at level 1 or higher in Mathematics or Pāngarau and a minimum of eight credits at level 2 or higher in English or Te Reo Māori (four credits in reading and four credits in writing) must be achieved. For programs with a limited number of places, universities have opted to have additional criteria in their selection systems based on the weighted average scores of the NCEA results (NZQA 2005a). Applicants are ranked according to their best eighty credits at level 3 or higher over a maximum of five approved subjects weighted by the level of achievement attained in each set of credits. As noted above, excellence earns more weight than merit, which, in turn, holds more weight than achieved. Not achieved gains a zero weighting. The average scores are weighted for the number of credits attained in each standard to produce a GPA used for limited entry university admission decisions.

There are two major implications which result from employing the NCEA results to make university admissions decisions. The first is that for open entry programs, where only university entrance is required for admission, the main requirement is the acquisition of the correct combination of credits rather than the acquisition of credits at high levels of achievement. Gaining merit or excellence does not increase the probability of gaining entry because differential weightings are not given to these higher grades. Some have argued that such a quantity-based system leads to many students claiming that there was little to motivate them to aim for merit or excellence because these higher grades carried no extra value (Meyer et. al. 2006). The second implication applies particularly to limited entry courses, where higher GPA requirements are set for admission into particular degree programs. As the GPAs are calculated across subjects, with no allowance for potentially different difficulty of the standards or examinations, attaining achieved, merit, or excellence in one standard is assumed to be similar across standards. Students, however, have reported a perception that standards differed in their level of difficulty and the time required for completion of a unit or achievement standard differs across subjects (Meyer et al. 2006).

ALTERNATIVE NCEA MODELS FOR UNIVERSITY ENTRANCE

The current model for using the NCEA results to determine entry into open and limited entry university courses as agreed between the NZQA and the universities is only one of many possibilities. A major purpose of this analysis was to assess which NCEA admission application provides the best predictive validity for a student's success in university and to evaluate the effects on the ethnic and socioeconomic composition of the student body. In order to do this, various models were developed to take into account different attributes of the NCEA performance. One model included giving greater emphasis to quality by taking into account excellence and merit awards while another model emphasized quantity by counting the number of credits achieved. Another attribute considered was the inclusion or exclusion of failed credits. Given the expressed concerns about the equivalence of standards, one model gave differential weighting to credits based on the difficulty to pass the examination and gain credit. This last measure was an approximation of a weighting by difficulty through the cumulative frequency of students who achieved each grade of excellence, merit and achieved. Each grade was weighted by the proportion of students who did not achieve it. This method is based on the assumption that courses where fewer students across the nation attained excellence or merit were harder than those for which many gained these grades. It is possible that some courses were taken by only a few students very different to the rest of the cohort. This possibility, however, is unlikely to significantly affect the models because of the small number of students who took these courses, though it might negatively affect perceptions of the fairness of admission decisions made on this basis.

Table 20.1 summarizes the ten NCEA models tested in this analysis. All "quantity" models assessed the number of NCEA level 3 credits achieved by students in university-approved subjects. "Quality" models involved calculating a measure) of the NCEA results (excellence = 4, merit = 3, achieved = 2, not achieved = 0). "Difficulty" models calculated the total score taking into account the proportion of students who failed to achieve each grade (achieved, merit, excellence) in each standard. The different models were also assessed according to whether "not achieved" credits were included or excluded. Note that all models used results from NCEA level 3 university approved subjects only (i.e., the NCEA model which is in use at present has not been tested; only part of it).

Each of these models was assessed in terms of the three objectives of this analysis. The first was to compare the correlations between the first-year university GPA with each of the models as well as with Cambridge results. The second was to assess how well different NCEA models predicted success and which features of the NCEA have the greatest predictive power: e.g., were university GPAs more predictable from the quality or quantity of credits? The third objective was to establish whether the implementation of particular models would change the profile of potentially successful students who would be eligible for entry to university. Of particular interest was the potential impact on currently underrepresented groups of students (e.g., Maori, Pacific, and students from low-decile schools).

THE EMPIRICAL STUDY

The ten models theoretically developed above needed to be empirically tested. Hence, a national data set of students (n = 29,161) who sat the NCEA

Table 20.1   List of models assessed against first-year grade point average

Model No.	Model Name	Type of Model	Description	Type of Measure
1	Credit model	Credit based	Total number of credits gained. Including only University Approved subjects/standards	Measures quantity only
2	GPA model	GPA based	Weighted mean of the scores gained in all Standards, weighted for the number of credits of each standard assessed.	Measures quality/level of competency only
3	Cumulative model	Based on GPA and Credit	Sum of the credits gained each multiplied by the scores achieved	Measures both quantity and quality
4	GPA with difficulty	Based on Credit and GPA adjusted for difficulty	Weighted mean of the scores gained in all Standards, weighted for the number of credits of each standard assessed.	Measures quality/level of competency only
5	Cumulative with difficulty	Based on Credit and GPA adjusted for difficulty	Sum of the credits gained each multiplied by the scores achieved	Measures both quantity and quality
6	GPA with "not achieved" excluded	As No. 2 but excludes "Not achieved"	Weighted mean of the scores gained in all Standards, weighted for the number of credits of each standard assessed.	Measures quality/level of competency only
7	Credit with "not achieved" excluded	As No. 1 but excludes "Not achieved"	Sum of the credits gained each multiplied by the scores achieved	Measures quantity only
8	Cumulative with "not achieved" excluded	As No. 3 but excludes "Not achieved"	Weighted mean of the scores gained in all Standards, weighted for the number of credits of each standard assessed.	Measures quality/level of competency and quantity
9	Cumulative with difficulty with "not achieved" excluded	As No. 5 but excludes "Not achieved"	Sum of the credits gained each multiplied by the related scores	Measures both quantity and quality
10	GPA with difficulty with "not achieved" excluded	As No. 4 but excludes "Not achieved"	Weighted mean of the scores gained in all Standards, weighted for the number of credits of each standard assessed	Measures quantity only

Note: All models used the NCEA Level 3 results of university approved subjects only.

final examination in 2004 was analyzed alongside data of the students from that cohort who enrolled in academic programs at the University of Auckland in the 2005 academic year (n = 2,832). The data included all NCEA results as well as gender, ethnicity, enrollment status at the university, programs enrolled in, courses taken, course grades, and qualifications gained.

The NCEA results comprised two measures. The first measure comprised a mean NCEA GPA score, which was calculated from University Approved subjects at NCEA level 3 (see above). This is similar but not identical to the GPA currently derived by the universities from the NCEA results for admission decisions for limited entry programs. The second was a binary measure, which indicated whether a student had qualified for university entrance. Scores based on the 10 models were calculated from these data. The GPAs from first-year results were calculated using the University of Auckland prescribed model: A+ = 9, A = 8, A- = 7, down to C- = 1, D or E = 0. Then, a predicted GPA for each student was calculated by linear regression of the NCEA GPA with the first-year university GPA achieved by students who actually studied at the university.

Students' ethnicity was identified from the NZQA data set. Students could report up to three ethnicities; if they reported more than one ethnicity, a priority rule was invoked whereby one ethnicity was chosen in the following order: Maori, Pacific, Asian, Pakeha, other. This system of classification could, no doubt, be contested. In the final sample, the proportion of Asian students was far greater than the New Zealand population statistics, and there were correspondingly fewer Pakeha and Maori students (see table 20.2).

The first set of analyses related to the predictive power of NCEA results, as modeled in various ways. The highest correlations with first-year GPA

Table 20.2   Distribution of all NCEA students' ethnicity vs. University of Auckland first-year students

Ethnicity	New Zealand NCEA		The University of Auckland first-year students	
	No.	%	No.	%
Pakeha	17,242	59.1	1,258	43.7
Maori	2,866	9.8	118	4.1
Pacific	2,019	6.9	212	7.4
Asian	5,342	18.3	1,137	39.5
Other	1,572	5.4	150	5.2
Total	29,041	99.6	2,875	99.9
Missing	120	0.4	2	0.1
Total	29,161	100	2,877	100

were generated by the quality-related models (GPA model, 0.66; GPA with difficulty, 0.66); then the models that incorporate difficulty (cumulative with difficulty, 0.66; difficulty, 0.65; cumulative with not achieved excluded, 0.66; GPA + cumulative with not achieved excluded, 0.63); then the NCEA credit model, 0.52; and the GPA with not achieved excluded, .51. The best predictors are GPA, then difficulty, and the least successful predictor excludes the not achieved weightings.

Testing the Equity: The Impact of the Models on Different Student Groups

A particular concern is the predictive correlations between the credit and GPA NCEA models across the 10 ratings of socioeconomic status for New Zealand secondary schools. It can be seen in figure 20.1 (note that the vertical axis represents a correlation between NCEA and first-year performance, not level of achievement), that one of the features of the GPA method is that the predictive correlations are systematically higher than the credit-based model, particularly for the lowest two deciles (although it is noted that the predictive correlations for the lower decile schools are much lower than those for higher decile schools, and this needs further research to understand why this might be so). Using the number of credits model, the correlation remains above 0.5 for students coming from decile 3 schools and above, but drops to .36 for decile 1 students. It is likely, therefore, that the NCEA GPA model will allow more Maori and Pasifika students to enter the university, as these

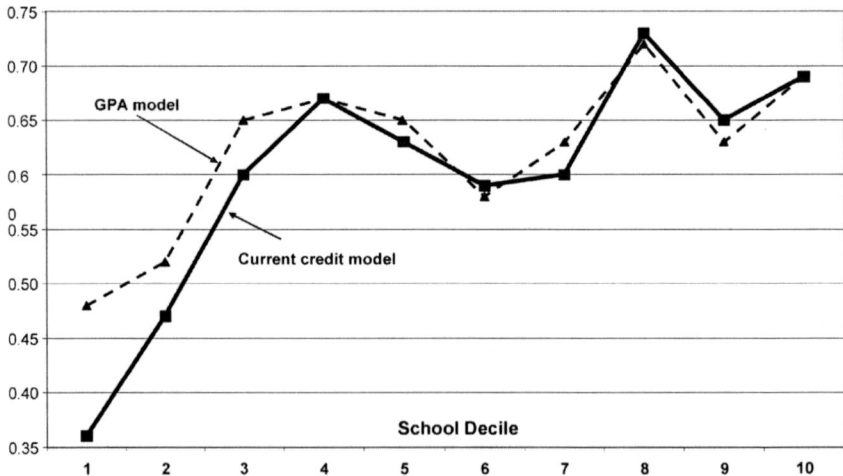

Figure 20.1.   Correlations of selected models with university GPA across the ten socioeconomic deciles of secondary schools

students are dominant in schools from the two lowest deciles. We next turn to such an analysis.

An important implication of the differential relationship between the NCEA models and the university GPA is whether a different composition of students with a higher probability of passing university courses would be eligible for entry to university if different models were used. Given that an NCEA GPA score could be calculated for every student in the national database, a regression equation was used to estimate their university GPA (R2 for this model was 0.44). An alternative entry was simulated for entry to university. Recall that the current credit-based model requires gaining twenty-eight credits in two university-approved subjects (fourteen in each) and another fourteen credits in no more than any two other subjects, that is, in total, forty-two level 3 credits. The students under this alternative model also had to meet numeracy (level 1) and literacy (level 2) criteria.

The alternative NCEA GPA model developed was based on fewer credits (thirty-six university approved credits) but based on quality only, namely, on the grades within those credits. The benchmark of thirty-six university approved credits was established, since the absence of such a benchmark would allow students to achieve very high grades in a very small number of credits that do not adequately test their knowledge base, skills, and abilities, nor adequately prepare them for university study. As only 1 percent of the students who entered the university had fewer than thirty-six credits (these students were admitted through other admission criteria than the traditional NCEA track), it was decided that thirty-six credits were adequate to evaluate a students' secondary school performance. It should be noted that the decision to require forty-two credits—comprised partially from university-approved subjects, partially from non-university-approved subjects and partially from compulsory credits for literacy and numeracy—was made as much for breadth as for predictive and other reasons. Thus, it is acknowledged that the features of these models are informed more by statistical than academic judgments and, that for this reason, the universities are unlikely to depart from the current forty-two-credit model without consideration of these other features.

In terms of quality, the current admissions policy requires only twenty-eight credits from university-approved subjects while the other fourteen credits can come from approved or nonapproved subjects. The regression analyses (r = 0.63; with similar simulated GPAs) predicted that those who entered under the alternative model would have had the same high probability of passing first-year courses should they have been allowed (and chosen) to enter and study. The regression analysis demonstrated that a minimum NCEA GPA of 2.32 (falling between achieved and merit) predicted first-year university GPA of 2.0 or higher, therefore, this NCEA GPA (2.32) was set as the minimum for entry provided that at least thirty-six credits were obtained from university-approved subjects together with a minimum of eight credits in level 1 in numeracy and eight credits in level 2 in literacy.

Under this alternative NCEA GPA model, there were very few additional students who would have qualified for entry to university (false positives = n = 1,253; 4.3 percent). Similarly, very few students who currently qualify for entry would be excluded by the adoption of the new model (false negatives = n = 1,623; 5.6 percent). Thus, if the current criteria through which the entry to university is awarded were replaced with the new NCEA GPA model, the total number of students who would gain entry to university would be reduced by 1.3 percent (370 students). This is probably not a desirable outcome, so it is assumed that an additive approach would be taken in any reconsideration of university entry criteria, that is, a dual admission model would be adopted which would include both the current credit-based model and the alternative GPA NCEA-based model. In practice, students' achievement would be assessed against both the credit and the quality models and students who met the university entrance criteria by at least one of the models would be admitted to the university.

In the remainder of this section, the profile of 1,253 students who would qualify for entry to university under the alternative NCEA GPA model, but do not currently do so, are considered. As can be seen from Table 20.3 the model has proportionately greater impact on Maori students eligible for entry than other ethnic groups (n = 138, 16 percent of the 2004 cohort entering the University of Auckland). There would also be a small percentage increase in the number of Pacific students (n = 62, 14 percent of 2004 the cohort entering the University of Auckland). The percentage of Pakeha and Asian students would decrease slightly, though their actual numbers would potentially increase (832 Pakeha, 162 Asian, and 66 other).

It is noted that the above analysis was derived from data from one university only but the national sample included 29,161 students. This means that the students who would be awarded with university entrance by the dual admission model would have university entrance for any university, assuming that the correlations between the NCEA GPA and university first-year GPA is not significantly different across universities. Although there is no reason to believe that this assumption is unlikely, further research using data from other universities may clarify this issue.

Given the higher percentage of Maori and Pacific students in low-decile schools, it is not surprising that higher percentages of these new students would come from decile 1 and 2 schools (see figure 20.2). It is noteworthy that, the effect of the Dual Admission policy would be greater on students in the lower school decile than on students from the lowest individual socioeconomic status deciles. This indicates that, within the population of those who live in low-income neighborhoods, the school-related factors have greater impact on student outcomes than the individual or family resources available to them.

Table 20.3   Students in New Zealand NCEA Level 3 cohort, and those eligible for entry under the current credit-based model and the alternative dual admission model

	New Zealand students		Current credit model		GPA model		Dual admission model	
	f	%	F	%	f	%	f	%
Pakeha	17,242	59.4	10,320	68.2	10,351	68.4	11,143	68.0
Maori	2,866	9.9	872	5.8	891	5.9	1,010	6.2
Pacific	2,019	7.0	437	2.9	435	2.9	499	3.0
Asian	5,342	18.4	2,817	18.6	2,758	18.2	2,979	18.2
Other	1,572	5.4	697	4.6	707	4.7	763	4.7
Total	29,041	100.0	15,143	100.0	15,142	100.1	16,394	100.0
Missing	120		4				6	
Total	29,161		15,147		15,142		16,400	

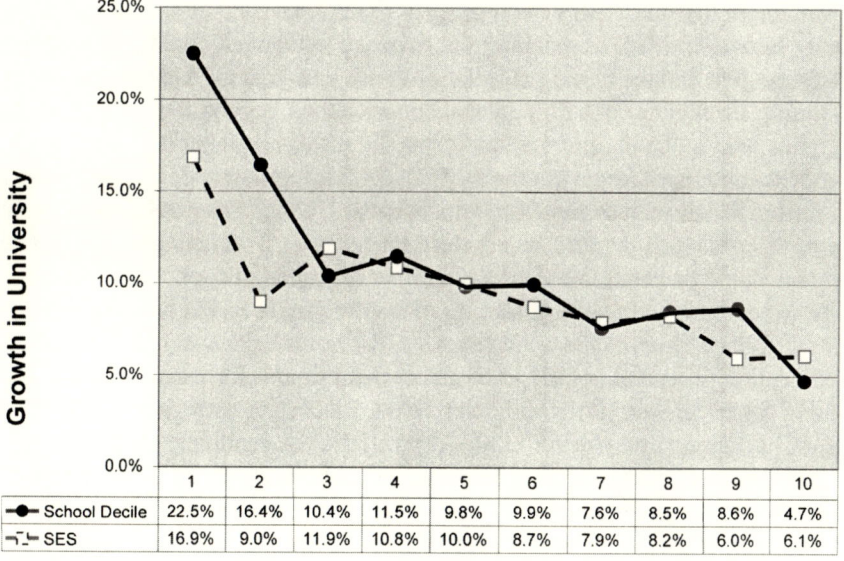

	1	2	3	4	5	6	7	8	9	10
School Decile	22.5%	16.4%	10.4%	11.5%	9.8%	9.9%	7.6%	8.5%	8.6%	4.7%
SES	16.9%	9.0%	11.9%	10.8%	10.0%	8.7%	7.9%	8.2%	6.0%	6.1%

SES / School Decile

Figure 20.2.   Percentage increase of students from each school decile and socio-economic status entering under the dual admissions model compared with the current credit-based model

DISCUSSION AND SUMMARY

The first part of this chapter established the robustness of the new NCEA models in comparison with similar secondary school assessment systems. It was found that the best of the NCEA models is up to five times $(0.66^2/{\sim}0.30^2)$ more effective in predicting first-year students' GPA during their first year at university than most other assessment systems (Goldberg and Alliger 1992; Kuncel et. al. 2001; Morrison and Morrison 1995). The higher correlation between the NCEA and university success may be due to the similarities in the assessment and the subsequent wash back on the teaching systems. Both require ongoing assessments involving a variety of tasks (projects, essays, portfolios) throughout the year, together with a final examination. This NCEA correlation is important particularly because the NCEA is a new assessment system in New Zealand and there have been too few investigations into its predictive relationships. As J. Strachan (2001, 258) suggested, "What must be ensured is that the potential for improvement offered by the NCEA does achieve the aims sought by the change, and does not repeat the negatives of the past."

The analysis presented in this chapter further investigates features within the NCEA systems that could be highly relevant for policy decisions relating to admission to degree programs at the university and the first-year results. It was found that the level of competency (NCEA GPA) that students achieve may be as important as reaching the required number of credits. The NCEA GPA models had the highest correlations with first-year GPA at the university. Aiming for higher GPA may increase motivations beyond merely collecting credits, while placing more attention on the discriminations between the excellence and merit levels (all the meaningful information under a credit model needs to be between achieved and not achieved, which is not necessarily what was desired when the four levels were introduced). Teachers have suggested that it would be better to reduce the number of credits to allow increased quality of teaching and learning leading to higher grades in the NCEA (Hipkins et. al. 2004). Much of the criticism of NCEA has been driven by the students' perception that there is little to motivate them to aim for excellence because these higher grades carried no extra value. Rather the emphasis has been on credit accumulation (Meyer et al. 2006). If NCEA candidates aspire to succeed in university, it may be appropriate to shift this emphasis from minimum passes in more credits to higher achievement in fewer credits.

Further analysis of the 1,253 additional students who would be admitted under the proposed dual admission model showed that this would increase the numbers from those groups most underrepresented at university. In proportion to the 2005 the University of Auckland cohort, 16 percent more Maori and 14 percent more Pacific students would have qualified for entry to the university, with the highest proportion of additional admissions given to students coming from low decile schools. It is important to note that this is a merit-based model; the students qualifying for university admission under this dual admission model would be eligible based on their NCEA achievements, which would be of sufficiently high quality to predict that they would be likely to pass their degree level courses. The students' eligibility would not be based on their ethnic affiliations or the decile level of the schools they had attended. The dual admission approach would thus be likely to maintain high success rates in the student body, while increasing the number of students from underrepresented groups at the university. A recent analysis (which employed different statistical procedures but applied the same concept of dual admission model) of two consecutive cohorts of students who sat the NCEA examinations in 2005 and 2006 identified similar positive effects on equity in enrollment in bachelor's programs at the university (Turner, Shulruf et. al. 2008).

In conclusion, it should be noted that the NCEA was introduced with intentions surpassing the aim to merely prepare students for entrance to university, and rightly so. Nonetheless, the NCEA appears to be an effective secondary school assessment system, particularly when appropriately used for university admission purposes. It is, therefore, suggested that the dual admission model is more equitable than any other single admission model; it enhances equity using merit rather than race or socioeconomic status–based criteria. Although the dual admission model thus far only has been tested in New Zealand, the fact that three consecutive cohorts of students could have benefited from that model strengthens the argument for its generalizability across jurisdictions and educational systems.

This chapter is based on studies undertaken as part of Starpath project, University of Auckland.

REFERENCES

Anae, M., Anderson, H., Benseman, J., and Coxon, E. *Pacific Peoples and Tertiary Education: Issues of Participation.* Auckland: Auckland Uniservices Ltd., 2002a.
————. E. *Pacific Peoples and Tertiary Education: Issues of Participation. Final Report.* (No. D-Anae.M0201). Wellington: Auckland Uniservices prepared for Ministry of Education, 2002b.
Black, P. *Report to the Qualifications Development Group Ministry of Education, New Zealand on the proposals for development of the National Certificate of Educational Achievement.* London: School of Education, King's College, 2001.
Brown, H., and Burkhardt, R. "Predicting Student Success: The Relative Impact of Ethnicity, Income, and Parental Education." *AIR 1999 Annual Forum Paper*, 1999.
Bucks, B. *Affirmative Access Versus Affirmative Action: How Have Texas' Race-Blind Policies Affected College Outcomes?* Dallas: The University of Texas at Dallas, 2005.

Deaton, R., and Schutz, G. J. *Examining the Predictive Power of the ACT and High School GPA*. Florida: Tennessee Higher Education Commission, Southern Association of Institutional Research, 2001.

Dobric, K. *Discourses in Qualifications Policy Adoption in New Zealand, 1996–2000: Identifying Power Imbalances in a Transformative Process*. Paper presented at the First International Congress of Qualitative Inquiry. University of Illinois at Urbana–Champaign, 2005.

Donnelly, N. "Berkeley Weighs Its Options for Preserving Student Diversity." *The Journal of Blacks in Higher Education 19* (1998) 29–32.

Epple, D., Romano, R., and Sieg, H. *Admission, Tuition, and Financial Aid Policies in the Market in Higher Education*. New York: National Bureau of Economic Research, 2005.

Friedlander, J. "From Open Admissions to the Honors College: Equal Opportunities at the City University of New York." Paper presented at the Hurst Seminar on Higher Education and Equality of Opportunity: Cross-National Perspectives. Ben-Gurion University of the Negev, Beer Sheva, Israel, 2008, 3–5 June.

Goldberg, E. L., and Alliger, G. M. "Assessing the Validity of the GRE for Students in Psychology: A Validity Generalization Approach." *Educational and Psychological Measurement, 52*(4) (1992) 1019–1027.

Gray, M. C., Hunter, B., and Schwab, R. G. "Trends in Indigenous Educational Participation and Attainment, 1986-96." *Australian Journal of Education, 44*(2), (2000):101–17.

Guri-Rozenblit, S. "Providing Higher Education to Socially Disadvantaged Populations." *Studies in Higher Education, 14*(3), (1989):321–29.

Halsey, A. Trends in Access and Equity in Higher Education. "Britain in International Perspective." *Oxford Review of Education, 19*(2), (1993):129–40.

Hipkins, R., Vaughan, K., Beals, F., and Ferral, F. *Learning Curves: Meeting Student Learning Needs in an Evolving Qualifications Regime: Shared Pathways and Multiple Tracks: A Second Report*. Wellington: New Zealand Council for Educational Research, 2004.

Jones, M., Yonezawa, S., Ballesteros, E., and Mehan, H. "Shaping Pathways to Higher Education." *Educational Researcher, 31*(2), (2002):3–11.

Kuncel, N. R., Hezlett, S. A., and Ones, D. S. "A Comprehensive Meta-analysis of the Predictive Validity of the Graduate Record Examinations: Implications for Graduate Student Selection and Performance." *Psychological Bulletin, 127*(1), (2001):162–81.

Lipset, S. M., Rothman, S., and Nevitte, N. "Does control diversity improve university education?" *International journal of public opinion research, 15*(1), (2003):8–26.

Loury, D., and Garman, D. "Affirmative Action in Higher Education." *AEA Papers and Procedures, 82*(2), (1993):99–103.

Meyer, L., McClure, J., Walkey, F., McKenzie, L., and Weir, K. *The Impact of the NCEA on Student Motivation*. Wellington: College of Education and School of Psychology, Victoria University of Wellington, 2006.

Ministry of Education. *Participation in Tertiary Education (August 2002)*: Ministry of Education, New Zealand, 2002.

———. *Maori Student Retention, Completion and Progression in Tertiary Education* (No. D-MOE04). Wellington: Ministry of Education, New Zealand, 2004.

———. *Economic Outcomes for Maori from Tertiary Education* (Fact Sheet): Ministry of Education, 2005a.

———. *Maori in Tertiary Education: A Picture of the Trends*: Ministry of Education, New Zealand, 2005b.

Mohr, J. W., Bourgeois, M., and Duquenne, V. *The Logic of Opportunity: A Formal Analysis of The University of California's Outreach and Diversity Discourse.* Santa Barbara: University of California, 2004.

Morgaman, P., Desai, A., Leone, D., McIntyre, B., Moore, E., Stuart, J., et al. *Post-secondary Progression of 1993–94 Florida Public High School Graduates: 2002 Update* (Research/Technical). Tallahassee: Florida State Council for Education Policy, Research and Improvement, 2002.

Morrison, T., and Morrison, M. "A Meta-analytic Assessment of the Predictive Validity of the Quantitative and Verbal Components of the Graduate Record Examination with Graduate Grade Point Average Representing the Criterion of Graduate Success." *Educational and Psychological Measurement, 55*(2), (1995):309–16.

NZQA. *Assessment and Certification Rules and Procedures for Secondary Schools.* 6.3.1 Approved subjects (2004).http://www.nzqa.govt.nz/ncea/acrp/secondary/contents.html (accessed June 23, 2004).

———. *How Grade Averages Are Calculated.* 2005a. http://nzqa.govt.nz/ncea/results/gradeaverages.html (accessed April 20, 2006).

———. *Secondary School Qualifications—A Guide for Students.* 2005b. http://www.nzqa.govt.nz/publications/docs/secsc-qual-guide.pdf (accessed April 24, 2006).

———. *University Entrance Standard.* 2006. http://www.nzqa.govt.nz/ncea/ue/index.html (accessed April 26, 2006).

Rigol, G. W. *Admissions Decision Making Models, How U.S. Institutions of Higher Education Select Undergraduate Students.* (New York: The College Board, 2003).

Schmid, C. *Challenges and Opportunities of Community Colleges.* Paper presented at the Hurst Seminar on Higher Education and Equality of Opportunity: Cross-National Perspectives, (Ben-Gurion University of the Negev, Beer Sheva, Israel, 2008, 3–5 June).

Scott, D. *Pathways in Tertiary Education 1998–2002.* Wellington: Ministry of Education, 2004.

———. "Retention, Completion and Progression in Tertiary Education in New Zealand." *Journal of Higher Education Policy and Management, 27*(1), (2005):3–17.

Skilbeck, M., and Connell, H. *Access and Equity in Higher Education An International Perspective On Issues and Strategies.* Dublin: The Higher Education Authority, 2000.

Smart, W. *Outcomes of the New Zealand Tertiary Education System: A Synthesis of the Evidence.* Wellington: Ministry of Education, 2006.

Smyth, R., McClelland, J., Lister, P., Steenhart, K., Sargison, A., Westwater, K., et al. *OECD Thematic Review of Tertiary Education: New Zealand Country Background Report.* Wellington: Ministry of Education, 2006.

Strachan, J. "Assessment in Change: Some Reflections on the Local and International Background to the National Certificate of Educational Achievement (NCEA)." *New Zealand Annual Review of Education* (11), (2001):245–74.

Strathdee, R. "The Qualifications Framework in New Zealand: Reproducing Existing Inequalities or Disrupting the Positional Conflict for Credentials." *Journal of Education and Work, 16*(2), (2003) 147–64.

Tienda, M., Alon, S., and Niu, S. *Affirmative Action and the Texas Top 10 Percent Admission Law: Balancing Equity and Access to Higher Education.* Paper presented at the Hurst Seminar on Higher Education and Equality of Opportunity: Cross-National Perspectives, Ben-Gurion University of the Negev, Beer Sheva, Israel, 2008, 3–5 June.

Turner, R., Shulruf, B., Li, M., and Yuan, J. *The Impact Upon Population Subgroups of University Entrance Criteria Based Upon a Form of NCEA Grade Point Average.* Auckland: University of Auckland, 2008.

University of Auckland. *2001 Calendar.* Auckland: University of Auckland, 2001.

Index

AAU. *See* Association of American Universities

ability, student, 48, 63

academic(s): in China, 131, 136–37; diversity *vs.* quality of, 65–67; in Hong Kong, 130; integration, 279; in Japan, 131; neoliberalism and freedom in, 132–34; preparation, 28–31, 35–36, 73–74, 82, 84; success and capital theory, 282–86; success *vs.* self-confidence, 263; success vs gender, 277–79; in Taiwan, 136–37

"Academic Excellence Project," 135

The Academic Ranking of World Universities, 131

access, 17–18, 122n8; community college, 25, 32–35, 53; to Dutch higher education, 271–72; equality *vs.*, 45–46, 235–37; in France, 255, 258–63; to Grandes Écoles, 256–59; to higher education, 202–4; incentives and subsidies, 107, 108, 114, 119; minority, 4, 53, 89–92, 93–94; policy, 46–47, 53, 54; of poor through student loans, 103–4, 106–7, 117–18; registration processes and, 261–63, 266; social class *vs.*, 258–61; for students with mental health difficulties, 299; success *vs.*, 32–35; to tertiary education in Korea, 145, 149, *150*; VWO for, 273

Access to Higher Education Program (AHEP), 204, 211–12; extracurricular activities of, 206, 210; participants of, 204, *205*; reflection/evaluation of, 208–9; school division of, 206, 210; scope/funding of, 204; self-confidence and, 211; structure of, 205–8; student eligibility to, 204–5, 213n3; student response to, 209–11; success of, 210–11; "Toward University" component of, 205–9; tutoring and, 206; university division of, 206–9, 210

accountability, of institutions, 18

Achieving the Dream 2002 (AD), 29, 30–31

activism, student, 90–91, 249n13

ACTs, 63, 96

AD. *See* Achieving the Dream 2002

Adelman, Clifford, 87n5

Parisian Institute of Political Science, 253–54, 263, 265
Park, Hwanbo, 6
Pasztor, Adel, 8–9
Peres, Shimon, 201
performance, measuring, 32–35
Peterson, Carol, 133
Philippines, student loans in, *110–11*, 114, 116, 118, *120*
Pissarro, Jaochim, 88n13
poor families: debt aversion of, 106, 122n2; financial aid to, 103–4, 106–7, 117–18; targeting student loans to, 108–13
population: of Africa, 225; of India, 163–64, 167, *169*, 180nn5–7, 184; of Israel, 184
poverty, 31; informational, 19, 119; line *vs.* eligibility of student loans, 109–11, 122n4; World Bank/IMF programs to alleviate African, 218
Poverty Reduction Strategy Papers (PRSPs), 218
preparatory classes (CPGE), *257*, 258, 265
"Prestige and Quality in American Colleges and Universities," 4, 68n1
pre-university diploma (VWO), 273; dropout rates, 276; graduation rates of, 277
pre-vocational education, Dutch (VMBO), 273, *274*
The Princeton Review, 76
privatization, 8, 18, 125, 137; in Africa, 222, 232; consequences of over, 153–54; in Ghana, 237–38, *238*; in higher education, 146; historical origins of, 147–49; in India, 173–75, 177, 181n15; in Israel, 21n1; in Korea, 145–54, 156–57; modern, 149–53; public education *vs.*, 147; quality of instruction *vs.*, 18, 21n1; of tertiary education, 6; of universities, 126–29, 231–33
procrastination, 300

professional courses, 172
"Programme for Promoting Academic Excellence of Universities," 130
"Promoting Access of the Poor through Student Loans in Asia," 5–6
Proposition 209 (California), 45, 69
protective discrimination, 167–68, 180n8
PRSPs. *See* Poverty Reduction Strategy Papers
public education: diversity and, 272; privatization *vs.*, 147
public funding, 18, 152; in Ghana, *236*
public good: education as, 152, 154, 156–57; private good *vs.*, 232
public research universities, 61–62
public schools, segregation in, 77
public universities, cutbacks in, 18
publishing, 130, 136–37

quality, of education, 172, 175, 176, 190, 240. *See also* twinning programs

Raab, Jennifer, 83, 84, 87n3, 88n12
race: academic goals *vs.*, 32; admissions *vs.*, 15, 19, 44–45; affirmative action *vs.*, 44–45; college experience *vs.*, 96–98; degree completion *vs.*, 34; enrollment *vs.*, 41–42; of students in remedial courses, 30–31
RAEs. *See* Research Assessment Exercises
rankings, 13–14, 16, 17, 65; in Asian higher education, impact of "world-class," 132–38; of Asian universities, 129–32, 135; of Chinese universities, 130–31; diversity and, 65; government funding *vs.*, 134; of Hong Kong universities, 129–30; of Hunter College, 76; of Korean universities, 157; LSAT/GMAT scores *vs.*, 63–64; SAT/ACT scores *vs.*, 63; selectivity and, 14; of Singapore universities, 131–32;

About the Contributors

Miriam Amit served for over a decade as the national superintendent of mathematics for the state of Israel, in charge of the development and implementation of educational policy. Since returning to Ben-Gurion University she has been head of the center and the Department of Science and Technology Education. She has also spearheaded extensive projects for excellence and academic access of students from Israel's socioeconomically disadvantaged areas. Her research interests include: mathematics and their application in education, development of scientific excellence, and socio-cultural aspects of math and science.

Pamela Blackmon is assistant professor of political science at Penn State University, Altoona. Her research and publishing interests include changes in the policies of the International Monetary Fund and the World Bank and on the economic reform processes of Kazakhstan and Uzbekistan. Her first book, *In the Shadow of Russia: Reform in Kazakhstan and Uzbekistan*, is forthcoming with Michigan State University Press.

Josiah A. M. Cobbah is a principal lecturer and administrator at the Ghana Institute of Management and Public Administration (GIMPA). He holds a PhD (geography) and a juris doctor from the University of Cincinnati. His research interests include human rights and development, the African business environment, leadership, and contemporary educational administration.

Steven J. Diner is chancellor of Rutgers University–Newark. He has written extensively on the history of American higher education. He is president of the Coalition of Urban and Metropolitan Universities.

Matt Evans is assistant professor of political science at Penn State University, Altoona. He has published books and articles on government and public policy in the Middle East. His book, *An Institutional Framework for Policymaking* (Rowman & Littlefield 2007), examines the effect of informal institutions on policy implementation. He is also coeditor of an anthology entitled *Reform and Democracy in Local Government of Countries in Transformation* (2007). His research interests include comparative politics, public policy, Middle East, electoral competition, political communication and regional planning.

Judith Naomi Friedlander is professor of anthropology at Hunter College (CUNY) and is currently serving as director of academic programs at the college's Roosevelt House Public Policy Institute. She has served as an academic dean at SUNY Purchase, Hunter and the New School for Social Research and written on questions of ethnicity in Mexico and France. Her publications include: *Being Indian in Hueyapan* and *Vilna on the Seine:Jewish Intellectuals in France since 1968.*

Gaële Goastellec is a sociologist, head of research unit at the Observatory Science, Policy and Society, University of Lausanne, Switzerland. She works on higher education policies in an international comparative perspective and has been part of the Fulbright New Century Scholar program 2005–2006 with a research on equity policies in access.

Ayelet Harel-Shalev is a postdoctoral fellow in the Politics and Government Department and the Centre for the Study of European Politics and Society, Ben-Gurion University. Her forthcoming book is titled *The Challenge of Sustaining Democracy in Deeply Divided Societies: Citizenship, Rights, and Ethnic Conflicts in India and Israel* (Lexington 2010). The book is based on her PhD dissertation, which won the Israeli Political Science Association prize for outstanding doctoral dissertation, 2006. Her research focuses on comparative political studies; Indian politics and society; ethnic conflicts; and Israeli politics and society.

John Hattie is professor of education at Auckland University. His current areas of interest are measurement models and their application to educational problems, including item response models, structural equation modeling, measurement theory, and meta-analysis.

John N. Hawkins is professor emeritus of social sciences and comparative education at UCLA and senior consultant at the East-West Center on the International Forum in Education 2020 Project. He has authored and edited several books and articles on educational policy and planning in the Asia region the most recent of which is *Changing Education: Leadership, Innovation and Development in a Globalizing Asia-Pacific*.

Sue Jackson is senior lecturer in disability support at the London College of Communication, University of the Arts London. Her experience includes more than thirty years teaching, working closely with students with a range of mental health difficulties, researching the impact of this illness on their learning and developing strategies to ensure their success in higher education.

Narayana Jayaram is professor and dean, School of Social Sciences, Tata Institute of Social Sciences, Mumbai, India. He has previously taught sociology at Bangalore University (1972–1999) and Goa University (1999–2003), and was the director of the Institute for Social and Economic Change, Bangalore, India. His areas of interest include sociology of education, theory and methods, political sociology, and the sociology of diaspora. He served as visiting professor of Indian studies at the University of the West Indies (St Augustine), Trinidad and Tobago (1994–1996). His publications include *Higher Education and Status Retention*; *Housing in India* (coedited with R. S. Sandhu); *Introductory Sociology*; *Social Conflict* (coedited with Satish Saberwal); *Sociology: Methods and Theories*; *Sociology of Education in India*; *The Indian Diaspora* (ed.); *Keywords: Identity* (with Aziz Al-Azmeh, Wang Bin, David A. Hollinger, Mahmood Mamdani and Emmanuel Renault); *On Civil Society: Issues and Perspectives* (ed.); and *Social Research Methods: Persistent Issues and Emergent Trends* (special issue of *The Indian Journal of Social Work*, 67 (1 & 2), 2006 (guest ed.). He is the managing editor of *Sociological Bulletin* (Journal of the Indian Sociological Society).

Ki-Seok Kim is professor, Department of Education, Seoul National University. He is also Co-CEO of Educators without Borders, Korea.

David L. Kirp is a professor at the Goldman School of Public Policy at the University of California at Berkeley. His fifteen books, which span the field of social policy, include *Shakespeare, Einstein, and the Bottom Line: The Marketing of Higher Education* (Harvard University Press 2005).

Fred A. Lazin is the Lynn and Lloyd Hurst Family Professor of Local Government in the Department of Politics at Ben-Gurion University of the Negev

(Israel). He has written and edited ten books dealing with public policy in the United States, Israel and developing countries, Israeli politics and society, and Jews in American politics. He received the Israel Political Science Association's award for the outstanding English language book on politics in 2005 for *The Struggle for Soviet Jewry in American Politics; Israel versus the American Jewish Establishment.* In 2010–2011 he will be the Seymour and Lillian Abenshohn Visiting Professor of Israel Studies at American University in Washington, DC.

Ka Ho Mok is chair professor of comparative policy, concurrently associate vice president (external relations) and dean, Faculty of Arts and Sciences, the Hong Kong Institute of Education (HKIEd). Before joining the HKIEd, Professor Mok was associate dean and professor, Faculty of Social Sciences of the University of Hong Kong. He also served as founding director and chair professor, Centre for East Asian Studies, University of Bristol. He has researched and published extensively in comparative policy, with particular focus on comparative development, policy and governance in East Asia.

Noga O'Connor is a visiting assistant professor of sociology of education at the University of Iowa. Her research focuses on higher education as a mechanism of social reproduction.

Hwanbo Park is a PhD candidate and a lecturer in the Department of Education at Seoul National University. His research focuses on access and equity in higher education, and international trends in the privatization of higher education. He is also a project manager with Educators Without Borders (EWB).

Adél Pásztor is a lecturer at the Department of Social Sciences, Northumbria University, UK. Her current research focuses on access to higher education and participation of nontraditional students.

Carol Schmid is professor of sociology at Guilford Technical Community College. Her research areas include higher education and inequality with emphasis on the community college, race and ethnic relations in international comparison, and global social problems

Boaz Shulruf is the deputy head of the Centre of Medical and Health Sciences Education at the Faculty of Medical and Health Sciences, University of Auckland. His main research interest is in assessment and measurement in education, health, social sciences and cross-cultural psychology. His recent publications include articles on student pathways in the secondary and tertiary education; admission policies; and collectivism and individualism.

Don Stewart was professor of chemical technology at the Papua New Guinea University of Technology, and during a career at the University of Melbourne he was director of the International Development Technologies Centre, Assistant Dean, International of the Engineering Faculty and Head of International House. He has a particular interest in supporting international students from developing countries.

Charles Tien is an associate professor of political science at Hunter College and The Graduate Center, CUNY. His recent publications on race and politics have appeared in *Polity* and in the *Du Bois Review: Social Science Research on Race* and in *PS: Political Science and Politics*.

Sarah Tumen is senior analyst at the Central Forecasting & Modelling Unit, Education Information and Analysis Division, Ministry of Education, New Zealand. Her research interest is in longitudinal trends of student progression in the education system in New Zealand and economic factors affecting student outcomes.

Rick Wolff is a senior researcher at Risbo, a research institute of the Erasmus University Rotterdam. His work focuses on the success of students from ethnic minority background in Dutch higher education, compared to that of White Dutch students. At present he is writing his PhD-thesis on the subject.

Adrian Ziderman, formally senior economist for human resources at the World Bank, Washington, is Wolfson Professor Emeritus, Economics Department, Bar-Ilan University, Israel.

Breinigsville, PA USA
14 December 2010
251411BV00003B/4/P